Teaching in Elementary and Secondary Classrooms

Teaching in Elementary and Secondary Classrooms

Building a Learning Community

Johanna Kasin Lemlech
University of Southern California

Upper Saddle River, New Jersey
Columbus, Ohio

Library of Congress Cataloging-in-Publication Data

Lemlech, Johanna Kasin.
   Teaching in elementary and secondary classrooms : building a learning community/
Johanna Kasin Lemlech.
     p. cm.
   Includes bibliographical references and index.
   ISBN 0-13-097695-4
   1. Elementary school teaching. 2. High school teaching. 3. Classroom environment. I. Title.
LB1555.L435 2004
371.102—dc22   2003058111

Vice President and Executive Publisher: Jeffery W. Johnston
Executive Editor: Debra A. Stollenwerk
Editorial Assistant: Mary Morrill
Production Editor: Kris Robinson-Roach
Production Coordination: WordCrafters Editorial Services, Inc.
Design Coordinator: Diane C. Lorenzo
Cover Designer: Eric Davis
Cover Image: Getty One
Production Manager: Pamela D. Bennett
Director of Marketing: Ann Castel Davis
Marketing Manager: Darcy Betts Prybella
Marketing Coordinator: Tyra Poole

This book was set in ITC Garamond by Pine Tree Composition, Inc. It was printed and bound by R.R. Donnelley & Sons Company. The cover was printed by Phoenix Color Corp.

Photo Credits: p. 185 by Scott Cunningham/Merrill; all other photos by Paula Goldman.

Copyright © 2004 by Pearson Education, Inc., Upper Saddle River, New Jersey 07458. Pearson Prentice Hall. All rights reserved. This publication is protected by Copyright and permission should be obtained from the publisher prior to any prohibited reproduction, storage in a retrieval system, or transmission in any form or by any means, electronic, mechanical, photocopying, recording, or likewise. For information regarding permission(s), write to: Rights and Permissions Department.

Pearson Prentice Hall™ is a trademark of Pearson Education, Inc.
Pearson® is a registered trademark of Pearson plc
Prentice Hall® is a registered trademark of Pearson Education, Inc.
Merrill® is a registered trademark of Pearson Education, Inc.

Pearson Education Ltd.   Pearson Education Australia PTY, Limited
Pearson Education Singapore, Pte. Ltd.   Pearson Education North Asia Ltd.
Pearson Education Canada, Ltd.   Pearson Education de Mexico, S.A. de C.V.
Pearson Education—Japan   Pearson Education Malaysia, Pte. Ltd.

                                                                10 9 8 7 6 5 4 3 2 1
                                                                    ISBN 0-13-097695-4

*This text is dedicated to my newest and youngest grandchildren,
Maxwell and Spencer Walshaw (ages 3 and 2).
I hope that they have
caring and kind teachers
who value curiosity and the joy of learning.*

Educator Learning Center: An Invaluable Online Resource

Merrill Education and the Association for Supervision and Curriculum Development (ASCD) invite you to take advantage of a new online resource, one that provides access to the top research and proven strategies associated with ASCD and Merrill—the Educator Learning Center. At **www.EducatorLearningCenter.com** you will find resources that will enhance your students' understanding of course topics and of current educational issues, in addition to being invaluable for further research.

How the Educator Learning Center Will Help Your Students Become Better Teachers

With the combined resources of Merrill Education and ASCD, you and your students will find a wealth of tools and materials to better prepare them for the classroom.

Research

- More than 600 articles from the ASCD journal *Educational Leadership* discuss everyday issues faced by practicing teachers.
- A direct link on the site to Research Navigator™ gives students access to many of the leading education journals, as well as extensive content detailing the research process.
- Excerpts from Merrill Education texts give your students insights on important topics of instructional methods, diverse populations, assessment, classroom management, technology, and refining classroom practice.

Classroom Practice

- Hundreds of lesson plans and teaching strategies are categorized by content area and age range.
- Case studies and classroom video footage provide virtual field experience for student reflection.
- Computer simulations and other electronic tools keep your students abreast of today's classrooms and current technologies.

Look into the Value of Educator Learning Center Yourself

Preview the value of this educational environment by visiting **www.EducatorLearningCenter.com** and clicking on "Demo." For a free 4-month subscription to the Educator Learning Center in conjunction with this text, simply contact your Merrill/Prentice Hall sales representative.

Preface

The theme of this text is teaching for learning in the classroom community. As an educator for more than forty years, I have found teaching personally rewarding and challenging. When teaching, I am learning from my students—by the questions they pose, the discussion that is stimulated, and the expansion of knowledge that occurs. I detect learning in students by observing their active engagement and participation, the spark that is visible in their eyes, the questions and insights they share, and their interest and excitement when clearly expressed.

Learning is natural for all individuals, but some experiences offer more opportunities for learning than others. The old adage that "teachers are born, not trained" has *not* been corroborated by research. Underqualified and unprepared teachers result in chaotic and rigid classrooms and unplanned and thoughtless curricula.

This book is written for novice teachers, be they student teachers, beginning teachers, or interns. Teachers who fail or quit the profession do so primarily because they do not feel successful in helping students read, write, or achieve the standards deemed appropriate. Sometimes teachers give up because they have not learned to balance their personal and professional obligations. In my work with students in the public schools in grades K–12 and my students at the university, I have learned that when students (of all ages) work together in democratic classroom communities *and* are supported by teacher and administrative efforts, the classrooms become exciting environments, with students and teachers more engaged in meaningful activities.

When teachers and students are able to share their zeal for learning, teaching is not burdensome; it is not routinized; it is not dehumanizing. Instead, teachers feel fortunate to be in a profession that emancipates the spirit and thoughtfulness of all individuals. In addition to sharing my experiences in democratic classroom environments, I show how such environments can be recognized and created. I focus on some of the dilemmas teachers face in dealing with students who lack self-discipline or who have not experienced a supportive environment or an engaging curriculum. I describe successful teaching lessons—techniques and strategies implemented every day by thoughtful, accomplished teachers.

This book is what is professionally described as a *methods* text. It focuses on the learner (both the teacher and the student), the environment for learning, and the process of teaching. Lesson examples or teaching episodes are content-based in order to demonstrate understanding and implementation of pedagogical content.

I believe that, to be a good teacher and to enjoy the profession of teaching, teachers need to be competent in the following areas:

- Establishing a classroom community
- Knowledge of their subject matter and how to plan appropriate experiences for students' learning
- Delivering instruction for students' learning (pedagogical knowledge)
- Ability to understand students' differences in experience, culture, language, gender, family, and community
- Understanding motivation—what kinds of experiences stimulate learning and how to use motivation for different types of learning—including classroom management
- Assessing what students know and don't know—strengths and weaknesses
- Seeking information, assistance, and resources when needed
- Ability to analyze and reflect on their own teaching and students' learning

We live in a very diverse pluralistic society, and as teachers we must strive to teach all students to the best of their abilities. To do so we must continue our own learning. My goal is to contribute to learning about teaching.

Special Features in the Text

1. *Teaching Hints.* Critical content, such as teaching English language learners or differentiation of instruction, is followed by a box entitled "Teaching Hints." The hints abstract the key information into simple methods for teaching.

2. *Did You Know That . . . ?* These boxes identify significant research that relates to the content of the chapter. Again, it is done in abstract style so that the reader recognizes the important information without a lengthy explanation.

3. *Teaching Scenarios.* Using fictitious teachers' names, classroom episodes are presented in every chapter. The scenarios are referred to as the content of the chapter is developed.

4. *Advance Organizer* and *introductory paragraph.* These elements begin every chapter. The advance organizers are in question form to assist the reader with an outline of the chapter and to serve as an overview. The introductory paragraph is another means for providing an overview of the chapter topics.

5. *The Interstate New Teacher Assessment and Support Consortium (INTASC)* issues and standards are addressed in each chapter. The specific standards dealt with are listed at the beginning of each chapter.

6. *Teaching Problems.* These end-of-chapter exercises relate to the content of each chapter. They can be used as lead-ins to class discussion or as individual or partner challenges to think about and work out.

7. *Lesson Plans.* Both daily activities and long-range teaching units are presented, with special hints for creating a teaching unit.

8. *Help* and *Support.* Chapter 13, "Growing as a Professional," shows new teachers how to obtain help and support from colleagues, mentors, and administrators. In this chapter suggestions are made as to whom to go to and what you can expect from these three groups in the school community.

9. *Professional Lexicon.* This glossary, which defines key words that are boldfaced in the text, appears at the end of the book.

Introduction

The thirteen chapters of this book are *integrated,* similar to a curriculum, so that each is linked with what follows. This means that significant issues are revisited in different contexts throughout the text. However, this does not mean that the chapters must be read in the order presented here. Two of the chapters are unique in a "methods" book. Chapter 2 focuses on how to observe in classrooms. It emphasizes the four commonplaces of teaching: the learning environment, the students, the teacher, and the subject field that is being taught. Chapter 10 focuses on how to monitor students' performance. Examined in this chapter are the ways that teachers can guide students' work, diagnose their problems, recognize individual differences, and differentiate instruction when needed.

The advance organizers that begin each chapter are intended to "set the stage" for the content and provide an organizing structure for the chapter. The paragraph that follows the advance organizer provides a quick overview of the chapter for the reader. The teaching problems at the conclusion of each chapter are related to the content of the chapter and contribute motivation for class discussion or professional interaction between and among peers. Because the content of the text is integrated and touches on important professional knowledge and pedagogy, a single behavioral objective for each chapter would be misleading and a disservice to the reader. However, significant professional teaching standards have influenced the content of this text; these standards are discussed next.

Professional Standards

Three national groups have concerned themselves with professional teaching standards. The National Council for Accreditation of Teacher Education (NCATE) oversees teacher education programs to ensure that the credential program provides appropriate content and practice to inform the beginning teacher and assess the performance of the teacher candidate.

The second group is a consortium of thirty-two states concerned with both assessment and support for the beginning teacher. The Interstate New Teacher Assessment and Support Consortium (INTASC) has developed ten standards for beginning teachers to assess their growth and development during their intern year or beginning year of teaching and to provide necessary support to improve their performance. Those standards are *integrated* throughout the content of this text and identified after the advance organizers. Each chapter touches on several of the INTASC standards.

The third group, the National Board for Professional Teaching Standards (NBPTS), has compatible standards with INTASC designed for more experienced teachers. Those standards are identified in Chapter 12. The INTASC standards on the inside back cover and the table on the inside front cover identify key issues for each standard and the chapters that relate to the standard.

Acknowledgments

A book about teaching is created not only by the author, but by all the individuals who have influenced and contributed to the author's education. These individuals include not only the educators we recognize as great historical figures, but the people with whom we interact on a daily basis and who tell stories about their experiences in schools, their children's experiences, the teachers who have invited me into their classrooms, and my colleagues in school systems and at universities.

Specifically, I want to thank Hillary Hertzog, who authored Chapter 12, "Integration of Technology for Teaching and Learning." Dr. Hertzog, who teaches at California State University, Northridge (CSUN), is a recognized specialist in the use of technology in the curriculum; she coordinates the Carnegie Project for a New Era at CSUN.

Margo Pensavalle coordinates the student teaching program at the University of Southern California; her discussions and insights about the problems of student teachers and new teachers contributed to many ideas and teaching episodes in this text.

Agodi Alagbe, principal of the Felton School in Lennox, California, helped with the student surveys concerning classroom routines and the definition of a democratic classroom community.

Many individuals used precious time to review the original proposal and drafts of the text. I compliment them for their suggestions and tenacity to use their own publication time to help me with this project. These professors include the following people: Sue F. Abegglen, Culver-Stockton College; Judy Arnold, Lincoln Memorial University; Allan F. Cook, University of Illinois, Springfield; Amy Cox-Petersen, California State University, Fullerton; Joyce Lynn Garrett, Boise State University; Dorene Huvaere, Lewis University; Donna Jurich, Knox College; and Mitzi Lewison, Indiana University.

Paula Goldman is a phenomenal photographer who captures the precise moment of interest and excitement in her choice of when to snap the picture. Because she takes so many excellent classroom pictures, it is very difficult to limit how many are chosen for publication.

The teachers and principals of the Santa Monica Unified School District in California deserve a great deal of credit for opening their classrooms for the pictures in this book. At the McKinley School, Principal Wendy Wax helped identify teachers and classrooms. At Lincoln Middle School, Hank Harris provided access and Jeanne Davenport provided opportunity for fine pictures of the action in her classroom as well as coordinating permission statements from parents. Ilene Straus, principal of Santa Monica High School, and her administrative assistant, Leslie McGee, coordinated pictures and permission statements. Ms. McGee also helped set up the timing for picture shoots at the other schools.

Sitting at a computer too many hours a day causes physical problems, as many are aware. So I must thank two individuals who provided physical therapy and saved me from depression and the surgeon's skills. Michele Zeolla is an outstanding Registered Physical Therapist who diagnosed my problems, exercised patience, and sometimes submitted edicts that helped me overcome the disease of computerese. Leslie Granowitz taught me to enjoy Pilates and with it increased my strength and posture. As an ex-teacher, she also contributed many ideas for helping new teachers and wisdom about professional problems that often make teaching a revolving-door career choice.

Samantha Stieger, my granddaughter, spared her schoolwork and used her talent to create the graphs and figures used in the text, and her sister Lauren contributed stories about her high school experiences that helped enrich this book.

Dave Nelson, science chair and physics teacher, contributed information about a project he required of his senior advanced placement students at Oak Park High School.

A special thank-you to Linda Zuk, who has guided this text from manuscript to book with sensitive understanding of the author's wishes and concerns.

My husband, Bernard, who should be mentioned first, endured my highs and lows as I progressed through the text, *and* gave up golf time and vacation time so that I could complete the task. He exercised compassion and good sportsmanship throughout the project—as always.

My appreciation to Debra Stollenwerk grows with each text that I have written. Her impact on this text is particularly significant. She set the stakes high, communicated points of emphasis, and cheered me with her e-mailed sense of humor. I also want to thank Mary Morrill, Debra's assistant, who helped me by answering publication questions, most of which were contained in the author's manual that I failed to read!

Brief Contents

Part 1 The Classroom Community: Teachers and Students 1
CHAPTER 1 Developing the Classroom Community 3
CHAPTER 2 Classroom Observation 27
CHAPTER 3 How Students Learn 53

Part 2 Teacher Planning 67
CHAPTER 4 Lesson Planning 69
CHAPTER 5 Unit Planning and Professional Responsibilities 85

Part 3 Classroom Management 109
CHAPTER 6 Classroom Management for the Classroom Community 111
CHAPTER 7 The Classroom Community: Resolving Problems, Focusing on Student Behavior 138

Part 4 Instructional Strategies 161
CHAPTER 8 Selecting from an Instructional Repertoire 163
CHAPTER 9 Higher-Order Teaching Strategies 191

Part 5 Guiding and Assessing Students' Performance 217
CHAPTER 10 Informing Instruction Through Monitoring Students' Performance 219
CHAPTER 11 Informing Instruction Through Assessment 238

Part 6 Technology and Professional Problem Solving 265
CHAPTER 12 Integration of Technology for Teaching and Learning 267
CHAPTER 13 Growing as a Professional 286

Contents

Part 1 The Classroom Community: Teachers and Students 1

CHAPTER 1
Developing the Classroom Community 3

Advance Organizer 3
Leading the Classroom Through Trust, Respect, and Responsibility 4
Building Community—What Can Teachers Do? 5
  The Classroom Environment 6
  Teaching Methodologies 6
  Subject Field Content 6
  Resources and Tools 7
  Interaction with Students 7
Building Community—What Can Students Do? 7
  The Classroom Environment 7
  Teaching Methodology 8
  Subject Field Content 8
  Resources and Tools 8
  Interaction with the Teacher 8
Good Teaching and Student Learning 9
Leadership in Democratic Classrooms: Contrasting Teacher Control and Student Control 10
Discipline Systems: What They Do and What They Negate 11
  Behavior Modification Systems 12
  Other Systems 13
Helping Students Develop Responsibility and Self-Control 14
Encouraging Communication and Teamwork in the Classroom 15
Diversity in the Classroom Community 16
Encouraging Student Effort and Participation 18

Culturally Responsive Teaching 19
Characteristics of the Democratic Classroom 20
   What Do Students Like? 20
   What Decisions Do Students Make? 21
The Effective Teacher 22
   Subject Field Knowledge and Curriculum Planning 22
   Understanding the Students You Teach 23
   Instructional Approaches 23
   Classroom Management 23
   The Classroom Environment 24
   Student Participation, Decision Making, and Communication 24
   Effective Teaching 25
Chapter Summary 25
Chapter Review 25
Teaching Problems 26

CHAPTER 2
Classroom Observation 27

Advance Organizer 27
The "Walkaround" and the "The Buzz"—What Should You Observe When You Visit a Classroom? 28
The Environment 31
   Classroom Organization 31
   The Social/Emotional Climate of the Classroom 35
The Students 36
   Lucia Martin's Classroom 36
   Gerry Alred's Classroom 36
   Roger Ives's Classroom 36
   Jean Cantor's Classroom 36
The Teachers 37
   Lucia Martin 37
   Gerry Alred 37
   Roger Ives 38
   Jean Cantor 38
The Subjects 38
What Would You Like to See in Lucia Martin's Classroom? 39
General Organizational Considerations 40
   Where Students Sit 40
   Other Considerations 41

The Classroom Climate 41
Casual Versus Focused Observation 42
Valuing the Democratic Classroom Environment 42
Specific Techniques for Classroom Observation 43
- *Scripting* 44
- *Interviewing* 44
- *Videotaping* 44
- *Diagramming Interaction* 44
- *Audiotaping* 46
- *Anecdotal Record* 46
- *Checklists* 47
- *Case Study Narrative* 47
- *Ethnography* 48

The Visible and the Invisible 49
What Rules Tell Us 50
- *Teacher and Student Relations and Teacher Authority* 50
- *Individual Needs* 50
- *Classroom Interaction* 51

Chapter Summary 51
Teaching Problems 51

CHAPTER 3
How Students Learn 53

Advance Organizer 53
Developmental Considerations 54
- *Constructivism* 56
- *Multiple Intelligences, Learning Styles, and Natural Differences* 57
- *How Can Teachers Take Advantage of Students' Multiple Intelligences?* 58
- *Learning Styles* 60
- *Reflection and Impulsivity, Field Independence and Dependence* 61

Societal Considerations 62
- *Societal Impact* 63
- *How Do Societal Problems Affect Lesson Planning?* 64

Subject Matter Considerations 64
Differentiation of Instruction 65
Chapter Summary 66
Teaching Problems 66

Part 2 Teacher Planning 67

CHAPTER 4
Lesson Planning 69

Advance Organizer 69
Jim Sierra's Classroom 70
Novice and Experienced Teacher Lesson Planning 71
What Should Teachers Consider When Planning Lessons? 72
   Hands-On Experiences 73
   Real-Life Problem Solving 74
   Service Learning and Problem Solving 74
   Planning for the English Language Learner 75
   Group Work 76
   Collaborative Learning 77
   In-Depth Learning 79
   Appropriate Resource Materials and the Use of Technology 80
   Family and Community Participation 82
Chapter Summary 84
Teaching Problems 84

CHAPTER 5
Unit Planning and Professional Responsibilities 85

Advance Organizer 85
What Should Teachers Consider When Planning Lessons? 86
Time Management and Teacher Planning 91
Lesson Planning and Curriculum Concepts 93
   Interdisciplinary Teaching 94
   Clustering Lessons by Using a Theme 94
Unit Planning 95
   Jim Sierra's Unit Teaching Plan 96
   Discussion of Mr. Sierra's Unit Teaching Plan 99
What Do You Do if the Lesson Plan Fails? 101
Additional Planning Considerations 102
Things to Think About When Planning a Unit 103
   Balance 103
   Semester or Yearlong Planning 104
   Student Participation Through Webbing 104
   Data Retrieval Charts 105
   Backward Problem Solving 105

Chapter Summary 107
Teaching Problems 107

Part 3 Classroom Management   109

CHAPTER 6
Classroom Management for the Classroom Community   111

Advance Organizer   111
Classroom Management and Discipline—Not Synonymous in Democratic Classrooms   112
  Orchestrating Classroom Life   *113*
  Planning Curriculum   *113*
  Organizing Procedures and Resources   *114*
  Arranging the Environment   *115*
  Monitoring Student Progress   *115*
  Anticipating Potential Problems   *116*
Getting Started—Grouping   116
Large-Group Instruction   117
  The Sense of Belonging   *118*
  Focus on Classroom Management   *119*
Small-Group Instruction   121
  How to Begin   *121*
  Group Size   *123*
  Group Roles   *123*
  Group Procedures   *123*
  What Can Go Wrong? Anticipating Group Work Problems   *124*
  Should You Ever Skip the Evaluation Discussion?   *126*
  Teacher Responsibilities During Group Work   *126*
Anticipating the First Day of the Semester   127
  Classroom Management in the Elementary Classroom—Lucia Martin   *127*
  Classroom Management in the Secondary Classroom—Roger Ives   *130*
Classroom Management and Motivation   132
Classroom Management and School Socialization   132
Class Size   133
Maintaining Class Attention   133
Management-Focused Problem Solving   135
  Elementary Classroom—Lucia Martin   *135*
  Elementary Classroom—Jim Sierra   *135*

Middle School Classroom—Gerry Alred 135
High School Classroom—Jean Cantor 136
English Language Learners 136
Chapter Summary 136
Teaching Problems 137

CHAPTER 7
The Classroom Community: Resolving Problems, Focusing on Student Behavior 138

Advance Organizer 138
Mr. Bemis's Classroom Management Problem 139
Freedom and Self-Control 140
Disruptions and Misbehavior 141
Misbehavior in the Classroom 142
Bullying 143
Signs of Bullying 144
Rudeness and Defiance 144
Nonaccountability 145
Interruption and Speaking Out 146
Social Skills and Interpersonal Relations 147
What Can Teachers Do? 148
Prejudice in the Classroom 148
Gang Activities 149
School Violence 151
Large Schools Versus Small Schools 151
What Can Schools Do? 152
Advantages of the Small-School and "Schools-Within-Schools" Concepts 153
School Environment and Supervision 153
Conflict Resolution 154
Students with Special Needs 159
Chapter Summary 159
Teaching Problems 159

Part 4 Instructional Strategies 161

CHAPTER 8
Selecting from an Instructional Repertoire 163

Advance Organizer 163
Authentic Teaching 164

The Direct Instruction Model of Teaching   165
   Gerry Alred's Classroom   166
   Analysis of the Lesson   167
   Lucia Martin's Classroom   167
   Analysis of the Lesson   168
The Comprehension Model of Teaching   169
   Lucia Martin's Classroom   171
The Advance Organizer Model of Teaching   172
   Pictures and Graphs   173
   Concrete Objects   173
Cooperative Learning   174
   Teacher and Student Behaviors for Cooperative Learning Groups   175
   Research Related to Cooperative Group Learning   176
   Recent Research   177
   Cooperative Groups Learning Models   177
   Motivation   178
   What Skills Do Students Need to Learn?   178
   Specially Designed Academic Instruction in English (SDAIE)   180
Questioning Strategies for Expository Teaching Lessons   180
   Precision Questioning   181
   Clustering of Questions   181
   Are There Some General Rules About Asking Questions?   182
   Are There Some No-Nos When Asking Questions?   183
   Wait Time, Reinforcement, and Increasing Interaction   183
Discussion Strategies for Democratic Classrooms   184
   Democratic Behavior During the Class Discussion   185
   The Teacher's Role   186
   Discussion Variations   186
   Discussion Problems   187
Teaching with Standards   188
   Content Versus Performance Standards   188
Chapter Summary   189
Teaching Problems   189

CHAPTER 9
Higher-Order Teaching Strategies   191

Advance Organizer   191
The Relationship of Inquiry and Constructivist Teaching   192
Inquiry Teaching Models   193
The Constructivist Teaching Model   194
The Divergent Questioning Model   195

Divergent Questions and Wait Time　197
The Concept Attainment Model　197
　　Gerry Alred's Classroom　197
　　Phases of Concept Attainment　200
　　Examples of Concrete Representation　200
　　Motivation and Assessment　200
The Group Investigation Model　201
　　Jim Sierra's Classroom　201
　　Analysis of Sierra's Group Investigation Lesson　203
　　Phases of Group Investigation　204
　　How Group Investigation Differs from Cooperative Learning　206
Why Concepts Are Important　207
　　The Taba Questioning Strategy　208
　　Jim Sierra's Classroom　208
Students' Questions as Means for Critical and Creative Thinking　210
　　Backward Problem Solving and Webbing　210
　　Whole Class/Small Group　211
　　Encouraging Creative Thinking　212
　　Analysis of Cantor's Lesson　212
Using Gestures to Emphasize and Communicate Meaning　213
Using Resources for Inquiry and Problem-Solving Teaching Strategies　214
　　The Case Study Approach　214
Chapter Summary　215
Teaching Problems　216

Part 5　Guiding and Assessing Students' Performance　217

CHAPTER 10
Informing Instruction Through Monitoring Students' Performance　219

Advance Organizer　219
Teacher Responsibility for Student Performance　221
What Is Monitoring?　221
　　Controlling the Classroom Environment　222
　　Encouraging Complex Thinking Skills　223
　　Monitoring English Language Learners and Students with Special Needs　223
　　Monitoring Each Student's Contribution to Group Assignments　224
　　Providing Guided Practice and Social Interaction　225
　　Partner Work and Coaching　227
Communities of Learners　228
Reinforcing Students' Progress　229

  Homework 230
   Monitoring and Feedback for Homework 230
  Behavioral Monitoring 231
  Sharing Student Work with Parents 232
   Parent-Teacher Conferences 232
   Unplanned Conferences 236
   Teacher-Parent-Student Conferences 236
  Chapter Summary 237
  Teaching Problems 237

CHAPTER 11
Informing Instruction Through Assessment 238

  Advance Organizer 238
  What Is Assessment? 239
  Authentic Assessment 239
   Assessing Students' Ideas and Ways of Thinking 240
   Assessing Students' Content Knowledge and Understanding 242
   Assessing Students' Communication Skills 245
   What Teachers Learn 246
  Student Portfolios 247
  Rubrics 248
  Standards and the School Curriculum 249
   Content-Based Standards 252
  Teacher-Made Tests 255
   True/False and Yes/No Tests 256
   Multiple Choice Tests 256
   Essay Tests 257
  Standardized Tests 257
  Fear of Tests 259
  Judging and Grading 259
   Judging and Grading English Language Learners 261
  Chapter Summary 261
  Teaching Problems 262

Part 6 Technology and Professional Problem Solving 265

CHAPTER 12
Integration of Technology for Teaching and Learning 267

  Advance Organizer 267
  Computer Technology for Student Learning 269

Using Technology to Differentiate Instruction: Computer-Based Learning (CBL) 273
The Thinking Connection—Problem Solving, Project-Based Learning, and Problem-Based Learning 275
Technology as a Student Tool 276
- *Writing: Word Processing and Desktop Publishing* 277
- *Organizing Data: Spreadsheets and Databases* 278
- *Using Graphics: Multimedia and Presentation Software* 278

Technology as a Teaching Tool 279
Technology as a Support Tool 280
Technology as an Assessment Tool 280
Technology as a Communication Tool 282
Organizing and Planning for Technology 283
Chapter Summary 285
Teaching Problems 285

CHAPTER 13
Growing as a Professional 286

Advance Organizer 286
Interpersonal Relationships with Peers, Mentors, and Administrators 287
How Can Peers Help Each Other? 287
- *Advantages of Peer Relationships* 288
- *Time—The Inhibitor of Professional Development* 288
- *Program Quality Review in California* 289

Collegial Relationships 290
- *Coaching* 291
- *Teacher-Mentor Relationships* 292
- *Relationship with Administrators* 293

Obtaining Help, Support, Assistance: Typical Beginning Teacher Problems 294
- *Lesson and Unit Planning* 294
- *Time Management* 295
- *Student Diversity* 295
- *Behavior Problems* 295
- *Small-Group Teaching* 296
- *Instructional Strategies* 297
- *Relationships with More Experienced Teachers* 297
- *School Policies and Procedures* 298

Whom Can I Ask for Help? 299
    Another Beginning Teacher 299
    Teacher-Mentor 299
    College Adviser 299
    Experienced Grade-Level or Content-Area Teacher 299
    Department or Grade-Level Chairperson 300
    Principal or Assistant Principal 300
    Additional Resources 300
    Professional Organizations 301
Participation in School and Professional Organizations 302
    How Is National Board Certification Accomplished? 302
    What Should Teacher Portfolios Contain? 304
Professional Ethics 305
Balancing Personal and Professional Responsibilities 306
Chapter Summary 306
Teaching Problems 306

Appendix A   Answers to Selected Problems   309

Appendix B   John Washington's Health, Physiology, and Physical Education Unit   311

Professional Lexicon   317
Bibliography   321
Name Index   327
Subject Index   331

PART 1

THE CLASSROOM COMMUNITY: TEACHERS AND STUDENTS

Chapters 1–3 introduce the concepts of society, the environment of the classroom, and the learner. These three concepts interact and affect the building of a classroom community. Chapter 1 focuses on the societal challenges that teachers face. Chapter 2 introduces the learning environment of the classroom and how that environment affects both teacher and student responsibilities. Chapter 3 addresses the developmental needs of students, how they differ, and how they learn.

CHAPTER 1

Developing the Classroom Community

ADVANCE ORGANIZER

These questions can be used as a framework to assist you in integrating professional knowledge and understanding of the content of this chapter.

1. There are two important goals that schools should achieve, but controversies affect their accomplishment. Identify the goals and explain how the controversies affect teaching.
2. In a democratic classroom community, student learning and quality teaching go hand in hand; what factors affect student learning?
3. How can teachers build a sense of community in the classroom and why is it important to do so?
4. How can student diversity be used as a teaching advantage?
5. How does culturally responsive pedagogy affect students?
6. What are the characteristics of a democratic classroom community?
7. What should an effective teacher know and be able to do?

 The following INTASC issues and standards are discussed in this chapter: Numbers 1–7, 9, 10.

The major purpose of this chapter is to define in professional terms the meaning and implications of a classroom community. To do so, I discuss some of the challenges that confront teachers and some of the ways that students respond to these challenges; the diversity of the modern classroom; and the importance of encouraging classroom communication, participation, and teamwork to improve the community of the classroom.

Leading the Classroom Through Trust, Respect, and Responsibility

In Gerry Alred's sixth-grade classroom, students were studying civil rights; they were focusing on the concept of intolerance. Students selected specific topics to research, such as ethnic jokes, graffiti that makes fun of gays, bullying on school playgrounds, and the drawing of hate symbols in the halls and on desktops. The topics served as the basis for grouping the students. Each group was to gather evidence of intolerance related to its topic and create a historical timeline that matched the evidence.

As the students joined their groups, Ms. Alred noticed that two students who had selected the ethnic joke group were not attending their group meeting. When she confronted them, they admitted that they didn't like working with the Cuban students in their group. Alred quietly talked to them about their beliefs. She decided to stop class work and, without naming the students, she asked the class, "What should we do when after selecting a group topic, someone decides not to work with a particular group of classmates?"

The students thought about the problem posed by the teacher and a discussion ensued. Responses included the following:

"We made a class rule that we must respect all of our classmates. It doesn't sound like this is happening."

"It isn't fair to quit a group and leave them shorthanded."

"We had the right to select our topic; it isn't responsible to change your mind when we have already started to work."

"If someone changes his mind it disrupts all the other groups and that's not fair."
Finally one of the students concluded—and the class was clearly in agreement—"It's your job, Mrs. Alred, to see that our class works cooperatively and that our rules are enforced."

Throughout our democratic history, schools have been expected to accomplish two major purposes: *literacy education* and *preparation for citizenship*. Neither political party allegiance (liberal or conservative) nor diverse educational theories have affected public acceptance of these purposes. Yet how these purposes are to be accomplished has always elicited great debate. Both attainment of literacy and readiness for citizenship responsibilities have been entrusted to teachers.

Debate about literacy education often focuses on *time* spent teaching the "three Rs" (reading, 'riting, and 'rithmetic), meeting *uniform standards* in these subject fields, and what else in the curriculum is considered *basic* for a literate educated person. This text will focus on how teachers fulfill their responsibilities to provide an outstanding culturally responsive education for students and some of the problems that confront them.

The debate over preparation for citizenship is even more complicated than that over literacy education. To participate in a democracy, citizens need experience in making choices and intelligent decisions. Gerry Alred entrusted her students to engage in a serious discussion and come to a rational decision. Their comments indicate that they had a common set of beliefs about life in their classroom. Citizens must share their viewpoints by engaging in discussion or discourse (Noddings, 1999). Yet in many schools students are given very few opportunities to make decisions. They are compelled to attend school with preset hours and a preset calendar. The curriculum is chosen for them and taught when the system deems it appropriate. They are given relatively few opportunities for elective subjects or sustained study in subjects of choice. They seldom engage in socially current or historical debates and rarely select how they will complete assignments or the tools and resources they will use—even though we recognize the need to attend to cultural diversity, learning styles, and multiple intelligences. In fact, students rarely decide when to go to the bathroom, get a drink of water, or communicate with peers. Yet despite these vagaries of the system, teachers and students can do many things to build community.

Building Community—What Can Teachers Do?

All human beings, young and old, have the need to belong to something, and that "something" must be larger than just their own family. The feeling of belonging involves bonding with others through cooperative activities, companionship, mutual respect, caring about each other, and the construction of common goals. To build a classroom **community,** it is necessary to do the following:

1. Provide opportunities for students to connect with each other through common cooperative work activities.

2. Help students develop respect for each other's rights and responsibilities.

3. Involve students in setting common classroom goals for work and behavior.

4. Build character through reflective caring attitudes.

Many conditions in our schools evolved through historical tradition and are often controlled by traditional state and district policies. Though some school faculties are attempting to reshape their school environment and district policies, under most circumstances teachers must accept the rules and regulations of the education system that employs them. However, teachers do have much to say about life in their own classrooms. Teachers can control the (1) classroom environment; (2) teaching methodologies; (3) time and emphasis of subject field content; (4) resources and tools; and (5) interaction with students. Each of these aspects of classroom life affects how students learn, how students feel about schooling, and the development of a class community. Let us briefly consider these items.

The Classroom Environment

Many terms are used to describe the **environment** of the classroom, such as *climate, milieu, structure,* and *instructional setting*. The environment encompasses a number of different concepts—for example, how the classroom looks, which includes the bulletin boards, the arrangement of chairs and tables or desks, the equipment and resources in the classroom, the ventilation, the neatness or clutter, the quietness or buzz of activity, and the tone of compatibility and comfort or discord.

Teaching Methodologies

Teachers have great control over *how they teach*. Does the teacher spend a great deal of time lecturing? Does the teacher elicit student participation? Do students work in small inquiry and cooperative groups? Are there whole-class discussions and debates? Is the teacher the center and focal point of all teaching strategies? Teachers can use a great variety of teaching strategies and so the question is, do they?

Did You Know That . . . ?

Students' problem-solving skills in mathematics improve when they are given the opportunity to discuss individual means and processes for working out problems. The communication process helps students organize and analyze their thinking and reflect on the strategies of others (National Council of Teachers of Mathematics, 2000, p. 60).

Subject Field Content

The National Board for Professional Teaching Standards (1990) identifies five professional teaching standards, which it calls *propositions*. Proposition 2 states that teachers know the subjects they teach and how to teach those subjects to students. Though teachers need to be cognizant of the professional standards in the content fields, they have a great deal of leeway in whether to explore topics in depth or superficially. They can provide time and opportunity for students' cooperative work projects and students' choices and interests. Teachers can integrate subject fields and demonstrate concept meaning in different disciplines, and they can tie present-day conflicts to historical social problems. Relevance to the students you teach and motivation to inspire learning are prime considerations for teacher decision making.

Resources and Tools

The use of materials for instruction affects methodology, time, content, varied perspectives, and even the room environment. If computers are used in the classroom, then space must be considered. If a wide variety of texts are to be used, then bookcase access must be considered. If students will work on hands-on projects during class, where will they work? What materials will be needed? Should students work in small groups or with a partner? Each of the subject fields and grade levels requires specific materials, such as science texts, kits, videos, craft materials, math manipulatives, flannel boards for beginning readers, and chart racks. The list is endless and teacher decision making vast. Each decision affects students' sense of belonging and connection to others in the classroom.

Interaction with Students

Some teachers are warm and enthusiastic, while others pride themselves on businesslike behaviors; regardless of personality style, all teachers can learn about their students' knowledge and cultural experiences. Interaction with students describes the ways teachers talk to and care about their students, recognize individual differences, and provide learning experiences that are developmentally appropriate and geared to students' interests and needs. Classroom management and discipline are related to teachers' respect for and commitment to their students and their understanding of how students learn. Ms. Alred considered it important that her students discuss inappropriate behavior in her classroom.

None of these elements are separate entities; they do not stand alone. Each is integrated with the other elements of teacher decision making. Planning your classroom environment affects classroom management; selecting instructional strategies affects management and resources; time and emphasis of content affects interaction with students. Each of these components will be discussed throughout this text.

Building Community—What Can Students Do?

Students can control only those aspects of classroom life to which the teacher grants them access. This may include making decisions about the classroom environment; expressing preferences for teaching methodologies, time, and emphasis regarding curriculum choices; use of materials and resources; and permission to interact with others. Students are pretty savvy about the choices and decisions they are allowed to make, and they recognize when teachers respect and care about them. If we think about these elements that have traditionally been considered the domain of teachers, we can get a picture of the kinds of decisions that students are capable of making in a genuine classroom community.

The Classroom Environment

In some classrooms students contribute to the way a room looks with their own projects, pictures, experiments, and portfolios. Young students contribute experience stories and charts. Older students may contribute provocative questions recorded on bulletin boards. Students may be made responsible for setting up the room and maintaining a healthful environment. If given the opportunity, students may suggest optimal space for computers, learning centers, and supplies. In a trusting, respectful climate students will contribute to a general good feeling about the classroom.

Teaching Methodology

Students enjoy the opportunity to express whether they prefer work on solo projects, with partners, or in small groups. Typically they like variety in the way a class is conducted. The same routines every day become boring. Though students want to know what to expect and the specific goals they are to accomplish, they need motivation and opportunity to choose *how* they may achieve the desired outcome. (In an English/language arts class, may they illustrate, dramatize, or write their own conclusion or development of a novel? May they select what they are to read? May they express their personal story or perspective about what they read?)

Subject Field Content

If students become hooked on Civil War battles or Galapagos Island turtles, may they sustain their interest and explore in depth? May they study divisions of labor during World War II that affected gender and racial differences? Do they have the opportunity to scan what is expected of them and choose how they will go about studying specific issues? May students share their own experiences and compare them with the concepts in their textbooks?

Resources and Tools

Should students select their own materials and tools? May they explore content on the Internet? Will students need to share texts and computers, and if so, will they select whom they work with and how they go about it? Should students be expected to use home and library resources? What will happen if students do not have access to the needed supplies? What choices will students be allowed to make? May they select "critical voices" in addition to the standard textbook chapter?

Interaction with the Teacher

If students do not understand a concept or an assignment, are they comfortable in asking the teacher for help? Do students smile and joke with the teacher? Do they trust the teacher and share personal experiences and problems? Do they speak respectfully to the teacher and recognize that respect should be reciprocal? Can students expect fair and honest responses and treatment from their teachers? Sometimes students are fearful in the classroom because of teacher retorts or sarcasm. When students respond similarly, it is frequently caused by lack of a positive relationship with the teacher. Should students be allowed to discriminate against other students?

Students' decision-making powers vary greatly in schools and classrooms. Much depends on the building of a classroom community in which there is an environment of mutual respect and trust. If students are subjected to ridiculous rules and are required to memorize them, be tested on them, and have their parents/guardians sign them, students recognize that teachers and administrators do not respect or trust them. Too often school rules are focused on dress codes (no hats, no cowboy boots, no cut-off jeans) and "thou shall not" activities such as entering the classroom before the bell rings, using the bathrooms except during recess periods, or communicating in languages other than English.

If schools adopt **authoritarian** regulations and teachers do not reject them, it is impossible for students to develop a sense of belonging or to feel that they are in an environment that trusts and cares about them. As a consequence, students' self-esteem, motivation, and acceptance of personal responsibility are undermined. Darling-Hammond (1997) proposes **authoritative** schools that allow students to make choices and decisions and require them to take responsibility for outcomes. When problems arise, the teacher and students problem-solve and discuss the consequences. (This will be discussed in depth in Chapters 4 and 5.) When teachers demonstrate that they care about their students, respect is mutual and students learn to accept responsibility for maintaining a democratic learning environment.

Teaching Hints

1. Involve students in setting classroom rules.
2. Involve students in sensible and real choices and decision making.
3. Provide many opportunities for group problem solving.
4. Ensure communication among students and interact personally with every student.
5. Verify students' understanding of work tasks.
6. Act authoritatively, not as an authoritarian.

Good Teaching and Student Learning

Teachers who demonstrate good practice recognize that the goal of a democratic classroom community is achievable only in an environment that supports genuine student learning and teaching that is geared to meet the diverse needs of the student population. Student learning can be measured only when students demonstrate the application of what they are taught; they must use knowledge in a purposeful way. Sizer (1992) describes "Community of Learners" classrooms where students work as researchers and share knowledge with classmates. Teachers are responsible for selecting meaningful contexts for studies and providing a supportive democratic community. Gerry Alred demonstrated these concepts: a supportive democratic environment, students working as researchers, student choice in learning activity, a meaningful context for study, and the sharing of students' knowledge.

National concern about school performance and professional accountability has emphasized the need for rigorous standards in both teacher preparation and continuing professional development. Three national groups have helped set standards for the teaching profession. The National Council for Accreditation of Teacher Education (NCATE) monitors teacher education programs to ensure appropriate course work and field work for prospective teachers. A special task force of more than half the states formed a consortium to set standards for teacher licensing, the Interstate New Teacher Assessment and Support Consortium (INTASC). The third group, the National Board for Professional Teaching Standards, created standards for advanced teacher certification to improve both teaching and learning.

Although Gerry Alred is a beginning teacher, she is interested in achieving National Board Certification (NBC). Her interest in NBC can be attributed to her teacher preparation; to obtain a teaching credential she was required to submit a teaching **portfolio,** and her portfolio helped her obtain her teaching position. Achievement of NBC means that a teacher is recognized for commitment to the profession and excellence in teaching. It is a process that encourages teachers to examine their own practice using standards defined by teachers and other stakeholders who are dedicated to professional development and student learning. Portfolio development requires self-study.

Portfolio development for teachers is similar to the student portfolios required in many schools. It is not sufficient for students to display a finished product, such as a science experiment. Students must analyze their work by identifying the process of development, what went wrong, the corrections they made, and what they learned from the process. Teachers must engage in a similar process of self-analysis of their teaching lessons.

National Board Certified teachers are dedicated to student learning and are professionally rewarded nationally and explicitly by their school districts. They serve as spokespeople for the teaching profession. They are honored as role models and frequently advise and mentor student teachers, new teachers, and colleagues seeking NBC. School districts typically reward NBC teachers with salary increases and bonuses. In most states teachers' personal costs for certification fees are reimbursed. The certification process, portfolios, and self-study for National Board Certification are discussed in Chapter 13.

Leadership in Democratic Classrooms: Contrasting Teacher Control and Student Control

There are several different perspectives on teacher versus student control of the classroom environment. Many years ago Lewin, Lippitt, and White (1939) studied the leadership style of three summer camp leaders. One leader assumed complete control of his team by assigning all tasks to be performed and complete instructions for procedures. Another leader provided no guidance to his team at all concerning their tasks. The third leader motivated his group by raising questions and provided time for the team to share decision making concerning their projects. After a period of time had elapsed, each leader left his group alone. In the first group with the authoritarian leader, the team continued to work for a while, but fighting and bickering characterized the period. In the second group with the laissez-faire leader, absolutely nothing was accomplished. In the third group with the democratic leader, the team continued work quite contentedly and accomplished as much as they had when the leader was present.

The researchers concluded that both the authoritarian-led and democratic-led teams were able to complete their projects, but the democratic leadership produced more contented and happier campers. Certainly less time is expended when teachers *tell* and *direct*, but also it is clear that students do not learn democratic processes and decision making unless they get an opportunity to participate in making choices.

In the teaching episode that opened this chapter, Gerry Alred did not need to stop class work to discuss the case of the two students who refused to participate in their group, but the teaching of democratic processes demanded it. We teach by what we do and what we ignore. If teachers abandon their leadership responsibilities, they lose control of their classroom, but if they trust and share responsibility with their students, they can create a classroom community that is fair and comfortable because everyone shares responsibility. Neither anarchy nor authoritarianism is valued in our society.

Discipline Systems: What They Do and What They Negate

Discipline is often misinterpreted by equating it with classroom management. As you will see in Chapter 6, the definition of classroom management makes no mention of discipline. Discipline denotes behavior that can be good when it is self-imposed and internally motivated or bad when it means that the individual fails to control his or her own behavior according to group norms.

In a democratic classroom all of the individuals in the classroom are the *community* and as such they refer to themselves as *us* or *we:* "We make the rules in *our* classroom." "We wrote a class song and a class newspaper." "Our class is considered the best . . ." Dewey (1944) tells us that a community has common aims, beliefs, aspirations and understandings; he called it "like-mindedness" (p. 4).

When a classroom community sets rules for behavior, it is committing its members to ways of governing themselves for the good of everyone. An individual who chooses to disregard class rules is distressing the whole community because he or she is not contributing as a social member. Gerry Alred appealed to the classroom community to apply the social rules of behavior they had defined.

Now let's see how **discipline systems** differ from the concept of a democratic community. Although the teacher is the ultimate authoritative figure of the classroom, in a democratic structure the teacher maintains an environment that encourages class members to actively participate in defining and affirming how the classroom is to be governed. When a discipline system is installed, the teacher's role changes to authoritarian and students' participatory roles change to compliance. The teacher sets the rules and enforces them to ensure obedience.

In some discipline systems the teacher offers incentives for compliance in the form of presents, points, time off, or candy. These are considered rewards or reinforcers for good behavior. Students who defy and fail to yield to the system must endure the consequences.

These may include public reprimands, exclusion from activities, detention, special assignments, and notes to parents/guardians concerning the student's misbehavior. The consequence is intended to serve as a negative reinforcer.

Behavior Modification Systems

Behavior modification systems are rooted in stimulus-response theories prevalent in the twentieth century and are used frequently in present-day schools. Based on Skinner's beliefs about learning, rewards are used to strengthen desired behavior and punishment is used to weaken negative behavior. An example of a popular behavior modification system is Canter and Canter's *Assertive Discipline* (1992), which focuses on teachers' rights to establish classroom rules and to enforce them through identified consequences.

The classroom environment is designed to ensure student obedience. Students are expected to know the rules, which are typically sent home for parents' signatures and displayed on the bulletin board. Along with the rules are the consequences for infractions. The first time a student disobeys a rule, the teacher places the student's name on the chalkboard. The second offense of the day gives the student a check by his or her name and requires 15 minutes of detention; on the third offense the student receives a double check and 30 minutes of detention; each check increases detention until the fifth offense, when the student is sent to the principal's office and parents are called. Ultimately the student can be required to leave school.

Another discipline system is Gordon's *I Messages* (1974), which focuses on the "ownership" of problems. The teacher must decide whether the student or the teacher owns the problem. When the student owns the problem, he or she is told to deal with it by coming up with a plan to solve the problem. Gordon believes that discipline in the classroom is a matter of communication.

Token economies are discipline systems based on bestowing rewards (such as play money or tokens) for appropriate behavior and taking the reward away when students misbehave. At set times students may exchange the tokens for tangible rewards: free time, early privileges to go to lunch, candy, and so on.

Contracting systems are used when teachers think the problem is that students need to be held to a formal agreement in order to complete their work. The contract spells out a timeline and a reward for the student when work is completed on time. Both the teacher and student sign the contract.

What's Wrong with Behavior Modification Systems?

1. Reinforcement principles rarely work past primary grade levels, and primary-age students can rarely read the rules and do not understand the consequences.
2. Older students resent taking "rules and consequences" home to parents and tend to make fun of them.
3. Teachers spend too much class time at the chalkboard writing and checking names and bestowing or taking away rewards.

4. Actual problem behavior is never dealt with on a personal or classroom community level. Students know only when they have disobeyed the rules.
5. Parents learn about their child's behavior only when the child repeatedly misbehaves. Since behavior can be good as well as bad, why shouldn't parents be contacted when students behave appropriately?

Other Systems

Jones and Jones (1986) try to focus on positive means to enforce appropriate student behavior. Teachers and students define classroom rules to deal with all contingencies. The rules are posted for all to see. A five-step plan is used when students fail to follow the rules:

1. The teacher tries a nonverbal admonishment—pointing.
2. The teacher tells the student to "check yourself."
3. The teacher asks the student which rule he or she violated.
4. The teacher tells the student to move away from the group to a designated spot in the classroom to develop a plan for improving his or her behavior.
5. The teacher sends the student to the discipline officer of the school (principal, assistant principal, and so on) to develop a plan for improving his or her behavior.

Glasser (1986, 1996) focuses on students who consistently misbehave. He believes the teacher should make a list of his or her personal reactions to the misbehavior. Then the teacher must analyze the list to see if he or she can identify what works and what doesn't work when interacting with the student. The teacher should attempt to improve relationships with the student. The student should be asked to identify the misbehavior incidents at a conference with the teacher. Conferences continue until the student can develop a plan to improve behavior. If all else fails, the teacher may invoke an in-school suspension, out of the classroom. Ultimately the student's parents will be called to help deal with the problem. Glasser's program is called *reality therapy* and he has written several books dealing with motivating students. He suggests that teachers should function as classroom managers.

One problem related to discipline in the classroom is *misinterpretation* of the student's reason for lack of conformity. Instead of questioning the clarity of the instructions given to students, whether students understand the assignment, the relevance and meaningfulness of the task, and the capability of the student to perform the task, the teacher usually assumes that the misbehaving student is dilatory or devilish. Discipline systems are not attuned to examination of the *causes* of student problems. They are intended to reinforce teacher authority and ensure student compliance; therefore a democratic community is antithetical, and sharing, respect, trusting, and caring become difficult for the teacher to demonstrate and achieve. (See Kohn, 1996, for more on the effect of punishment in the classroom.)

> **Teaching Hints**
>
> 1. Speak respectfully to students, not sarcastically.
> 2. Involve students as a community of learners to solve discipline problems.
> 3. Speak quietly and personally to misbehaving students and provide opportunity for students to "state their case."
> 4. Question your own instructions and behavior instead of blaming students.

Helping Students Develop Responsibility and Self-Control

There are only two basic means to encourage student responsibility and self-control. The first is to insist that students work through the process of defining classroom government. This means they must discuss how their classroom will operate. The teacher may need to present organizational problems. For example, "We are going to be doing quite a bit of group work this semester; we need to decide (1) how to arrange our tables and chairs and (2) how we determine who works together. Do you want to always work with the same people? Should you work with your closest friends? How should groups be selected? What problems should we anticipate?"

These decision-making questions engage students in realistic thinking about how they will work best in this classroom. Students know very well that on many occasions they will want to work with others who are not their best friends. Sometimes they will want to work alone. They know that some group work should be arranged by interests, not permanent placements, but they need to work through these solutions. These are choices we want students to make.

Another discussion needs to be addressed—wasting class time. If you are using a discipline system, you can threaten the students with detention or taking away privileges, but if you want a democratic classroom community you might say, "We all know that our classroom time for our projects is limited; how can we make sure that we use our work time during class wisely and eliminate some of our out-of-class work?" This is not a veiled threat; it is a realistic decision that students must think about: getting to class on time and being ready for work. This may include thinking about obtaining necessary resources for their projects: Computer use? Passing out textbooks? Obtaining felt pens, crayons, large paper, floor space? Who will do what? When students are involved in choices, they will feel more involved in the decisions that are made and more accepting of responsibility to see that the decisions work.

The second means to build responsibility and self-control is to appeal to students' expectations. Once students have made decisions about the process for running their class, involve them in assessing whether things are going as they anticipated. "Do we need to make some adjustments?" "How can we help each other accomplish our goals?"

Classrooms are rarely ideal environments. If students have never had the opportunity to participate in making decisions that affect their life in the classroom, they will need your patience and most of all they will need to see that you are trustworthy. If the decisions you ask them to make are irrelevant, they will know it. For example, consider questions such as, "Should we give special work assignments to classmates who are not ready on time?" or, "Do you want to read this book by Laura Ingalls Wilder first or the book by Beverly Cleary first?" If students are going to be required to read *both* books, and not a choice of one or the other, they won't really care which one they read first, and they won't consider the question a real decision.

Students need to make decisions if for no other reason than they need the practice in order to grow into mature thinking adults. Choosing needs to be taught at school; it is a significant part of the socialization experience. Another way that teachers help students accept responsibility begins in the primary grades. Teachers often set up monitor charts or "helper" charts, which distribute classroom responsibility to the young students. These charts identify the jobs that need to be done in order for the room to run efficiently. The helper charts are usually changed weekly so that students rotate their responsibilities.

Though a helper chart sounds silly for a secondary classroom, there are still jobs that need to be carried out during each class period, and students can be given responsibility, thereby relieving the teacher of some preparations. In secondary classrooms students can be responsible for taking attendance, setting up work tables and supplies, tutoring, and communicating resource information and school news. In some secondary classrooms teachers reserve one bulletin board for each class and students are responsible for displaying work that reflects their class studies.

Encouraging Communication and Teamwork in the Classroom

When students are given the opportunity to share knowledge with each other, they reap the benefits of improving communication skills and learning to value teamwork. Earlier in the chapter there was mention of the value of students discussing their problem-solving methods. Suppose that during the discussion students question each other concerning the process used to solve a problem, and the teacher suggests that students who are questioned go to the chalkboard and demonstrate (teach) their method to the rest of the class. This is a very meaningful and purposeful way to encourage students to share knowledge and recognize that they can learn from peers. All learning does not need to emanate from the teacher. When students share learning they are taking on responsibility to apply what they know for others' benefit and at the same time they are encouraging their classmates to be actively engaged in the process.

Collaborative learning is another means to encourage student teamwork, recognize the value of diversity, and improve communication. It is not unusual for students, particularly students with limited English proficiency, to misunderstand the teacher. But learning from other students may be comprehensible. Working in small teams with each person responsible for a specific component allows team members to work in their own unique ways and then share the benefits of multiple intelligences and individual expertise.

Another advantage of teamwork is that students learn so many different ways to inquire from classmates and generate new experiences and skills from classmates. Teamwork can embrace diversity instead of insisting that everyone follow the same route and process. However, teamwork must be carefully planned, both in the composition of the groups and in work assignments that are challenging.

Diversity in the Classroom Community

Public school classrooms in the United States enroll students who differ in race, ethnicity, social class and income, language, nationality, citizenship, physical size, gender, sexuality, religion, culture, disabilities, capabilities, multiple intelligences, and combinations of all of these. Many large school districts have students representing a hundred different languages. An example is Minneapolis (Johnson & Taylor, 2001); Los Angeles urban schools often have as many as fifty different languages in *one school*.

Since the classroom contains so many societal differences, it is difficult for teachers to include curriculum that represents all human differences; however, teachers can make a point of specifying that "Today we will hear and read about the story of a specific group of individuals and their perspective about . . ." Students need to learn that each group has a different story and different perspectives. As a consequence it may be necessary to include different approaches to every subject in the curriculum.

The most important concept that we must recognize when teaching in such diverse classrooms is that heterogeneity is an advantage because it can be used to improve both teaching and learning. When the teacher uses collaborative teaching strategies, students can share their experiences and knowledge and are not as dependent on the teacher as the only source of information. One California school that had a limited number of Hmong children decided to reorganize and have multigraded classrooms, because some of the

Student diversity is highlighted in this student-designed bulletin board.

older children had mastered English and could help other children and interpret for the teachers. Though teaching units had to be planned to meet the needs of students at different levels of schooling, it was apparent that student teams improved the learning capacity of all of the students.

Aside from the formal curriculum, students' diverse experiences enhance the concept of a democratic community and a multicultured society. Whenever teachers can connect students' experiences in planning the curriculum, students will be more interested and engaged in learning.

Did You Know That . . . ?

> There is "increasing evidence that academic achievement is related to teachers' ability to connect curriculum to learners' experiences and frames of reference" (Darling-Hammond, 1997, p. 126).

For many teachers, second-language learners pose problems. These students may be highly literate in their primary language despite the fact that they are English language learners (ELL). Though methods for teaching second-language learners will be discussed throughout the text, at this juncture it is important to recognize some basic practices to be avoided in multicultural classrooms. First one must recognize that ability grouping that uses reading English as the basis for placement does a disservice to all students. Second, ELL students who are taught exclusively by paraprofessionals are being short-changed because they are not receiving the benefits of a professional teacher. Manzo (1999) notes that insistence on correct pronunciation impedes development because students shy away from taking risks and many fear to participate in class discussions.

Still another problem in multicultural classrooms is the very old-fashioned practice of round-robin reading. A good observer will note that students count the number of paragraphs prior to their turn, fail to listen to their classmates, and fearfully await their time to be on stage. Inclusion does not apply only to students with disabilities; it must relate to *all* students in the classroom so that they have equal access to every facet of education. Diversity in the classroom community means that all students will:

- Interact with the best teachers
- Use the best facilities, including equipment and materials
- Share the wealth of school support
- Interact with other students
- Study all subjects
- Prepare for all vocations (Lemlech, 2002)

Encouraging Student Effort and Participation

In a democratic community, student involvement and participation are of prime importance. Lesson planning and organization are necessary. Lesson content needs to be relevant to your student population and take advantage of students' prior experiences. Initial motivation for a lesson needs to "capture" your students, and your enthusiasm and attitude toward encouraging students to ask questions, respond to content, and reflect on how the lesson fits with their past experiences will demonstrate your support and regard for your students.

Lesson planning and organization should include a variety of activities to appeal to the diverse learning styles and multiple intelligences of your students. Plan to accomplish your goals in a variety of ways. (There is no one best activity to accomplish a goal.) In planning and organizing your learning experiences, consider the elements of time and space. How much time will be needed for the variety of activities? Will some activities need more time than others? (If so, what will students do if they complete their activity ahead of the rest of the class?) Space considerations should include deciding whether students will work at desks or in free space in the classroom.

Your regard and enthusiasm can be demonstrated by looking directly at the student who is asking questions or making a comment and then looking at the rest of the class and encouraging others to comment. Your own responses, both verbal and nonverbal, demonstrate your interest and that you are listening to what students are saying.

Early in the chapter the significance of providing opportunity for student choice and decision making was emphasized. Will your lesson provide "wiggle room" for students to choose method, process, or product? Will students be challenged by the content, topic, and issues? If they are learning a specific skill, may they choose how to demonstrate their competence?

Did You Know That . . . ?

Differentiation of instruction can be accomplished when teachers provide opportunities for students to choose activities and means to complete work assignments. There are three ways to differentiate instruction: (1) *content* complexity or depth; (2) *process*, the means by which students accomplish the task(s); and (3) *product*, students' choices for demonstrating learning.

Effort is encouraged by teacher recognition and respect. A pat on the back, a direct question to the student about his or her work, and suggestions or ideas and opportunities to tell others how and what they are doing will demonstrate your interest and affirmation. We cannot underestimate the power of effort in learning and in the development of intelligence. Effort helps the mind grow; when students are treated as thinking beings, they gain confidence in their own abilities. Good thinkers recognize the value of both challenges and errors. We learn through both. Resnick (1999) states: "*Intelligence* is knowing what one does (and doesn't) know, seeking information and organizing that information so that it makes sense and can be remembered. In short, one's intelligence is the sum of one's *habits of mind*" (p. 39).

Culturally Responsive Teaching

> Jim Sierra, an elementary teacher in a large urban school district, selected as a curriculum theme "Patterns of Change." His topic in social studies was to be communities around the world. He asked his class, "How many of you were born in other countries? How many have parents born in other countries?" He discovered that five students were not citizens and were born in Oman, India, Korea, Japan, and Mexico. Another six students were born in this country, but their parents were from El Salvador, Colombia, Mexico, Japan, Hungary, and Russia. Using that information, he planned lessons to be used as "field trips" to different communities. The students knew they were studying patterns of change in several subject fields, and Mr. Sierra now shared the idea of studying communities of the world. He asked the students to help frame questions for their inquiry. Their questions included the following:
>
> 1. What customs in our parents' or our native country differ from those in our present community? In what ways are they different?
>
> Many of the students who were not from foreign countries acknowledged that their families or their parents had lived elsewhere in the United States, and so the students asked another question:
>
> 2. Are there communities in the United States where the customs are different from those in this community? In what ways?
>
> Mr. Sierra grouped the students heterogeneously in small groups and each group planned how they would go about their inquiry and decided on additional questions they would need to ask.

Culturally responsive teaching can be defined as sensitivity to the backgrounds, experiences, and contexts of the students you teach. Crocco (1998) states that the curriculum of many school systems seems to be a philosophy based on "one size fits all" and "one teacher fits all"—and this author would add "one standard fits all." But these facetious premises are not congruent with a democratic education.

The school is the only social institution responsible for teaching citizenship participation in a democratic culture. Yet, sadly, schools and classrooms are too often managed autocratically and without consideration for the demographic fit of the students in the classroom. Studies such as that planned by Mr. Sierra, who also will encourage the students to look at gender differences, can be considered sensitive to cultural differences and similarities. By encouraging his students to direct their own inquiry, Mr. Sierra is supporting their participation in a democratic learning environment.

Characteristics of the Democratic Classroom

Can students characterize a democratic classroom? To obtain a picture of what students consider important, a varied group of twenty-five students from age 7 to 16 were interviewed. The students were Latino, Caucasian, and African American; had varied income, gender, and language backgrounds; and attended schools in diverse parts of the Los Angeles and extended communities. They were asked the following questions:

1. What distinguishes a class you like from one you don't like?
2. Do you get to make any decisions in the class you like? Tell me about the decisions you make.
3. In the classes you like, what does the teacher do to make the class interesting and pleasant to be in? What do students get to do?
4. If you were to advise your teachers, what would you tell them about their class to make it more enjoyable for students? (How would you make it better?)
5. What do you think is the meaning of a democratic classroom?
6. In your opinion, what are the characteristics of a democratic classroom?

The students clearly knew what they liked and what they did not. Even the oldest students were unable to define a democratic classroom, but when it was explained to them, their responses were to laugh out loud! Typically the response was, "You're joking, aren't you?"

What Do Students Like?

Students' responses differed very little. They liked classrooms that were cheerful with lots of pictures on the walls and hanging exhibits (such as inflatable animals). In terms of teacher behavior, they liked teachers that used lots of activities instead of lots of lectures. They identified group work and projects as favored activities.

An insightful comment by one student expressed the thoughts of several: "He explains one idea well and then lets us practice it." In a drama class a student commented, "The teacher explains something and then she actually demonstrates it; then the students get to act and the observers get to give feedback." An eighth-grade student praised her math teacher, who didn't lecture, taught through the use of math games, and allowed group work: "We learn from each other, and we take group tests."

In general, a number of the students were not complimentary of their teachers. One honor student said, "I hate all of them equally." When asked to explain, she said, "Well for one thing, tests don't match lectures or the work we do." Students also objected to the same routines used in many of their classes. "You come in, correct homework, listen to a lecture, and take a quiz." Elementary students definitely favored their teachers more than middle or high school students.

What Decisions Do Students Make?

Not many, according to this sample. Some students said they were able to choose whom they worked with and the kinds of projects to make. In drama class the student praised the teacher for allowing students to select their own character roles and play scripts. The majority of students said they never get to make "real decisions." However, other students in the sample disagreed and said, "Everyone gets to shape the class." (It is important to remember that these students were of diverse backgrounds, lived in different communities, and attended several different school districts.)

Despite the conflicting reactions of this random sample of students, certain characteristics of democratic classrooms are recognized by students, teachers, philosophers, and researchers (Darling-Hammond, 1997; Dewey, 1944; Morton, Autry, Johnstad, & Merrill, 1998; Ochoa-Becker, 2001) as shown in Table 1.1.

TABLE 1.1   Characteristics of Democratic Classrooms

Teacher Behavior	Student Behavior
Shares decision making with students	Helps define classroom standards
Emphasizes student responsibility and sense of belonging to classroom community	Recognizes responsibility to classroom community
Requires student discussion if infractions of rules occur	Participates in community decision making
Plans curriculum that attends to cultural diversity	Participates in curriculum decisions that include activities, processes, and products
Plans inclusive curriculum that includes gender studies and attention to immigrant and minority students and second-language learners	Is expected to behave respectfully toward peers and teacher
Speaks respectfully and caringly to students	Expresses interests and needs
Demonstrates enthusiasm and listens attentively to students	Interacts positively with teacher and peers
Encourages student participation in discussion and small heterogeneous group work	Participates with peers in planning activities and projects
Encourages student problem solving and risk taking	Shares and demonstrates problem-solving skills and insights

The Effective Teacher

With the aforementioned characteristics in mind, how does an effective teacher differ from one who is not? Suppose you are beginning your teaching career and you intend to implement the characteristics of a democratic classroom as described in this chapter. To the extent that you succeed in doing so, you will be able to study your performance (using Table 1.1) and determine your relative success. However, another significant way to self-evaluate your own effectiveness is to review the National Board for Professional Teaching Standards identified in Chapter 13.

Learning to teach is a developmental process, and even the most experienced teacher recognizes that he or she has not mastered some elements of teaching. Good teachers are always learning—and good is a relative concept. An effective teacher tries to build mastery in the following areas:

1. Subject field knowledge (depth) and curriculum planning
2. Understanding the students he or she teaches (developmental levels, backgrounds, experiences, interests, and needs)
3. Appropriate use of a variety of instructional approaches that lead to problem-solving and critical-thinking skills
4. Classroom management skills, including organization and planning skills
5. Design of a classroom environment that motivates student learning
6. Facilitation of student participation, decision making, and communication

Each of these elements will be briefly described here, with a referral to the appropriate chapter in this text for in-depth information.

Subject Field Knowledge and Curriculum Planning

Your undergraduate education prepares you in the different subject field disciplines; however, knowledge is never static, so you must continue education in any or all of the subjects that you teach. We often hear the story of the great physicist or mathematician who was asked to teach a lesson in an elementary or secondary classroom, and the students were bored to death. Teaching is not easy and professional preparation is critical. However, teachers do need a rich background of knowledge in the areas that they teach.

Knowledge of the discipline by itself is not enough. Teachers need to select the major concepts in the discipline that are appropriate for the students they are teaching. These concepts must be transformed for curriculum planning. Judgment is needed concerning breadth versus depth. *Covering* the subject field means just touching on topics in the discipline. When teachers do this, students perceive only a fraction of what the discipline is about and quite often lose interest as a consequence.

In-depth teaching about a few major concepts is sometimes referred to as "digging a hole," to achieve critical, penetrating knowledge versus superficial understanding. Projects and other research products provide the means for students to construct new conceptual ideas and connect them with what they already know. Higher-order thinking skills are developed when teachers provide opportunity for in-depth learning. (Chapters 3 and 4 will help you learn more about planning for learning.)

Understanding the Students You Teach

> Kito was a new student in Karen Adazzio's seventh-grade social studies class. Ms. Adazzio had only a little bit of information about him. She knew that he was from Japan and spoke English even though he had been in the United States just a couple of months. When Kito was asked to join a group of students for work, he sat with the students but did not contribute. His individual assignments and homework were excellent, but his class participation was nil.

Karen Adazzio needed to meet with Kito's parents to find out more about him and discuss his apparent shyness in class. She needed to find out if the work in class was difficult for him or too easy. (Why were his home assignments excellent?) Were his language skills adequate or did he fail to participate because he was fearful of talking? How did his prior education in Japan differ from education in the United States? What were his special interests? Ms. Adazzio was concerned that cultural differences and family life for Kito were so different that he was having a hard time adjusting to life at school.

Teacher effectiveness depends on many factors. The physicist and mathematician were ineffective in the classroom because they lacked understanding of the students they were trying to teach. Developmental levels, motivation, diversity, language skills, individual differences in learning styles, and special skills all affect how students learn, and teachers need to be cognizant of these factors. (How students learn will be discussed in Chapter 3.)

Instructional Approaches

The student interviews discussed earlier revealed that classroom routines need to be varied. A diet of pasta every day is boring—and fattening! Some students do need more directed instruction than others; however, all students appreciate variety. The authoritarian teacher tends to offer "formula teaching" lesson plans, but these formula plans rarely provide for higher-level thinking skills and problem solving. The one lesson plan for all fails to consider multiple intelligences, multiple skills, critical thinking, student engagement, motivation, and boredom.

Instructional approaches must match desired goals. If your intent is to improve students' kicking skills for soccer, then students will need the opportunity to practice kicking the soccer ball. If your intent is to develop critical thinking, then the lesson plan must provide for decision making, perhaps with a focus on controversial issues. Teacher effectiveness is determined by the match between teacher intent and student accomplishment. (Instructional approaches are discussed in Chapters 8 and 9.)

Classroom Management

This aspect of teaching receives more attention in professional education than perhaps any other element of teacher effectiveness. Quite often "practice" teaching places a higher premium on the preservice teacher's ability to control the classroom than his or her ability to demonstrate a repertoire of teaching skills. Obviously the reason for this concern is that unless you have the attention of your students, it is impossible to present a lesson or motivate an activity.

Classroom management reflects the teacher's ability to plan lessons that are so well organized that neither teacher nor students are wasting time. This means that instruction materials are appropriate and ready. If grouping is needed, a plan has been thought out, and if space is an issue, this has been considered. Since most lessons expect students to perform some tasks, good classroom management requires that teachers monitor student performance and offer assistance as needed. Because there are always unexpected events in classroom life that may include misbehavior, equipment that breaks down, fire drills, and loudspeaker messages, the effective classroom manager anticipates problems and has prepared students for these happenings. (Classroom management is discussed in detail in Chapter 6.)

The Classroom Environment

Visualize a prison cell. No pictures. No fresh air. No interaction with others. No personality. No freedom. Sameness. This is the way some classrooms are perceived by students. The classroom environment reflects the personality of the teacher and the students who live there, whether it be all day or for one long period of the day. The environment can make a statement about what students are learning, how they are challenged, what they are producing, and how they are motivated.

The environment (milieu) also reflects the culture—patterns of behavior—that pervade this classroom. If one whole bulletin board displays a chart with class rules and consequences for infringement, it tells the story of teacher control and student submission. But if the bulletin boards display students' original work, provocative questions, controversial issues, and pictures that capture the imagination, a whole different impression of teacher and learners is communicated. The effective teacher uses the environment, physical and cultural, as a teaching tool. (Learn more about the classroom environment in Chapter 2.)

Student Participation, Decision Making, and Communication

Ochoa-Becker and colleagues (2001) succinctly reflect on the importance of student participation in a democratic learning environment: "To involve students in shaping the curriculum by responding to their interests, asking them to decide what classroom rules are needed, and letting them make judgments about infractions in their classrooms mean teachers need to give up control, power, and time" (p. 269).

At the beginning of this chapter two significant goals of schooling were identified: literacy education and citizenship education. Both of these goals require that students have not only the opportunity, but the requirement of communication. The second goal, citizenship, also requires that students engage in decision making.

Unless students actively participate in class discussions and teachers monitor small-group discussion, there is no way for teachers to know the extent of student participation. Interaction with peers is of prime importance. The research of Piaget, Vygotsky, and Dewey confirms the need for learning experiences that enable students to participate in social interaction (Glassman, 2001; Osterman, 2000). Osterman notes that participation in dialogue facilitates the development of ideas. If students spend the majority of school time listening to lectures and pencil-pushing on worksheets, they are missing out on the social/cultural experience that schools can offer. (The process and context for social interaction and appropriate learning experiences will be discussed in Chapters 3–9.)

Effective Teaching

To be an effective teacher it is important to engage in self-study and peer coaching. Self-study involves both professional education and the study of your own teaching performance. Review Table 1.1 in this chapter. Peer coaching involves teaming with a trusted partner or colleague—who need not be teaching at the same grade level or subject field. Peer coaching requires that you and your partner have the opportunity to observe each other teach or at least watch videotapes of teaching episodes. (Both self-study and peer coaching will be discussed in Chapter 13.)

Chapter Summary

Essential elements of a classroom community were discussed in this chapter with an emphasis on how teachers can achieve a learning community. Emphasis was placed on the need for students and teachers to have mutual trust and respect, and for teachers to encourage student responsibility and facilitate students' interactions. Culturally responsive teaching that capitalizes on students' diversity was illustrated through a teaching scenario. The chapter concluded with the characteristics of the democratic classroom and the significant competencies of an effective teacher.

Chapter Review

Match each concept with the corresponding description. Review the chapter sections if you need help. Answers are given in Appendix A.

Concept	*Description*
Diversity	Names and checks
Democratic community	No controls
Authoritarian teacher	Student choice, decision making
Punishment	All things big and small
Rewards and consequences	Teacher knowledge, democratic control
Stimulus/response	Instructional approaches to teaching
Discipline systems	Sensitivity to students' experiences and backgrounds
Token economy	Student compliance
Rules	Supreme deity
Pedagogy	Positive and negative reinforcement
Student control	Environment
Teacher control	Means to assert teacher control
Milieu	Student involvement, choice, decision making

(continued)

Concept	Description
English language learners	Skinner's theory
Laissez-faire	Standards for classroom government
Culturally responsive teaching	Second-language learners
Assertive discipline	Credits and debits

Teaching Problems

1. Ginny was just beginning her teaching career. During her practice teaching, her master teacher used a system of writing students' names on the board when they misbehaved. There were few discipline problems in the classroom and the system seemed to work; however, Ginny didn't like the idea of embarrassing students this way. Suggest some ways that Ginny can control her class without shaming students.

2. Al was a middle school teacher of life science. He knew very little about second-language teaching, but he had several students in one of his classes that were English language learners. He was concerned that these students did not understand his directions and could not perform the experiments. What would you suggest that Al do to help these students?

3. A group of teachers were gathered in the teachers' dining room gossiping about their classroom problems. Several of the teachers commented that they believed their principal expected classrooms to be extremely quiet places; yet they did not agree. Should you be able to hear a pin drop in the classroom? What are the issues involved?

Teaching Problems are intended for self-study or as discussion starters. You may want to share your ideas with a colleague.

CHAPTER 2

Classroom Observation

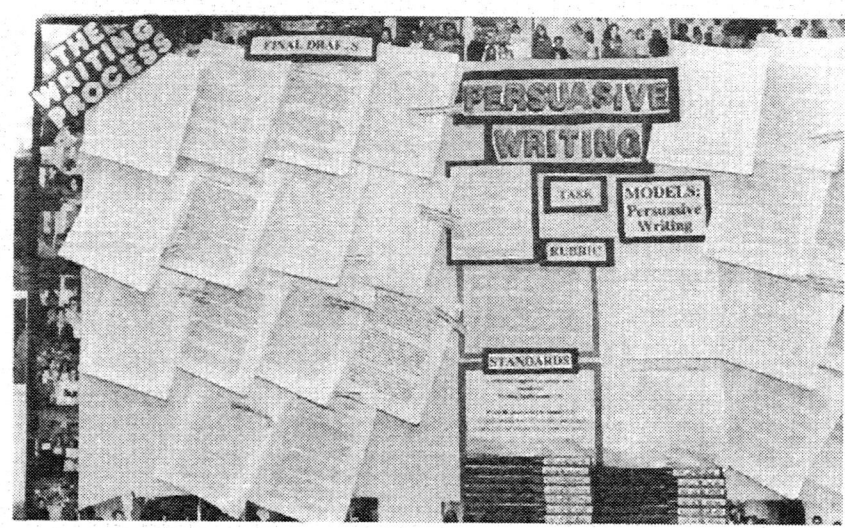

ADVANCE ORGANIZER

These questions can be used as a framework to assist you in integrating professional knowledge and understanding of the content of this chapter.

1. In what ways do four "commonplaces" of the classroom (environment, students, teacher, subject matter) affect life in classrooms?
2. Explain why both what you observe in classrooms and what you do *not* observe are equally significant.
3. What aspects of a democratic classroom environment should teachers consider for self-study?
4. Casual observation and focused observation are different; what techniques can be used to study classroom life?

 The following INTASC issues and standards are discussed in this chapter: Numbers 2, 3, 5, 6, 10.

The focus of this chapter is what and how to observe in classrooms. Four aspects of every classroom are significant: the environment, the students, the teacher, and the subject matter. Readers are asked to determine how these components affect the life of the classroom community. The four commonplaces of classroom life are used to analyze life in four classrooms: Lucia Martin teaches second grade, Gerry Alred teaches sixth-grade social studies and science in a suburban middle school, Roger Ives teaches middle school mathematics in a Southern school district, and Jean Cantor teaches English literature at an urban high school. The teachers are different not only in where they teach, but also in their teaching styles. None of the featured teachers is intended to be "perfect."

The "Walkaround" and "The Buzz"—What Should You Observe When You Visit a Classroom?

It is Sunday evening and Lucia Martin is nervous thinking about the next day at school. It will be the fourth week of the semester and Lucia is in her first year of teaching. She decides to call her friend Maida, who is now an experienced second-year teacher.

"Look, Luce, calm down. What's the big deal? So what if the principal wants all the teachers to walk around the classrooms and see what they're like and how they differ?"

"I'm scared, that's what if. What if my kids are awful, the lesson falls apart, and the room is a mess when they arrive? I've tried to remember what my master teacher's classroom was like the first day that I visited. I don't know what Ms. Jenkins expects of her teachers."

"You took pictures of your student teaching classroom; did you look at those when you set up your room?"

"No, Maida, I forgot. I should have done that, but it's too late to change anything now. I'll probably be teaching math when they come. The walkaround begins at 2 P.M. I just called because I needed someone to empathize."

"I know it will go fine, Lucia. Relax and enjoy showing off your classroom and students. Call me tomorrow night."

Monday afternoon Lucia heard the knock on her classroom door and a group of teachers entered with Ms. Jenkins. They were touring the elementary wing of the school. Lucia taught in an urban school that included grades K–12. The elementary school, middle school, and high school each had its own assistant principal, staff, and faculty. The school was on a year-round schedule. One-third of the teachers were always "off track" and would not return to teach for nine weeks. These teachers were visiting as part of a continuing-education plan.

Lucia's friend Maida taught in a relatively small school district with a traditional school schedule. Her calendar year began after Labor Day and she was on a typical two-semester plan. Though they taught in different school settings, they talked frequently about their teaching problems. Both Maida and Lucia were subject to the state's new teacher assessment and support program.

Ms. Jenkins, Lucia's assistant principal, recognized the value of teachers observing in each other's classrooms and hoped to initiate a coaching plan to encourage teachers to collaborate and develop strategies for improving the curriculum and instructional program of the school. Ms. Jenkins did not suggest *what* teachers should look for in the classrooms, but she did intend to lead a debriefing session to assess the impact of the visitations. Had she made suggestions, her observation plan might have been similar to Figure 2.1.

The Environment

- Is it comfortable in the classroom—not too hot or too cold?

- Is the environment interesting and motivating? What is displayed on the bulletin boards? Is there evidence of multicultural/multiethnic interests? Do displays reflect an interdisciplinary approach to teaching and learning?

- If students' work is displayed, does it indicate authentic and individual creation or "copy work"? (Are all papers alike?)

- Is the furniture arrangement conducive to group work, student interaction, and direct instruction?

- Is there consideration of students' need to see (boards, charts, teacher, other students) and to hear?

- If room standards (rules) are displayed, do they demonstrate motivation for students to work together cooperatively and respectfully? Are they what you would expect in a democratic community?

- If you were a student, would you want to work in this classroom?

The Students

- When you enter the classroom, what are students doing? Do their work tasks look interesting and meaningful?

- Does it appear that the tasks consider individual differences?

- If the teacher is not teaching, is there a comfortable buzz or pin-drop quiet?

- Is there evidence that students control some of their own work tasks and learning projects? Do they make choices and decisions?

- Is there evidence that students work together in small groups?

- Is there evidence that students interact and communicate as needed?

- Do students appear to have the freedom to move around as needed?

FIGURE 2.1 **When Observing in Classrooms, What Do You Look For?**

The Teacher

- Do you feel welcome to visit?
- What is the teacher doing? (Lecturing, initiating work tasks, monitoring, working with an individual or a group, observing?)
- Does the teacher appear to be comfortable and confident in his or her own teaching?
- Is there evidence that the teacher uses a variety of teaching approaches?
- Is there evidence that the teacher considers individual student differences?
- When the teacher talks to students (or when students talk to the teacher) is mutual respect apparent?
- If a classroom discussion is occurring, is discourse among students encouraged?
- Is there evidence of instructional planning? (Lesson notes? Organization of materials? Timing? Pacing?)
- Does the classroom appear well managed? (Do students move about freely without disturbing others?)
- Is there access to materials, computers, paper, and other items? Is there a natural flow to events in the classroom?
- Would you like to spend time in this classroom with this teacher?

Subjects

- If it is an elementary classroom, is there evidence that all subject fields are taught? (A daily schedule? Learning and/or interest centers? Work displayed? Manipulatives? Texts, media, computers, other resources?)
- If it is a secondary classroom, is there evidence of an interdisciplinary approach, an integrated approach, or a focus only on the specific subject that is taught?
- Is there evidence that teaching is both expository and inquiry oriented? (What are students doing/producing? What is displayed? What is the teacher doing now?)
- What evidence is there that teaching is current and consonant with subject field standards or state frameworks?
- Is there evidence of long-term planning and teaching through thematic or subject field units?

FIGURE 2.1 (*Continued*)

When observing in classrooms there are four major areas of interest. The first that usually strikes your eye is the *environment* of the classroom. Is it attractive? Ask yourself, "What is life in this environment like? Does it reflect democratic values?" The second item that you normally focus on is the *students* in the classroom. What are they doing? Do they seem content? Does it appear that they make work/task choices? The third area of interest is, of course, the *teacher*. What is he or she doing? The fourth component that needs attention is the *subject(s)* being taught. (See Klein, Tye, & Wright, 1979.)

As you study Figure 2.1, ask yourself what other questions you would add to each of the commonplaces of classroom observation.

Using the four commonplaces we will take a virtual field trip to several classrooms. Beginning in Lucia Martin's classroom, we will observe the *environment* that the visiting teachers observed. As indicated in Chapter 1, there are two interpretations to be considered: the organization of the classroom and the social/emotional climate of the classroom.

The Environment

Classroom Organization

The way in which the classroom is organized tells much about the way you intend to teach. The term **synomorphy** refers to the compatibility of the physical environment and the learning experiences you intend students to engage in. The layout of your classroom will either facilitate or inhibit movement and encourage or discourage students' interaction, group work, and class discussions.

In Lucia Martin's second-grade classroom she wants students to engage in whole-class discussions. To facilitate this she has her tables arranged in an open **E** formation (see Figure 2.2). Only the students seated in the middle portion of the **E** need to move their chairs for class discussions. (They move their chairs to the front of the room, facing the rest of the class.) She was also concerned about conserving space for small group work. She intends to use the front and sides of the room and the tables on the sides of the **E** to provide space for group work.

Upon entering the classroom, the visitors noted that most of the students were focused on the teacher, who was presenting information about three-dimensional shapes to the students. Some abstract solid wooden blocks were arranged on the floor of the classroom. Her objective was to have the students differentiate between two- and three-dimensional figures. The students were seated at their tables; they were not prepared for a discussion.

Further observation of the classroom revealed a chart rack that displayed "Our Classroom Rules," a display of library books, and some tadpoles swimming in an aquarium with a question in front of it asking, "How are the tadpoles changing?" There was a calendar on one of the bulletin boards and cursive writing letters displayed on another board. A large apple box on a cupboard held files arranged for each student's work. Windows were open and the room was airy and cheery. The visitors stayed about ten minutes and then waved goodbye. Ms. Jenkins thanked Lucia and the students for allowing them to visit.

If you were a visitor in Lucia Martin's classroom, what would impress you?

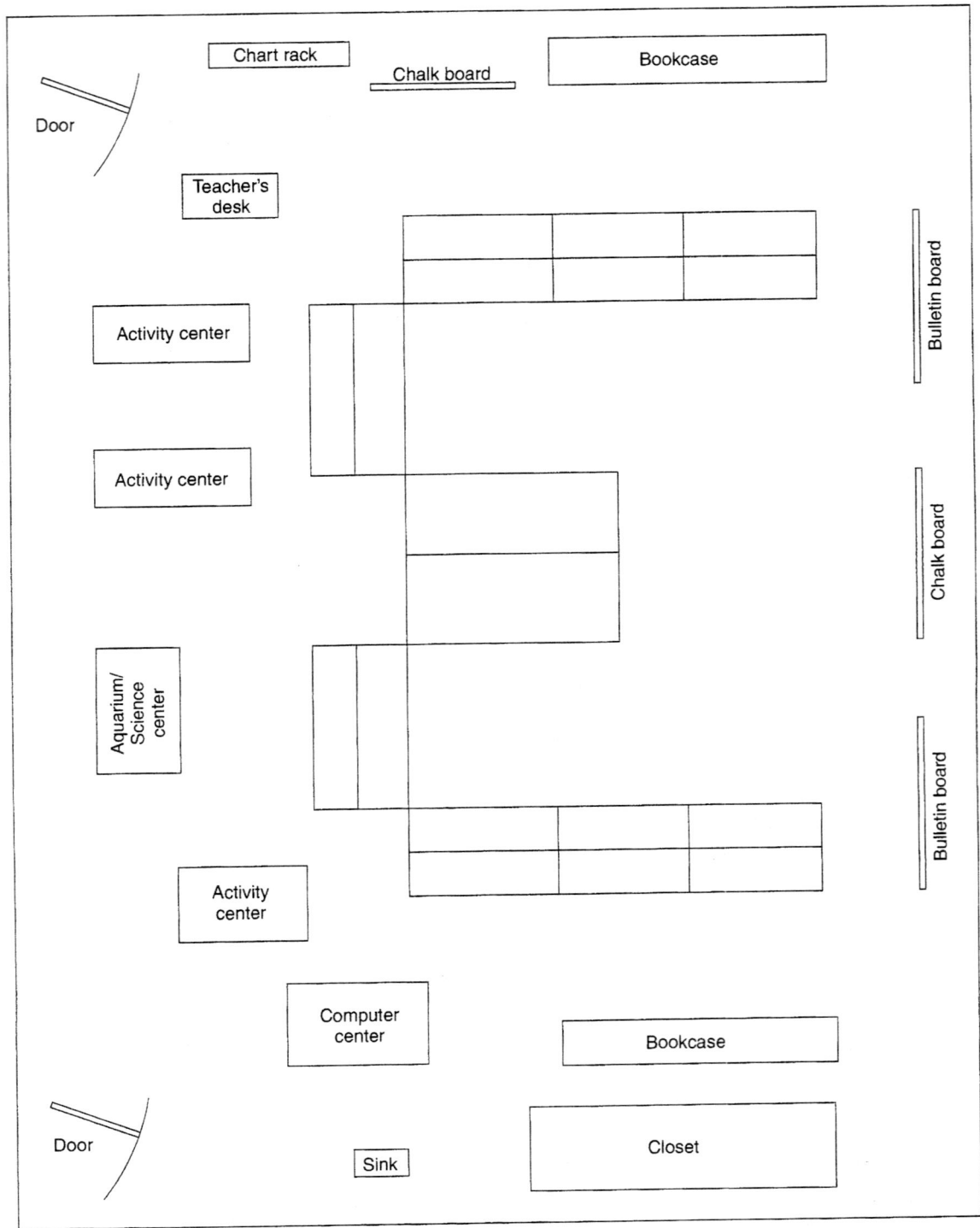

FIGURE 2.2 Lucia Martin's Classroom

Let's visit several more classrooms to see how they differ.

Gerry Alred teaches sixth-grade social studies and science in a middle school located in a suburban school district. She is a very serious and dedicated teacher. Her classroom is arranged with tables in groups of three to accommodate six students. The triads are placed around the room with a space in the middle for the use of a computer and liquid crystal display (LCD) placed on an overhead projector. Her bulletin boards are extremely interesting and always reflect current issues. On one board she has a chart of all of the U.S. presidents and their vice-presidents, the opponents who ran against them, and the number of electoral votes received by both the winners and losers. On another bulletin board she has a world map with flags on the different countries that represent where some of her students were born. A third bulletin board focuses on environmental problems. This board has pictures and stories by her students concerning worldwide pollution problems. Her bookcases hold fiction books about different periods of American history, great inventors and inventions, and reference books. Periodically she has dioramas made by students and realia that reflect the two subjects she teaches. (See Figure 2.3)

Did You Know That . . . ?

In 1916 Dewey wrote about the importance of the classroom environment. He said: "The only way in which adults consciously control the kind of education which the immature get is by controlling the environment in which they act, and hence think and feel. We never educate directly, but indirectly by means of the environment. Whether we permit chance environments to do the work, or whether we design environments for the purpose makes a great deal of difference. And any environment is a chance environment so far as its educative influence is concerned unless it has been deliberately regulated with reference to its educative effect" (1944, pp. 18–19).

Roger Ives teaches ninth-grade mathematics in a Southern school district. He is a very active, enthusiastic young teacher. He enjoys moving about the classroom and getting students motivated to learn through the use of games, simulations, and inquiry activities. His classroom is set up with desk-chairs; each chair has an armlike desk attached to one side. Some of the desk-chairs accommodate left-handed students. The chairs are arranged in small groupings throughout the classroom. They can be moved easily to accommodate different types of activities and groupings. He also has a space along the wall with several computers. One of the bulletin boards in Roger's classroom displays pictures and math problem stories written by his students. The caption reads: "How can you solve these problems?" A bookcase displays math games, video series, and simulations to be used on the computers. Elsewhere in the room are calculators, concrete instructional materials, and math puzzle books. The room appears cheerful, but crowded.

Jean Cantor teaches English literature at a small urban high school in the Midwest. She often collaborates with one of the history teachers on teaching projects that involve students in both classes. Her classroom features four tables arranged in squares around

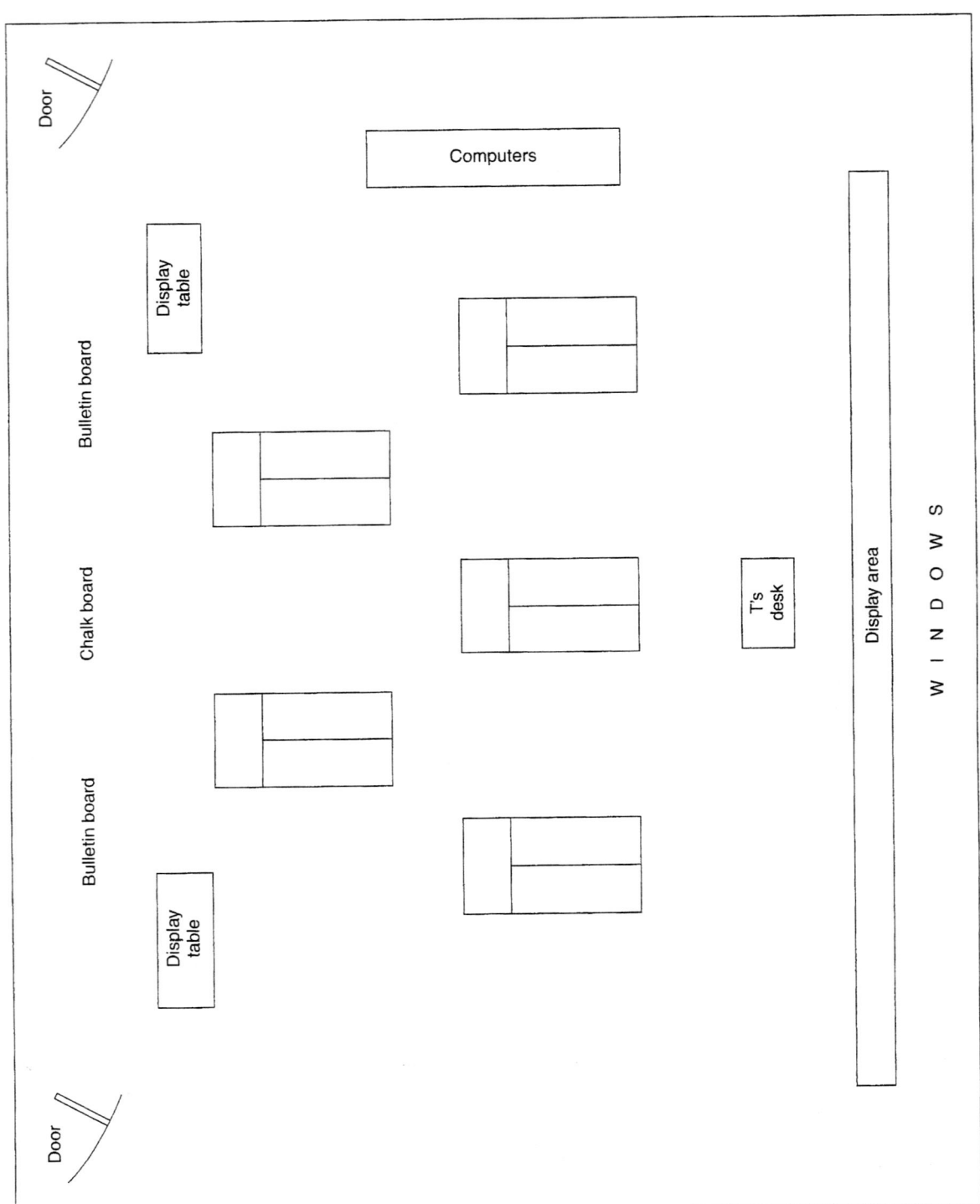

FIGURE 2.3   Gerry Alred's Classroom

the classroom. Since some students automatically have their backs to the front of the classroom, the students need to turn their chairs around for presentations and discussions.

Book jackets and short synopses of books cover one of the bulletin boards. On another bulletin board is a timeline with different authors' names printed on it. On a third bulletin board is a list of questions in bold manuscript print. The list begins with the title "What Do You Know About the Author of Your Book?" Underneath the title are questions that include the following:

Where was the author born?

What early experiences did the author have that may have affected his or her writing?

How old was the author when he or she wrote the book?

Who or what do you think influenced the author?

The Social/Emotional Climate of the Classroom

Ten minutes of observation in a classroom does not reveal a great deal about the climate of the classroom. A cursory look around Lucia Martin's classroom indicated that not all students were attending to her presentation. Lucia acted a bit nervous—no doubt because she had visitors—but teacher nervousness is usually communicated to students. The room was unnaturally quiet except for three students in the back who were whispering; students were not asking questions, and the teacher did not verify understanding. With the display in the front of the room, one might also question whether all students could see.

When we entered Gerry Alred's classroom, she was giving students directions for joining their groups. (They were studying intolerance.) She displayed several books related to the topics the students had selected. She called attention to a reference guide about extremist symbols, logos, and tattoos. She reminded the students that they could select their own reference materials even if they were not in the classroom. When it was clear she was done with preliminary talk, the students changed their seats to join their groups. One student asked how much time they would have to work and Alred responded. The room was noisy and Alred did not say anything about it, expecting that it would quiet down when the students were involved in their tasks. After a few minutes she began to monitor the groups' work, listening intently to their planning and discussions.

Roger Ives's classroom was buzzing. Our virtual field trip to Roger's classroom began at the beginning of the period, and as the students filed in they immediately began work on a problem that was on the bulletin board. Obviously there was no rule that forbade them to consult with friends, and students quickly formed small groups and began to discuss the problem confronting them. The teacher was consulting his seating chart to determine attendance. Every now and then a student would approach and he would laughingly provide clues. After ten minutes Ives held up his hand and the students quit work, many changing back to their own assigned seats.

How would you characterize the social/emotional climate of the three classrooms described in this section? How did the environment affect life in these classrooms? Which classroom(s) reflected the characteristics of a democratic community?

The Students

Lucia Martin's Classroom

There was a display of three-dimensional blocks at the front of the classroom, but the students did not appear particularly interested. Students seated at the back part of the **E** probably did not have a good view of the blocks. Three students on the south side of the **E** were whispering. One student was sneaking a candy bar and another student was playing with something in his lap—probably a handheld computer.

Gerry Alred's Classroom

Students entered the classroom in twos and threes talking and engaging in some horseplay. They did not settle down until Ms. Alred raised her hand and looked directly at students who were still talking. When she indicated that she wanted to talk to the students, some students moved their chairs for a better view of her. The students appeared respectful and interested, and one student immediately raised her hand and asked whether they would be able to work on their projects.

After the signal to join their work groups, students prowled the classroom for research materials. Several students went to the computers for Internet searches. Students appeared at ease and did not seem to anticipate a reprimand for a somewhat noisy start on their group work. Several students approached Ms. Alred with questions and she reminded them to raise their hands in their group and she would come over and help them.

Roger Ives's Classroom

Students seemed challenged and interested. They were talking about ways to solve the problem on the chalkboard. Once in a while a student would look at his or her watch and remind others of how much time they had left. Most of the students were completely ignoring the teacher and concentrating on their warm-up problem, except for two of the students who were talking intently about their homework from the previous night and not taking part in the warm-up activity.

Jean Cantor's Classroom

When we entered the classroom the students were sitting at their tables browsing through their notebooks, talking to each other, and seemingly unconcerned that class was about to begin. Ms. Cantor was looking at her notes for the class. She called the students to order and began to lecture. Students hastily began to take notes. Toward the back of the room a girl wrote a note and nudged the student next to her to pass the note to a friend. The note began to travel across the room. Ms. Cantor noticed and frowned. Some students smiled; others looked guilty. The lecture continued without further interruption. Finally Ms. Cantor stopped and announced that there would be a quiz tomorrow. The students groaned and began to protest. The classroom was noisy. The bell rang and the students dashed out of the room.

How would you describe student motivation and behavior in the four classrooms described in this section?

Did You Know That . . . ?

> The environment we work in has a profound effect upon us. An enriched environment produces growth in the cortical neurons of the brain. Researchers' studies of rats' brains found that they were able to solve more complex maze problems when they lived in enriched environments (Wolfe, 2001).

The Teachers

Lucia Martin

Polyhedra are three-dimensional shapes that have faces, edges, and vertices.* Lucia Martin has displayed a tetrahedron, hexahedron, octahedron, icosahedron, and dodecahedron. She has them on the floor in the front of the classroom. Her intent is to have the students draw them and describe their characteristics. She has not motivated the lesson and the students do not appear to know what she wants. She expects the students to talk about what they see and she intends to pass around the five shapes. She begins the lesson by calling on Frank and asks: "What can you tell us about these shapes?" He responds, "Ah . . . I don't know."

She quickly calls on Billy. "What can you tell us about the shapes?"

Billy responds, "Well, they are all different."

"I know, Ms. Martin," responds Jane.

Lucia ignores Jane and calls on Rex.

Rex thinks a moment and then says, "Do they all have a different number of sides?"

"Good thinking, Rex. How many notice how the shapes are different?"

Lucia finally begins to tell the students a little bit about three-dimensional shapes and identifies their characteristics. She then selects students to come up, pick a shape to take back to their table for other students to touch, and get ready to draw it.

Gerry Alred

Alred is a strong believer in constructivist teaching. She wants her students to be actively involved in what they study. As noted in Chapter 1, she tries to maintain a democratic classroom environment and works hard to see that students have curriculum choices and decisions to make. As the students work on their projects, she sits in on the different group meetings, asking questions and giving some feedback to them, suggesting additional lines of research.

---

*Lesson content suggested by W.G. Cathcart et al. (2000). *Learning Mathematics in Elementary and Middle Schools.* Upper Saddle River, NJ: Merrill/Prentice Hall.

Roger Ives

Roger always keeps his students busy. He believes that there should be something for the students to do the minute they enter the classroom. His warm-up activity, as he calls it, is usually quite intriguing. When we entered his classroom the students were working on a license plate subtraction problem. Even though his students were mostly eighth- and ninth-graders, he used manipulative materials and had students studying math theories using the Internet and taking part in math simulations.

Jean Cantor

Jean Cantor says she believes in active-learning, problem-solving, and inquiry activities for students; yet she consistently lectures to her students. She expects them to take notes, study, and pass weekly quizzes. Her lectures are well organized and carefully planned. She works from notes, uses a lectern, and expects students to act maturely. She teaches her classes as if the students are in college.

How would you characterize the teachers described in this section? Do they appear comfortable in their role as teachers?

The Subjects

Lucia Martin is teaching about regular polyhedra, which are three-dimensional shapes with sides of the same length and angles that are equal. The study of three-dimensional shapes helps students develop spatial sense. Learning experiences include drawing, measuring, and constructing these geometric figures. Students should be given opportunity to discuss, compare, and classify the shapes. Verbalization about the shapes should precede other activities. The study of shapes helps students develop geometric thinking and is suggested in the standards of the National Council of Teachers of Mathematics (NCTM, 2000).

Jean Cantor's students are in the process of reading *The Catcher in the Rye* by J. D. Salinger. Though the book was written in 1951, it has maintained great appeal for teenagers. Cantor has lectured the students concerning the book's historical significance and present-day authenticity. The students are given a choice of a number of books to read; their present assignment is to compare their book of choice with the Salinger novel. The students were required to read the Salinger book. Many of the students are organizing their analysis based on the questions that Cantor has displayed on the bulletin board, which were integrated in her lectures.

In the two examples of subject field assignments, have the teachers selected significant content? Are the learning experiences (activities) appropriate and consonant with the teachers' beliefs about how students learn?

Classroom observation requires a great deal of insight and knowledge about teaching and classroom life. The perceptive observer thinks about not only what is visually apparent, but what is *not* apparent, *and* what ought to be evident. This type of thinking involves observing the environment of the classroom and considering the needs and interests of students. It involves watching the interaction patterns among students and teacher, observing student and teacher behaviors, and attending to *what* is taught and *how* it is taught.

Teaching Hints

To achieve a democratic learning community, students need:

1. Challenging work tasks
2. Authentic choices and opportunity for decision making
3. Active involvement in work assignments
4. Opportunity for interaction with others

What Would You Like to See in Lucia Martin's Classroom?

Think about the *environment,* the *teacher,* the *students,* and the *subject* Martin was teaching—mathematics. Make a list of what you think should be seen and what should be happening in Lucia Martin's classroom. Compare your list with the following analysis.

Since Lucia teaches in an urban school district, we can assume that there is a great deal of student diversity in her classroom. Yet the environment of the classroom did not reflect that diversity. We did not see pictures that demonstrated multicultural education. No student work was exhibited, and there was no evidence that Lucia was providing for individual differences. Teachers frequently consider individual differences through the use of specially designed centers to assist ELL students and students with varied abilities and interests.

Bulletin board displays and exhibits usually reflect what is taught in the classroom. We do not know that Ms. Martin taught *all* subjects of the curriculum. There was no evidence that time is provided for the arts and literature. We did not see a daily schedule displayed that would tell us what is taught and when it is taught.

Think about Ms. Martin's teaching performance. Lucia conducted a mini-discussion with her students. We would anticipate that there should have been student questions, greater participation, and more interest in the lesson. This was not evident. In fact, we saw that Lucia called only on boys to answer her questions and failed to encourage students to respond or to widen the involvement of the class.

Consider the teacher's intent (goal). How was Ms. Martin going to have the students compare two- and three-dimensional shapes? Were the students going to have the opportunity to touch and see—up close—all of the shapes? It is generally recognized that young elementary children need concrete experience and active participation. This can occur through the use of manipulatives, experimentation, questions, and discussion. But the children in Lucia's classroom were sitting a distance from the three-dimensional blocks. In fact, we do not know whether they could all see the shapes. Drawing the shapes requires the development of geometric thinking and spatial sense. We do not know what prior experiences the students have had, but we might question the ability of all students to be successful in this activity.

General Organizational Considerations

When you observe in a classroom, it is natural to notice furniture arrangement and classroom accoutrements, such as computer centers, exhibit areas, and space for direct instruction. It is vital that you consider your overall room arrangement prior to assigning students' seats. For example, where will you place texts and other resource materials? Do you need a computer center? Will you need a demonstration table in the front of the room? Do students have access to supplies? Have you thought out traffic patterns in the room? For example, if students need to obtain paper, sharpen pencils, or find a dictionary, will they be able to do so without disturbing others?

Suppose that you intend to work with small groups of students for skill lessons. Have you considered space for this to occur? Usually you will want to use the chalkboard; this may require space in the front of the room so that you do not have your back to the majority of the class. This decision will dictate the arrangement of tables, chairs, and traffic patterns in the rest of the classroom. After planning the overall design of your classroom, you are ready to decide where students will sit.

Where Students Sit

Studies have shown that students who sit in the front of the classroom do better and get higher grades than students who sit in the rear of the classroom. Observational studies also have revealed that teachers tend to call on students who are in close proximity to where they are teaching (Acheson & Gall, 1997). Seat location can affect:

- Student participation
- Student interaction with teacher and other students
- Student status with peers

Let's find out why these factors can affect students' performance. Most teachers make presentations from the front of the classroom. Now suppose that the teacher calls only on students who sit close to where he or she is teaching. If this practice is habitual, other students will learn that there is no point in trying to be involved because the teacher will not call on them. In fact, as long as they are quiet, they can ignore whatever is happening in the classroom.

Recalling the short discussion in Lucia Martin's classroom, perhaps you noted that she called only on boys. When a girl volunteered information, she was disregarded. In addition, we do not know whether the students who were named had raised their hands to contribute or Martin just called on them. Some students raise their hands to talk because they know that the teacher will never call on students who *know* the information, and as a consequence they may use this as a ploy to evade participation. Sometimes where students sit motivates them to talk out to get attention because they can find no other means to participate in the class.

Occasionally teachers choose to seat students by ability. Though this practice is frowned on, teachers do this so that students can be grouped for specific skill activities. The consequence of this practice is that other students "catch on" and recognize where the smart students sit and where the dummies sit.

Other Considerations

First, when planning where to seat students, consider whether any of your students has a disability that requires a specific location in the classroom. Plan the location for students with special needs before considering other students. At the secondary level you may want to invite students to choose their own seat and remind them that this privilege is valid unless it is abused. Elementary students typically like a place to call their own, but they should be reminded that seat locations will be changed periodically.

You may want to consider the physical size of your students to be sure that all students can see the chalkboards. Try to plan your own teaching position so that you are not always standing in the front of the classroom. Mix boys and girls and blend ability groups. Interaction is the most important ingredient to develop a democratic classroom community.

Talk to your students about work behavior. Remind them that their best friend may not be the best working partner. Ask students to write down the names of peers they would like to work with, and try to honor their choices and see how it works out. Students with special problems, such as shyness or aggressiveness, may need to be considered in the overall plan, but do not assume that students have problems before they emerge. Chapters 4 and 5 will help you work through these problems.

The Classroom Climate

On our virtual field trips to different classrooms we viewed different teacher styles for managing the social/emotional climate of the classroom. Lucia Martin probably communicated her nervousness. Gerry Alred's students were motivated to work on their group projects. Roger Ives's classroom was a bit hectic, but the students were challenged and interacting with classmates.

The classroom that is "pin-drop" quiet communicates to visitors that student interaction is discouraged. We may also infer that in these classrooms students work alone and learning activities rely on textbooks; assessment occurs through testing, not through student projects. Though classrooms should not be noisy places, one wonders how excessive quiet affects students' psyche. The buzz of Roger Ives's classroom and the obvious interactive environment of Gerry Alred's classroom provide a different picture. Here we can infer that student communication is valued. Students are expected to be problem solvers, thinking beings with ideas and viewpoints. Assessment of these students occurs through teacher observation and student performance, such as projects, experiments, exhibitions, and testing.

Did You Know That . . . ?

> Researchers generally associate school and classroom climate with the effectiveness of the school. Students tend to excel academically when teachers have high expectations for student achievement, exhibit high morale, treat students positively, involve students in active learning activities, and promote positive social relationships among students (Griffith, 2000).

Casual Versus Focused Observation

The police typically have problems with eyewitnesses. The reason is simple; we observe everything, but we do it casually. We look out the window of our home and see birds, squirrels, the car speeding down the street, and our neighbor carrying out the trash, but rarely can we identify the type of birds, the make of the car, or what our neighbor was wearing. Casual observation is somewhat meaningless.

Researchers in the 1960s and early 1970s believed that classroom observation should focus on the teacher, and they focused specifically (and only) on teachers' presentation skills and monitoring behaviors (Rosenshine & Furst, 1973). But teacher educators and classroom teachers believed that observation research needed to focus on all aspects of the classroom: the context of teaching, students' engagement, the learning environment, the instructional process, and the significance of what was being taught. Figure 2.1 provided a more structured observation by identifying four categories to focus attention.

It is generally recognized today that classroom observation should be purposefully focused on specific questions or problems and should consider the context of the situation (time, subject, students, general environment). Though it is often useful to visit a classroom to perform a nonspecific observation, such as our virtual field trips to classrooms, this should occur prior to a focused, problem-centered observation.

Valuing the Democratic Classroom Environment

Let us consider some of the questions or problems that teachers consider important to observe for self-study of their own teaching.

If you were observing this classroom, what "commonplaces" would focus your attention?

- *Interaction*—Do I provide opportunity for all students to participate in discussions? Do I encourage student-to-student interaction?
- *Questioning skills*—Do I ask open-ended or closed-ended questions? Are my questions motivating?
- *Seatwork*—Are students actively engaged? Do I provide for individual differences?
- *Motivation*—Do students appear motivated and interested?
- *Instruction*—Is there enough variance in my teaching strategies? Do my strategies match my goals? Am I using teaching models correctly?
- *Decision making*—Am I interpreting correctly what students know and don't know and selecting appropriate content and strategies?
- *Classroom management*—Why do students seem to wander around the classroom? Why does it take so long before students start their work? Am I too authoritarian as a teacher?

Obviously teachers can ask many questions when trying to improve their teaching performance, and the preceding list represents just a few categories. You may want to construct your own list. Let us now look at how observation research can be used to provide some insight concerning these questions.

Specific Techniques for Classroom Observation

Jean Cantor was really upset about the note-passing that occurred in her English literature class. She asked a teaching colleague to sit in on her next session. Her colleague asked her: "What do you want me to look for? What is your instructional goal for the lesson?"

Cantor responded, "I want the students to engage in problem solving concerning what motivates authors to write about certain themes in their novels."

"Let's work this out together then," her colleague responded.

The two teachers decided that notes should be taken at Cantor's next class session on the presentation and on what students were doing.

Cantor's colleague scripted some direct quotes and many notations from the lecture that Jean delivered. The colleague, sitting in the back of the room, also watched what students were doing and their reactions. When the class was over, Cantor's colleague talked with several of the students. In her interview with the students she asked them, "What ideas did you get from the lecture? What surprised you?" After school the colleague shared her notes with Cantor and the two teachers analyzed the lesson.

The teacher friend asked Jean, "Do you think the students engaged in problem solving?" Cantor responded, "Well, I guess I expected that they would do so in their own minds, but in class all they did was take notes—and obviously some of them didn't even do that!"

> After an extended conversation about teaching strategies, Cantor noted that if she wanted students to problem solve, she would have to stop lecturing and provide opportunity for students to investigate and discuss among themselves the books they were assigned to read. She decided to work with her friend to design some new teaching strategies that would be more motivating.

It is important to note that Jean Cantor's colleague reported to her on only the questions that she had requested. She did not focus on anything else that might have occurred.

Scripting

Scripting a lesson is frequently used in observation research and lesson planning. In observation, it is a means to record key statements or questions that a teacher makes; in lesson planning, it is used to record what you anticipate students will respond. In this situation the observer recorded key statements and notes on Cantor's lesson and also focused on what the students were doing during the lecture.

Interviewing

Interviewing students is a productive and insightful means to find out if students' perception of the class experience is the same as what the teacher anticipates it to be. Without students' perception it is not possible to know "what worked" and "what didn't."

Videotaping

Now let us suppose that Lucia Martin recognizes that her classroom discussions are not real discussions and she wants some help. She asks a colleague to *videotape* one of her classroom discussions. (Videotaping could be done by a student as well as by another teacher.) She may view the videotape by herself or with her friend.

Diagramming Interaction

During the discussion in Martin's classroom, the students were sitting in a square so that they could all see each other. Martin also was seated with the students. She began the discussion with a question and then she called on a student to respond. The "discussion" continued in this manner. Martin decided that she wanted her friend to help her analyze the videotape.

Martin's friend drew a picture of the square and students' positions in it. As suggested by Acheson and Gall (1997) she then began to draw arrows from the teacher to the designated student. If the student responded she drew an arrow from student to teacher. It was soon apparent that only the designated students responded and that Martin was in complete control of the so-called discussion because there was no student-to-student interaction.

Martin noted another happening as she studied her friend's diagram. She realized that all her questions were directed to boys. She ignored the girls in the class. She had asked about ten different questions, but she never elicited responses from girls.

With her friend's prodding she made a third discovery. When students responded they directed every response to her. They never looked at their classmates. As a consequence there were no add-ons by other students to the original response; students expected the teacher to either answer or ask another question.

If students are seated in their own seats, it is possible to use your seating chart to record who is speaking and to whom and how often. It also simplifies counting the number of students who participate in the discussion, the number of males and females who are involved in the discussion, and the teacher's role. (In a real discussion the teacher should not be the central focus; students should be talking to their classmates.)

Roger Ives is concerned about his classroom management skills. Roger decided to ask his assistant principal to sit in on a class meeting.

Roger's instructions to the assistant principal were to observe the students and see if he was providing clear directions. "After my initial warm-up activity, I have difficulty getting everyone's attention on the day's lesson."

At the beginning of class, the assistant principal toured the classroom, visiting the groups of students working on the license plate problem. She noted that the students were very animated and involved in their task. When time was called, the students were somewhat disappointed because many had not finished. Roger's remark to the students was, "There will be time at the end of the period to share your ideas on how to solve this problem."

Ives expected the students to put their work aside and listen to him as he began the day's lesson. "Today we need to study . . ."

After Ives' presentation he checked for student understanding and had students do some practice problems using the concept he had taught. As the end of the period approached, he called on students to talk about the license plate problem, but time ran out and he told students, "Tomorrow we'll get to it."

Roger's assistant principal had taken a few notes, and she had some thoughts that she wanted to put down on paper. She suggested that they talk in the afternoon. In the meantime, she categorized her notes using four headings: motivation, clarity, fragmentation, and timing.

Before reading further, use the four categories to critique Roger's lesson.

At their meeting she asked Roger what meanings the headings had for him. They then discussed the four aspects of the lesson that she had observed. Her ideas follow: (1) The assistant principal believed that the warm-up exercise was motivating and a great idea, but it should lead in to the context of what the lesson will be about. (2) The warm-up inquiry experience should be discussed immediately when time is called so that students' attention does not lag. (3) Postponing the discussion of the initial activity and moving on to a new mathematics concept fragments learning for the students and causes them anxiety and lack of motivation to pay attention. (4) The whole class period needs to be organized with timing carefully considered. (5) As to Roger's concern about the clarity of his direction, the assistant principal believed that he was very clear and that students understood the new concept.

Audiotaping

Audiotaping is another means to observe, and you can do it without assistance of anyone but your students. Suppose you want to find out whether you have motivated your students and whether all students participate during group work. You can place a tape recorder in each group and ask students to run it while they are engaged in their small groups.

You should still be monitoring your groups and providing whatever assistance they need, but the tape captures the complete experience. Give each group a number, identify the students in each group, and then number the tape. At your leisure you can listen, identify voices, take notes of group accomplishments and problems, and get a clear idea of what you taught by the responses of your students. The audiotape provides a fine means to reflect on your lesson and ask yourself not only "What worked?" but "What did I forget?"

Anecdotal Record

The **anecdotal record** is a means to study individual students who may not be performing to your expectations or may be having a particular problem, as well as an informal and objective means to observe behavior and describe specific events. You will want to describe the context of the observation—what is happening in the classroom, the time, the subject, the learning experience, and what the subject of the observation is doing. You will need to do this over a period of several days to perhaps a couple of weeks.

You may study your written record each day or after several days and try to interpret why the behavior is as it occurred. You may want to try to alter your own performance and check to see how that affects the behavior of the subject. The ultimate task is to plan action to mediate the problem. In some cases your anecdotal record should be given to a specialist (nurse, counselor, resource person) to assist in both the interpretation and the prescription. An example of the anecdotal record will be given in Chapter 5.

Some anecdotal records are used to record a single event in order to study a specific classroom problem. It is written very objectively, describing precisely what happened. Here is an example.

> Students are working in small groups studying causes of school violence. Marta leaves her group and goes over to another group to talk to Sally. At first Sally seems to respond to Marta, but then Sally shakes her head and pushes Marta away. Sally's group seems to be angry to be bothered by the interruption; they are staring at Marta. Marta stamps her foot and in a loud whisper says, "You'll be sorry for this." Marta's face is red and Sally looks angry.

Marta has no doubt disturbed two groups of students. You have not heard the initial discussion between Sally and Marta, but you decide it warrants further investigation. What do you think the teacher should do?

Checklists

Checklists provide a relatively simple means to collect objective data about student and teacher performance. The trick is to develop a checklist that is specific and identifies all of the behaviors that interest you. The checklist can be used after the lesson with a videotape; otherwise you need a partner to observe. Partner observation will make the checklist more objective. However, it is important to recognize that use of a checklist means that the observer is wearing "blinders" because the context of teaching is ignored, as is any other behavior that is not identified on the checklist. Figure 2.4 exhibits a checklist that focuses on teacher behavior; Figure 2.5 focuses on student behavior.

Case Study Narrative

Case study narrative observation may be performed when the observer has a great deal of time to spend in observing the classroom. The purpose of the case study is to describe every aspect of classroom life that relates to the study of a specific question or problem. For example, five New Zealand researchers (Alton-Lee, Diggins, Klenner, Vine, & Dalton, 2001) studied teacher management of the learning environment during social studies instruction. These researchers wrote narrative accounts of the school and classroom environment, a description of the social studies content to be taught to the students, students' experiences that related to the unit, the pedagogy used by the teacher, and challenging

---

Y = yes, N = no

___ Motivates lesson enthusiastically

___ Makes eye contact with students

___ Relates new content to familiar content

___ Provides examples and nonexamples of new concept

___ Asks students lower cognitive questions to check for understanding

___ Provides feedback and corrects any misunderstandings

___ Asks open-ended questions to extend thinking

___ Encourages students' questions and discussion

___ Uses appropriate lesson materials and resources

___ Clearly states directions to students

___ Matches learning activity to lesson goals

___ Verifies student understanding of learning activity

FIGURE 2.4   Teacher Behavior

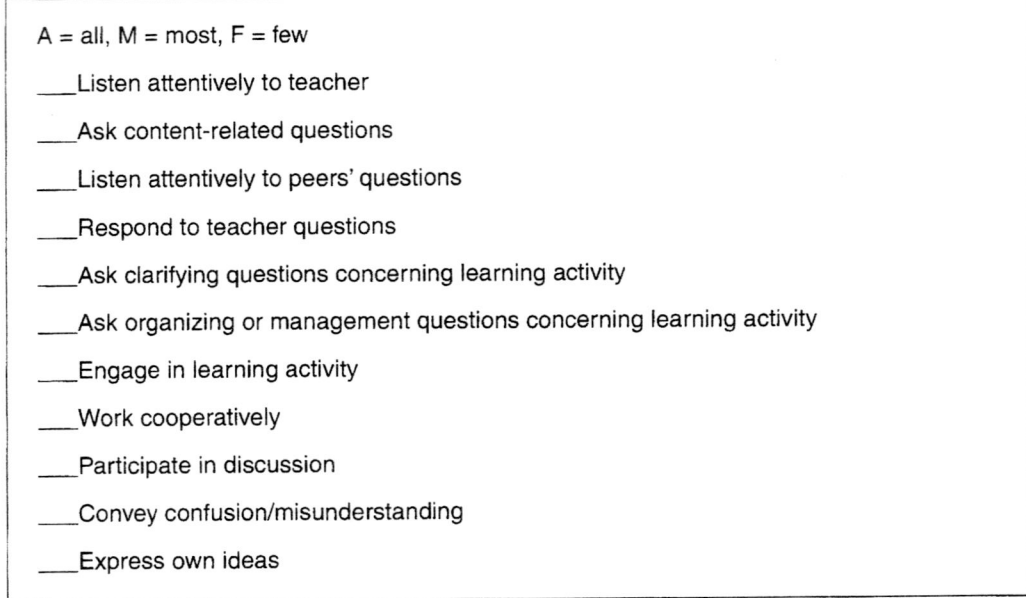

FIGURE 2.5 Students' Behavior

classroom problems that confronted the teacher. Through study of the narrative accounts, the researchers (and the teacher) reflect on how the strategies teachers use (may) help to build learning communities.

 Did You Know That . . . ?

"[Students'] shared stories and understandings can serve as reference points for supporting individual learning as a teacher assists students to generate more links between what they already know and new information" (Alton-Lee, Diggins, Klenner, Vine, & Dalton, 2001).

Ethnography

Ethnography is similar to the case study. The observer writes in narrative style and focuses on the study of culture in the school or classroom. The observer selects a specific aspect of culture and writes a "thick description" of what is observed. The intent is to understand and interpret life from the perspective of those observed. Through use of narratives, the observer tries to capture meaning as shared by the participants, thereby sharing interpretations with others.

Suppose that a teacher is concerned that he or she is unable to establish a democratic learning community in the classroom because the diverse ethnic groups do not seem to relate to each other. The teacher asks assistance from a friend, who agrees to spend time in the classroom and on the playground observing and talking to the students. Context, dialogue, and incidents are recorded. The observer is seeking to find out if the diverse groups interact and if there is integration of individuals across ethnic lines.

Both the observer and the teacher study the narrative accounts of what happened, interviews, and dialogues, and each interprets on his or her own. Insight from this research concerning group relationships has the potential to help the teacher understand ways to get the groups to work together and to develop a learning community to improve the social and cultural environment of the classroom.

The Visible and the Invisible

Nothing is more important when visiting a classroom than identifying what isn't in the classroom but should be; what is taught and what is left out; what is spoken and what is hidden. These elements—the invisible curriculum, the unspoken management tactics, the teaching strategies that never happen—are very powerful encumbrances that affect what students learn.

We know that the arts are supposed to be taught in elementary schools. But how often do we see evidence that they are taught? How well have teachers been prepared to teach the arts? Do schools stock materials and resources for teaching the arts? Is transportation available to take students to art centers and museums? What we encounter here is purposeful and traditional neglect of the arts curriculum.

What else? In the secondary schools the *other* social sciences are often omitted: political science, economics, anthropology, and sociology. In the humanities, too little time is provided for communication skills in both the elementary and secondary curriculum. The curricula that are not taught become missed opportunities for students.

Now let's look at some teacher messages. In an elementary classroom we hear, "If you do not quiet down and pay attention, we will *not* be going out for P.E. today." What's the real message here?

1. The teacher needs to discipline and punish students.

2. Students are restless and need to move around.

3. The teacher does not value physical education and believes it is a "frill" subject.

If you said "2" and "3" you are correct. This teacher is broadcasting, loud and clear, that physical education does not need to be taught. We do not have enough evidence to know about the teacher's classroom management system, but number 1 is not the way to manage the classroom.

If we want to learn more about a classroom, we need only to check the wastebasket at the end of the day. The scraps of paper will tell us about the drill curriculum, the pictures that were not valued by the teacher, the notes that were passed surreptitiously, and the spelling list and homework assignments that were forgotten. These items are visible, but we need to search for the invisible.

What Rules Tell Us

The rules chart pinned to an elementary classroom bulletin board states:

1. Our desks are to be kept neat and clean.
2. We do not bother our neighbors.
3. We do not waste paper or time.
4. We ask permission to sharpen pencils and to leave the classroom.
5. We do not wander about the classroom.

The following rules are given to eighth-grade students to take home and obtain a parent signature:

1. Students are to arrive on time to class and be ready for work when the bell rings.
2. Your textbook is to be brought to class every day.
3. Homework will be assigned three days per week and is due the following day when class begins. No excuses.
4. Students are not to pass notes or talk to their neighbors except during group work.
5. All work assignments are to be neat and when completed at home, typed.
6. If you are absent, you are expected to contact the teacher or another student to find out what you have missed.

Now none of these rules sounds obsessive, but let's think about what they tell us about teacher-student relationships and authority, individual needs, and classroom interaction.

Teacher and Student Relations and Teacher Authority

It would appear that both sets of rules are designed to ensure teacher authority and quiet classrooms. The teachers will tell students when they may talk. The standards to be enforced are quiet and orderliness. It is reasonable to assume that teacher-directed instruction is of prime importance to these teachers, and very limited interaction either between teacher and students or among students will occur.

We may assume also that the teacher fears student talk because it may lead to an out-of-control classroom. As a consequence, learning experiences will be limited to those that ensure teacher control. So we have limited opportunities for the development of communication skills and limited opportunities for problem-solving experiences because such activities would involve student talk, group experiences, movement, and sharing of a variety of resources.

Individual Needs

The rules in these classrooms suggest rigidity of instructional routines, procedures, and instruction. The eighth-grade teacher knows in advance that homework will be necessary three days per week and that no excuses for nonconformity will be accepted. The teacher has stated what students must do, but not what the teacher will do. For example, we do not know whether time will be devoted to checking and talking about homework, which is something that students have a right to know.

One can assume that the rigidity of standards (no excuses) means that individual needs of students will not be considered. In addition, the code of silence also affirms that individual ideas and opinions that should be expressed during class discussions and peer activities are not to be encouraged.

Classroom Interaction

If students are discouraged from talking to their peers, appropriate social behavior is not developed. In the elementary classroom we can guess that the teaching of social studies is neglected, as well as any other content field experience that requires social interaction.

The rules chart and the rules students are required to take home tell us a great deal about life in the classroom. We can also take another look at the teacher behavior checklist in Figure 2.4. Any observation technique that specifies a particular area of observation ignores all other aspects of classroom life. An observer in Cantor's classroom could score her positively on most of those behaviors, yet she does not seek students' interests, needs, and opinions. It is possible that the literature curriculum is quite limited and that teacher authority is emphasized while student interaction is neglected.

Chapter Summary

There are lots of ways to see in classrooms, from everyday observation to more sophisticated focused observation. In between the everyday, casual observation and focused observation are the clues about classroom life that need great reflection. These clues relate to what we don't see and should, what we don't hear and should. This chapter is intended to extend your thinking about life in classrooms and suggest a variety of means to observe, and thereby to improve teaching and learning.

Four observable commonplaces of the classroom were identified and each was demonstrated through teaching scenarios. Where students sit was correlated with the potential effect on students' performance. A number of techniques for focused observations were explained. These included narrative, technological, and checklist procedures. An important focus of the chapter was the significance of reflecting on hidden meanings and curriculum omissions that can be interpreted from classroom visitations.

Teaching Problems

1. Mathew is an eighth-grade student in a middle school that has block scheduling and team teaching for mathematics and science. The two subjects are often integrated by the two teachers. Lately Mathew has had a strange problem. He suddenly begins to cough until he gets red in the face and claims that he is choking. He then asks to leave the room. Since most of the period Mathew is fine with no signs of illness, the teachers do not think he is really ill. How can they study the problem to determine the cause of Mathew's sudden and mysterious malady?

2. You are observing in a third-grade classroom and as you tour the room you are interested in the bulletin boards that display students'

work. On one bulletin board are watercolor pictures the students have made. On another bulletin board are "creative" stories. Close examination of the pictures and the stories reveal that the pictures are almost all alike and the stories are too similar. What do these bulletin boards tell you about life in this classroom?

3. You are visiting in a tenth-grade history classroom. The bulletin boards are sterile; there are no exhibits or anything of interest. The teacher confides in you that she is having difficulty with her first-period class. She states that only about half the students pay attention to her instructions. The other half ask irrelevant questions, doodle on scraps of paper, and clearly lack interest. What does the classroom environment and the teacher's problem tell you about her? How can the teacher engage in self-study to discover on her own why she is having a problem?

4. Focus on a classroom problem that disturbs you. Record the following information.
   1. Identify who is involved in the problem.
   2. Identify the behavioral action(s).
   3. Record dialogue/conversation.
   4. Record what happened—specifically—but without bias or interpretation.
   5. Use your data to reflect on causes and consequences.
   6. Consider ways to resolve the problem. (What do you need to do?)

CHAPTER 3

How Students Learn

ADVANCE ORGANIZER

These questions can be used as a framework to assist you in integrating professional knowledge and understanding of the content of this chapter.

1. Considering the characteristics of the democratic classroom community, how should teachers deal with the following aspects of diversity when planning lessons?
   a. developmental levels
   b. language proficiency
   c. ability
   d. life experiences
   e. multiple intelligences
   f. learning styles
2. How do the problems and concerns of society at large play a role in lesson and curriculum planning?
3. Identify and describe four ways that teachers can differentiate instruction.

 The following INTASC issues and standards are discussed in this chapter: Numbers 1–10.

In this chapter three important concepts are considered when teachers reflect on how students learn: (1) students' diverse physical and individual development, (2) societal problems and priorities, and (3) the subject field of focus. In addition, philosophical and psychological theories of learning affect the ways in which teachers consider lesson planning. Constructivism, multiple intelligences, and learning styles affect teacher planning.

Developmental Considerations

Individuals differ cognitively, affectively, and in psychomotor abilities. If identifying a student's grade level really provided a "label" for what students can do, teachers would not have to consider individual differences. But realistically we know that identification of grade level tells us very little about the individual student. Jean Piaget (1969), a Swiss psychologist, recognized that children mature at different rates, but progress through similar stages on the road to maturity. His study of developmental patterns generated behavioral characteristics of four stages of development.

The *sensorimotor stage* affects the child from age 0 to 2 years. This is recognized as the prelanguage stage and is critical to the development of thought. By the end of this stage the child experiences concepts of space, time, causality, and intentionality.

The *preoperational stage* affects the child from age 2 to 7. Language develops and the child learns to categorize and label objects. Categorization requires differentiation, and at the beginning of this stage the child tends to generalize about objects; for example, all vehicles are considered "cars," but through play, experience, and hands-on activities, the child learns "classes" of cars such as race cars, SUVs, trucks, and convertibles. The size of objects becomes important in the process of differentiation; big and little, fat and thin are relatively easy, but the preoperational individual has difficulty recognizing that an object that is fat and squat may hold the same amount of liquid that a tall and thin vessel will hold. Piaget described this as the concept of **conservation,** and he concluded that the child at this level has difficulty recognizing **reversibility.** The implications of these concepts affect the planning of learning activities.

Teaching Hints

Teachers of K–2 students need to plan activities that require students to categorize objects, such as rocks, rods of different sizes, pictures of animals, blocks, and stacking rings or cups.

The preoperational child lacks certain social skills because of the tendency toward **egocentrism**. The child knows what he or she wants, but is not conscious and aware of others. Social interaction is vital for the child in order to learn to be reflective and recognize others' beliefs and viewpoints. Group work is extremely important if students are to learn to accommodate their behavior and ideas to those of their classmates.

> ### Teaching Problem
>
> Suppose a first-grade teacher placed flannel airplanes on a flannel board in front of the class. Eight airplanes were placed in a row, and eight more directly below. The teacher asked the students if the two rows contained the same number of airplanes. The students responded "yes." Then the teacher spaced the bottom row of airplanes farther apart than the top row and once again asked the students if the rows contained the same number of airplanes. This time the students responded "no." Explain what this tells you about the developmental level of the students and what learning activities you should plan to help them.

The *concrete operations stage* generally affects students from age 7 to 11. Logical thought can be expected of the student when dealing with concrete problems and situations. If studying about a desert environment, students will need pictures of what the desert is like, animal adaptation to the desert environment, and the plants that grow in that environment. Students cannot be expected to visualize problems associated with desert life unless they have had the opportunity to see the desert environment.

The *formal operations stage* affects students from age 11 to 16. No longer constrained by the need to provide concrete materials, teachers can plan problems that involve abstract thought and scientific reasoning. Students can organize data by classifying, seriating, and corresponding, and most students can subject thought to inference, implication, and hypothetical situations. To facilitate logical thought, students need opportunities to consider "if-then" types of problems. For example, in a health education class adolescent students were asked, "If the government relaxed auto emission requirements for SUVs, what might some of the consequences be for society at large?"

> ### Teaching Problem
>
> You are teaching adolescent students in a health education class. You have recently read that drug companies are not producing enough serum for children's vaccinations. Yet the vaccinations are required for school entrants. Plan a motivating question to involve your students in if-then thinking concerning the consequences of the situation.

Lev Vygotsky (1962), a Russian psychologist, also studied developmental patterns. He noted egocentric behavior in young children; however, he ascribed different reasons for it. Vygotsky believed that the preoperational child engages in egocentric talk as a natural language developmental pattern because the child is engaging in inner speech and talking to himself or herself. Piaget theorized that social development preceded language development, but Vygotsky believed that learning precedes development. Vygotsky's theories suggest to teachers that social interaction, particularly between older and younger students, will facilitate learning development. Vygotsky called this the **zone of proximal development** because the young child profits from the assistance of the older student and learns to carry out tasks that otherwise would be too difficult.

Both Piaget and Vygotsky advocated active learning experiences and believed that teachers should plan activities in which students are engaged in discovery, problem solving, and experimentation. They believed that students need to interact with their environment and that students learn through their own construction of knowledge. This process of building knowledge through active experiences is called **constructivist learning theory.**

Constructivism

Constructivism is an inquiry learning approach that takes advantage of students' own experiences to develop challenging problems that will engage students in active learning. Students' prior experiences serve as building blocks to assist them in integrating new knowledge with concepts already learned. Students' experiences serve as a bridge to facilitate learning new content and information. When teachers plan active learning experiences, students participate in hands-on activities, raise questions about a topic that interests them, determine how they will go about their inquiry, and demonstrate their ability to apply what they have learned. A model for constructivist teaching will be given in Chapter 9.

Brooks and Brooks (1993) have studied the environment of constructivist-oriented classrooms. They tell us that constructivist teachers rely on learning activities that use primary resource materials and data, consider their students "thinkers," seek students' viewpoints, and assess students' work through observation and by what students produce. An example follows.

> Gerry Alred is teaching about how immigration to a new country affects patterns of behavior for both the immigrants and the citizens of the country. She asked her students: "In what ways do immigrants have to adapt to their new country and in what ways do citizens of the country modify their ways of living?" To assist students' thinking, she drew a circle on the chalkboard with the word *immigration* in the middle. As students came up with ideas, she drew lines from the circle to their concepts. She explained that their ideas demonstrated what they knew about immigration and that they were constructing a concept web that would direct further inquiry.

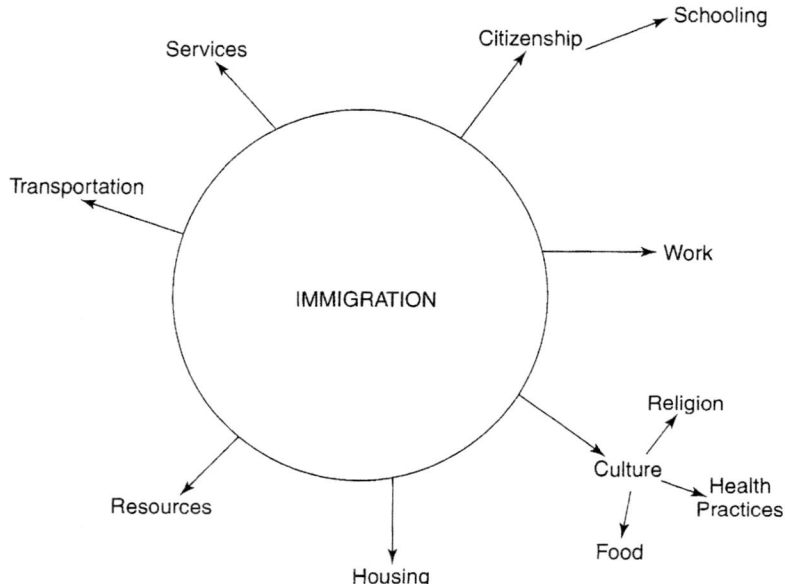

In what ways do immigrants have to adapt to their new country, and in what ways do citizens of the country modify their ways of living?

FIGURE 3.1 **Concept Web**

Multiple Intelligences, Learning Styles, and Natural Differences

Intelligence relates to the special *ability* or *capacity* that an individual has related to a specific content or subject field. Howard Gardner (1993, 1995) has identified eight different intelligences that affect human behavior. He considers all of the intelligences equal in impact and challenges teachers to appeal to the natural differences among students by providing multiple means for students to respond to learning tasks using their special abilities.

Each identified intelligence suggests different areas of ability; the first two have been more valued in the schools.

Linguistic intelligence defines the individual with special ability in word usage. This person may use language to express sounds, rhythms, and meanings of words. Poets tend to display this capacity.

Logical-mathematical intelligence is exhibited by the individual who can detect logical or numerical patterns. Scientists and mathematicians display this intelligence.

Spatial intelligence is displayed by engineers, surgeons, sculptors, painters, sailors, and other individuals who can use spatial models to solve problems. Artists also demonstrate this capacity in their use of dimension, perspective, and spacing.

Musical intelligence is demonstrated by both the public who appreciate music and the artist who produces it through the use of rhythm, pitch, and timbre.

Bodily-kinesthetic intelligence is exhibited by athletes, dancers, surgeons, and craftspeople who use their bodies in a variety of ways that demonstrate skills of coordination, balance, and dexterity.

Interpersonal intelligence is demonstrated by individuals who are particularly sensitive to others' moods, meanings, intentions, and desires. Parents, politicians, teachers, and therapists typically are strong in this area of intelligence.

Intrapersonal intelligence is demonstrated by individuals who are insightful about their own needs, capacities, strengths, and weaknesses and use this insight to guide personal behavior.

Naturalistic intelligence is the capacity to instinctively and intuitively discriminate and appreciate nature, and art in nature. Botanists, biologists, and artists demonstrate this ability. Often this person is an environmentalist and loves animals and natural objects.

How Can Teachers Take Advantage of Students' Multiple Intelligences?

Certainly teachers cannot design eight different lessons to appeal to all students; however, lessons can be varied so that students can apply their special abilities in responding to learning tasks. Project work can provide opportunity for students to demonstrate understanding and communicate to others through creating artwork, building models, writing reports and stories, using technology to create multimedia projects, using cameras and tape recorders, and interviewing specialists. It is important to remember that learning tasks in different subject fields should provide different opportunities and elicit different responses from students.

Gardner emphasizes that intelligence is not a fixed entity, cannot be measured by a single test or number, and does not predict the individual's future success in school. The theory of multiple intelligences can be implemented in a variety of ways. When teachers provide real-life contexts for problem solving, the natural capacities of students will emerge. The learning activities planned by Gerry Alred in Table 3.1 provide examples of ways **multiple intelligences** can be included in lesson and unit planning. The majority of Gerry's learning experiences require small-group work.

Teaching Problem

Using Gerry Alred's learning activities for several of the concepts, identify the multiple intelligences she considered in her planning.

TABLE 3.1 Lesson and Unit Planning Using Multiple Intelligences

Lesson Topic	Learning Activity
Citizenship	Read about citizenship requirements; interview INS person; chart demographic maps of immigration; create a timeline of immigration cycles; graph population groups and points of entry, settlement, and native country. Share findings in class discussion.
Culture	Share ethnic music, art, food, literature; listen, cook, create, view, and appreciate; paint murals; read folk tales; role-play how it feels to be an immigrant resident in the United States.
Work	Investigate immigrant jobs, special talents, and problems obtaining and keeping jobs. Share findings in class discussion. Write stories about the talents of immigrant residents.
Schooling	Interview new and naturalized citizens; inquire about problems and second-language learning; graph language abilities in own school and school district. Report findings.
Recreation	Study sports activities of different cultures; participate in games of different cultures.
Transportation	Create a transportation model to exhibit freeways and roads; study means of transportation for immigrants to job sites.
Health	Experiment with food spoilage and cleanliness; graph progress.
Housing	Locate ethnic "pockets"; find out why groups locate where they do. Go on a field trip to sections of the city to see visual signs of changes in the population. Study and report on living conditions. Correlate transportation to jobs and where people live.
Services	Find out what services people need and what is available to immigrant residents. Locate family services and immigrant residences. Share findings in class discussion.
Resources	Inquire: What resources does the city have that attracts immigrant populations? What resources are needed to assist new residents? Share findings in class discussion.

Reading to children develops their interest in reading, helps to focus attention, improves listening skills and comprehension, and develops linguistic intelligence.

Learning Styles

Learning style relates to the individual's cognitive, affective, and psychomotor *preferences* and *characteristics* for ways to learn. For example, to understand a new concept or remember someone's name, I need to see it in writing because I know that I remember things better when I see them than when I just hear them. Because students have different learning styles, it is important that teachers present information using a variety of teaching methods.

After studying how children and adults learn in a variety of settings, Dunn and Dunn (1987) isolated eighteen elements that affect individuals' learning. They noted that individuals react to four key preferences: *environment, emotionality, physical needs,* and *sociological preferences.* These four dimensions of learning style affect people as shown in Table 3.2.

Reviewing several of these elements, it is clear that the individual who needs to move around may prefer hands-on activities and involvement in learning experiences. The student who prefers to work with an adult may need more teacher monitoring than the student who likes to interact with peers. The student that prefers open-ended tasks is self-motivated, while the individual who needs structured lessons may need immediate feedback on how he or she is progressing.

If you recall the discussion of seating in Chapter 2, you can see that the environment may strongly affect students' work and participation. Some students prefer to be seated with others in small clusters, while others may prefer more space. Some students like seats near the window, while others are bothered by too much sun and light. Too much teacher attention may inhibit the work of some students, while others may prefer frequent interaction and monitoring.

TABLE 3.2 Dunn and Dunn Learning Styles

Learning Factor	Description
Environment	Individuals may be affected by sound (noise or quiet), light (dimness or brightness), temperature (too hot or cold), physical design (seated too close, distant, far from instruction, or too close to teacher).
Emotionality	Individuals may be affected by motivational needs (structured lessons or openness and choices), persistence (stays with study until concluded or gives up easily), responsibility (assumes responsibility for task completion and jobs or lets things slide and prefers passivity).
Physical Needs	Individuals may be affected by perceptual strengths (prefers to listen, to see, or to feel), mobility (needs to move about or sit still), intake (needs frequent food or drink), time of day (works best in the morning or the afternoon).
Sociological Preferences	Some individuals may prefer group work and interaction with others; some individuals work best alone, prefer to work with a partner, or work best with an adult.

Did You Know That . . . ?

> When teachers need to present detailed information to students, the students will understand and recall the information better and for a longer period of time if the material is presented dramatically. Nuthall (1999) and Nuthall and Alton-Lee (1995) studied teachers' lessons presented verbally, visually, and dramatically. They learned that verbal instruction had the weakest effect on student learning.

Reflection and Impulsivity, Field Independence and Dependence

Clinical psychologists also have studied students' learning styles. Yando and Kagan (1968) recognized that some students tend to respond without considered thought while others tend to reflect. Students who blurt out responses to questions and cannot wait to listen to their peers may be impulsive learners, and students who hesitate before responding need to process conceptual knowledge; thus they respond reflectively.

Classroom Application Teachers need to help both types of students. For the *impulsive* learner, some nonverbal maneuvers may help. First, establish eye contact with the student; then try gesturing by pointing to your head and then to your lips. Try to convey that you want the student to think before responding. If absolutely necessary say to the student, "Jay, I want you to think for a moment before answering the question." Or, "Jay, I know you want to respond, but let's give some of your friends a chance."

The *reflective* learner's conceptual tempo may be quite deliberate and therefore slow, and it is possible also that the student is shy. Increase your "wait" time to give the student opportunity to think out the response. Sometimes it may be advisable to call out the student's name and say, "Chris, what do you think about . . . ?" This approach lets the student know that it is his turn to talk and that you will wait for him. More about questioning techniques will be discussed in Chapter 9.

Field-dependent learners tend to be distracted by irrelevant information. As a learner confronted with story problems in mathematics, this student may have difficulty ignoring unneeded data and focusing on the details necessary for solving the problem. *Field-independent* learners can ignore the irrelevant details in the problem and concentrate only on the significant data.

When teachers lecture and students are required to take notes, field-dependent learners may try to fill their notebooks with everything the teacher has said, thereby missing the substance and significance of the lecture. The field-independent learner may take scant notes because of concentrating on what he or she considers significant.

Classroom Application Observe your students and monitor their efforts. When students cannot sort out the significant from the irrelevant, ask them questions, probe their responses, suggest ways to clarify their thinking, and remind them of the purpose of what they are doing. When students are required to take notes from a text or a presentation, ask to see their notes so that you can detect the field-dependent learner. Field-dependent learners will benefit from study questions that direct their reading and note-taking. Examples of such questions appear at the beginning of each chapter of this text.

Societal Considerations

Lesson planning involves consideration of three factors: developmental capabilities of the learner, the needs and interests of the society we live in, and the subject field we are teaching. As you become acquainted with your students you learn about their cultural identity, ethnicity, social class, and nationality. Sociologists have contributed a great deal of information about how the family influences socialization. For example, we know that the early years of family life are critical to the child's development of intelligence. An enriched family environment that includes books, newspapers, music, games, travel, and family discussions influences personality, temperament, and general behavior.

The ways students are punished or rewarded affect their behavior. If parents provide opportunities for reasonable discussion of problem behavior, the student learns to reason, reflect, and accept criticism. But if the student is subjected to verbal and/or physical abuse, then the individual learns to resort to the same when confronted with similar situations.

In short, the interactions experienced in the family circle carry over and influence future behavior.

Race and cultural differences also affect behavior in the classroom. Many children are taught at home that it is impolite for a young person to make eye contact with an adult. This is particularly true for Hispanic, African-American, and Navajo students. Some parents do not believe that they should visit school and hold a conference with their children's teachers. Collaborative planning by parent and teacher are not valued by some cultures. When holding a conference with students' parents, it is important that you are seated at the same level as the parent. You do not want to appear overbearing and impolite. Verbal, nonverbal, and written communications with parents will be discussed in Chapter 10.

Sex roles are influenced by the family, the peer group, and the community. In some cultures girls are still discouraged from enrolling in solid academic studies, and boys may be expected to be macho and involved in mechanical arts. However, it is even more likely today that both parents are working or that children are raised in single-parent families. As a consequence, sex-role socialization may occur in the neighborhood, the school, and community organizations. It is important that students' education at school is nondifferential and not sex **stereotyped** and that students experience a variety of activities and experiences. Both curriculum materials and teacher behavior must be unbiased to ensure that students experience gender equity in their education.

Classroom Application   Lesson planning and methodology need to be *culturally responsive*. Multicultural students often respond more positively to small-group learning experiences instead of teacher-directed instruction. Teachers need to demonstrate respect and caring for all students in a democratic classroom environment. Understanding that your students are *individuals* means that the curriculum must be racially and culturally inclusive if students and parents are to respond positively. If the only voice heard in the classroom (and in curriculum materials) is eurocentric, many students, perhaps the majority, will not be motivated to study.

Societal Impact

The impact of society on the curriculum should not be underestimated. Lesson planning is affected by standards set by state and district requirements. Certain subjects are expected to receive more instructional time than others. Some subjects are considered superfluous, and as a consequence teachers in these specializations find it difficult to obtain jobs. Societal problems affect the school environment (violence), the curriculum (blood-transmitted diseases), and even methodology (second-language instruction).

A variety of societal problems that affect student motivation to learn cannot be ignored. Problems of poverty and homelessness are prevalent in every region of the country. Students subjected to these problems feel powerless; some are passively resigned, while others resort to bullying their classmates. Child abuse is another problem that affects students from all social classes and throughout the world. Teachers are often the first to recognize when a student is being abused. Both teachers and school nurses are responsible for reporting incidents of abuse.

How Do Societal Problems Affect Lesson Planning?

As teachers we cannot ignore the problems of our students. We know that a good education will help students in adult life to overcome many of these problems. Our task is to provide relevant curriculum and learning activities that relate to students' experiences. Gerry Alred's immigration unit should include *why* immigrants leave their native land, *what* expectations they have, and *what* problems confront them. She then needs to lead to the fact that immigrants are not alone in having to respond to these problem situations.

The democratic classroom environment is ideal for creating relevant curriculum to link the needs of learners with the community at large. Whether or not students are multicultural and multiethnic, all students in our country need to learn about citizens' rights and responsibilities, how people's customs may differ, and the problems of our society. It is important to note that social psychologists have long told us that values are caught, not taught. Thus, if teachers are expected to teach about democratic values, they must be practiced in the classroom.

Teaching Hints

Students succeed when—

1. They are not hungry.
2. They have access to materials and resources to do their homework.
3. There is a caring adult who encourages them.
4. They have empathetic classmates who serve as buddies and tutors.

Teachers succeed when they acquaint themselves with the needs and interests of their students and facilitate the aforementioned advantages.

Subject Matter Considerations

The third element that affects teacher planning is the content that you need to address. Subject matter is *what* you teach, and pedagogy is *how* you teach. When you consider subject matter you also need to address pedagogy, because you can't have one without the other. Choosing what to teach is not as nebulous as it sounds. Teachers have suggestions from national organizations that specialize in each subject field, textbooks that provide a programmed approach, and district and state requirements. Because of the variety of sources and suggestions as to what you teach, it is extremely important that your decisions consider the students you teach, societal interests, your own background knowledge, and the materials and resources that you have available.

Reviewing Figure 3.1, we see the concepts the students suggested for their study of immigration, and in Table 3.1 we see that Gerry Alred made some decisions concerning the ways these concepts would be studied. In her long-term planning, she determined that her theme for a teaching unit would be "interdependence of people," and she selected immigration as the first focal point of the unit. In choosing the activities in Table 3.1, she needed to consider the learning styles of her students and their abilities for reading, interaction, technology, and to provide for multiple intelligences through differentiation of tasks to achieve her goals. Before we go through the actual planning process, let's look at one more concept that influences your choices of learning experiences.

Differentiation of Instruction

Differentiation means that you have considered all the ways that your students are unique individuals, and your planning considers individualization and personalization of instruction. Your lesson planning takes into account the ways some individuals excel and that others need different opportunities for success. There are four major ways that teachers can plan lessons to differentiate instruction.

1. *Content* can be modified by "depth studies," in which students study fewer concepts, but study them in depth to satisfy their need for learning everything about the concept. Or, content can be covered superficially and students learn less about more! Content can be varied by where you begin a unit and lesson, the focus of lessons, complexity, and simplicity.

2. *Process* of instruction can be differentiated by changing your teaching strategy and the purpose of your lesson. You will need to decide whether students will do research on the Internet, interview people, problem-solve in small groups, experiment, write letters and stories, or research papers. Once again, all of these things can be happening at the same time as you consider individual needs.

3. *Product* is what students produce, and they may be given a variety of choices to demonstrate their learning. The students using the computer may be required to keep a log of their Web sites and then create a multimedia production. Interview groups may need to script their interviewees and then graph their findings. Some students may prefer to write an individual research report.

4. The *environment* for learning can be differentiated by providing a variety of tools and resources, using learning centers or learning packets and workstations. Some students may need to work in the library; others may work outside or in other classrooms.

The trick to differentiating instruction is to provide equal access to multiple pathways to accomplish the learning goal. Students need choices and all students need a challenging curriculum. Chapter 4 will look at two different lesson plans to see how an experienced teacher and a novice teacher implement several of the concepts discussed in this chapter.

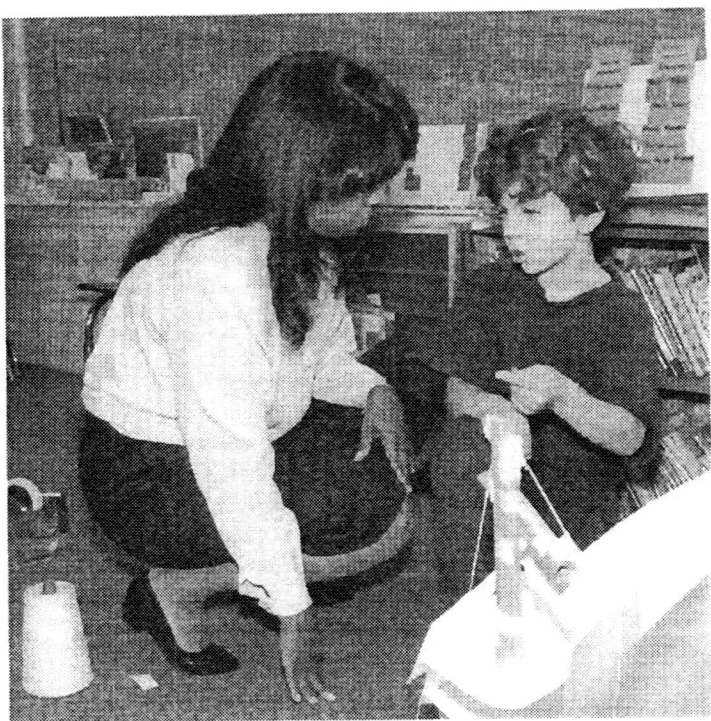

Listening to students describe their work plans helps to individualize and differentiate what students do.

Chapter Summary

This chapter focused on three components that influence the planning process: the learner, society, and subject matter. Philosophical and psychological factors also influence teacher planning. Beliefs about how to facilitate children's learning such as learning styles, constructivism, and multiple intelligences also affect teachers' planning processes.

Teaching Problems

1. A first-grade teacher has planned to take her students on a walking trip around the community to study plants: their parts, their needs, and their enemies. Plan a list of activities for them when they return to class that will incorporate multiple intelligences and provide for a variety of learning styles.
2. Identify the multiple intelligences and subject fields integrated in the following activities:

a. Share research findings in a class discussion.
b. Role-play immigrant residents.
c. Graph language ability in your own school.
d. Locate ethnic "pockets" in your city.
e. Use the Internet to research citizenship requirements in different countries.
f. Experiment with food spoilage.

Check your answers with those given in Appendix A.

PART 2

TEACHER PLANNING

Chapter 4 provides information on lesson planning, the important components of the plan, and the types of experiences that students need. Novice and experienced teachers' planning processes are compared. Suggestions are made for family and community participation. Chapter 5 addresses the teacher's need for long-term planning, including things to think about when planning a teaching unit, what to do if your lesson plan fails, and the different ways to jump-start unit planning, such as webbing and backward problem solving.

CHAPTER 4

Lesson Planning

ADVANCE ORGANIZER

These questions can be used as a framework to assist you in integrating professional knowledge and understanding of the content of this chapter.

1. How can novice teachers ensure effective lessons?
2. What issues should teachers consider when planning lessons?
3. How can all students participate in service learning?
4. Suggest ways to help English language learners.
5. How does group work help teachers differentiate learning and instruction?
6. How can families and the community involve themselves in the school program?

 The following INTASC issues and standards are discussed in this chapter: Numbers 1–10.

In this chapter we will look at actual lesson plans by both novice and experienced teachers. A special section will consider the needs of ELL students, and group work is discussed in this chapter (as well as in Chapters 8 and 9). Collaborative learning, which includes cooperative groups and teamwork, is discussed, as well as the impact of resources on teachers' choices and decisions. The chapter concludes with the ways in which teachers can include the family and community in the life of the classroom.

Jim Sierra's Classroom

Jim Sierra was teaching his students about the causes of the American Revolution.* He read to the class a short story about John Adams and his cousin Sam Adams. After concluding the story he wanted to engage the students in a discussion about the Boston Massacre. Jim was a novice teacher; to ensure that his lessons would go smoothly, he liked to script his opening questions and anticipate some of the responses that students might make. By anticipating students' responses he felt he would have a better idea as to whether his questions were on target. Jim's scripted questions were as follows:

1. *"In the story that I read to you, what were some of the things the British did that outraged the colonists?"* Jim anticipated that with encouragement and probing the students would give the following responses: (1) the forced housing of soldiers in the colonists' homes; (2) the seizing of John Hancock's ship; and (3) the influx of troops marching and training on Boston Common.
2. *"In what ways did the colonists antagonize the British troops?"* Jim intended to take notes on the chalkboard of students' responses to the questions.
3. *"Do you think the British or the colonists were more responsible for the massacre? Be sure to state your reasons."* This question was intended to encourage thinking in greater depth during the discussion.
4. *"Why did John Adams agree to defend the British soldiers and should he have done so?"*

After the discussion Jim intended to tell the students that the next day they would role-play the jury and trial of the eight British soldiers accused of murder.

---

* Lesson content suggested by *The Bill of Rights in Action* (1999, Winter), p. 1.

Novice and Experienced Teacher Lesson Planning

Jim Sierra's Lesson Plan

Subject: Social Studies, Language Arts

Purpose: (1) To appreciate that there are two sides to every dispute. (2) To recognize that popular opinion is not always "fair." (3) To participate in whole-class discussion concerning the causes of the American Revolution. (4) To write stories or draw cartoons about the Boston Massacre.

Resources: Historical literature, writing materials

Procedure/Teaching Strategy

Motivation: To listen to a story about a major incident prior to the American Revolution.

1. Read story to students about Boston Massacre.
2. Discuss story; ask questions: (a) In the story I read to you, what were some of the things the British did that outraged the colonists? (b) In what ways did the colonists antagonize the British troops? (c) Do you think the British or the colonists were most responsible for the massacre? Be sure to state your reasons. (d) Why did John Adams agree to defend the British soldiers and should he have done so?
3. Tell students we will role-play the trials tomorrow.
4. During language arts, have students write stories about the massacre or draw cartoons with captions about the massacre.
5. Time: Two class periods.
6. Assessment: Students' stories and cartoons; role-play.

Experienced Teacher's Lesson Plan

Subject: Social Studies, Language Arts

Purpose: Discuss British and colonists' beliefs about the Boston Massacre; recognize diverse points of view; write stories and draw cartoons about the massacre.

> **Procedure**
>
> 1. Motivation: Read story about John Adams and the Boston Massacre.
> 2. Hold class discussion about the causes of the massacre.
> 3. Tell students: Role-play of soldiers' trials tomorrow.
> 4. Language arts: write stories or draw cartoons about the massacre.

Both teachers taught virtually the same lesson. Jim Sierra's plan was more detailed because he felt insecure about raising appropriate questions to guide the class discussion. Although most student teachers dream of the day when they can discard the lesson plan, the reality is that to be an effective teacher, you need purposeful lessons and you need to anticipate students' reactions.

Both lesson plans *integrated social studies and language arts*. The content was drawn from social studies, but students' learning experiences (listening to a story, discussion, story writing, and captions) all drew on language arts goals. In addition, students who chose to create cartoons were exhibiting their art ability.

Multiple intelligences were provided for by having the students engage in discussion (interpersonal intelligence) and write stories and captions (linguistic intelligence). Students who drew cartoons were using their spatial intelligence. Both interpersonal intelligence and linguistic intelligence will be demonstrated in role-playing.

Constructivist learning was evident by the questions asked by Jim Sierra (and intended by the experienced teacher). Jim was guiding the students to deliberate and judge the integrity of both the British and the Boston colonists. Students needed to form their own opinions concerning responsibility for the incident and why John Adams, a patriot, would choose to defend the British soldiers.

Learning-style needs also were accommodated by the teachers. Students who prefer to listen were motivated by the story reading; students who prefer group work were accommodated by peer interaction during the discussion; students who prefer to work alone were accommodated during the writing and cartooning activity.

Differentiation of instruction is evident in the teachers' plans, first by holding a whole-class discussion in which students can respond at will, and second by encouraging students' choice in ways to demonstrate their understanding. Content is self-modified by the students in what they choose to add to the discussion. Process is differentiated by first reading a story to the students, holding a class discussion, and then assigning the writing activity. Product is differentiated by what students produce—a story or a cartoon.

Assessment is accomplished by seeing the students' accomplishments, the class discussion, and the role-plays.

What Should Teachers Consider When Planning Lessons?

An analogy for lesson planning is climbing a ladder, step by step. Contemplation of each step is important, and care must be exercised so as not to skip a step and fall. The analogy for falling in lesson planning is failing to achieve an effective lesson and very possibly observing the collapse of your classroom management.

A teacher needs to make seven basic decisions every time he or she plans a lesson:

1. *Goal/purpose:* What is the intent of the lesson? What do you want students to understand or learn to perform?

2. *Content:* What will be the substance of the lesson? What big ideas do you want students to gain?

3. *Resources:* What materials will be needed for you and for the students?

4. *Teaching strategies:* How will you teach the lesson? You will need to consider students' *ability, grouping,* and *space* for activities. (The teaching strategies are how you will *deliver* the content.)

5. *Procedures:* How will the lesson progress, step by step?
   Motivation: How will the lesson begin?
   Development: How will the lesson proceed?

6. *Time:* How much time will be needed for the lesson?

7. *Assessment:* How will you know what students have learned?

Hands-On Experiences

Hands-on learning is aimed at a variety of students' needs, including the following:

- Manipulative experiences
- Concrete experiences
- Spatial, musical, and bodily-kinesthetic intelligences
- Preference for perceptual experience

It is sometimes assumed that only the very young elementary student needs hands-on learning, but all learners gain understanding through concrete and manipulative experiences. Hands-on experiences include laboratory problem solving, service learning projects, computer and calculator experience, music and art productions, and body movements. Learning experiences in science, mathematics, dramatics, and social studies motivate students when hands-on activities are included. Realistic involvement in problem-solving activities outside of the classroom are another means to provide students with hands-on learning.

Did You Know That . . . ?

There are three levels of learning: concrete experience, representational or symbolic learning, and abstract learning. Abstract concepts are more comprehensible when students have had prior involvement experiences, such as real-life problem solving (Wolfe, 2001).

Real-Life Problem Solving

A variation of hands-on learning occurs when students are involved in problem solving that takes them outside of the classroom. A Los Angeles elementary teacher emphasizing diversity wanted her students to taste food from different ethnic cultures. She suggested that this could be a monthly treat and asked the students how it could be accomplished. Students suggested that their mothers would enjoy being involved. The teacher said this was a great idea, but that another option might be restaurants in the neighborhood within walking distance. She then suggested that the first lunch be Mexican food, and the students should investigate whether it would be more economical to go out for lunch or have their mothers prepare the lunch. The students discussed the menu. They were then divided into work groups. Three groups were to visit supermarkets and determine the cost of buying the ingredients for making the food. Two groups were to investigate the cost of eating out at two local restaurants. The students gathered the data and realized that it would cost less to have their mothers make the food—which, of course, did not consider their mothers' work time involved in the process.

Service Learning and Problem Solving

Still another variation of hands-on learning and problem solving occurs when students are actively involved in citizenship projects. In a middle school health class, students were asked to be involved in "Operation Cheer-Up," which focused on visits to seniors confined to rehabilitation centers and nursing homes. The students were divided into teams and each team was assigned a specific center. They were then to visit the site and find out what kinds of activities would cheer up the residents. Students came back to class with their information and team activities were planned in class. Each team was then responsible for carrying out its plan. Teams were to prepare albums to describe their activities and experiences. The albums were to include interviews with the residents and staff of the center, photographs, descriptions, and the students' personal reflections concerning the needs and problems of seniors confined to resident care.

High school students are counseled that college applications ask about their involvement in service learning. Typically, history and social science teachers take the lead and help students get involved in societal-problem projects. A project sponsored by a biology teacher focused on people with AIDS. Students were asked to help out on Saturdays or Sundays at a storefront food center. Volunteers at the center assisted in cutting up vegetables for soups and stews, washing and preparing chicken and meats for roasting, and making gravies and sauces. At the end of the day, the students delivered the meals to the homes of people with AIDS. Introduction to the individuals receiving the food had a tremendous impact on the students. The students were required to write a paper that described their involvement, what they learned, and the myths held by the general public about AIDS.

All of these projects are considered "hands-on" because students are involved in active learning, seeking knowledge, problem solving, manipulating materials and resources, and both in-class and out-of-class experiences.

Did You Know That . . . ?

Students in the Philadelphia public schools are required to participate in service learning activities for promotion to grades 5 and 9 and for graduation from high school. Projects require an essential question, research and investigation, problem solving, and reflection. Projects must be based on real-life community needs. The implementation of service learning in the curriculum also requires professional development for Philadelphia's teachers (Hornbeck, 2000).

Planning for the English Language Learner

Suppose that in your classroom you have a number of ELL students who are diverse in their primary-language knowledge. As a consequence, even if you were competent in one or more of these languages, you would not be able to converse with *all* of the English learners. One of the first rules in teaching this diverse group of students is to credit these learners with language skills that were acquired in their primary language and that will transfer to the second language. In other words, you must recognize that second-language learners are not lacking language skills. Your task then is twofold: (1) to build their self-esteem by demonstrating respect for their language and culture, and (2) to provide comprehensible academic instruction in English. Nieto (2002) notes that effective teachers build on students' prior knowledge and experiences (p. 13). She emphasizes the importance of *additive bilingualism,* in which the teacher builds into the curriculum students' native cultures, experiences, and languages.

The methods for providing comprehensible instruction are really not very different from what you normally do. For students learning a second language, it is difficult to process information quickly because it is necessary to grasp the meaning of spoken language and convert it from their natural, primary language into the second language. So the first rule is to *speak slowly.*

To facilitate the learner's understanding of what you are presenting, you need to *be dramatic* and *use concrete objects* whenever possible. Being dramatic means using gestures, facial expressions, and exaggeration of emotions. Pretend that you are playing charades.

To facilitate the second-language learner's participation, *provide plenty of time* for the student to respond to questions. If the language comes out convoluted, accept it, but then repeat it correctly for the rest of the class: "Jennie had some difficulty with her English, but this is what she means: . . . ."

Try to present information using very *simple language* and provide as *many examples* as possible. Also, do not shout; the second-language learner is not deaf. Too often when a person does not understand what is being said, the speaker seems to believe the listener did not hear.

Hands-on learning is particularly helpful for the second-language learner. Sensory activities help ELL students express themselves. Working in small cooperative groups facilitates the learning of language, and if there is another student with greater proficiency, pairing the students for mentoring and tutoring will be beneficial.

> **Teaching Hints: Helping English Language Learners**
>
> 1. Speak slowly.
> 2. Exaggerate expressions.
> 3. Use concrete materials, objects, and pictures.
> 4. Increase wait time when anticipating responses to questions.

Group Work

Responding to students' developmental needs, learning-style preferences, and effective teaching all require that students have opportunities to work alone, in whole-class instruction, and in small-group activities. Earlier in the chapter it was noted that some students prefer working alone while others prefer group interaction. Some types of instruction are best performed for the whole class because large-group instruction is an efficient means to provide information needed by all students. However, small-group instruction tends to be more open-ended, facilitates student involvement and differentiation of instruction, and can use students' diversity advantageously. (Chapter 8 will discuss grouping procedures and the management aspects involved in both large- and small-group teaching.)

Both Piaget and Vygotsky favored peer interaction for social growth. The act of exchanging information and expressing personal viewpoints helps students recognize others' knowledge, values, and beliefs. Interpersonal relationships build communication skills, interpersonal trust, and leadership and decision-making skills. These skills also assist students when they need to resolve conflict situations.

In Chapter 1 teacher Gerry Alred used small groups to study civil rights. Students selected the topic they wanted to study in depth, and their choice determined their group. When a classroom problem arose, she asked for guidance from the class as a whole, and her students reinforced group responsibility. A review of Table 3.1, which depicts Alred's choice of learning experiences, will reveal that many of them require group investigation.

Most research on group work cites the advantages of **heterogeneous** grouping versus ability grouping. With ability grouping, students tend to label their classmates as either very bright or very dumb; this becomes a self-fulfilling prophecy, and the self-confidence of students in low groups plummets. In heterogeneous grouping, all students can contribute in self-selected tasks, and they learn from their classmates through sharing and peer tutoring. Low-ability students perform better when working in a heterogeneous group. Though one might expect that high-ability students would benefit greatly from **homogeneous** grouping, the actual effect is negligible (Marzano, Pickering, & Pollock, 2001).

Small-group work can be effective in all subject fields. In Chapter 2 Roger Ives permitted the students in his math class to form their own small groups as they began work on a warm-up problem at the beginning of the class period. Heterogeneous grouping can be *formally* arranged by the teacher or *informally* accomplished by students.

Formal Grouping. In Table 3.1 Gerry Alred has identified the concept of citizenship for students to study; the activities require that students interview a U.S. Department of Homeland Security person; chart demographic trends in immigration; and graph population groups and points of entry, settlement, and native country. Each of these activities could be assigned to a group and Alred could designate the individuals for each group. Her reasons for doing so might include using student diversity, assuring an appropriate mix of student abilities, and managing students with problems.

Informal Grouping. Students can be informally grouped as Roger Ives did, very casually and cooperatively as groups of students gathered together. Students can also be grouped by interest, as in Gerry Alred's class; by their choice of specific resources (computer, library, laboratory experiment, learning center); or even by clothing (such as groups of students wearing tennis shoes, sandals, and boots).

Duration of Group Assignments. Group assignments may last for a single work period or for a week, month, or semester. Duration depends on the students involved and the activity. However, a general rule is that group assignments should be flexible so that students have the opportunity to work with many different classmates. If students work with the same individuals over a long period of time, much of the value of grouping may be lost, and students tend to get tired of each other.

Collaborative Learning

Cooperation, teamwork, affiliation, alliance—all are integral meanings of collaborative learning. Let's refer back to Gerry Alred's classroom where they were studying about societal intolerance. One of the groups had selected the topic of ethnic jokes. There were five students in the group. The group's first task was to plan how they would go about their inquiry. The group decided that one student would serve as "leader" and another as "recorder." Then they began their discussion.

Leader (Jeanne): OK, how should we start collecting information?

Victor: I think we need to decide how far back in time we want to go.

Jane: Maybe we should ask Mrs. Alred.

Ralph: Why don't we begin to gather information and see how far back it goes?

Leader: Yeah, that's sounds good; maybe we will only find information for the last decade or so.

Christopher: Let's decide who is doing what and then we'll decide the historical time period when we have some information.

Bobbie: I think that's a good idea; I'll list our names and let's make some decisions.

Randy: How about if Joe and I work the Internet and see what we can find?

Shelly: I'd like to look for some old Anti-Defamation League bulletins and see what I can find.

Leader: I'll start looking through some of the texts.

Doris: I wonder if it is possible to find some old vaudeville actors; they certainly did routines featuring ethnic jokes. I'll hunt that out.

Group work requires practice, and the students in Gerry Alred's class obviously had participated in collaborative learning often enough to go about their tasks without a great deal of teacher supervision. When planning for group work, it is important to define a distinct purpose for students working together. If the purpose is practice of a skill, then group membership may be extremely important. Will some students serve as tutors? Will the groups be homogeneous in ability or heterogeneous? Will the whole class be practicing the same skill or will it be differentiated? Will all groups use the same resources and have the same needs? Evaluation would focus on whether all group members were proficient in learning the skill.

In the preceding example, the students were heterogeneously grouped. Each group in the classroom had a slightly different topic. Groups needed different resources, and each group member selected a task to contribute to the group project. The groups were involved in inquiry activities. Whole-class discussion followed each group work session. Unlike a skill-learning task, group projects may take several days or a week or more. The product will differ by group decision. Group projects are shared with the entire class.

Planning for group activities differs depending on the learning purpose. Process, product, and the roles of group members differ; all depend on the purpose and what is to be accomplished. It is also important to recall that all students do not necessarily like working in groups. However, that does not mean that they should not do so. It does mean that group activities should not be the sole teaching strategy used. Teaching strategies must be varied so that students are not bored. This will be discussed in Chapter 8.

Small-group work provides a means for teachers to differentiate learning and instruction.

In-Depth Learning

Satiation is an interesting concept in teaching methodology. Too much skill and drill bores students and, as a consequence, attention lags and students become indifferent and forget the meaning of what they are doing. But when satiation means that students have the opportunity to explore a concept until they are satisfied that they have discovered what they want to know, satiation is motivating and serves as an advantage to learning.

Still another aspect of satiation is the not-so-fine line between *covering* a topic and *in-depth teaching* of a topic. Coverage is, by definition, superficial learning. In-depth teaching can be compared to digging a trench. When something is of interest or particular significance, learning dictates that one must find out everything about the topic that is developmentally appropriate for the student. It would not make sense to read a page in a textbook about immigration in the United States without studying the waves of immigration, where people settled, the problems of immigrants, and the jobs they filled.

Classroom Application Figure 3.1 (Chapter 3) is a concept web created by students' brainstorming about the topic of immigration. It represents what students wanted to know about how immigrants and citizens adapt and modify their ways of life as they live together in the United States. In-depth teaching is often motivated by students' interest and questions. In the following episode the students had been studying worldwide climate changes. It was a beautiful summer day, and the temperature was in the 80s. The sky was bright blue with scattered clouds. As class began a student spoke out, directing his comment to his science teacher, Andrea Mitchell.

> *Student: Did you notice the fluffy marshmallow clouds?*
> *Other students nodded and chuckled and Billy said, "Yeah, they look like balls of cotton piled on top of each other."*
> *Teacher: Does anyone know what kind of clouds those are?*
> *Student: I've heard of stratus clouds. Is that right?*
> *Student: I don't know what kind they are, but can you see through clouds?*
> *Teacher: That's an interesting question, Tess. Who else has a question about clouds?*
> *Student: Do pilots fly through the clouds? Can they see in them?*
> *Student: The clouds look so close today; how high up are the clouds?*
> *Student: We didn't have clouds yesterday; what makes them form?*
> *Teacher: Wow! You've asked a pack of questions and they are all good. Why don't we spend some time studying about clouds and see if we can find out the answers to your questions.*

The study of clouds was clearly not on the teacher's agenda at this time, but this is an example of the "teachable moment." The students were interested; they needed no motivation to begin an in-depth study of clouds. The teacher would change gears; write the students' questions on the board; find information in their science books about condensation for them to read, and then in small groups have them calculate cloud height and diagram cold and warm air fronts. Students' questions would probably take them into a study of precipitation and the water cycle, which would lead them back to their original study of climates. (In the preceding dialogue, note that the teacher did not correct the student's incorrect response about cloud types. The correction would occur when the students discovered the three basic types of clouds.)

Appropriate Resource Materials and the Use of Technology

Many teachers believe that the first thing to do when deciding on a unit or topic for study is to investigate what resources are available for students' use. Though it is certainly important for teachers to anticipate the need for learning materials prior to a lesson, students also may be made responsible for selecting appropriate materials for study purposes. Resource materials can be categorized as print and picture materials, laboratory materials, technology tools, people resources, place resources (field trips), and manipulative materials. Before you select or personally develop resource materials, you need to decide (1) what students should learn, (2) how students should be organized (whole class, heterogeneous groups, individual work), (3) your teaching strategy, and (4) time allotment.

Print materials are certainly the most common and dominant instructional tool used in the classroom. Textbooks, both current and old, can be used for research purposes to gather data and to confirm or contradict hypotheses. But textbooks should not be used in a lockstep fashion that serves to direct the teaching program. The textbook should not be the sole print resource used in the classroom. Newspapers, magazines, cartoons, and pictures are all valuable resources.

Teaching Hints: Print Material Planning

1. Preview what students are to read and verify that they will understand abstract concepts and new vocabulary.
2. Structure what students are to read with guiding questions and verify that students understand the purpose of why they are reading.
3. Verify that students have the needed skills for reading the material.
4. Anticipate reading skill needs. (If students are to read graphs, teach the skill when needed.)
5. Verify students' comprehension after they have read the material.

Laboratory materials include all activities that involve students in group experiments. Elementary teachers typically have science kits for experimentation; secondary teachers may have formal laboratory centers for student use. The materials for these activities need to be anticipated and carefully planned. The quantity of materials needed must be available and the distribution and grouping of students must be considered. Some experiments require specific safety regulations, which must be communicated to students and understanding verified.

Technology planning requires much the same familiarity with the content as textbooks. The concepts and ideas students will gain using the Internet, laserdisc, or other media materials must be anticipated and carefully planned. Classroom stations for computer use must be arranged and work time anticipated. It may be important to block out time that infringes on other subject fields. However, the Internet allows for great integration of subject fields; thus it is important that content themes are planned. If students are to surf the Internet, try out some of the sites before they begin. You may even want to consider listing the sites they may visit.

Technology in the classroom requires cooperative grouping, and so group planning must be considered. When students complete their work it will be important to evaluate group processes. What did students learn from each other? While one student worked on the computer, how did the others contribute? How did they decide what data were important? How did they decide on the use of the data? What did they produce? Technology is discussed in depth in Chapter 12.

People resources require either invited guests visiting the classroom or student interviews of experts in the field or within the school. When inviting guests it is important to verify their expertise and their ability to talk to your students. Almost legion are the stories about invited scientists who come to the classroom to share their research and students are bored silly because they do not understand a word being said. Both students and the invited guest must be prepared.

Before students are allowed to interview others out of the classroom, interview questions should be discussed. If students are working in groups, then each group should plan the interview questions. It is even advantageous to have students role-play the interview situation and to practice both open-ended questions and structured interview questions. Young students are typically better off with structured questions from which they do not deviate. Older students may practice asking open-ended questions and probing for responses. Students need to anticipate the nuances of the interview situation and be prepared for unexpected responses.

Field trips are always popular with students, but they too require advance planning. Visit the site before you take your students. Prepare students with guiding questions and a frame of reference. Students should be well aware of the purpose of the field trip and how it will be evaluated. Use students' existing knowledge and experiences to introduce and motivate the trip. Decide whether students are to take notes, appreciate without note taking, take cameras, sketch, or use tape recorders. If students will be returning directly to school, plan a class discussion to debrief them on the experience.

Manipulative materials sometimes are considered the most difficult to prepare in advance. They may include **realia** in the social studies; instruments, including rhythm sticks for music; art supplies such as paints, charcoal, glue, and scissors; egg crates, tiles, assorted shapes, and counting materials for mathematics; and microscopes, magnets, and dry cell batteries for science—the list is endless.

Manipulative materials depend very much on the developmental needs of the learner, the multiple intelligences to be accommodated, and the purpose of the lesson. Once again, planning for the use of resources means consideration of what students are to gain from the lesson, how you intend to teach, and the organization of the class.

Family and Community Participation

Since the early 1950s, researchers have recognized the value of family involvement in children's education. Many schools have parent advisory boards that meet several times a semester to discuss the school environment, school organizational problems, classroom needs, and student problems. Parents in many schools contribute to the school environment through landscaping, painting classrooms and outside walls, assisting with plumbing and electrical problems, and building special equipment for teachers' use.

Teachers typically meet the parents for the first time at "Back to School" night. The purpose of this occasion is to get acquainted, talk to parents about the curriculum you will be teaching, and provide an opportunity for parents to ask questions and discuss their concerns about the program. Avoid talking about individual students; focus the conversation on your teaching philosophy and your instructional approach. If parents have special concerns about their child, circulate a sign-up sheet for individual conferences.

Since parents will be observing the classroom environment, it is a good idea to call attention to technology, resources, learning centers, and anything else that will influence the instructional program. If possible, particularly at the elementary level, have work samples of students' work available, but be certain that you have samples from *all* of the students.

Family involvement in the classroom and school is a high priority in schools across the nation. Joyce Epstein, director of the Center on School, Family, and Community Partnerships at Johns Hopkins University, suggests that schools involve parents in meetings and activities concerned with parenting, communicating, volunteering, learning at home, decision making, and collaborating with the community (Allen, 2000). Parents often need help in learning how to assist their child with homework, how to listen to their child, and how to monitor their child's work and play activities. A teacher might encourage parents' participation in a physical fitness unit by having students share information at home and by inviting the family to school to see their work.

Frequently in the modern family, both parents (or a single parent) are working; thus time is of a premium. Many schools communicate with parents via e-mail if it is available in the home. Telephone calls in the evening are another way to communicate, but these calls should be focused on the "good" things that students do, not the bad! When students have problems at school, you need to find a way to meet personally with the parent or guardian. (This will be discussed further in Chapter 10.)

Parental help is often needed if students are to have the opportunity to go on field trips. Parents can serve as experts to lead class discussions in areas of expertise, serve as instructors for club programs, work as aides and tutors in classrooms, help translate during parent conferences, and suggest resources in the community. High schools have discovered that if parents attend sporting events and help supervise dances, fights and general disorder are less likely to occur.

Though not often recognized, the community also shares in the socialization process with the school and family. Students' academic success is a concern of and a benefit to the community, and for that reason individuals, organizations, and businesses are often interested in partnership activities and are quite willing to supply resources to schools and students. Sanders (2001) reports that more than 400 schools in the United States are members of the National Network of Partnership Schools.

Did You Know That . . . ?

Community involvement in school-based programs benefits students, schools, neighborhoods, parents, and society at large. Community-school partnership activities include mentoring, tutoring, job shadowing, and academic enrichment that may include providing students and schools with equipment and supplies (Sanders, 2001).

Planning for family and community involvement should be a schoolwide responsibility. Each school has different needs and special problems. These needs may be related to culture, language, school environment, and school organization. In one inner-city school, the school faculty was dismayed because of lack of attendance at parent conferences and back-to-school programs. The problem was rectified when the parent advisory board explained that meetings had to occur in the evening instead of the late afternoon. At another school, graffiti on school walls and theft of equipment were constant problems until adults in the community offered to be vigilant and call the police if they observed any shenanigans. The link between school, home, and community must be a concern of the entire school faculty.

FIGURE 4.1 Lesson Planning Concepts

Chapter Summary

This chapter contrasted novice and experienced teachers' lesson plans. Grouping procedures, service learning, and the needs of English language learners were discussed. The importance of considering resources available to the class and the relevance of the materials for the developmental needs of the class affects the quality of the lesson and the effectiveness of the teacher. The importance of communicating with the family and involving the community in school-related activities was also emphasized.

Teaching Problems

1. Figure 4.1 summarizes the concepts discussed in this chapter. Using the three planning components—the learner, society, and subject matter—identify how each of the concepts exhibited in the figure affects the planning process.
2. Plan a lesson for English language learners; identify who the learners are and incorporate their native cultures and experiences.
3. Select a grade level in elementary, middle, or high school and plan a service learning project. Identify the purpose, the problem-solving experience, and how you will assess students' reflections.
4. In your school community, discuss the ways in which parents are involved in the school program. Suggest some alternative activities that would facilitate the link between school and community.

CHAPTER 5

Unit Planning and Professional Responsibilities

ADVANCE ORGANIZER

These questions can be used as a framework to assist you in integrating professional knowledge and understanding of the content of this chapter.

1. Why is it important to allow societal problems to influence lesson planning?
2. Good teachers recognize the importance of time management both in and out of the classroom. What can teachers do to help themselves personally and professionally?
3. The following curriculum concepts affect the design of long-term plans: continuity, sequence, integration, and interdisciplinary teaching. Can you explain how these concepts are used?
4. Webbing and backward problem solving elicit ideas and understandings from students. How can these techniques be used for unit planning?

 The following INTASC issues and standards are discussed in this chapter: Numbers 1–5, 7, 9, 10.

Traumatic incidents affect the classroom community and teachers cannot ignore them. The beginning of this chapter describes how three teachers (high school, middle school, and elementary school) planned lessons after September 11, 2001, that used appropriate subject matter and provided opportunities for students to express their fears and sadness. The balance of the chapter considers teachers' professional responsibilities and provides examples of curriculum concepts for long-term planning. Two teaching units are presented as examples.

What Should Teachers Consider When Planning Lessons?

The three lessons that follow demonstrate how a societal problem affects teachers' planning and how teachers can incorporate subject matter content and respond to developmental needs. On September 11, 2001, nineteen terrorists gained control of four airplanes and crashed them into the World Trade Center in New York City, the Pentagon in Washington, D.C., and the Pennsylvania countryside. After a day off from school most school districts resumed classes, and teachers were confronted with planning lessons to cope with students' fear and anxiety. Most teachers provided time for students to voice their concerns. Both elementary and secondary teachers planned lessons that encouraged students to discuss the problems and their concerns and to write about their feelings in journals or as formal compositions.

Jean Cantor—High School Lesson Plan

Date: September 13, 2001

Goal: To engage students in societal problem solving; to provide a constructive means for students to express thoughts, feelings, and relieve tension.

Content: Oral and written language expression; creative writing to express personal experiences or feelings.

Resources: Daily newspapers, Internet: *www.nytimes.com* and *www.latimes.com*

Teaching Strategy: Whole-class discussion, individual writing, whole-class discussion

Time Allotment: One class period; first period

Procedures and Key Questions

1. Focus students' thinking on "what the United States should do." Elicit students' feelings and concerns about the tragedy. "Today is different from all other

days we have experienced, and we certainly cannot continue with our normal class activities without acknowledging how this experience affects us. Let's take some time to problem-solve about what our country should do and to share some of the things that bother us."

2. Provide as much time as needed for students to debate the issues, ask questions, and discuss the traumatic events. Then ask (if not already discussed), "Do you think the United States should retaliate?"

If students say yes, then ask, "What actions should we take?" Follow up with, "How do you anticipate the terrorist attack will affect our way of life?" and "What if our volunteer military force is not sufficient? Would you be willing to serve if you were 18 years old?"

3. Suggest a writing activity in the form of a letter or article for the opinion section of the newspaper addressing the points we have talked about that you think are critical.

4. "I will provide some writing 'starts' to help you review your thoughts, but you may deviate and choose your own beginning and purpose."
   a. Nothing seems normal . . .
   b. Today I want to forget about . . .
   c. I've been deeply touched by . . .
   d. I am grateful that . . .
   e. We cannot escape . . .
   f. Our country must take some risks . . .

5. Suggest that students may want to share ideas with a partner before writing.

6. Tell students that there are copies of newspaper articles available if they want to read them and articles on the Internet from the *New York Times* and the *Los Angeles Times*.

7. Walk around and provide assistance as requested.

8. Ask students if they would like to share their work and provide opportunity for sharing and further whole-class discussion.

9. Collect papers that are finished, or have students complete their work at home.

Assessment: Students' oral contributions and compositions/letters for review.

Unlike most class days, Cantor's eleventh-grade students began the school day quiet and somber. She chose not to ignore the tragedy; thus she deviated from the typical class meeting, yet at the same time she wanted to teach in a manner appropriate to her subject field and to the students who were taking her class.

Cantor set the tone for the class period by expressing her own perspective ("Today is different from . . .") She hoped that this would encourage students to talk about how they felt and what they were afraid of. She used a whole-class discussion to accomplish this and her intent was not to cut the discussion short. She then went on to challenge the students with additional questions.

The writing activity was planned to accomplish several purposes: cathartic written expression and reflective problem solving. Her time allotment was probably inaccurate because students' oral participation on this particular day would likely consume more time than she had planned. Her idea of providing writing phrases to initiate thinking about written composition was a good idea, and the phrases helped the students review the discussion and engage in reflection about the challenges we face. She also recognized that some students might not want to conform to her suggestions and desire a different direction.

She suggested writing partners to help students develop their ideas. This is a traditional means to assist students in creative writing; however, for this occasion, it may have been redundant after a long class discussion. She also provided copies of newspaper articles for the students to review and suggested use of the Internet for articles in the *New York Times* and the *Los Angeles Times*.

Cantor monitored students' work by providing assistance as needed. Her class discussion was intended as a culminating aspect of the lesson. It may or may not have been successful because if the students' compositions were emotional, they may not have wanted to share them. She would further assess students' work by reviewing the papers when completed. When grading creative writing, the teacher evaluates the mechanics of writing, not the creative aspects.

Lee Jensen—Middle School Lesson Plan

Date: September 13, 2001

Purpose: Provide a means for students to express feelings using visual art processes.

Content: Applying media, techniques, and processes to create an art production; reflection on the merits of own work.

Resources: Paper, paints, clay, easels.

Teaching Strategy: Individual visual art productions; whole-class sharing and discussion.

Procedures:

Motivation: Acknowledgment of need for expression by teacher and students.

Key Questions: "Would you like to draw, paint, or sculpt how you are feeling today?" (Motivation)
"What message did you want to communicate?" (Assessment)
"Why did you choose the medium you used?" (Assessment)

Review/Assessment: Students will assess their own work by communicating their intent and explaining whether the selected medium was appropriate.

After September 11, there was no way that schools could ignore students' need for consolation. Before class began, Lee Jensen, a middle school visual art teacher, set up a variety of paper types and sizes, crayons, watercolor and tempera paint, easels, clay, and charcoal. When the students took their seats, she asked, "Would you like to draw, paint, or sculpt how you are feeling today?" The students quickly agreed that artwork was an ideal means to express their feelings. Jensen had students raise their hands to tell her what medium they wanted to use, and she dismissed them to the various centers to begin their work.

Though the students worked relatively quickly, middle school students want a lot of detail in their art productions, and they are very critical of their own work. Most did not finish in the single class period, and the teacher assured them that they could complete their work on the following day. Only two students had chosen sculpture and they were working on figures to depict the rescuers. The rest of the students were using either crayon or paint and were producing pictures of the towers, people jumping out of buildings, firefighters and police officers, symbolic pictures with flags wrapped around people and buildings, and even cartoon figures to tell their story.

The next day in class when the students had completed their work, the teacher asked them to talk about their artwork. "What message did you want to communicate?" "Why did you choose the medium you used?" When the students talked about their art production, some held their picture up for their classmates to see, but others kept their work hidden. Middle school students are extremely sensitive and evaluative concerning their own artwork.

Lucia Martin—Elementary School Lesson Plan

Date: September 13, 2001

Purpose: Oral and art expression to communicate feelings and concerns; written expression to practice functional and creative writing; reading of own compositions.

Content: Language arts: oral and written expression; visual arts to express characteristics of community workers.

Resources: Pictures for motivation, art paper and crayons, lined paper for writing.

Teaching Strategy: Language experience approach to teaching reading.

Time Allotment: 90 minutes

Procedures:

Motivation: Show class pictures of community workers. Tell them: "We've been studying public services in our city. I know that you have been watching a lot of television since the tragedy in New York City. Who can tell us how these workers have been helping the people in New York?" (Allow as much time as needed.)

Development: Encourage students to talk about their feelings and concerns. When students have concluded, ask, "Would you like to draw pictures about all the people who were helping others?" (About 35 minutes)

When students conclude, bring them back up to front of the room and ask them to tell the class about their pictures. (Sharing time about 20 minutes.)

Ask students to write letters to the New York police, fire, and emergency personnel. Dismiss students to tables; pass out paper; provide time to sharpen pencils if needed. (Writing time 25 minutes.) Read stories if time permits, or read stories tomorrow.

Assessment: Oral expression, pictures, and written work.

Although reading instruction was usually taught at the beginning of the school day, Lucia Martin decided that on this day students needed a language experience lesson. She invited the students to come to the front of the classroom and sit on the floor in front of her. During social studies her class had been studying community services and so on this occasion she displayed some pictures of police, fire, and emergency medical personnel performing their jobs.

Lucia began by stating, "We've been studying public services in our city. I know that you have been watching a lot of television since the tragedy in New York City. Who can tell us how these workers have been helping the people in New York?" There was no hesitation in responding to the question.

"They have been rescuing people."

"I saw a fireman carrying a woman out of one of the buildings before it collapsed."

"I saw a policeman helping a man look for his wife."

"The ambulances were going back and forth to the hospitals."

"Yes, and I saw people being carried out on carts with wheels."

"Those are called gurneys," said Lucia, and she wrote the word on the board.

"Fire and dust were everywhere and the firemen and policemen were wearing masks."

"There were women fire and police persons helping too," said one little girl.

Lucia let them continue and almost all of the students had something to say. Finally she asked the students, "Would you like to draw pictures about all the people who were helping others?" The students responded positively and she dismissed them to their tables and distributed paper and crayon boxes.

When the pictures were completed, the students were again invited back to the front of the room to share their work. Lucia Martin called on students to tell the class about their pictures. The students held their pictures up for others to see and then told the story of each picture. Then Martin asked the students, "Would you like to write a letter to the fire fighters and police officers in New York City? Or would you like to write a story about your picture?"

The students chose to do both; some wrote letters and others told the story of their pictures. As they wrote, Martin toured the room observing the students as they created their stories and letters. If a student asked for help with spelling, she wrote the word on a piece of paper so the student could copy it.

> The next day students read their stories aloud to their classmates. (What students write, they can read. This is a basic premise of the language experience approach to reading.) Pictures, letters, and stories were displayed on the bulletin board in the classroom, and some were forwarded to New York City.

Note that all three teachers included in their lesson plans not only their key questions to be asked in class, but directions to themselves so that they would not forget what they needed to do. Although most experienced teachers would not need to do this, novice teachers are more comfortable with explicit plans.

Each of these teachers had to construct the lesson plan on one day's notice. The plans responded to a major calamity and required sensitivity to students' fears, grief, and depression. Each plan had to be appropriate for the developmental level of the students and each had to consider appropriate subject matter. The high school teacher challenged students' knowledge and conscience; the middle school art teacher used visual arts to help students deal with terror; and the elementary school teacher used the basic skills of third-graders to communicate through discussion, drawing, and story writing.

Did You Know That . . . ?

> Providing tangible rewards, such as food, time off, and good-student awards, tends to undermine intrinsic motivation for the rewarded activity. To facilitate intrinsic motivation, it is more important for teachers to plan interesting learning activities, offer more student choice, and ensure challenging work tasks. Intrinsic motivation "promotes creative task engagement, cognitive flexibility, and conceptual understanding of learning activities" (Deci, Koestner, & Ryan, 2001).

Time Management and Teacher Planning

It is not unusual for teachers to plan lessons with little advance notice or time. It is only unusual when the planning must respond to a major tragedy. Ideally lessons are outlined well in advance of delivery, but teachers need to respond to their own personal well-being as well as professional responsibilities. Many outstanding and conscientious teachers forgo their teaching career because they never learned to balance their personal and professional responsibilities. Time management and advance planning are the keys to a successful professional life.

Though student teachers dream of the time when they are not responsible for a lesson plan, experienced teachers know that planning not only improves teaching but keeps them tension-free. Because most elementary teachers do not have a free period during the school day to plan lessons, time becomes a valuable commodity. Secondary teachers can take advantage of a planning period, but since they are often planning for different grade levels and great diversity of students, one period is still not enough to engage in long-term planning. So what can teachers do?

1. *Plan at school.* Try to resist the temptation to do all of your planning at home. The resources you need for lessons are available at school, and carrying them home means that you need to remember to bring them back! Though it may be difficult to separate your professional work from your personal life, it is important that you establish a life away from school. Teachers need time to enjoy movies, read fiction, participate in politics, and in general enjoy the cultural life of the community. You also need time to satisfy your home chores. Too often teachers stay up till midnight doing their planning for the next day, and then the next day, they are too tired to do a good job!

2. *Plan with a colleague.* The idea bank sometimes runs dry; it helps to work with other teachers to develop short- and long-term plans. Critique each other's ideas and plans. Work out teaching strategies together. It may even be possible to teach some lessons as a team. Share resources for lessons; this may mean that you do not have to run around on your own corralling all the supplies you will need.

3. *Reflect on successes and failures.* What worked and what didn't? Profit from past mistakes. Review yesterday's lesson plans; do you need to reteach, reconceptualize your plans, or continue on? This is another time when it helps to work with other colleagues to discuss and problem-solve why a lesson was successful or not.

4. *Log your use of time.* In order to take advantage of available time, it is important to document how you are using time in the classroom. When you arrive in the morning, what do you do? If you are recording grades, how long does it take? How often do you have committee meetings and how long do they last? Examine your log to find ways to save time. For example, if you have volunteers in the classroom, could someone record your grades, duplicate class materials for you, water the plants, help with bulletin boards? Would it save time to record homework and grades using a computer program? Could e-mail be used to communicate with other committee members? Time saved can be used for planning.

5. *Use block scheduling.* Middle school and high school teachers are finding that block scheduling makes planning easier because they are not teaching as many different students and subjects each day. Planning for a longer class period increases the opportunity for the use of technology and project work for students. Hands-on learning experiences are more motivating for students, increase the time teachers can work with small groups of students, and decrease interruptions resulting from discipline problems. DiRocco (1999) found that block scheduling improved student achievement, teacher morale, and the overall school climate. Time management also is discussed in Chapter 13.

Did You Know That . . . ?

In Folkston, Georgia, Charlton County High School, grades 7–12 experimented with block scheduling. They found that content could be covered in greater depth in a 90-minute block and that teacher preparation time was reduced. In addition, teacher burnout and student absenteeism declined (Hannaford, Fouraker, & Dickerson, 2000).

Elementary teachers also find that planning their subject load in blocks of time facilitates their integration of subject fields and allows them to vary physically active learning experiences with more concentrated study experiences. Elementary blocks of time typically include language arts, social studies/science, physical education/health, and the arts (music, drama, art).

6. *Bank time.* Schoolwide rescheduling to bank time is another means of helping teachers find time for working with colleagues. Many schools add from fifteen minutes up to an entire period to the school day four days a week. Then on the fifth day the time "banked" is used for teaming with other teachers, staff development, or grade-level or subject field meetings.

Lesson Planning and Curriculum Concepts

It is not customary for a lesson plan to evolve in isolation from other lessons; each should fit into an overall plan. This is true with both skill-oriented lessons and concept-based plans. Three curriculum concepts serve as criteria for both short- and long-term plans: **sequence, continuity,** and **integration.**

Sequence of a single lesson or a group of lessons deals with the order of presentation. Just as you consider how to begin a lesson (motivation), you also need to consider the progressive development of the lesson; the same is true for a group of lessons in an overall unit plan. Sequence is often determined by the learners' stages of development. One of the most obvious examples of sequence is the traditional development of social studies units. The kindergarten and first-grade curricula focus on the individual, the classroom group, and the family. As the student progresses through the grades, the curriculum moves further away from the individual to the study of city, state, national level, and global concerns.

Skill-based lessons are even more concerned with sequence as a criterion for teaching. Addition is taught before subtraction or multiplication. In geometry, simple axioms are the basis for more complex principles. The geometry student needs to base decisions on prior understandings.

However, there is some controversy about how sequence is determined. Some educators believe that all teaching within a subject field should be logically determined, organized in discrete step-by-step progression from simple to complex and concrete to abstract. Others believe that abstract concepts should be introduced to the learner first, to serve as an organizing structure for what follows (whole to parts). Much depends on the subject field and the nature of the learner. Of greatest importance is for teachers to find out what students know and what they don't know.

Continuity is a subtle determiner of lesson and unit planning. For many school districts and teachers, the use of grade-level textbooks determines when certain topics and concepts are to be taught. But students' maturity is a better determiner for what is taught and when. Again, the social studies curriculum is a fine example. Fifth-graders are introduced to U.S. history, and eighth- and eleventh-graders are reintroduced to U.S. history; as students mature, the conceptual content can be more complex and presented at greater depth. Continuity as a criterion helps articulate content from one level to another.

Integration of skills and content across the curriculum was first practiced by elementary teachers because of the wide array of subjects they needed to teach and the limitation of time to accomplish the task. Studies by developmental psychologists recommended the practice because it helps the learner draw on existing knowledge as a structure for incorporating and understanding new knowledge.

Integration also takes advantage of the "teachable moment," which means that teachers teach *what* is needed *when* it is needed. Moss and Fuller (2000) describe a middle school program that integrates the curriculum with the arts. The teachers were focusing on the Renaissance period; they used two visual aspects of the period, art and architecture. The class studied the masterpieces of the period, visited museums, and created their own buildings including a replica of the Sistine Chapel. This required not only history and the arts but mathematics and physics as they studied structural components of the buildings.

Reviewing Gerry Alred's lesson planning (Table 3.1), we can see that she integrated social studies (citizenship), mathematics (timelines, demographic studies), language arts (creative writing, discussions, literature), music and art (mural painting, ethnic music), physical education (cultural sports), and science (food spoilage experiments). Integration allowed her to link subject fields and learning processes and helped students see relationships in time, space, actions, concepts, problems, and judgments. Integration makes both teaching and learning more relevant.

Interdisciplinary Teaching

Using concepts from different subject fields (disciplines) is another way to enrich the lessons you teach. **Interdisciplinary teaching** differs from integration because the student learns how different disciplines consider similar problems or concepts. For example, a geographer may study how different ethnic groups *modify* the environment they live in, whereas a sociologist may study how the same groups *adapt* to their environment, and the social psychologist and the mathematician may study trends in social behavior. Using different lenses, each discipline may use similar data to gain knowledge and understanding.

Concepts should be thought of as tools for generalizing and focusing inquiry in a discipline. In geometry, the concept of rules suggests that mathematical laws serve as a basis or structure for more complex means of study. In political science, the concept of rules means that humanmade laws govern human behavior. In sociology, the concept of laws is used to explain the norms of different cultures. The concepts you select for study serve as the "big ideas" of your teaching unit.

Clustering Lessons by Using a Theme

A **theme** is a broad, overarching concept that helps tie the content of lessons together to make them more meaningful. For example, the concept of *change* may encompass knowledge of time (years, eras), growth, environment, behavior, and technology. The identification of a theme serves as a goal to integrate study. For this reason it is useful to define your theme to communicate with students and others. The definition is often called a **generalization.** An example of a generalization about change could be as follows: *Change is a natural phenomenon that affects patterns of behavior.* This statement tells the learner and other professionals (as well as parents) precisely what it is about change that will be studied.

The theme may be selected after you identify your content, or the theme may facilitate your choice of content. The generalization helps you formulate key questions and select and organize your learning experiences. In the teaching unit example that follows, Mr. Sierra began with the selection of a theme and generalization, then identified his content and related key questions.

Unit Planning

Unit planning is a means for teachers to engage in long-term planning over the course of a month or even an entire semester. Unit planning may occur among a group of teachers or as a solitary activity. Major advantages of unit planning include specification of subject field goals, and resources can be anticipated and gathered well in advance of when they are needed. The unit plan differs from individual lesson plans because procedures for individual lessons are not specified.

When you are planning a unit, the plans should not be rigid, but should leave room for flexibility based on students' interests, needs, and unforeseen events. The unit serves as a guide for the semester calendar. Topics can be allocated a certain number of days or weeks as estimated. Figure 5.1 suggests a unit planning process based on (1) your existing knowledge of your students, their needs, interests, and abilities; (2) your knowledge of the subject to be taught; and (3) your knowledge of teaching strategies.

---

1. Select a theme to encompass the entire unit.

2. Write a sentence about the theme so that it is meaningful.

3. Identify topics in each subject field that will be integrated in the unit.

4. Identify goals or specific objectives.

5. For each topic, identify content (big ideas).

6. Write key questions focused on each "big idea." These questions will help you identify appropriate learning experiences.

7. Select learning experiences/activities to match the questions. These experiences may incorporate objectives and guidelines for how performance will be judged.

FIGURE 5.1   Unit Planning Process

Jim Sierra's Unit Teaching Plan

Sierra decided that his theme would be migration; his generalization was that migration to the West during the period from 1820 to 1860 influenced the development and statehood of all the western and southwestern states. His content ("big ideas") included the following:

1. People migrate to attain religious and/or political freedom and/or to improve economic conditions.
2. Migration affects individuals' ways of life and their relationships with others.
3. Home life on the frontier affected economic and cultural ways of life.

Sierra's next task was to identify the *key questions* that would serve as "triggers" to help him select appropriate learning experiences. The questions needed to fit his big ideas.

1. Who were the early settlers of the West, and what influenced them to migrate westward?
2. What were the main routes that led to the West?
3. In what ways did pioneer life affect behavior?
4. Why did migration to the West affect relationships with Native Americans, Mexicans, and other nations?
5. How were disputes with other nations settled?

Figure 5.2 outlines Mr. Sierra's unit teaching plan.

The students were stunned by the transformation of their classroom. They straggled in after recess to find a small tent in one corner, pictures on the chalkboard, and models of boats and a covered wagon. Mr. Sierra smiled and told them to walk around and look at the exhibits.

Though the students didn't know the types of boats they were looking at, in fact, the models included flatboats, keelboats, and a steamboat. Mr. Sierra followed the students around the room, listening to their comments and questions. After about 10 minutes he flipped the light switch to get attention and then asked the students to sit down so that they could discuss the exhibits.

Mr. Sierra: Kelly, I heard you ask a number of questions about the boats; would you like to share your thoughts?
Kelly: Well, I wondered what kind of boats these are and where were they used.
Mr. Sierra: Who else would like to comment on their thoughts?
Emma: I recognized the steamboat, and I think it was used on the Mississippi River. (Mr. Sierra smiled, but did not comment.)
Jennie: Who used these boats, Mr. Sierra?
Fred: I looked at the pictures and the people must be early pioneers.

Who were the early settlers of the West, and what influenced them to migrate westward?	• Direct instruction—how to find and use primary resources.
	• Students will read diaries of pioneer travels to the West, using the Internet and textbooks.
	• Students will listen to and sing folk songs about the West.
	• Problem solving/group investigation—What were Americans seeking?
	• Advance organizer—to structure research on the ways people earned a living in the 1820s and 1830s.
	• Concept attainment—using the concept of manifest destiny.
What were the main routes that led to the West?	• Direct instruction—how to read topographic maps.
	• Students will choose groups based on the form of transportation they are interested in: covered wagons, wagon trains, keelboats, flat boats, or steamboats. Groups will be responsible for (a) constructing a model of their selected form of transportation; (b) researching trails, inland waterways, or ocean travel around the cape; (c) drawing a map of their proposed trip; and (d) studying the environment to find out what tools and other supplies they will need for their trip.
	• Groups will calculate and research number of miles to be traveled and length of time for travel.
In what ways did pioneer life affect behavior?	• Students will select literature books to read about the Oregon Trail, the gold rush, the Mormon Trek, and early explorers.
	• Whole-class discussion to develop a concept map depicting pioneer life (sleep facilities during travel, housing when settled, food, recreation, education, tools, work, clothing, health, and religion).*
	• Group investigation—using items on the concept map.
	• Group investigation—roles of men, women, and children.

FIGURE 5.2 Sample Unit Teaching Plan: Migration

In what ways did pioneer life affect behavior? (con't.)	• Role-play of family life. • Whole-class discussion on how pioneers had to adapt to their new environment. Since many of the pioneers had to leave possessions behind, decide what they would leave in their prior home, what they would take, and what they would make in their new abode.
Why did migration to the West affect relations with Native Americans, Mexicans, and other nations?	• Problem solving—How did the pioneers affect the life of Native Americans? In what ways did the Native Americans help the pioneers? Write a story about the westward migration from the perspective of Native Americans. • Investigate what problems developed between American and Mexican pioneers; where did the Mexican pioneers settle? • Use Internet resources, maps, and texts to learn what other countries claimed territory in the West. Who were the first settlers to reach California? Why did American pioneers rush to California and what was the impact of the new settlers in California?
How were disputes with other nations settled?	• Students will read about the Louisiana Purchase and the clash between the Mexican government and Texas. • Group investigation—Oregon was claimed by Great Britain; what was the basis of the claim? • Group investigation—How did the United States acquire Texas and Oregon? How were California and New Mexico conquered? • Whole-class discussion on the role of early pioneers in the settlement of the West. • Group reports—Reports should consider the "fairness" of the early pioneers in their relations with others.

*See Figure 5.4.

FIGURE 5.2 *(Continued)*

The comments and questions continued until finally Mr. Sierra told the students that they would be studying the American settlers who explored and settled in the western United States. Sierra had used the **arranged environment** technique to motivate his students' unit study in social studies. The arranged environment initiated the unit and provided Mr. Sierra information about what his students knew about the early pioneers and what interested them.

Discussion of Mr. Sierra's Unit Teaching Plan

Mr. Sierra used a variety of teaching strategies that included both whole-group and small-group class organization. His direct instruction and concept attainment lessons were delivered to the whole class. The advance organizers for the lessons were used to alert the students to the data they needed to acquire and to help them structure their data. The organizers were written on the chalkboard for the students to refer to. The concept map developed through class discussion also served as an advance organizer. The concept map used the technique called *webbing,* which will be discussed later in the chapter.

Students chose their groups based on the form of transportation they wanted to study. The group investigation/problem-solving lessons were all group-oriented, and the groups were responsible for researching the evidence they needed, taking notes, and ultimately writing a group report and presenting that report orally to the class. The teaching strategies (direct instruction, advance organizer, concept attainment, group investigation) will be explained in Chapters 8 and 9.

Organization of the unit demonstrates that Mr. Sierra's learning experiences were sequenced to motivate and to develop more complex understandings. His arranged environment excited the students about what they would study. He could have initiated the unit with a story or with just pictures, but the models were definitely more motivating. Next he taught the students to read physical maps because they would need this skill to recognize the difficulties the pioneers faced. By planning their own exploration to the West, the students were able to confront the problems of traveling through unknown territory. The unit culminated with students recognizing the hardships of pioneer life and the difficult relationships forged during this period. Student reports and discussion provided evidence of student learning.

Integration and *interdisciplinary study* were accomplished through many of the learning experiences: literature, oral and written language, reading, use of the Internet, music, drama, art, mathematics, and science. In the social sciences, Mr. Sierra included history, geography, sociology, and political science. By teaching skills when students needed them, Mr. Sierra integrated subject fields. By selecting activities that incorporated other subject fields, he used the advantage of interdisciplinary study.

Multiple intelligences were accommodated through the variety of learning experiences that focused on linguistic intelligence (research, writing, discussion), logical-mathematical intelligence (travel calculations), spatial intelligence (mapmaking, construction activity), musical intelligence (songs), bodily-kinesthetic intelligence (role-play, movement, and group work), inter- and intrapersonal intelligence (independent and peer group work), and naturalistic intelligence (study of the environment). The group work organization allowed students to select experiences that were most appealing to them.

Understanding for *English language learners* was facilitated by the use of group work. Peer interaction and interpretation will help the student who is having difficulty learning English. Through careful guidance, Mr. Sierra ensured that students were paired with peers who could help them.

Did You Know That . . . ?

> Several key factors affect differentiation of instruction. Students learn best when:
> 1. Learning experiences are related to their interests and life experiences.
> 2. Learning opportunities are based on natural contexts.
> 3. Classrooms and schools create a sense of community; students need to feel respected and significant (Tomlinson, 2000).

Differentiation of Learning Experiences Though it is not possible to provide a variety of learning experiences in every lesson, most of the activities that Jim selected allowed for a variety of experiences that included verbal and written work, drawing and constructing, and performance activities using role-playing and music. Most of the actual work was done in small groups, allowing students to select the tasks for which they would be responsible.

What the Unit Does Not Tell Us

Continuity. We do not know what was taught before the unit or what will follow the unit. We can only assume that the students were studying American history and the movement westward, the acquisition of territories, and the beginning of statehood. We can assume also that Mr. Sierra will next teach about the Mexican War.

Time. We do not know how long the unit will last and probably neither does Mr. Sierra. Much will depend on the students' ability to do research, construct their modes of transportation, draw their maps, and perform their calculations. In all likelihood this unit will last about four weeks.

Appropriateness. With slight deviations this unit would be appropriate for grades 5, 8, and 11. High school students would not be interested in the construction activities. Nor might the class spend time singing songs, but you might have students research the folk music of that period and discuss its relevance to the pioneer culture. The research activities, the study of relationships, and the calculations would all be appropriate for eleventh-graders.

Simulations and Field Trips. Though it is not clear from Figure 5.2, Mr. Sierra could have planned simulations about pioneer travel, problems, and life on the frontier. These will be discussed in Chapter 12. Most local museums have exhibits that would be useful for this unit of study and a field trip could be planned. Using the Internet, Mr. Sierra could also plan or have the students plan a virtual field trip using several of the sites that are available about the westward movement.

Assessment. Clearly Mr. Sierra intends to use performance experiences for assessment. The discussions, reports, and performance activities will allow him to evaluate what students are learning and what they need to learn. We do not know whether he will administer teacher-developed paper and pencil tests.

Figure 5.3 illustrates a shortcut method to plan a teaching unit. This synopsis of the curriculum planning process assumes that the content and key questions demonstrate unit goals and that the learning experiences clearly express performance objectives.

What Do You Do if the Lesson Plan Fails?

For each of Jim Sierra's learning experiences he needed to construct a procedural lesson plan. On the day that students were to use Internet resources, each group assigned two students to work at the computer. There were five computers in the classroom. Approximately one-third of the students would need to use the Internet.

On this particular day the students went to the computer and the Internet connection failed. They waited and waited and became restless and upset. If they were not given something else to use, they would be disturbing the entire class. But Jim had prepared for such an emergency. He had viewed the sites and their links that students would use and printed out some of the materials. He talked quietly to the students and handed out the duplicated materials. He explained that these materials covered only several of the sites they could research on the Internet, but that this would help them until they were able to work on their own.

The students were disappointed, but work time was used to good advantage and Jim's lesson was saved. Internet connections can complicate lesson planning. Whenever a lesson depends on equipment (hardware), there is the element of chance and so it is important to plan ahead and have alternative procedures ready.

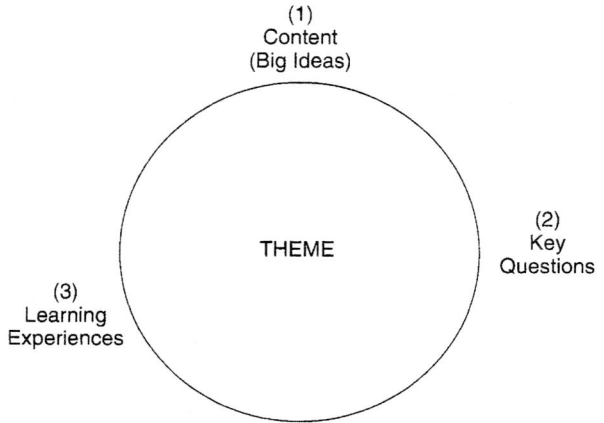

FIGURE 5.3 Synopsis of Curriculum Planning Process

Did You Know That . . . ?

Teachers in the Pittsford Central School District in New York learned to differentiate instruction:

1. Collaborate and share planning ideas.
2. Begin planning by finding out what students know.
3. Plan flexible grouping of students.
4. Encourage student responsibility.
5. Give students choice over content, activity, or product.
6. Ensure fair grading of students' work (Pettig, 2000).

Additional Planning Considerations

Interruptions are usually an unknown entity that affects the timing of lessons. Disruptions, whether caused by student problems, loudspeaker bulletins, schoolwide scheduling changes, or messenger notes, can cause lessons to bomb. When they occur, it is vital that you have good control of your classroom; however, in terms of lesson planning, you always need to think through a variety of means to conquer these ill-timed events. Experienced teachers often do the following:

1. Shorten the lesson by eliminating excess practice and holding fewer activities and less discussion.
2. Assure the students that additional time will be allowed, later or tomorrow.
3. If an alternate lesson will serve the same purpose, switch plans and explain to the students that you are doing so because of time constraints. Of course this means that you are aware of other means to accomplish the same objective.
4. Extend the lesson through student discussion and sharing of what they have accomplished; postpone the planned activities for the following class meeting.

Student disinterest may be caused by several factors: lack of understanding, lack of relevance, or lack of participation. All three of these factors result from inadequate planning. If students do not have the background and structural knowledge to *understand* the lesson, they are going to be bored and will not mentally attend to the lesson. Students' existing knowledge is a significant component in planning a lesson.

Relevance is related to students' experiences in the home, community, and peer group. Lessons that use examples totally unrelated to students' lifestyles may be unfathomable for them. To capture students' interest and imagination it may be necessary to start with what students know about and then help them journey to the unknown.

Participation is a significant factor for all age groups. Participation may occur through performance, experimentation, and peer-group work, or through student participation in planning and framing what is to be studied. Authentic student decision making, which was

In a relaxed environment, the teacher is providing direct instruction to a small group of students.

discussed in Chapter 1, is one way to motivate student involvement in learning. Mr. Sierra involved his students in planning by having them construct a concept map focused on pioneer life. By doing this, the students decided what they needed to investigate instead of Mr. Sierra telling the students what to do.

Things to Think About When Planning a Unit

Balance

Elementary teachers need to consider their whole curriculum when planning a teaching unit. It is important to ensure **balance** among the subject fields for which you are responsible. Teaching units are generally focused on substantive concepts, not skills. Skills are integrated within the teaching unit and taught separately as needed. For example, one does not develop a unit that focuses on phonics or multiplication, but one could focus on historical literature and incorporate all of the necessary reading skills. The arts, science, mathematics, health, and physical education all need to be considered so that none are slighted in curriculum planning.

Secondary teachers who are subject field experts also need to consider balance, but in a different way. Teachers need to guard against their own biases and interests in curriculum planning. It is a temptation to select topics that are particularly interesting to you personally and reduce the time allotment for those topics that don't interest you. It is natural to spend more time and to be more motivated in areas that you are passionate about, but it is important to consider what your course is supposed to cover!

Semester or Yearlong Planning

Consideration of standards and testing and bombardment with new topics, ideas, and news make it extremely difficult for the classroom teacher to schedule everything that subject field experts and society want in the curriculum. Unit teaching using comprehensive, wide-ranging themes helps facilitate planning; however, it is still necessary to block out available time so that you are not overwhelmed and feeling guilty about untaught lessons. The best way to do this is to develop a calendar timeline of your expectations for teaching the different aspects of your course.

Despite the benefits of planning ahead, you must think about a number of other considerations. Not all subject fields should be converted to a timeline curriculum. It is more important to respond to students' learning abilities than it is to adhere to a "coverage-oriented" curriculum. Language arts in the elementary and middle school does not lend itself to scheduling. Literature, arts, and music are sometimes shortchanged when a timeline curriculum is implemented. Balance, integration, interdisciplinary teaching, and flexibility are significant factors to consider when you are scheduling curriculum.

Student Participation Through Webbing

Webbing is a brainstorming technique to stimulate thinking about a topic or problem. Mr. Sierra used the strategy as a motivation technique to encourage student participation in curriculum planning and as a means to facilitate in-depth thinking about the problems and culture of the early pioneers. Figure 5.4 demonstrates what Mr. Sierra elicited from student participation.

Webbing is considered a nonlinear graphic system that helps individuals recognize connections among content threads. Social and physical science laboratories have used the technique for many years, and recently teachers have adopted the technique to assist in their own curriculum planning of teaching units.

Teaching Hints

Webbings help to:

1. Select content and see connections to integrate subject fields.
2. Encourage nonlinear thinking (brainstorm ideas).
3. Identify patterns and relationships among concepts.

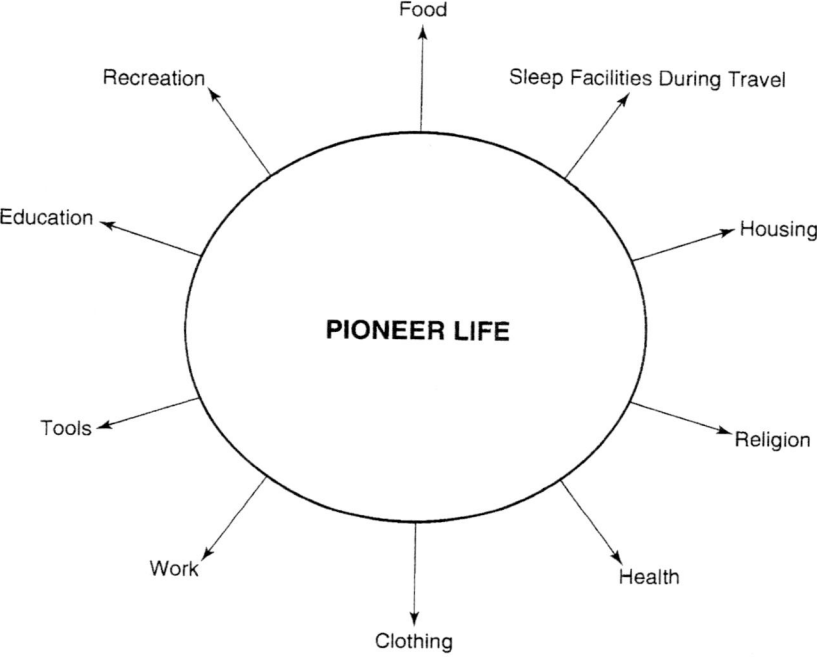

FIGURE 5.4 Concept Map

Data Retrieval Charts

As students engage in small-group inquiry, they need to share their information so that the whole class benefits from their collective research. The data retrieval chart is a way to preserve the data for continued use. Suppose that students were studying the concept (and theme) of culture in different societies. The data retrieval chart shown in Figure 5.5 allows them to compare aspects of culture across several societies.

As groups reported during class discussion, the information was entered on the chart and the discussion focused on how the cities differed. This facilitated understandings of the similarities and differences among the different societies. Knowing the categories on the chart helped the students search for data to prepare for the class discussion.

Backward Problem Solving

Backward problem solving can be used as a unit planning technique. In a science class the students were discussing environmental problems in their own community. The teacher asked the class, "In the best of all possible environments, what would you consider ideal?" The students agreed that a clean environment where waste was not a hazard and where everyone accepted personal responsibility for protecting the environment was what they would consider "ideal."

	Tokyo	New York	London	Mexico City
Housing				
Customs				
Food				
Religion				
Recreation				
Transportation				
Services				
Work				

FIGURE 5.5 Data Retrieval Chart

It is important for teachers to plan time for individualized assistance. Students appreciate teacher attention and guidance.

Next the teacher asked the students, "How do we get there? How do we manage change?" The teacher drew a circle on the board and wrote in the middle, "Clean Environment/Patterns of Change."

The students then began thinking about what would facilitate the ideal they had defined. Their ideas included the following:

1. Explaining changes in weather and earth disasters. (How have weather patterns and natural disasters affected us?)

2. Adjusting to changes in technology. (How do we adjust to technological patterns of change?)

3. Hazardous waste disposal. (How can we find safe and cost-effective means to dispose of waste?)

Backward problem solving focuses on the desired outcome and then engages students in thinking about how to achieve the outcome. It is a slight variation of webbing and takes advantage of students' ability to plan their own learning tasks.

Chapter Summary

This chapter discussed the basic decisions that teachers must make both when planning individual lessons and when engaging in long-term unit planning. Individual lesson planning was demonstrated through the work of three teachers who coped with traumatic circumstances. A sample teaching unit was analyzed to demonstrate both the decision-making process and the major considerations that need to be made for long-term planning. These decisions included how varied learning activities can accommodate multiple intelligences, differentiation, integration, interdisciplinary concepts, and second-language learners. A synopsis of lesson planning to "fast-start" the planning process was exhibited. The chapter provided significant curriculum concepts that affect the selection and organization of learning experiences. Concluding the chapter were two alternative methods for planning a teaching unit.

Teaching Problems

1. Suppose your students do not appear to understand the lesson you have planned. What could be the problem(s) and what should you do about it? Remember the adage, "When students fail, the teacher has failed."

2. How should teachers cope with school/community/societal tragedies that affect the students they are teaching? Did the three teachers in this chapter teach appropriate lessons? How would you handle similar circumstances?

3. Construct a webbing concept map using the theme of "systems." Use Figures 3.1 and 5.4 for review.

4. Let's see what you can do with some of the ideas in this chapter.
    a. Identify several long-range goals in a subject and grade level of your choice.

b. Identify some "big ideas" (content) that fit your goals.
c. Match some learning activities to one of your content ideas and one of your goals.
d. Critique your work using the analysis of Jim Sierra's sample unit.

5. Read the teaching unit in Appendix B. Discuss the unit, using considerations of individual differences, multiple intelligences, sequence of lessons, interdisciplinary content, integration, and assessment.

PART 3

CLASSROOM MANAGEMENT

Chapter 6 defines classroom management and contrasts what it is and what it is not. The chapter discusses grouping for both large and small groups. The characteristics of each are identified and suggestions are made for classroom management and anticipating group work problems. Chapter 7 focuses on student behavior and the variety of problems that may occur in the classroom community, such as rudeness, defiance, bullying, and nonaccountability. Suggestions for handling these problems are made, including conflict resolution through role-playing and classroom meetings.

CHAPTER 6

Classroom Management for the Classroom Community

ADVANCE ORGANIZER

These questions can be used as a framework to assist you in integrating professional knowledge and understanding of the content of this chapter.

1. Classroom management differs from behavioral management and student discipline. What are the significant characteristics of classroom management that help teachers create a productive learning environment?
2. In what ways do group activities contribute to democratic socialization? What are the advantages and disadvantages of large- and small-group instruction?
3. Students need to practice working and learning with their peers in small groups. How does a teacher begin the process? What roles and procedures may facilitate the process?
4. What you do on the first day of class often sets the tone for the balance of the semester. What planning decisions that affect classroom management need to be made?
5. Traditional classroom management problems can be alleviated very simply. Explain the concepts of *with-it-ness*, *ripple effect*, *overlapping behavior*, and *classroom problem-solving meetings*.
6. Why should teachers anticipate and plan fill-in activities?

 The following INTASC issues and standards are discussed in this chapter: Numbers 2–5, 7, 9.

I view classroom management as an instructional approach and an integral part of teaching. When students are motivated by challenging tasks and there is no lag time, managing a room full of students is easy. The characteristics of classroom management are discussed in this chapter as well as how effective management techniques contribute to a productive learning environment. The advantages and disadvantages of large and small groups along with the procedures for implementing grouping techniques are charted for you. Examples of key concepts related to effective management are provided. The ways in which management techniques relate to the socialization process and influence learning are significant factors in this chapter.

Classroom Management and Discipline— Not Synonymous in Democratic Classrooms

> Some years back I recall an incident in which the noise from an adjoining classroom was so deafening that it was disturbing my sixth-grade class. I decided to walk next door to see what was happening. I entered the classroom and looked at the students, and they looked at me. Silence was immediate and I turned on my heel and walked from the room.
>
> After school my young colleague came over and asked, "How did you do that?" I responded, "I don't know."
>
> But in retrospect, I do know. Experienced teachers develop a certain persona, a presence, that communicates to students, "I expect respect." And I communicate to students that respect is reciprocal.

The presence that experienced teachers develop is rooted in students' knowledge that you understand them, support them, will treat them fairly, and hold high expectations for their scholarship and behavior. Most important of all is to communicate to students that you sincerely care about them.

In order to understand the concept of **classroom management,** it is necessary to identify exemplars of what it is and what it is not. Table 6.1 makes the distinction.

The definition of classroom management that is used in this book is as follows:

> Classroom management is the orchestration of classroom life: planning curriculum, organizing procedures and resources, arranging the environment to maximize efficiency, monitoring student progress, anticipating potential problems, Lemlech, 2002, p. 67).

Good classroom management is not difficult, but it does require systematic thinking concerning students' needs for productive learning and your own needs to teach creatively.

TABLE 6.1 Classroom Management

Positive Elements of Classroom Management	Negative Elements of Classroom Management
Arrange a comfortable, caring, and respectful social environment	Display a list of preset rules for classroom behavior on the bulletin board; require students to copy them and obtain parents' signature
Plan a curriculum that considers developmental needs, in-depth learning, and relevance to students	Display a list of punishments for rule infractions
Students and teacher jointly decide on classroom standards and organizational procedures for obtaining materials, movement, and communication in the classroom	Threaten students with communication with parents and other authority figures
Monitor students' progress and communicate progress with students	List students' names on the chalkboard for behavioral and academic infractions
Anticipate potential classroom problems; engage in class discussions of emergent problems openly with students at appropriate times	Prejudge potential discipline problems

The key concepts used in the definition of classroom management are a means to explore success in the classroom.

Orchestrating Classroom Life

In a democratic classroom everyone knows what is expected of them—both students and teacher. The teacher is like an orchestra leader, blending focused presentations, students' study tasks, group work, independent work, relaxation, resources, unique needs, and classroom schedules (timing). The teacher/conductor needs to know where everyone is and what is happening in the classroom. Like the orchestra leader, the teacher knows when to emphasize and strengthen certain work tasks and when to trust that the class/orchestra will accomplish what is expected without too much supervision. The blending process is accomplished through the other components in the definition.

Planning Curriculum

Jim Sierra had planned a unit on electrical energy. His overall goals were to have students understand how electrical circuits are closed and opened, the concept of electromagnets, and how to produce electricity. His intent was to involve the students in recognizing the role of switches to turn the flow of electricity on and off, investigate how to light a bulb using dry cells, how to develop series and parallel circuits, how to construct electromagnets, and how to make simple machines.

All of Sierra's plans required hands-on activities for the students. He had to decide how to motivate the students to get them involved. He would need to gather materials for hands-on exploration. Although all of the materials would not be used the first day or two of the unit, he knew he had to think it through in order to accomplish his goals.

Curriculum and instruction are two sides of the same coin, and so Jim had to decide on appropriate instructional strategies. How would he begin? Should he demonstrate techniques or have students discover how to make circuits and electromagnets? Should students work in groups or independently? The students were new to him; he didn't know how well accustomed they were to group work. Was the classroom arranged appropriately for hands-on work tasks? If students ran experiments, should they be required to write down their processes and conclusions?

Sierra's planning tasks took him several hours as he detailed a plan that would no doubt take about three weeks of class time. He decided that his unit would integrate science, industrial arts, and mathematics.

Jim Sierra's Decision Points Jim needed to make some very basic decisions that would affect the success of his lessons. These included the following:

1. Unit goals
2. Content
3. Instructional strategies
4. Grouping decisions (whole class, small groups, independent work)
5. Time (how much would be needed)
6. Class activities
7. Materials and resources
8. Evaluation (how he would assess what students were learning)

Organizing Procedures and Resources

While planning his teaching unit, Jim Sierra made decisions about his theme, goals, and content and the integration of subject fields. As he considered what he was going to teach, he recognized that a number of additional decisions would affect his success and the management of his classroom.

His first decision that would affect teaching and learning was how he would deliver the content. He decided that much of the unit would occur using an *inquiry instructional strategy* approach to motivate students to discover the major concepts for an electrical energy unit. To accomplish this, he recognized that students would need to work in small groups because independent work would require too many materials.

As he thought this out, he noted that small-group experimentation might take longer than he had originally scheduled for science. But since he would be integrating other subject fields he decided to rearrange his daily schedule to provide more time if it were needed.

Actual class activities would need to be somewhat flexible, depending on students' progress and conceptual understanding. He knew that his first activity would be to motivate interest in electrical energy and set up a strategy for students to recognize that switches affect the electrical circuit. From there he intended that students would get acquainted with equipment needed for making circuits to light bulbs.

Materials and resources were vital to his lessons. His next task was to make a list of needed materials. These included dry cells, copper wire, wire strippers, flashlight-size light bulbs, paper clips, pieces of tin, some wood for making machines, and science textbooks. Since students would be working in groups, he recognized that the distribution of materials would be a problem. He decided to find a number of shoe boxes, each of which would serve as a science kit for a group of students.

If students were working in groups he knew that he would need to be walking around offering suggestions and monitoring progress. He thought it would be a good idea if students were responsible for keeping track of the assumptions they made and the processes they used to develop concepts about electrical energy. Their written work would reflect their thinking and give him another means to evaluate their progress in addition to what they produced.

Arranging the Environment

Respecting and caring about each other were important ingredients in Jim Sierra's classroom organization. This meant that students would need to be considerate of each other in sharing materials, listening to each other's ideas, and being willing to experiment with assumptions that may not reflect their own thoughts.

Work places would need to be arranged so that five students could work comfortably together. Since he had thirty students in the class he anticipated six work groups. His tables were arranged in an E formation and would require the movement of some chairs. There were open spaces in the classroom where books and other materials were kept. He decided that some of these spaces would accommodate work groups.

Noise was another factor to consider. If some groups were too loud it would interfere with the thinking and work of other groups. He would need to caution the students about this. He also needed to decide where to keep the shoe boxes for easy access—and then it occurred to him that as students began construction of different electrical projects, these too would need storage space. He was beginning to feel quite stressed and recognized that he had some serious decisions to make. Finally he decided to empty a cupboard to be used for students' work projects. The shoe boxes would need to be kept in an open bookcase.

Monitoring Student Progress

Sierra knew that he would be teaching some specific concepts to the whole class, but many activities would occur in small groups. When teaching the whole class he knew that he would be questioning students to verify understanding. Small-group work would require constant monitoring by sitting with each group and observing their work. His decision to have students record their thinking processes would provide another means to assess their progress. He would use a group reporting process at the end of each work period so that students could discuss what they accomplished and share ideas with other groups.

Anticipating Potential Problems

Jim was holding his head! He recognized there were many potential problems that he needed to think about. He decided to make a list.

1. His class was new to him, and he too was somewhat inexperienced; therefore, he was concerned about getting started with grouping and group processes.
2. Maintaining a democratic classroom environment was very important to him. If students were noisy and unruly during group work, would he be able to keep control of the class and preserve his own composure? Would students continue to act respectfully when working with each other?
3. Cleanup time after experimenting and project work would need to be quick but orderly. He needed to plan a system to alert students when it was time to clean up.
4. Safety precautions would need to be taught to the students when studying electricity and working with tools.
5. Material and tool needs would be ongoing. For example, when constructing motors and telephones, students would need to use pieces of wood for a base. This would involve cutting pieces of wood, using saws, saw blocks for safety, hammers, and nails.
6. Because he was integrating subject fields, he would need to communicate to students the purpose(s) of what they were studying, so that they wouldn't think this was "play" time.
7. He needed to remember that he wanted students to "discover" energy concepts, and he should not be tempted to "talk and deliver" the concepts to them. Patience was to be his watchword! (Talking is not teaching.)
8. One last task would be to design a science experiment record sheet for students to use to write down their assumptions and testing processes. (See Chapter 11 for Sierra's science record form.)

Getting Started—Grouping

Students are not workers to be ordered and commanded. They are learners, and in democratic environments they need to understand what they will learn and how to behave in both large- and small-group settings because the two settings differ dramatically. Large- and small-group experiences contribute to students' citizenship socialization, group identity, and group responsibility. Both approaches need to be part of a teacher's instructional repertoire.

Large-Group Instruction

When we attend a concert, a play, or a movie, we are experiencing a certain group identity with others in attendance because of a common purpose(s): to appreciate, relax, or even critique. We have been socialized to know that during these events we need to be relatively quiet so as not to intrude on others' enjoyment. Both in the home and in school we teach students to care about others and restrain our own behavior so as not to disturb other attendees at these events. Participation is limited to expressing appreciation during breaks in dialogue or performance.

Whole-class teaching in the school environment has other characteristics. Passivity is not necessarily valued. As you will see in Chapter 8, teachers often make presentations or perform demonstrations, but then elicit student responses through specific questioning techniques. Large-group instruction is an efficient means to communicate to the whole class at the same time. This assumes, of course, that the whole class *needs* the same information, skill, or presentation.

When teaching the whole class simultaneously, it is necessary to verify students' understanding. So if Sierra wants to demonstrate how to use the dry cell battery to light a bulb, it would be prudent to ask students "How did I use the dry cell?" "What do you notice about the copper wires connected to the battery?" Similarly, when Sierra gives directions to the whole class, verification of his own clarity and students' attention is a good classroom management technique.

There are advantages and disadvantages to the use of all teaching strategies. For example, large-group instruction focuses attention on the teacher; if the teacher is dynamic and has captured students' attention, then theoretically students' involvement will be assured because they are not distracted by other students or other happenings in the classroom. But if the lesson is not going well and the teacher lacks enthusiasm, students' attention may lag and deviant behavior is probable. Teachers have "holding power" when they present a good lesson or give significant information to students in a large-group setting. If the lesson is poor and students' attention wanders, then groups of students may act up or engage in private conversations, and classroom management problems emerge. The advantages and disadvantages of large-group instruction are reviewed in Table 6.2.

Table 6.2 clearly reveals conflicting features in the use of large-group instruction. An advantage should be that students' focus of attention is on the teacher, but since it is more difficult to keep the attention of the whole class, there is a tendency for some students to carry on their own personal activities and disrupt the large group.

Still another problem is that teachers tend to feel they must exercise their authority when working with the entire class, and this can undermine a democratic environment. When several students are disruptive in a large-group setting, teachers may be tempted to make examples of them. This causes what Kounin (1970) calls the **ripple effect:** Other students in the class feel embarrassed when their classmates are "put down" and they in turn begin to display the same disruptive behaviors.

No one can deny that large-group instruction is an efficient means to present information to all students at the same time, but the teacher must consider whether control problems emerge because instruction is unsuited for all of the students or because physical problems cause inattention. By anticipating the potential problems inherent in large-

TABLE 6.2 Characteristics of Large-Group Instruction

Advantages	Disadvantages
Helps create a sense of belonging to the class community.	Shy students hesitate to participate or share ideas in whole-group environments.
Encourages students to focus on the teacher. The teacher has "holding power."	It is more difficult to keep the attention of all students; some students may be distracted, bored, and disruptive.
Efficient means to teach a skill or present significant information to the entire class at one time.	Instruction is not differentiated and teacher focuses on fictional average students.
	More difficult for all students to physically see, hear, and participate.

group instruction, teachers can arrange seating patterns so that all students are physically accommodated; planning motivating large-group instruction can minimize distractions and disruptive behavior.

Did You Know That . . . ?

> Classes tend to be quite large in Japanese classrooms (forty students). To minimize control problems, teachers often honor students by asking them to lead a lesson or begin class by calling the group to order. As a consequence, students experience firsthand what happens when some students are unruly and fail to pay attention. In this way Japanese teachers help students reflect on appropriate classroom behavior (Zorpette, 2001).

The Sense of Belonging

Earlier I provided the example of attendance at a concert or play and audience behavior. Another factor affecting behavior is that the audience *chose* to attend. They had a like-mindedness because (with rare exception) the experience was ego-satisfying. But students assigned to a classroom generally do not choose to be there, so it is very important to develop a sense of identity and belonging. Effective teachers do this in a variety of ways.

Gerry Alred put up a bulletin board that displayed where members of the class or their families were born, and she ensured that students were acquainted with each other's heritage. Senior classes at elementary and middle schools often write class songs to the tune of popular music to express their identity as seniors. High school students often select class mascots and names to describe their class and year of graduation.

In Salt Lake City, Utah, industrial arts students at Granite High School made bobsleds using fiberglass during the 2002 Olympics. When asked on the *Today* show how they felt about the project, the students responded that it gave them a sense of pride, class spirit, and togetherness that they had never had before.

Service learning activities, described in Chapters 1 and 4, serve as unifying experiences for a class and have the potential to develop a sense of belonging. Undertaking a research activity with involvement of the whole class, producing a class newspaper, or writing a play and producing it are all activities that help to develop group responsibility, cooperation, and respect for classmates. A sense of belonging and group solidarity increase students' interest in schooling and caring about teacher and classmates.

Focus on Classroom Management

Your purpose for choosing to work with students as a whole group needs to be clear not only to you, but to your students as well. Let them know that you need to convey important information to them or to teach specific concepts or skills needed by the majority of the class. Your first management task is to gain the attention of *all* students. Alert the students with an opening remark appropriate to the age of your students. ("Boys and girls, I need your attention." "OK folks, please give me your attention." "Let's all look up here.")

Can you write your own list of teaching hints for large-group instruction?

Now you need to be patient; learn to *wait* while scanning the class. Do not try to begin talking until you have total attention. Do not try to talk over the students. Make eye contact with as many students as possible. Remember that you are not rooted to one spot in the classroom; you may want to walk around and stand by the students who are not attentive. Do not hold side conversations with a group of students. You may want to remind the class that you are waiting for their attention and that they are wasting their own time.

If you absolutely cannot get the students' attention, you need to do something dramatic. Turn off the lights, and standing by the light switch tell the students that it appears to you that they are not aware that you need to talk to them. Call their attention to the standards *they* set for respectful behavior in their classroom. (Setting standards will be discussed in the section on the first day of class, later in this chapter.) Discuss the standards with them; ask them how they would feel if you ignored them when they wanted to talk to you.

When you have their attention, speak in a normal-pitched voice—not too loud. In fact, it is sometimes a good technique to lower your voice so that students need to pay greater attention. While speaking, continue to scan the class and make eye contact with as many students as possible.

If while you are presenting information to the class, the attention of several students seems to wander, you should stop talking in *midsentence* and *wait*. Look at the students who are unruly or not paying attention. You do not need to say anything. When they recognize that you are waiting and return your attention, continue talking to the entire group. It should not be necessary to say anything to the students at this point in time. But you may want to have a private talk with them at a convenient moment about courteous behavior and your expectations for mutual respect.

Playground management can be difficult if you do not have a system for capturing students' attention.

To maintain student interest when you are teaching specific concepts or skills, ask frequent questions. Select students to respond from different parts of the room. You may even want to choose students who are *more* likely to let their attention wander. Whether you are teaching specific information or conveying information needed by the class, always verify understanding. ("Joe, how does this information affect us?" "Who can tell us what we ought to do about this?" "Why is it important to strip the ends of the copper wire?")

Teaching Hints: Large-Group Instruction Classroom Management

1. Select information, skills, or concepts needed by the majority of the class.
2. Elicit students' attention. Establish eye contact by scanning the room.
3. Verify that all students can see and hear.
4. Motivate interest.
5. Speak clearly in a normal voice; continue to scan the class and encourage eye contact.
6. Ask frequent questions to clarify information and verify understanding. Encourage students' questions and responses. Assure students that you will be available to provide assistance later if it is needed.

Small-Group Instruction

In contrast to large-group instruction, which is somewhat formal and requires student self-restraint, small groups focus on student participation. Small-group work emphasizes and fosters democratic behaviors. Most of the time the small group takes advantage of student diversity through heterogeneous grouping by differentiating content, work tasks, and work products. Students are expected to assist each other, share viewpoints, and learn to negotiate and compromise.

Piaget, Dewey, Kohlberg, and Vygotsky (Chapter 3) all advocated social **interaction** so that students can learn from each other, confront disagreements, and learn self-control and how to cooperate with others. Working in a small group, students soon recognize that the progress of the group depends on *all* members of the group. Group goals and interests need to be communicated among the members. Experiences of each student influence and contribute to the attainment of the collective interest and aims. Review Table 6.3 for a succinct differentiation between the advantages and disadvantages of small-group instruction.

How to Begin

In the best of all perfect school environments, students would begin small-group work in kindergarten, but this does not always happen—so let us assume that your students have rarely worked in small groups for either cooperative skill tasks or inquiry-oriented tasks. Your first task is to motivate class interest in content and tasks. Next you and the students need to talk about group work rules.

> "Suppose we were to work in five or six different groups in this classroom, where do you think we should locate our groups?" (Class decides where and whether chairs and/or tables need to be moved.)
>
> "For studying astronomy, what materials do you think will be needed?" (Class discussion.) "If everyone has to obtain his or her own materials, what will happen?" (Class discussion—mad rush, confusion; it will be better if one person in each group goes to obtain materials for the whole group.)
>
> "Since we will need five groups for our work tasks, what are some things we need to think about?" (Class discussion—noise, courtesy, attending to the task.) "Now suppose I need to talk to you during group work; how should I get your attention?" (Class discussion—lights, bell.) "Suppose you need to obtain assistance from me; what can you do?" (Class discussion—raise hands in group, eye contact.)
>
> "Since this is our first group work session, I am going to select the groups and we will practice moving to our designated locations." (Assign groups and locations; have each group move to its designated spot. If moving is too noisy or unruly, call them back and begin again!)

When you are satisfied, inform the class how much time they will have for working. Inform them that at the end of the designated time you will signal them and then it will be time for them to turn their chairs so they can all see each other and "We will have a discussion about our work."

TABLE 6.3 Characteristics of Small-Group Instruction

Advantages	Disadvantages
Fosters democratic behaviors: interaction, cooperation, respect, caring, assisting others	Democratic skills such as sharing, assisting, cooperation, negotiation, compromising need to be practiced
Requires communication among group members	Student alertness and consideration of group processes and noise factors need to be practiced
Motivates individual and group involvement and problem solving	Group reporting skills need to be taught
Necessitates listening to others and sharing own viewpoints	May subordinate individual interests and needs to accomplish group needs and goals
Necessitates development of group goals, task assignments, and responsibility	May subordinate subject field content to learn group process skills
Teaches negotiation, compromise, and decision making	Requires anticipation of time and scheduling needs
Fosters group learning	Increased motivation, involvement, and participation require teacher anticipation of potential problems
Promotes differentiation of instruction	
Frees the teacher to observe, listen, diagnose, and assist	

If students are too noisy during group work, stop them and discuss it. As they work, walk around and monitor whether they are on task, have assumed individual responsibilities, have appropriate resources, and are working cooperatively and respectfully.

The first work period should be short so that there is plenty of time to evaluate what has been accomplished. Begin the evaluation by asking each group to appoint one person to share substantive accomplishments (content and task). After group reports, open up the discussion to the whole class to allow students to direct comments and questions to specific groups. For example, in group 1 in Jim Sierra's class, William said, "We had difficulty connecting lights in a series." Group 2 had a suggestion for them: "Did you try to . . . ?"

When reports and discussion are over, ask groups whether they had the necessary materials and resources. "What will you need to continue your work tomorrow?" This will help you plan your lesson for the next day.

The second part of the evaluation should focus on group processes, and you may want to ask questions similar to the following:

1. When working in your group, did everyone get to participate? (Should they? Yes.)
2. Did you all agree on how to go about your task?
3. What did you do when you disagreed? How did you handle disagreements? What are some ways to solve these disagreements? (Try different ways to experiment/work. Compromise. Negotiate.)
4. Why should you listen to the viewpoints and ideas of all group members?
5. What was most difficult about working as a group?
6. What worked best?
7. What did you learn about working as a group?

Group Size

Five group members seems to be ideal in terms of interaction. I like odd numbers of students to settle disputes that require voting upon. There are times, however, when pairs are important for group work, in which case go with four group members.

Group Roles

Suppose your students had difficulty deciding on who should do what in the group. You may want to set up specific group work roles until your students are more experienced. You may make the choices or have each group designate the roles as soon as they meet together. Roles may include the following:

- Group leader—initiates discussion and keeps group on task
- Resource leader—gathers materials for the group
- Group recorder—takes notes on group plans and decisions
- Group reporter—uses notes, plans, and decisions to report to class during evaluation
- Cooperative leader—evaluates how well group worked together, judges how to improve group interaction; may report to class during evaluation time

Group Procedures

With a new class and/or inexperienced group work students, it is a good idea to walk them through procedures for working together. You may want to do this before they work or have them help decide on the procedures after their first experience. Jim Sierra used the following procedures for his electricity energy unit.

1. By group consent, decide on individual role responsibilities (leader, recorder, resource person, reporter, cooperative evaluator)
2. Group discussion to plan experiments and tasks to be performed
3. Group decision on who will do what during experiments (stripping wire, connecting batteries, drawing plans, testing)
4. Group discussion: what worked and why, what didn't work and why
5. Planning for class discussion
6. Cleanup activities

Can you write your own list of teaching hints for small-group instruction?

What Can Go Wrong? Anticipating Group Work Problems

Does Each Group Understand the Task? Before sending students off to their groups, it is a good idea to verify understanding of what they are to accomplish. Simply ask at least one member of each group, "What are you going to do today?" or, "Explain your group's work task today."

Do Students Have the Necessary Skills? Suppose that students will need to read or construct bar or broken-line graphs, but they have no experience with graphic techniques. Spend a few minutes teaching the whole class how to read, use, and make graphs to express quantitative data. Otherwise you will need to teach each group separately and there will be a great deal of commotion in the classroom as students confront a task with no experience for dealing with it.

Are Materials and Resources Available in Sufficient Quantity? Anticipate the work needs of students ahead of time. Otherwise students will be arguing and overly concerned that they will not have enough time to complete their work. This is one of the reasons why you need to ask students during the evaluation discussion about their needs for the next time they work together.

What Should Students Do if Their Group Completes its Work Before the Others Do? First, be sure that students understand that they need to have a group discussion to prepare for the whole-class discussion. During that group discussion, they should review their accomplishments and correct any errors. If this has been done, then the group needs an alternative assignment, which could be posted on the chalkboard so that groups can begin without disturbing you or other groups.

What Can You Do About Aggressive/Compulsive Talkers? If you have more than one student with this problem, put them in different groups and select one of them to be an "observer" for you. Instruct the student to take notes and observe the other group and report to you: Did everyone get to participate? (Why not?) Were group members respectful and courteous to one another? Try to elicit from the aggressive talker that one student

Having free choice of reading material motivates these girls to become interested in the sports section of the daily newspaper.

monopolized the group talk. Question the individual concerning how he or she thought others felt about this problem. If you only have one student with this problem, place a tape recorder in the group and then have this individual review the recording with you and respond to the same questions.

Providing for Multiple Intelligences When individual responsibilities within groups are to be decided, remind students that each of us has special talents and that group work allows us to take advantage of that. If a student is a tech whiz, then that person should lead computer searches. If one individual is terrific in math work, then he or she may set up how the group will report its data. The individual who leans toward art and nature could do the drawings to accompany a group report. Help students appreciate and value each other's talents and preferences.

Shy Students, English Language Learners, and Inclusion The group leader's role should be to encourage group participation of all group members. For the shy student, ask that student, "Marina, what do you think about this? How do you think we should go about . . . ?" For English language learners, poor readers, or students with disabilities, encouraging them to participate and recognizing their contributions is very important It may be necessary to pair students within the group for tutoring and mentoring. But the group leader needs to consider that this is his or her responsibility. Sometimes it is even a good idea to ask one of these students to take on the responsibility of leadership. The group role responsibilities should be rotated among members of the group.

Should You Ever Skip the Evaluation Discussion?

No. The evaluation discussion at the end of group work provides an assessment of progress, the need to remotivate, diagnosis of understanding, and planning needs for the next day. In addition, evaluation of group processes makes group work more productive each time students participate. Group work requires practice by both the teacher and the students. The evaluation contributes information on whether students are respectful, cooperative, and working democratically and what problems the group encounters. Plan class time so that the evaluation discussion is almost as long as the work time. Remember that communication among class members is our raison d'etre.

Teacher Responsibilities During Group Work

Your main work tasks occur in the planning for group work. If you have done a good job planning a stimulating and relevant problem for students and have considered resource needs and all of the management needs, then during group work you can enjoy the fruits of your labor. This does not mean sitting at your desk, but rather walking around the classroom, sitting in on several of the groups, listening to how they are proceeding, assessing their needs, noting the thinking process of individuals, writing down questions to ask them during the evaluative discussion, perhaps deciding on who to call upon because of an insightful comment, and—last of all—patting yourself on the back for planning so well!

Teaching Hints: Small-Group Instruction Classroom Management

1. Introduce the whole class to the problem or task.
2. Teach skill(s) to whole class if needed.
3. Verify understanding of group work problem or task.
4. Assign group members and physical space for work.
5. Identify amount of time for group work.
6. Remind students of how you will signal their attention and how they can signal you for assistance.
7. Verify group work rules and procedures, including cleanup responsibilities.
8. Monitor groups for on-task behavior, understanding, group needs, and use of resources.
9. Evaluate substantive accomplishments, group processes, and group needs.

Anticipating the First Day of the Semester

Four planning tasks should be accomplished before students arrive in your classroom. These are:

1. Establishing your room environment
2. Obtaining materials and resources
3. Deciding what and how to teach (content and process) for at least the first week
4. Scheduling what and when (timing)

Classroom Management in the Elementary Classroom—Lucia Martin

In an elementary classroom it is customary to devote each bulletin board to a different subject field. Lucia Martin had four bulletin boards in her classroom. Using pictures and questions under the pictures, she devoted one bulletin board to the science content she expected to teach, one to social studies, another to art and music, and the fourth to literature books.

She arranged her tables and chairs and then set up centers of interest in the classroom: a science corner, musical instruments, a library with book displays, math manipulatives, and a computer center. She organized her cupboards so that she had paper, pencils, scissors, crayons, paints, science supplies, chart paper, and bookcases filled with textbooks.

She made decisions about greeting students and getting acquainted with them. Then she planned a unit of study in science and social studies, which she intended to integrate. She planned some skill lessons in mathematics to diagnose students' needs. She also planned a spelling lesson for the first day of class and made preliminary plans for reading instruction and creative writing.

Next she decided how much time she would need for each subject on the first day of class and her scheduling ideas for the rest of the first week. Let's examine Lucia Martin's first day in the classroom and see how she carried out her plans.

8:30–9:00	Attendance, seating, greetings, room environment
9:00–9:30	Mathematics
9:30–9:40	Preparation for recess, school rules
9:40–10:00	Recess
10:00–11:30	Language arts, discussion of room standards
11:30–11:35	Preparation for lunch
11:35–12:20	Lunch
12:20–12:40	Storytime
12:40–1:20	Social studies/science

1:20–1:40	Physical education
1:40–2:00	Music
2:00–2:15	Review of day's work

As Lucia greeted students upon their arrival, she handed them a piece of tagboard and told them to use the black crayons on the tables to write their names and place the tagboard in front of them so that she could see their names. Students were allowed to select where they wanted to sit. She then took attendance and had each student raise his or her hand when she called names. When the student raised his or her hand she made a point of establishing eye contact with the student and usually made a comment such as "Glad to meet you," "Welcome," or "You did a good job writing your name."

Other school business included obtaining a lunch count of how many students were planning to eat in the cafeteria, and she placed a card with the number outside her door in a special box. Then she called attention to the room environment and asked the students, "What do you think we will be studying this semester?" She called on students to share their thoughts. Sometimes a student was interrupted by others and Lucia would ask, "Whose turn is it to talk now? How do you feel when someone interrupts you?" In this way she began to communicate to the students that they were expected to be respectful to each other.

For mathematics Martin had a handout for students to work some simple story problems; she monitored their work and provided assistance to students who seemed to have difficulty reading. After about 15 minutes she told the students, "Let's talk about the problems; who would like to go to the board and show us how you worked on problem number one?" She encouraged discussion of each problem and asked for alternative means to work the problems. She observed the students' work and recitation carefully. Sometimes when a student was not paying attention, she would walk over and stand next to that person.

To prepare for recess she reminded the students that each classroom had a special place to play and a special place to line up after recess. "Recess is also the time for you to use the lavatories and get a drink." She handed out balls and other physical education equipment and called groups of students to line up at the door. If a group was too unruly she had them sit down and asked a different group to "Show us how we ought to line up at the door." Martin walked the students out to the playground, showed them where to line up at the end of recess, and took them to their area of the playground for activity.

While the students were outside, Lucia prepared both drawing and writing paper and brought out a copy of the book *Madeline and the Gypsies* by Ludwig Bemelmans. Madeline's adventures were familiar to the students and a favorite for the age group. After recess, Lucia started reading the story aloud and from time to time asked the students what they thought would happen next. When the story concluded she asked the students to think about what other adventures Madeline might have with the gypsies, draw pictures of her adventures, and begin a story about their version of Madeline and the gypsies.

While the students worked, Martin called small groups of students to the front of the room to read with her. In this way she began to diagnose students' reading ability and get more acquainted with her students. In the small group she asked each student's name and had them tell something about themselves. As they did this she would look directly at the speaker, smile, and make an appropriate comment.

On two occasions Martin had to stop the students who were working on their pictures and stories. The second time she said: "We're having difficulty working up here, what do you think is the matter?" She took time to elicit students' responses: "Too many people are walking around the room and we're too noisy." Lucia nodded and said, "Do you suppose you can use soft voices while you work and only get up if you need a book or some paper?" The students nodded and she continued work with the students in the front of the room.

Towards the end of the language arts time, Martin decided it was appropriate to discuss classroom etiquette with the students. She began by telling the students, "You know, boys and girls, we need to live together like a family in this classroom. So that we can all get along together, what are some things we need to do and to remember?" In this way Lucia Martin elicited from the students some classroom standards for behavior. Sometimes the students needed prodding with a question, such as, "What should you do if you need help and I am working with a group of students here in the front of the room?" (We could raise our hand or try to catch your eye.) Ultimately the students came up with some significant thoughts.

- We need to respect each other and be polite.
- We need to talk quietly so as not to disturb others.
- If we need help from the teacher, we should raise our hand or wait until she sees us.
- When we need materials or need to line up at the door, we should walk.

Lucia wrote the students' standards on a chart and placed it on the chart rack to be referred to if necessary.

Lunch preparation was similar to recess preparation. She walked the students to their lunch tables and reminded them about their play area on the playground. Students eating in the cafeteria joined the cafeteria line.

The day progressed in an orderly manner because Lucia had anticipated most of the students' needs and her own teaching plans. Before dismissal she asked the students,

Teaching Hints: Classroom Management

1. Instead of handing students a list of rules that you have composed, elicit standards of behavior from them.
2. Remember that in a democratic environment, everyone must live by the same rules; if students compose them, the rules are more likely to be followed.
3. Make as few rules as possible and elicit them when students recognize the need.
4. As the authoritative leader of the classroom, be certain that you carry out the intent of the rule equitably for all students.

"What are some of the things we did today? What have you learned?" Knowing that their parents would ask a similar question when they arrived home, she "primed" the students so that they would be able to respond.

Classroom Management in the Secondary Classroom—Roger Ives

Roger Ives taught the equivalent of five periods per day. Block scheduling in which he integrated math, science, and health adjusted his schedule so that he taught 80-minute periods. His schedule was as follows:

8:00–9:20	Ninth-grade earth sciences, math, health
9:20–9:40	Recess
9:40–11:00	Tenth-grade biology, geometry
11:10–12:30	Tenth-grade biology, geometry
12:30–1:30	Lunch
1:30–2:50	Ninth- and tenth-grade global science, advanced geometry
2:55–3:10	Homeroom (house meetings; two days per week)

During the first and third weeks of the month students are in Mr. Ives's classroom on Monday, Wednesday, and Friday. During the second and fourth weeks of the month they are in his classroom on Tuesday and Thursday. During the alternate days of the week students take a humanities core that is integrated with social science. Other subject fields (electives, physical education) also are scheduled into 80-minute periods and meet on alternate days.

Roger's planning for the first day of school was similar for each of his classes. He stood at the door of his classroom and greeted students and told them to select where they wanted to sit. When the class was gathered and seated he immediately passed out a 3×5 card for students to write their name, phone number, and e-mail address (if they had one). In one period he taught both ninth- and tenth-graders; he told these students to identify their grade level.

Next he told the class a little bit about himself, his interests, his sports activities, and what he liked about teaching math and science. He then asked students to introduce themselves and tell a little bit about their own interests. As they did so, he would nod, make eye contact, and comment that he was pleased they were in his class.

After the introductions he began to talk about his goals for the class and specific information about what they would be studying and how he would integrate the subject fields. He explained that he liked to use a lot of hands-on activities and group work in the classroom, but he expected that each student would write an independent report explaining the group experiments, data, and conclusions. Though students would work together, their drawings and writing needed to be individually constructed.

He then passed out a three-page "policy" packet to each student. "You may read along as I discuss this." He told the students that when they entered the classroom there would be a short problem on the chalkboard for them to work on and that they could join any group of students and do the warm-up activity. After 10 minutes they would talk about the activity. Next they would go over their homework assignments, and he would collect them. "Note on your sheet that I have provided you with my grading system, which includes the number of tests, quizzes, and lab assignments. Class participation will be considered when determining your grade. If you miss an exam or fail to turn in an assignment I will expect you to meet with me and explain what happened. We will then jointly decide whether you qualify for a makeup test or extra time to complete the assignment."

Ives explained that he was available after school Wednesdays and Thursdays if students needed to see him or obtain assistance. He also gave the students his e-mail address for their use or their parents' use. He said he didn't believe in a lot of class rules, but he did have certain expectations. These were listed on his policy packet:

- Please arrive on time to class.
- Please have your materials with you every class meeting (notebook, pens, texts, and any other materials suggested during the prior class meeting).
- I expect a respectful attitude toward your fellow students and toward me, and let's all display a sense of humor.

He told the students to share his policy statements with their parents, but he did not require parental signatures. "You are old enough to value your own education and act maturely. OK, let's get down to work. We will begin with . . ."

Mr. Ives had a very straightforward, no-nonsense approach to managing his classroom. He anticipated what students needed to know about the teacher and the class and what was expected of them. Though students had no hand in "setting the rules," he did not threaten them, waste time outlining punishments, or have anything except simple procedural standards. He said nothing about talking to classmates, raising hands to be recognized, leaving your seat, or asking permission. Obviously he expected appropriate behavior from his students and would deal appropriately if he was disappointed. His use of a warm-up activity at the beginning of the class period was his means to settle the class down before he began to teach in earnest. It gave students a chance to come together and ready themselves for the day's activity.

Now let's look at some of the needs of middle and high school students.

Teaching Hint

Establish your instructional goals during your first class meeting and emphasize those instructional practices throughout the semester. Focus on active learning and student effort.

Classroom Management and Motivation

Roger Ives emphasized several factors that research indicates are extremely important to adolescents—and no doubt to elementary students as well. He informed students that they would be spending a significant amount of time working in groups on hands-on activities. This means that there would be plenty of opportunity for students to *interact with their peers*. He informed students when he would be available to give assistance, and he gave them his e-mail address for assistance. This conveyed *teacher support* when and if needed. His class rules informed students of the importance, and his expectation, of *mutual respect*. Finally he conveyed to students how their *performance* would be judged by identifying class requirements and grading procedures.

Findings by Ryan and Patrick (2001) indicate the importance of the social environment of the classroom in student motivation and engagement. Students need to interact with their classmates and work collaboratively in order to feel comfortable in class. Knowing that they have the support of their teacher builds their confidence in their own ability to regulate their work and communicate their needs. Emphasizing respect communicates to students that their ideas, contributions, and participation will not be made fun of—that the environment is "safe" for exploring and expressing their thoughts. Finally, Ryan and Patrick found that a social environment that embraces interaction, teacher support, and respect, and deemphasizes competition, thus encourages self-efficacy and motivation to learn. Kohn (2003, p. 27) emphasizes the importance of asking *yourself* the right questions: "What do these kids need—and how can we meet those needs?"

Classroom Management and School Socialization

School socialization begins in the primary grades. Many students have not had experience working and playing in an anonymous cultural environment with a large group of peers. This is particularly true for students from impoverished backgrounds. Nor have most students experienced time limitations, changes in tasks and activities, or challenges to produce products according to set criteria. Sharing materials and space, learning to control movement and impulse, the need to listen and respond at set times—these are all foreign to the majority of children. But with appropriate instruction and caring teachers, most children learn internal controls and develop work habits that remain with them throughout their years at school.

There needs to be a balance between rules and regulations that *control* children and rules and regulations that *facilitate* and *motivate* learning. Respectful, caring teachers recognize this balance and strive to provide as much freedom and individuality as possible to encourage students' passionate interest in different subject fields.

When elementary teachers are successful in the socialization process, middle and high school teachers have fewer problems to worry them. However, too often the early grades are socially repressive and students resist schooling, which can ultimately lead them to quit and drop out.

Class Size

Why do so many legislators advocate smaller classes and lower ratios of students to teachers? Though the legislators may not recognize why student achievement may improve in smaller classes, it is clear that both students and teachers have more opportunity for interactions and options for learning and teaching when classes are small and space is more adequate.

Students do not necessarily achieve greater gains in smaller classes unless the teacher is more qualified (a better teacher and credentialed), interacts more with the students, and uses a variety of teaching strategies. Gains from smaller classes are particularly evident for disadvantaged students, who profit most from teacher-student interaction (Biddle & Berliner, 2002).

Student behavior also is better in small classes (less than twenty students), probably because of greater teacher attention and interaction, less stress on the teacher, and a more conducive social environment. With smaller numbers of students, the teacher is less distracted and can spend more time on instruction and building better relationships with students. Again, these factors favor disadvantaged students. Biddle and Berliner found that achievement gains occur in most of the academic disciplines in the early grades and are retained throughout upper elementary grades, middle school, and high school. These researchers have found that the gains apply equally to boys and girls, all age students, and particularly disadvantaged students (p. 20).

Maintaining Class Attention

> Your math class is filled; all seats are occupied. You have just begun to talk about your semester goals when another student enters the classroom. Your dilemma is whether to (1) stop talking and tell the student you have no more room, (2) reprimand the student for being late, or (3) ignore the student and expect the class to do the same.

If you select (1) you will probably forget what you were saying and the class will begin their own conversations. If you reprimand the student (2), you will waste time and embarrass the student and your class. If you try to ignore the student (3), the whole class will watch to see what the student will do next!

The answer is what Kounin (1970) called **overlapping behavior.** This means that you attend to more than one event at the same time. You continue talking about your goals, but you also signal the student to come into the classroom and you quickly pull your own desk chair out for the student to sit and listen. Then when you assign a task to the class you quietly go and talk to the new student and decide whether you can accommodate him or her in the classroom.

> You are working with a small group of students and you notice that several students sitting in the back of the classroom are talking animatedly about something other than their work. If you ignore them, there is a good chance that their behavior will be contagious to other members of the class. You are also taking the chance that the group you are working with will be too distracted to pay attention to you.

What you must do is give the group you are working with a task to focus their attention, and since you are not "rooted" to your chair, stroll back to those disruptive students and stand there giving them your very best *I mean it* expression. Very likely you will not need to say a word, and the students will be surprised at your **with-it-ness** (another of Kounin's descriptive classroom management behaviors). With-it-ness lets students know that you are not a pushover and that you are well aware of what is happening in the classroom.

> Still another annoying management problem occurs in the modern schoolroom when the loudspeaker blares or the telephone rings and disrupts your lesson, in which you were just about to clinch the most significant point of the lesson. It is no use; you need to stop either to listen and discuss the message or to answer the telephone. What do you do next to get the class back on track?

Admit that you (and the students) have been distracted. "Well, class, let's hope we are not disturbed again. Let's see if we can figure out what we were discussing." Some alternative group-focusing ideas that usually work are as follows:

1. If it is a middle or high school class, ask one or more students to read their last bit of notes aloud and encourage discussion of them.
2. With younger students, ask several students to relate the last bit of discussion and their understanding of it in their own words.
3. If students had been involved in a task assignment, ask several students to discuss their progress and then encourage everyone to get back to work.

At this point you should be ready to pull the threads of the lesson back together and say—with confidence—"I was about to help you/tell you/ask you to . . ."

Do not fear discussing classroom problems with your class. In a democratic classroom environment you want to involve students in management problems that directly concern them. Students are as concerned as you are about problems in the classroom. Meaningful learning involves confronting issues that affect our behavior. It is well worth the effort to abandon the content you were focusing on to discuss the issues that challenge the way we conduct class. Engaging students in classroom meetings about behavioral problems is a means to build student identity and a learning community in the classroom.

Did You Know That . . . ?

Hertzog (2002) reports that novice teachers typically have the following classroom management problems:

1. Keeping the majority of students busy while working with small groups of students

> 2. Behavioral problems related to the instruction of English Language Development students
> 3. Attempting to "cover" a textbook program versus using individual judgment about what is appropriate
> 4. Deciding whom to ask for help when experiencing difficulties
>
> Which of these problems trouble you?

Management-Focused Problem Solving

One of the problems that affects both novice and experienced teachers is the need for substantive fill-in activities when schedule changes, interruptions, or equipment failures spoil planned lessons. Fill-in activities need to be planned for use in emergencies. Perhaps the following activities will give you some ideas.

Elementary Classroom—Lucia Martin

Lucia Martin knew that her students had a continuing problem learning to use a dictionary productively because their alphabetizing skills were poor. Her fill-in activity was to write a list of spelling words on the chalkboard and have students alphabetize them. She challenged the students by selecting words that required looking at the second and third letters of each word.

Elementary Classroom—Jim Sierra

Jim Sierra's students had studied weather changes. Jim collected weather maps from across the country. When he needed a fill-in activity he passed out the maps and reviewed with the students a description of the six major North American air masses by drawing them on the chalkboard. The students discussed how the cold and warm fronts move, and then, working with a partner, the students listed the probable weather changes that would result from the location of highs and lows on the weather maps. They then shared their predictions and reasoning process.

Middle School Classroom—Gerry Alred

Gerry Alred displayed two large roll-down political maps of the world. She invited several students to come to the maps to see what they would notice. After several minutes the students responded that the maps were different. She asked the students at the maps and the class as a whole: "Why do you think these two maps might be different?" After a bit several students realized the countries might change their names. "Hmmm," responded Alred, "could there be other reasons?" "Maybe countries conquer each other," said a student. "Good point," replied Alred. "I'm going to pass out some current maps and some historical maps. You may also use textbooks, the Internet, and your own knowledge to find out the following." On the board she wrote: *Which countries changed their names? When did the changes occur? What major events caused the change(s)?*

Alred divided the students into groups using the tables where the students were sitting. Tables 1 and 2 studied Europe. Table 3 studied Africa. Table 4 worked on the Middle East and Table 5 focused on Asia.

High School Classroom—Jean Cantor

Jean Cantor had a collection of famous quotes and their authors. She distributed them in separate lists to her students and told them they needed to match the quote with the poet or author. The students were then required to write the context of the quote and their own interpretation of it. All of the quotes came from books the students had read. She advised them that they could use any texts in the classroom they needed and could work with a partner if they chose.

The professional teacher is constantly on the alert for creative and meaningful fill-in activities for occasions when time exceeds anticipated lesson plans. These supplementary activities need to be ready and relevant for the students you are teaching and can seldom occur if you teach "by the seat of your pants."

English Language Learners

Behavioral problems caused by ELL students who do not understand their task assignments reflect on the clarity of the assignment, your use of **sheltered English,** and verification of students' understanding. However, whatever the cause, the question you must consider is, what can you do about it now?

You have two choices, and both depend on your perception of the cause. If your presentation lacked clarity for these students, you could bring them together and use sheltered English with lots of body language and emotive expression while you go through the lesson again. Then you need to verify their understanding of the task by asking them to tell you (and the others) in their own words what they are supposed to be doing.

If you believe that English language learners understand the assignment but lack the language skills and/or confidence to carry it out, you should pair each student with a willing and knowledgeable peer who will mentor them so that they can meet the academic requirements of the lesson. Do not pair them with another English language learner unless that individual has more sophisticated skills than the individual who is having difficulty.

Chapter Summary

The definition of classroom management is the ways teachers can avoid discipline and control problems in the classroom. The social environment of the classroom is critical for working respectfully and supportively with students. Because students need experience working with their peers in both large and small groups, teachers need to carefully plan these activities to teach democratic participation and to achieve school socialization. Examples of teachers' planning activities for the first day of school were exhibited, and typical management problems for holding students' attention were discussed. The chapter concluded with ideas for substantive fill-in activities for classroom planning emergencies.

Teaching Problems

1. You are in the middle of a lesson when the school loudspeaker interrupts to urge students to sell magazine subscriptions for a fund-raiser. You are flustered; the lesson is ruined, and the students are gleeful. What can you do to settle them down? (Discuss alternate solutions with a colleague.)
2. You have been in the hall talking to a neighbor teacher. When you enter your classroom, students are sailing paper airplanes across the room. You thought your students were more mature and well behaved. You are disappointed and your first instinct is to punish them. What other options do you have?
3. Last night you went to the movies instead of planning lessons. Sometimes personal activities need to take precedence, but you can't teach by the seat of your pants. Consider your grade level and subject field(s) and plan several lessons that will not waste students' time and will contribute to their education.
4. Your students claim that they have never worked in small problem-solving groups. Describe how you will guide them.
5. Your students helped set their own classroom standards for respect, communication, classroom procedures, and group processes. If several students are not living up to those standards, what are some things that you can do about it? (Discuss this with colleagues.)
6. It is the first day of class and you have made a new-teacher mistake! You said it was time for recess and the students promptly got up and raced to the door, almost knocking you over. What should you do?

CHAPTER 7

The Classroom Community: Resolving Problems, Focusing on Student Behavior

ADVANCE ORGANIZER

These questions can be used as a framework to assist you in integrating professional knowledge and understanding of the content of this chapter.

1. In what ways does motivation affect student behavior?
2. How does student participation in valid decision making help alleviate misbehavior?
3. What are some common types of misbehavior in the classroom, causes, and remedies?
4. How does bullying affect the bully and the bully's target?
5. What are some ways to help students who lack responsibility for their work?
6. Prejudice is a serious classroom problem. Identify what teachers can do to deal with this problem.
7. Since the incident at Columbine High School, school violence has been studied by many researchers. What preventive steps can schools take?
8. Conflict resolution is an important teacher skill. Suggest ways teachers can defuse personal conflict situations and conflict that involves current controversies.

CHAPTER 7 The Classroom Community: Resolving Problems   139

 The following INTASC issues and standards are discussed in this chapter: Numbers 2–4, 6, 9.

Problems in group behavior exist among young children as well as adults. This chapter enumerates many of the problems that disrupt the classroom community, and suggests means to encourage and facilitate individual and social control. Situations include individual nonaccountability, prejudice, bullying, violence, conflict, disruptions, and misbehavior. In addition, the development of small community schools within large comprehensive schools is examined.

Mr. Bemis's Classroom Management Problem

Student misbehavior is sometimes triggered by teachers, as the following incident reveals. Ben Bemis, a middle school science teacher, began class by berating and threatening his students.

Mr. Bemis: Your assignment was to investigate the dumping of hazardous wastes and infer how this may affect our environment if we do not control it. You are experienced enough to know that you must document your resources, state your own viewpoint, and present opposing interpretations. I submitted your papers to a special computer program and discovered that the majority of the class copied what they read from Internet sources. No original ideas were presented, and as a consequence 70 percent of this class will receive an F on this assignment. I will *not* be returning your papers!

Kenneth (standing up and shaking his fist at the teacher): You can't do this. I don't remember any class session where you taught us how to cite the papers we use off of the Internet, and you are a lousy teacher!

Mr. Bemis: You will not shake your fist at me, young man, and you better sit down right now. I will not tolerate any more of your antics.

Other students (muttering): We've had quite enough of yours too! And you didn't tell us to provide opposing interpretations and viewpoints.

The class session went from bad to worse. Some students were obviously scared; most were belligerent and yelling. The teacher kept raising his voice and attempting to restore order, but he failed dismally.

If you were observing this session, whom would you blame and how would you characterize teacher and students? What advice would you offer Mr. Bemis?

Freedom and Self-Control

The essence of this chapter is the relationship between freedom and self-control. The reality of classroom teaching is that teachers must help students recognize and appreciate freedom, yet at the same time accept that living together in a classroom necessitates social control. For teachers, the important questions are as follows:

- How can we provide individual freedom to motivate interest and involvement in learning?
- How can we encourage empathy and understanding of classmates?
- How can we balance individual freedom, interpersonal conflicts, and the controls necessary for group living?

Motivation in the classroom affects both the teacher and the students. If external processes are used to reinforce desired behavior, both the teacher and students depend on classroom rewards—including grades. After a while it becomes difficult to continue to think up a reward system and constantly implement it. But if instead instruction is focused on students' satisfaction in learning (a cognitive perspective), the teaching effort is on appropriate choice of learning activities (tasks) and the emphasis is on intrinsic forces of motivation to influence students' effort. So both teachers and students are challenged to apply effort, and as a consequence they gain confidence through both the skills that are developed and what they learn from their own errors. The teacher who told her students that it was recess time, and watched them all rush to the door to exit, learned very quickly about the need to dismiss students in small groups! The student who constantly interrupts other students will learn, with appropriate guidance, that it is not socially acceptable to classmates to usurp their opportunities to contribute. Perhaps Mr. Bemis will examine his lesson plans to find out whether he taught the students problem-solving techniques for life science and how to annotate bibliographic sources.

Pastor (2002) tells the story of a little boy who constantly hit his classmates; his teacher would send him to the office to cool down. One day the principal admitted to the boy that she was extremely troubled by this situation and didn't know what to do about it. The little boy was chagrined that he was causing the principal such concern; he offered to think about the problem and see what he could do to stop himself from hitting other children. Upon reflection he decided on a plan of action, and the principal said that he was free to come in any time if he needed assistance. From that point on, the child quit hitting his classmates!

As Pastor reflected on the problem of the behavioral challenges she and her teachers were confronted with, she realized that just as academics need to be individualized, so does discipline. She concluded that too often the approach to classroom and school discipline policy was tied to Skinner's behaviorist theory and ignored human differences and growth. She likened school discipline policies to that of a penal system that fails to consider behavior and learning (p. 659).

It is extremely difficult to categorize the kinds of behavioral problems that teachers and administrators need to solve. Most obvious are the ones involving *misbehavior* (disobedience) and *disruptions* in the classroom. Another category should focus on the more subtle acts of behavior related to *social skills* and *interpersonal relations*. Finally, global attention has recently focused on the *violent behavior* of a small group of youngsters who have extreme psychological problems.

Obviously these three categories could be expanded, but they seem to encompass the majority of problems in schools today. Each will be explored in this chapter, with the focus on possible ways for teachers to avoid behavioral problems and help students learn to resolve their own problems. However, in order for students to learn to handle personal problems, teachers and administrators need to be positively involved to improve the school climate and willing to provide each other with mutual support.

Did You Know That . . . ?

Freeman, McPhail, and Berndt (2002) studied students' views of activities that facilitated learning and activities that impeded learning. Students identified active learning activities (building models, interaction with friends, and experiments) as facilitating their learning. Watching movies, drawing, and watching an experiment impeded their learning because they were easily distracted and tended not to pay attention. The researchers concluded that "students' choices in action patterns are not incidental but rather are critical to their growth as persons" (p. 336).

Disruptions and Misbehavior

Disruptions may be caused by events external to the classroom, such as loudspeakers, changes in school routines, visitors, notes from other teachers, or the breakdown of equipment. Each of these annoyances affects teaching plans and necessitates that students respond to the changes. The majority of these situations are beyond the control of the teacher, but teachers with good management skills know how to soothe their students and come up with reasonable alternatives.

A lesson that depends on the use of the Internet or perhaps a walk around school grounds on a reasonably good weather day may be spoiled by lack of Internet connections or rain. Although most teachers may have anticipated these problems with other resources, the situation provides a natural opportunity to involve students in lesson decisions by asking them, "What should we do about this?" The importance of **valid decision making** by students should not be overlooked. Asking students to help decide on alternative resources provides a means to model and teach respect and responsibility. Students in these two situations must choose another way to gain the information they need. Obviously it would be faster for the teacher to decide, but the time used for group discussion is a more valuable learning experience.

Misbehavior in the Classroom

Teachers are not professionally prepared to be psychological counselors—nor should they be. However, teachers are good observers and often can differentiate among students who are mistreated at home, students who need trained psychologists, and students who misbehave because of academic, personal, or social problems. It is important that when you experience behavioral problems in the classroom, you consider some of the possible causes of those behaviors.

Academic causes may include lack of interest and/or involvement in the lesson or activity, poor teaching, or lack of understanding of the content or task to be performed, which leads to "acting out." When misbehavior results from academic causes, students often seek more enticing activities such as talking or disturbing other students, getting up and wandering around the classroom, or demonstrating purposeful disrespect aimed at the teacher.

When these academic problems prevail over a period of time, students may become rebellious and develop consistent unacceptable work habits. Obviously it is important to explore these problems immediately with the student through a quiet one-on-one conference. You need to approach the problem in a caring and supportive manner, questioning why the student lacked attention, was easily distracted, and may need some tutoring or mentoring to gain understanding of the content or task. Good open-ended questions should provide the student with opportunity to explain his or her needs: "Yesterday I noticed that you were not really paying attention when I was explaining how to . . . I'd really like to know how to help you; can you tell me about the problem you were having?"

However, if you discover that the student does understand the content, but just enjoys disturbing others, then it may be time to call upon the entire class to discuss the problem that affects the classroom community. "Is it fair for one or two students to take advantage of the whole class by spoiling our lesson/using our time/creating a disturbance?" Generally students are quick to cite how the disturbance affected them and the inequity of attention caused by the problem.

If the behavior is unusual for this particular student, then observation techniques should be implemented to check whether the misbehavior occurs on a particular day, time, or subject. An anecdotal, situational record (Chapter 11) may be warranted to document the problem and gain insight as to the cause and possible remediation. If disturbances are pervasive, go back to Chapter 6 and think about involving the class in setting new standards that they will commit to upholding.

Misbehavior is less likely to occur in classrooms (and schools) where students are recognized as individuals with special needs. The importance of "knowing" your students cannot be overemphasized. Darling-Hammond (1997, p. 137) comments, "Environments that attend to students as individuals also help heighten the probabilities that school relationships will be characterized by respect and caring rather than by demeaning interactions, threats, and sanctions."

Sometimes tardiness to class poses a disturbance problem when the individual feels embarrassed and proceeds to enter in a manner that disrupts the entire classroom. If this occurs, it is far better to gesture to the student to sit down and be quiet, rather than make an issue of it during the middle of a lesson. Adopt an objective facade and question the individual in a respectful manner when the rest of the class is at work. Remember that if you make a scene in front of the whole class, you will end up embarrassing the entire group—yourself included. Both misbehavior and appropriate behavior are contagious!

Bullying

In a school situation, **bullying** is typically defined as intimidating, domineering, and overbearing behavior. Within the classroom the bully may be a loner who is an angry individual or one who seeks attention in any possible way. Behavioral activities may range from bumping and pushing others to gesturing, fighting, or making comments to incite riot. A private conference with the student may help discover the cause and possible means to alleviate the behaviors. For example, if the individual simply needs attention, giving this student some responsibility within the classroom or school environment may help to diminish the bullyish behavior. Sometimes asking the student to help mentor a peer or a younger child may encourage controlled behavior.

The individual who exhibits extreme anger may need the assistance of a trained professional and should be referred to the school counselor. The angry student needs help to understand why he or she feels anger, how to control the temper, and how to avoid incidents that motivate the angry feelings. After gaining some of this insight, the student can begin a self-help program, with the teacher and family providing positive feedback and encouragement.

Bullying may be physical or may involve name-calling and prejudicial behaviors. When there are several bullies in the classroom, the first action to be taken is to separate these individuals so that they are not seated together. The second action is to "invite" the students to an after-school conference with you. If you feel the need, also call in an assistant principal or another teacher to witness the conference. Third, be specific in your questions to the students, insist that each student respond, and provide ample time for their responses. This means that your questions must be planned, positively oriented, and appropriate to the age group of the students. Your objectives are to discover the purposes and causes of the students' behaviors and to help them recognize that they are hurting other students, disobeying school rules and policies, missing out on their education, and gaining nil. Olweus (2003, p. 16), who has studied bullying for the last twenty years, suggests that teachers meet individually with the bully and the victim, meet with the parents of each, and develop plans with the individuals and the parents for intervention.

The most important outcome of the conference should be to help these students develop empathy for others: "How would you feel if you were Edward and someone was deliberately making fun of you, or pushing you around?" "How do you think Jessica feels when you laugh at her speech? How would you feel if I were to laugh at you?" "Suppose you went to live in Mexico and didn't speak or understand any Spanish, what would it be like for you? What experiences do you think you would have?" "You and Jean used to be good friends; what is the matter? Why are you treating Jean this way?"

Did You Know That . . . ?

> There are gender differences in bullying behaviors. Boys feel that they must be rough and tough, according to Dr. William Pollack of Harvard University. Girls tend to use subtle means to bully others. They may turn their back on a friend, call each other names, and spread gossip. Girls will isolate others through body language or refusing to talk to the target of their bullyish behavior (Simmons, 2002).

Signs of Bullying

Both boys and girls exhibit similar signs when they are the targets of bullying. They often do not want to attend school, reject meeting with other students, and are extremely moody. They may appear depressed, tired, shy, and irritable. Sometimes they act out bullying behaviors themselves by taking out their aggressions on younger children and siblings.

Teachers and parents can help victims of bullies through communicating with each other about the problem and encouraging the victim to talk about the problem. Try to help the victim connect with other students and develop friendships and allies who will help when he or she is being attacked (Pollack, 2002).

Teaching Hints: Helping Victims of Bullying

1. Identify the type of bullying experienced by the victim and when it occurs.
2. Note that the presence of an adult eliminates bullying.
3. Help the victim by reminding him or her of personal rights.
4. Role-play what the victim should do when subjected to bullying.

Rudeness and Defiance

In the incident at the beginning of the chapter, Kenneth was obviously rude to his teacher. There were extenuating circumstances, but very likely Kenneth may have had a history of discourteous behavior. Kenneth's response to his teacher motivated other students' defiant reactions. In most cases the defiant student is asking for help, but is wary of requesting assistance from the teacher or does not know how to do so.

What should you do when a student is publicly rude to you? Clearly you cannot respond to the student in front of the whole class; you do not want to put on a show. "Ms. James /Stephanie/ (however you normally address your students), I realize that you are upset; please be seated, and we will have a chat in the back of the room in just a moment."

Continue on with the class in your normal speaking voice. Make sure that you clarify what the class is to do; ask if anyone needs assistance; put the class to work; exude confidence in your role as teacher. Next, approach the offending student, take a couple of complete breaths, and ask the student to accompany you to a quiet section of the classroom. Control your own personal feelings and take on the role of an expert listener. "Stephanie, please tell me what is troubling you. I want to know if I did something to hurt your feelings."

Now suppose Stephanie was not at her desk when the altercation occurred. Go and stand near the student, but not close enough to touch her. In a quiet voice tell the student that you will give her your full attention in a moment. Then continue on as suggested earlier. There are two basic principles in this situation. First, you want the class to know that you are not going to touch the student; second, you will deal with the situation in a calm adult manner.

Outright, vocal disrespect cannot be tolerated in the classroom. If you cannot deal with the situation through a personal conference reminding the student of classroom and school rules, then it may be necessary to send the student to the school discipline officer. This reality may require that you will allow the student to return to class only with a signed agreement that his or her classroom behavior will be monitored and that it must improve.

Nonaccountability

A student who consistently fails to complete work, meet deadlines or due dates, or return homework assignments lacks responsibility. However, there may be many reasons why the student fails to complete work: lack of understanding, lack of "tools" or a place to do homework at home, or absence of self-confidence and assertiveness.

Helping the student may require patience, setting contract goals, private conferences, and meeting with parents or guardians. The first step is usually a private conference between teacher and student to discuss the problem and try to determine the cause. Quite often students who are nonaccountable set very lofty and impossible goals for themselves and as a consequence "give up." Thus the teacher must help the student set realistic, achievable goals. If an elementary student can accomplish work on only three story problems, then set that goal and congratulate the student for the achievement. Next time help the student set a higher goal. For a middle or high school student who undertakes projects that are too complicated, assist the student in choosing a project that is less complex and can be accomplished in less time using fewer resources.

Though the foregoing may be the best way to deal with the problem, it is usually a good idea to let parents in on the situation so that both the family and the school can work together with the student to develop procedures for completing assigned tasks. Parents know their children best and can tell you if the student has home chores or extracurricular work that interferes with school work.

When talking with both the student and the parents, question how much time the student has for sleep. Middle school students are notorious for wasting time, watching too much television, and coming to school tired. One should also question whether there are too many homework assignments and whether these assignments are "busywork" or productive, application-level thinking assignments.

Private talks with students should focus on the ways adults are accountable in the workplace, community contributions, religious activities, and social situations. Help the student recognize that all of us are accountable and responsible to our peers, our family,

Work time is often disrupted by small skirmishes that can be settled by separating the students, talking quietly to them, or simply giving them an "I mean it!" stare.

and our friends. If none of this helps the student improve in work habits, it is time to obtain professional help from the school counselor or the family physician.

Interruption and Speaking Out

It's not a disease, but some students seem to feel the need to interject comments while others are speaking. For these students it often becomes a habit, and their interruptions lead to discontinuity during discussion time, when others are asking work-related questions, and during lesson presentations. Reasons for this are hard to pinpoint. It may be that the student rarely has anyone listening to him or her and so the classroom provides an audience. The student may be seeking attention or may be nervous, overly competitive, or just plain impulsive.

Several techniques are available to help the teacher deal with the "incessant interruptor":

1. Use the classroom community to help you. Turn to the class and say, "Mark has disrupted our discussion, and I see that many of you are annoyed." Then, depending on the age of the students you are working with, you can ask a variety of questions to obtain the community viewpoint:

- "How do you feel when you are interrupted?"
- "What can we tell Mark to help him remember to keep his comments to himself unless he is contributing to the discussion?"
- "Why is it important to listen to the flow of a discussion before speaking out?"

2. Stop whatever is happening in the classroom and focus on Mark. Ask him if he knows who was speaking. Wait for the response. Then ask Mark how he would feel if he were constantly interrupted.

3. Use nonverbal gestures while making eye contact with Mark. Shake your head and place a finger across your mouth, or hold your hand in the traditional "stop" gesture while making eye contact.

4. Calmly tell Mark that you want to talk privately with him when the discussion is over. During your private conversation, attempt to find out what causes him to interrupt so often. If it appears that the reason(s) is inoffensive and unwitting, set a goal with him to count how many times he interrupts and see if he can control himself to curtail the interruptions.

5. Sometimes the individual monopolizes conversation during group work. This was discussed in Chapter 6. Give the student a role to perform (group recorder) and see if that helps the situation.

Social Skills and Interpersonal Relations

> Sally's grades in her high school physics class suddenly dropped. She appeared sad and moody in class. It was clear to the teacher that something had to be wrong. When Sally was interviewed by the teacher, she denied that anything was awry; however, good observation and the right question finally got Sally to share her problem. The teacher observed: "I've noticed that you and Terry no longer seem to be friends. What has happened?"
>
> Sally burst into tears and confided that Terry seemed to have new friends now and was ignoring her. Sally did not feel that she had "done anything" to hurt Terry and was at a loss as to the cause.
>
> The teacher proceeded to hold a private conversation with Terry and learned that Terry thought that Sally had "broken" their friendship.

In this case a wise teacher noted the discrepant behavior, interviewed the students, and suggested that each girl write a letter to the other. The written interaction remedied the situation and the girls resumed their friendship. Written communication helps protect the writer's inner feelings and self-concept because they are not observed, yet still expressed.

Students' social skills with their peers often trigger many classroom problems because they intrude on the student's concentration, affect self-concept, and may lead to behavior problems such as interrupting class work. These occur primarily because of hurt feelings that result from being left out of social activities, feelings of isolation, inability to make friends, or not being invited to special events.

Though these problems happen more often at the middle school level, they can occur among upper-elementary students and less mature high school students. We tend to associate social problems primarily with girls, yet the data that emerges from incidents such as that at Columbine and other schools reveals that boys, too, are affected by isolation, prejudice, and the inability to "break into" the desired crowd.

What Can Teachers Do?

No matter what subject we teach, we cannot get into the heads and hearts of our students unless we provide opportunity for students to talk about their problems and their interests. The culture of the classroom must offer opportunities for students to express themselves, work within their peer culture to develop friendships, pose questions (even if those questions are unrelated to the subject field), and get involved. If students are expected to just sit and absorb, their minds go elsewhere. Peer groupings, student-posed questions about learning, and student exploration of the questions that interest them build a community of learners.

When you take the time to sit in on student groups and listen with the "inner ear," you develop the insight to counsel and guide young people not only to assume responsibility for their own knowledge but to help others. Provide a wealth of opportunities for students to experience real-world problems in the course or subject you teach; provide opportunity for all students to lead exploration into student-posed problems; and you will help resolve students' social problems while building subject field knowledge.

Prejudice in the Classroom

Prejudice has a significant effect on interactions in the classroom and school. Gordon Allport's comprehensive study (1954) of its origin and nature is considered classic. Allport defines prejudice briefly as "thinking ill of others without sufficient warrant" (p. 7). However, further study acknowledges that prejudice can be both favorable and negative. The words *without sufficient warrant* are critical to the definition.

Prejudice involves *prejudgments*. Individuals who will consider evidence and are flexible enough to reverse their judgment using that evidence as a deciding factor are not considered prejudiced. The integral components of prejudice have to do with attitudes and beliefs; the prejudiced individual has an attitude that favors or disfavors the target subject *and* is related to an erroneous belief. While it is sometimes possible to affect an individual's beliefs through rational discourse and evidence, it is more difficult (if not impossible) to change pre-existing attitudes.

The prejudiced individual uses *stereotypes* to justify and rationalize beliefs. For example, when talking about Latinos, some Caucasian students said, "They are clannish; they refuse to speak English; they are dirty and lazy." The students were using the stereotypes to justify their dislike of the Latino students. That the statements lacked truth and understanding never penetrated because the students had heard these statements from others.

Prejudicial attitudes are traditionally acquired in the home. Children hear their parents or other adults express beliefs and conclude the accuracy of those beliefs. Reinforcement of beliefs may occur in the school when students see the target group clustering together and participating in in-group communication. Though it is quite natural for English language learners to seek out other students who speak the same language, this is often disregarded. In the community, new immigrants will try to live close to others of the same nationality in order to gain assistance. The consequence, of course, is a ghetto community.

It is often said that *values* (which are beliefs) are "caught, not taught." So parents do not have to teach their children to distrust or hate other ethnic groups; when distrust or hate exists in the home, it just rubs off! However, since the school is a social agency and is so significant in the child's development, it is certainly possible to model appropriate behavior and influence students. For this reason, the development of the classroom community is important to our democratic way of life.

The teaching episode that opens Chapter 1 provides an example of prejudicial behavior in which students openly admitted that they didn't like working with specific ethnic peers. The teacher immediately referred the problem to the entire class, with the result that the students recognized that their classroom rules were in jeopardy. The community of learners in Ms. Alred's class decided that the rules should be upheld. (The rule in question was that students must demonstrate respect to all of their classmates.)

When prejudice is encountered in the classroom, teachers have several options. The first option is to take aim and target the problem by teaching directly about religious, cultural, and ethnic diversity. The second option is to teach about the problem through a variety of subject fields, such as history, English, and geography. Provide information and study problems involving different groups of people throughout history who have suffered as a consequence of discrimination. For example, many school districts customarily ignored black and Asian literature in favor of Western European and American literature. The third option is to develop a number of service learning projects that involve students in participatory activities within minority communities. The fourth option is to be certain that students participate in learning groups that are diverse in every conceivable way.

Teaching Hints: Prejudice in the Classroom

1. Create group projects and learning teams that involve students who are diverse in culture, race, and religion.
2. Teach directly about prejudice and stereotyping.
3. Use a variety of subject fields to teach about the roles and problems of diverse groups.
4. Role-play social problems encountered by diverse groups. "How would you feel if you were . . . and this occurred?"

Gang Activities

Most student group activities occur after school; while they may not even be linked to the school, most result from lack of recognition in the school environment. Student groups or gangs are made up of the jocks, the nerds, and social cliques of both sexes. When students become hostile, their behavior affects the classroom.

Gang activities are quite obvious in students' clothing, body language, humor, exclusiveness, and general behavior toward others. Observant teachers recognize the signs; while in some cases such groups may not cause a problem, in general, they do.

School approaches to control gang activity are limited. Community social agencies can help. Bateson (2001) writes about "the need to teach citizens to entertain multiple points of view" (p. 116). Schools and teachers are pretty good at helping students recognize what it would be like if they were the ostracized individual. The "out group" or the ostracized individual knows only too well how the gang operates and typically tries to distance himself or herself from conflict situations. But only through participation in a democratic community can we teach about the significance of diversity and require critical thinking about behavior and feelings. Teachers can help students recognize that there are alternative ways of thinking about problems, and that all individuals have the right to express their thoughts.

As a teacher I do not believe that I have the right to select certain values that I may consider "good" and then try to teach them. What I can do is guide students to respect their peers and accept responsibility for their own behavior. One approach is to provide opportunity for students to set their own goals for accomplishing learning in a subject field or a unit of study, and then hold them responsible for their actions. This is true for behavioral problems as well as academic problems.

Another approach is the class meeting model, in which students express their own viewpoint related to a specific value such as reliability, kindness, or caring. Ask students to provide examples of how these characteristics play out in their own behavior. Give them some examples to think about:

- "You are in the mall and you find a little boy crying and looking around for his parent. You do not see the parent nearby. What would you do in this situation?"

- "You were riding your bike over to a friend's house. In order to get there quickly, you were riding along on the sidewalk. Because of your speed you frightened an older woman who was carrying groceries. She dropped the bags she was carrying. What would you do in this situation?"

- "You are on the playground with your gang and all of you cluster around the drinking fountain, blocking the fountain from use by others. You see another student who wants to use the fountain. Would you ignore this? What would you do?"

Note that in these situations the question is not, "What could or should you do?" After obtaining a number of responses, ask students to pose several dilemmas and debate them. When possible, use dilemmas that are reality based, such as stories from the battlefields about "buddies" that are hurt or about killing or maiming innocent people in the villages of Vietnam, Iraq, or Afghanistan. The point is to push students to feel for others, consider emotion, and recognize the need for helpfulness and responsibility.

Recreational clubs may seem rather mild in terms of a cause of behavioral problems in the classroom; yet when these clubs or groups meet during classroom time, students who are left behind feel that they are not getting a fair shake because the only alternative left to them is more academic work. This situation occurs when students are pulled out of class to attend a band meeting, orchestra practice, or some other school activity (yearbook or newspaper committee meeting, football practice, drama club, photography club, and so on). School-related clubs need to offer something to every student if school time is to be used, so that the club program is inclusive and all students have time out—regardless of their grade point average.

Sports activities are often the key incentive that attract students to attend school. When these activities are curtailed because teachers feel there are more important areas of the curriculum to teach, students are missing out on physical fitness and interaction with peers. At the middle and high school levels, some schools prohibit participation if students' grades are below par; however, frequently the student who is poor in academic subject fields needs sports activities the most. Team sports are the raison d'etre of school for many students.

Did You Know That . . . ?

> Raywid and Oshiyama (2000) studied violent activity in large and small high schools and noted that small schools were more likely to make the school a genuine learning community. Rigid rules affecting dress, speech, and behavior make students feel anonymous. They concluded that schools need to cultivate students' acceptance of each other, empathy, and compassion.

School Violence

Prejudice, loneliness, isolation, personality problems, lack of supervision, parental mistreatment—all of these may cause students to be violent. The truth is we really do not know what makes some individuals exhibit violent behavior. Since the 1999 incident at Columbine High School, school districts have taken a number of steps to improve the safety of our schools: greater collaboration between law enforcement and school officials, realization by students that they need to report suspicions and threats to school officials, alerting school counselors to bullying activities, and greater community involvement in the prevention of violence (Bowman, 2002a).

Large Schools Versus Small Schools

Raywid and Oshiyama (2000) point out that when schools have a student population of several thousand, it is very difficult to develop a sense of community. Large schools breed alienation because students are anonymous entities; few teachers and administrators can associate students' names with their faces. School counselors in large schools are required to see too many students; their counseling is limited to programming classes, not detecting individual problems or providing traditional behavioral guidance.

In a synthesis of the studies of school violence, Raywid and Oshiyama found that the larger the school, the more violence, student alienation, and teacher dissatisfaction. There are also more behavior problems and greater difficulty in maintaining an orderly school environment. These researchers report that smaller schools have less truancy, discipline

Unsupervised areas of the school grounds are often the sites selected for school violence.

problems, substance abuse, and gang participation. In addition, students considered "at risk" are less likely to be alienated from their classmates in the smaller school environment (p. 445). Ark (2002) corroborates these findings. His studies indicate that smaller high schools have higher attendance rates and fewer dropouts. In addition, he states that teachers in smaller schools are more satisfied with their jobs and the students have higher grade point averages (p. 55).

What Can Schools Do?

Fundamental changes are needed in schools in order to build "community." Though it may not be possible to tear down the huge comprehensive high school or middle school that enrolls two to three thousand students, it is possible to create "schools within schools" in order to accomplish the qualities that motivate students to feel accepted as members of the school community and to develop personal relationships with teachers and peers.

By creating a variety of "community schools" within the larger structure of the overall school, attributes that enhance small schools can be modeled. Each community works as a team. The team, which can be composed of students at different grade levels or at the same level, stays together throughout the school experience. Each community has a theme and purpose that guides its curriculum; teachers work as a team to develop curriculum. Each community is autonomous and makes the decisions that affect the cohort of students and the teachers. Schools within schools have a population no larger than 200 students. Arrangements can be made among the different community schools to allow students to enroll in a special class within a different community when it is desired by the student.

> **Teaching Hints: Creating Small Community Schools**
>
> 1. Develop "community" schools that are organized as "schools within schools."
> 2. The community school has a team of students and teachers who stay together over a period of time.
> 3. Each community school has a theme and purpose; teachers develop collaboratively an interdisciplinary curriculum.
> 4. Each community school is autonomous; teachers work as reflective professional leaders and make it a point to know all of the students.

Advantages of the Small-School and "Schools-Within-Schools" Concepts

There are a number of personal, professional, and curricular advantages to breaking down a large school into smaller components or schools within schools. The personal advantage is that everyone knows everyone else. Teachers learn the names and personalities of the cohort of students. Students are together for several years and have the opportunity to make a variety of friendships. Students are not anonymous; teachers know when students are absent and present.

Professionally, teachers work reflectively with their colleagues to develop curriculum and make decisions that affect their professional lives. The students can contribute to set standards for their community environment and contribute to curricular teams with defined themes and purposes. Professional development can be designed by the teachers to enhance their own performance and effectiveness. Everyone is responsible for the environment of the community and the vision of the curriculum.

Student behavior and learning problems can be handled by teachers consulting with each other. Students have more access to professional help and can develop personal relationships with teachers because of the continuity and closeness of the community. Students are visible—and this is perhaps the most important point. In a relatively small community, everyone knows what is happening; no one can hide, and teachers can intervene quickly if problems emerge. Working professionally as a team, teachers can act before student behavior gets out of hand.

School Environment and Supervision

Every school has areas described as "unowned" (Astor, Meyer, & Behre, 1999). These public spaces, which are typically unsupervised because they are not viewed as anyone's responsibility, include hallways, stairs, bicycle rack areas, parking lots, sometimes lunch areas and cafeteria, areas of the playground, and the school library. They make wonderful hiding areas, and students interested in creating havoc use them to meet and to plot.

Though some of these areas are supervised by instructional or playground aides, uncertificated adults do not seem to make much of an impression on students. For some reason, when teachers take over the supervision there are fewer incidents of violent behavior. Rarely has there been any problem within classrooms where teachers are in charge. Since the Columbine incident, many schools are attempting to alleviate this situation by asking teachers to be more visible when students are changing classrooms, going out for recess and lunch, and leaving at the end of the school day.

> **Teaching Hints: Alleviating School Violence**
>
> - Teachers need to be more visible and monitor "unowned" space.
> - Use group work to diminish prejudice and bullying behavior.
> - Allow more time for students to practice communication skills and talk out disagreements.
> - Confer with students who are reacting to conflict situations; act as mediator.
> - Use role-playing as a means for students to resolve problems.
> - Evaluate with students their skills in resolving problems through compromise and negotiation.

Conflict Resolution

Conflict among students arises at every level of education. Some conflicts are at the personal level and pertain to students' interactions and beliefs; other types of conflict occur in the classroom when controversial issues are discussed. Regardless of the cause, students need to know how to handle disagreements so that they do not hold grudges or come to blows. We will examine two different types of controversies that result in student conflict—personal conflict and conflict involving a current controversy.

Personal Conflict Fifth-grade students have just returned to the classroom after playing basketball at lunchtime. Several of the students are hopping mad. The teacher, Mike Davies, recognizes that something happened and it will be impossible to teach without resolving the conflict. Mr. Davies inquires about the problem and students respond simultaneously, but clearly not in agreement.

> *Various Students:* John's team doesn't play fair. Bill purposely tripped Sam so he couldn't make a basket. It was Sam's fault; he ran into Bill. You're lying.
>
> *Mr. Davies:* OK. Let's stop this. Sam, tell me what you think happened.
>
> *Sam:* I was running down the court and Bill stuck out his leg so that I would fall.
>
> *Mr. Davies:* Bill, what happened?
>
> *Bill:* I was trying to guard Sam. He ran into me and fell, but I didn't trip him; he just fell.

Further inquiry by Mr. Davies demonstrated that the truth was somewhere in between what the two teams observed and were willing to accept. Mr. Davies decided on an experiment; he called four students to the front of the classroom and whispered to them. The students were asked to leave the classroom, then come back in and pretend to be physically fighting with each other. After several minutes, Mr. Davies stopped the "fight" and asked the class what they observed. As he had anticipated, the observations differed dramatically. Mr. Davies began to question the students: "You were all here, why do your accounts of what happened differ?"

The students responded, "We didn't expect to see our classmates fighting. We were all looking at different things. We didn't watch at the exact same moment."

"Now I wonder," said Mr. Davies, "if you can apply this incident to the playground squabble that occurred today." More classroom discussion resulted in the following realizations:

1. You see what you expect to see, not what necessarily happened.
2. Because we were competing, Sam's team assumed that Bill was not playing fair, and Bill's team assumed that Sam purposely fell.
3. We didn't ask for or listen to Bill's and Sam's explanations. Each team thought the other team was lying.

Mr. Davies summarized the situation and recommended that the students work on good sportsmanship and fair play. Had he not allotted time to play-act and discuss this situation, hard feelings would have carried over out of school and in successive encounters. More frequently than not, teachers can prevent future conflict by helping students clarify and reflect on different points of view.

Conflict over Controversial Issues Opposing viewpoints dealing with controversial issues are commonplace, and students typically handle the conflict without too much heat. However, teachers do need to be alert and help students recognize that there are always multiple ways to view an event. Let us observe in Ms. Echols's high school economics

---

Teaching Hints: Conflict Resolution

1. Allow time for students to vent their feelings and emotions.
2. Elicit personal statements from the combatants.
3. Clarify what happened and focus on different perspectives.
4. Help students define the problem, including the cause.
5. Elicit probable consequences of the problem.
6. Discuss ways to resolve the problem.
7. Decide on future actions to prevent conflict(s).

classroom. The students have reviewed some of the newspaper and journal articles that have been written about the Enron, Tyco, and WorldCom cases. Ms. Echols suggests a discussion about the three cases. She begins by asking, "What are the facts that we know about this problem?" (Students respond without being called upon; almost everyone participates.)

- Employees lost their retirement savings and their jobs.
- Stockbrokers lied to their clients about the value of the stocks they were selling.
- Bankers approved of the practice of inflating the stocks.
- The public lost money when people in the know, such as the chief executive officers (CEOs), sold out.
- The CEOs didn't admit that they were doing anything wrong in the way they were running their company, and they took advantage of what they knew.
- The accounting firm and company executives destroyed their work papers, and the profit-and-loss statements were not accurate.

Ms. Echols nods as she listens to the students. When it appears that the students have commented on most of what they know, she suggests a role-play in which groups of students act out the roles of the major participants. The groups include stockbrokers, employees, bankers, the public, and CEOs. Students select a group and each group meets as a caucus to frame their opening remarks.

Stockbrokers: Our job is to reel in the customers and promise them deals by "covering" the stock.

Employees: The company officers were bandits. They knew what was happening and they sold out before the stock bottomed out. Employees weren't allowed to sell their stock.

Bankers: We lent money to the companies because it looked like a good risk and the stockbrokers did a great job of peddling the junk.

CEOs: We only did what our contracts allowed us to do—buy and sell our stock options. We did nothing wrong.

The public: The stockbrokers "praised" the stock offerings and recommended them to us—the investors. We were taken in and cheated.

Ms. Echols comments that each group represented the perspective accurately. "Can anyone synthesize what has been expressed?" Jeremy volunteers, "Well, based on the opinions expressed and what we have read, it seems to me that these large companies lied to the public about their profits, and the stockbrokers helped by encouraging people to buy the stock. As a consequence, the public and employees lost their savings and the corporate bosses made out good!"

Ms. Echols suggests that each group choose one member to represent the group and the representatives will role-play the conflict of interest. Each group selects and coaches its representative. When the students are ready, Ms. Echols suggests that they tackle the question of social values: "Are there value questions that confront us, and if so what are they?"

Bob: Should the CEOs be paid these huge bonuses and perks? They cashed out and left everyone else holding the bag.

Louise: But if the CEOs don't get fat contracts, they won't take the job and will go to a competitor who is willing to pay it.

Mary: What we are looking at is the question of corporate honesty. That's the main social value and the question is, should a company be allowed to deceive the public about its profits and losses?

Sal: Big companies always lie when they are trying to sell a product; the public should expect it. It's your own fault if you invest too heavily in a single company.

Jeremy: Yeah, that may be true, but what about the employees who weren't given a choice in terms of their retirement funds? The employees did not have equal opportunity—that's a social and ethical value.

Ted (red-faced and confronting Sal and Louise): It seems to me that you are excusing dishonesty. Everybody lied to the public and the employees. Now they're caught and trying to say that this is the standard way of doing business.

Ms. Echols (facing class): Do you agree with the role-players?

Rena: The role-players seem to all agree that the value of honesty has been violated.

Ann: Yeah, and Jeremy says equal opportunity is in violation, but the major question that they raised is whether the company actions should be condoned because it is common practice in the business world.

Ms. Echols: Good summation. Let's have each group choose a new representative to discuss some analogies that demonstrate this point. Remember to coach your role representative.

New Enactment

Margie: The drug companies are a good example. They don't necessarily report their negative findings about new drugs and the public suffers.

William: That's true, but then the public sues and the FDA makes the company pull the drug off the market.

Glen: So are you saying that it is all right to lie to the public because they have recourse through the courts?

William: Of course not, but we all know it happens; it's business as usual.

Sue: The auto manufacturers are another example. They seem to always need to recall certain models—after fires, blowouts, and accidents. The public always gets hurt.

Ms. Echols: Those are good examples. Let's get back to the cases now, and the whole class should take part. What do you predict will be the consequences of this situation?

The discussion concludes with the whole class participating in projecting the consequences. There were several phases to the discussion; it is patterned after the *jurisprudential* teaching model (Joyce & Weil, 1999). The problem focused on a conflict among economic groups. The phases included the following:

1. An open discussion to identify the factual issues
2. A focused discussion of the perspectives of the groups involved in the problem
3. A caucus-type role-play emphasizing the social values that were violated
4. A second enactment with a focus on analogies that are similar to the original problem and may shed light on the consequences
5. A whole-class discussion focused on prediction of consequences for the current conflict

Caucus group role-play has advantages and disadvantages. Participating in a role-play is sometimes embarrassing for students. The shy, introverted student dislikes "being on stage" with everyone listening and watching. The aggressive student tends to "ham it up" for the audience. By using the caucus group role-play, the whole class feels involved. Groups are pulling for their spokesperson, whom they have coached. The spokesperson uses the ideas of the whole group while participating in the actual enactment. When dealing with conflict involving controversial issues, the caucus group method allows everyone to contribute ideas and beliefs, which can improve the thinking process.

The only disadvantage to the caucus group role-play is the possibility that a group may "railroad" someone into being the spokesperson. It behooves the teacher to closely monitor the groups when they are generating group ideas and preparing their representative for the enactment. When conflict deals with personal issues, such as the basketball skirmish discussed earlier, the caucus group is not as effective as having the individuals who were involved in the problem perform the role-play.

Teaching Hints: Caucus Group Role-Play

1. Teacher sets motivation related to a problem.
2. Class discusses the problem.
3. Students are divided into groups to discuss and decide on the group's perspective.
4. Groups choose and coach a spokesperson.
5. Spokespeople enact a role-play.
6. The whole class discusses the enactment.
7. Groups choose a new spokesperson.
8. The new spokespeople enact a new role-play.
9. The whole class discusses consequences and generalizes about the problem.

Students with Special Needs

We always need to be alert to the problems of students with special needs. The English language learner who has difficulty communicating questions about work tasks or participating in group activities needs a buddy for assistance. If there is no buddy, then the teacher must assume the responsibility. The teacher's responsibility does not end with providing instruction for the English language learner. It is critical that the whole class recognizes the need to be accepting, patient, empathetic, and willing to provide needed assistance.

Students with physical problems also need special assistance, particularly when the class is working in small groups. It is not unusual for a classmate to break a limb and have a temporary special need that involves the use of equipment for walking or sitting. If special needs are not considered, students will have too much time for distraction and behavioral problems will emerge. A wise teacher organizes work tasks and interaction so that all students can participate and classroom management problems are avoided.

Chapter Summary

If schools and classrooms have not developed a sense of community, behavioral problems escalate. These problems may progress from simple irritants of compulsive talking to bullying, prejudice, social and interactional problems, and even school violence. Teachers' skills are severely tested when students act out their behavioral problems instead of engaging in productive communication. Class meetings, student participation in decisions about class problems, teacher-student-parent conferences, and role-playing are some techniques that teachers can use to alleviate classroom problems. An important teacher skill is learning to use techniques for conflict resolution.

Teaching Problems

1. Ben was large for his age and constantly in motion. He wanted to be first in line or first to get supplies. To accomplish this, he would push other students aside. He was pals with several other boys in class, but the others were not really as irritating. Other students and their parents complained about him, and many of his classmates tried to stay away from him. On the playground, the playground supervisors considered him a menace. Obviously Ben was a genuine bully. You are his teacher and you have been asked by students, parents, and the playground supervisors to do something. What procedures will you follow?

2. You teach in a relatively affluent school district. Parents expect a lot from their children and the school district is known for its academic toughness. Recently there has been a string of robberies at the high school, both within the school and in the parking lot. Teachers are not paid particularly well as compared to larger districts nearby, and as a consequence teachers feel they are not responsible for supervising students during pass time between class periods, recess, lunch, or after school. The high school has not made any plans to prevent school violence or means to curb the robberies. What suggestions do you think should be made?

3. Marguerita appeared to be a loner. She rarely spoke in class; however, the teacher recognized that she was nervous about speaking English. Middle school students in this school tend to be cliquish and Marguerita was not included in any of the groups. In fact, the other students either ignored her or seemed to make fun of her. Her teacher concluded that her students were exhibiting prejudicial behavior. What can she do about it?

PART 4

INSTRUCTIONAL STRATEGIES

Instruction is the teacher's delivery system for teaching subject field content. Three teaching models are introduced in Chapter 8. These three models are considered **expository** strategies. Also included in this chapter is cooperative learning, research about it, and its advantages and disadvantages. Questioning strategies and classroom discussions are addressed, as well as typical discussion problems. The chapter concludes with information about teaching with standards. Chapter 9 focuses on **inquiry** teaching strategies. Several teaching models are explained along with classroom management hints. Questioning strategies are again discussed, but in this chapter the focus is on divergent strategies along with the concept of wait time. The use of resources and problem-solving techniques for inquiry teaching conclude the chapter.

Jigsaw chap. 8

Table 1 - 163-169
2 - 170-177
3 - 178-184
4 184-189

CHAPTER 8

Selecting from an Instructional Repertoire

ADVANCE ORGANIZER

These questions can be used as a framework to assist you in integrating professional knowledge and understanding of the content of this chapter.

1. Authentic teaching and authentic performance focus on quality teaching and students' active participation in their own learning. Can you contrast these concepts with scripted approaches in textbook manuals?
2. Expository teaching strategies are used to convey specific information and skills to students. How are these strategies used in democratic and constructivist classrooms?
3. Direct instruction requires three distinct practice activities. Differentiate the purpose of each of the three practice activities.
4. Cooperative groups can provide opportunities for students of different cultural and language groups to interact socially. What are the advantages and disadvantages of cooperative group strategies? How does cooperative learning affect achievement?

5. Wait time, reinforcement, and interaction are keys to good questioning strategies. How are these teaching techniques used, and how can they improve instruction for students who are not proficient in English?
6. Discussions in democratic and autocratic environments differ. What are the characteristics of discussions in democratic classrooms?

The following INTASC issues and standards are discussed in this chapter: Numbers 1–5, 7, 9, 10.

The major focus of this chapter is on expository teaching strategies. Three teaching models are demonstrated through teaching scenarios. Different types of cooperative teaching models that emphasize learning skills are featured in the chapter, and questioning strategies and classroom discussions are applied to teaching scenarios.

Jimmy: I don't understand why you are so upset with us, Ms. Alred.

Ms. Alred: Jimmy, don't you recognize that you are acting prejudicially and disrespectfully when you refuse to work with other students in the classroom?

Jimmy: I don't think I understand what you mean; I just don't like Roberto and Sonia. They're always talking Spanish.

Ms. Alred: We agreed at the beginning of the semester that we are a community and that in our community, we respect each other. I think perhaps we need to have a lesson that clearly explains what it means to be prejudiced. We will do that in conjunction with our spelling lesson.

Authentic Teaching

Authentic teaching means that we teach *what* is needed, *when* it is needed and relevant, and do so *appropriately*. In the foregoing scenario it was clear to Gerry Alred that Jimmy and perhaps other students needed to understand the concept of prejudice. She did not think she should wait for other occasions to teach about the concept. Instead she would integrate it with her spelling lesson that very day. She recognized the "teachable moment."

To fully understand the pedagogical principle of authentic teaching, we need to understand what it is *not*. Teachers' textbook manuals are sequenced in ways deemed appropriate by textbook authors. Often the chapters are considered to be short units of study. Because the textbook takes the pressure off the teacher to find resources and to sequence what is to be taught, teachers often accept the text's arrangement of content and suggestions for how the content should be delivered. But both the selection of concepts to be taught, the order of when it is to be taught, and the instructional method for teaching are geared to a fictional "normal" population that rarely matches the students you are teaching. As a consequence, if you follow the textbook manual you become a slave to the text. (This is often referred to as using the text as a bible.)

Teachers who accept the textbook as the guide for instruction sometimes feel guilty about departing from the text's suggested coverage. But students' texts are not designed to provide both breadth and depth of content, so without the teacher's professional knowledge, students receive a very lean diet of content. It is important to remember that content influences students' achievement, and your own professional development has helped you acquire knowledge about the subject field you are teaching; students' knowledge, development, culture, and experiences; and pedagogical principles to provide appropriate instruction. So pat yourself on the back and realize that you are competent to judge what is to be taught.

Authentic teaching also requires that students respond in authentic ways. This means that students are taught to recognize that knowledge taught by the teacher and the textbook reflect personal experiences and social contexts. Because other viewpoints should be sought, it is important that students learn how to seek alternative ideas and beliefs and learn to apply critical judgment to their own and others' values and perspectives.

Authentic performance from students involves participation in activities, application of concepts, extracurricular activities, and interaction with other students. In this chapter, expository teaching strategies will be examined; historically, this has meant that students were expected to be quiet and "consume" what was presented. However, instead of students' passive performance, the demonstrations will exhibit ways for students to apply knowledge and skills in relevant, meaningful ways. (Chapter 9 will demonstrate higher-order teaching strategies.)

The Direct Instruction Model of Teaching

At the beginning of each new academic year, the famed Wizard of Westwood, John Wooden, began the basketball season by demonstrating to his freshmen how to tie their shoelaces! Surely they must have known how to tie their shoes, you say to yourself. Yes, of course, but too frequently their shoes would become untied on the basketball court, and so Wooden gave a special demonstration on how to ensure that this would not happen. He would then ask the students to practice, and he would observe and make appropriate suggestions, if needed. During the actual training sessions on the basketball court, he could observe the application of the skill lesson.

Direct instruction is a teaching strategy that is used to *demonstrate* a skill or *present* very specific information. After the initial demonstration or presentation, three distinct practice sessions occur. The first practice session is used to verify students' understanding, and this occurs through the teacher's questioning of the students. The second practice session focuses on students' practice or use of what was taught, and the teacher walks around monitoring and guiding students' work. The third practice session involves students in the application of what they have learned; this may occur in the classroom or as an out-of-school activity.

> **Teaching Hints: Direct Instruction**
>
> 1. Demonstrate a skill or present specific information.
> 2. Provide structured practice through teacher questioning.
> 3. Provide guided practice with teacher monitoring.
> 4. Have students apply the skill or knowledge (authentic performance).
> 5. Assess the product.

Gerry Alred's Classroom

Gerry Alred began by saying to the students that she would like to tell them about an incident she experienced. She then pulled down a map of Europe and told the students that when she was an elementary student, she had several classmates from the Balkans. (She pointed to the area on the map.) Every time one of them was called upon to answer a question or tried to volunteer information, the class would laugh. "Their English is funny," some would say. Sometimes other students would hide their faces behind their hands, and giggle. After a while the new students refused to volunteer information and would shake their heads when the teacher called on them. When students were asked to form teams for play or group work, the Balkan students were never included.

"What do you think of the students in that classroom? Jeannette?"

"I think they weren't very caring. They were disrespectful."

"Billy, what do you think about it?"

"Well, you always tell us that we are a community and that in a community you care about each other. I think Jeannette is right."

"How would you describe the attitude of the students in that classroom? Jerry?"

"They weren't tolerant of people who were different."

"Yeah, Ms. Alred, just because those students hadn't learned English yet, the class wasn't respectful or tolerant."

"That's a good way of putting it, Maria. I think Jerry and Maria used a word we need to think about." Alred wrote the word *tolerant* on the chalkboard. "Does anyone know another word that would describe the behavior of the students in that classroom?"

Jimmy raised his hand. "OK, Jimmy, do you know another word that describes the situation?"

"The class was *prejudiced*, Ms. Alred. You used that word earlier when we were talking."

"I'm glad you remembered." Alred wrote the word *prejudice* on the chalkboard. "Who can give us a definition of these two words? Randy, can you help us?"

"I think the two words are opposites. *Tolerant* means that you accept other people and are respectful."

"Very good, Randy. They *are* opposites. Who can define *prejudice?*"

Milly raised her hand. "That's easy. *Prejudice* means that you are biased and probably disrespectful of other people's differences."

> George raised his hand. "People who are prejudiced are intolerant."
>
> "George, that's good thinking; let's write the word *intolerant* on the board, too. OK, class, let's take some time to write individual sentences or paragraphs about these three words. If you need some help, raise your hand. I'll come around and see how you are doing."
>
> The class went to work and Alred monitored their work. After about 10 minutes she called on students to share their sentences.
>
> "Tonight for homework, I want you to write a paragraph on how you think the immigrant students felt about their experience in the classroom and another paragraph about how you would feel if you were a student in that classroom. Be sure you use our three spelling words and see how many synonyms you can use for them."

Analysis of the Lesson

The lesson had three distinct phases:

1. *The presentation*—Alred told the story of her own experience.
2. *Structured practice*—Students answered questions, volunteered information, and defined the words. Alred gave positive feedback to verify that the information was correct.
3. *Guided practice*—Students wrote sentences using the three spelling words and shared their work with the class.

The fourth phase of the teaching strategy would occur in the homework assignment when students apply what they have learned. Fifth, the teacher would assess the quality of the product (the completed assignment).

The whole lesson probably took no more than 20 to 25 minutes. Alred kept the students quite active through her questioning, their contributions, and their written work. In a direct instruction lesson, it is important that the presentation be meaningful and motivating. It is important, also, that the teacher gives feedback when students respond. If a response is incorrect, then the teacher must immediately either give the correct response or call on other students to do so.

Lucia Martin's Classroom

> Lucia Martin gathered her students in front of her and said, "Sometimes we can guess what a story is about by looking for clues. What kind of clues do you think we should look for?"
>
> Roger spoke out first: "I'll bet you mean we should look at the pictures."
>
> Other students nodded and Lucia said, "Yes, you are right. I'm going to demonstrate." Lucia held up a Curious George book, and she proceeded to tell an abbreviated version of the story as she pointed to the pictures. "Now," she said, "I'm going to read the story to you and you check whether I guessed correctly what was happening in the story from the pictures." She read the story aloud and then asked the class, "What differences did you notice?"

Marci commented, "There was more detail in the real story."

"Good for you. What do you think about it, Jorge?"

"Well, I think the pictures made the story more fun and really gave clues like you said."

"Clifford?"

"The pictures tell me whether I want to read the book, so I like to look at the pictures first."

"That's a good point, Clifford. Any other comments? Marrissa?"

"Sometimes when I don't understand some sentences, I look at the pictures and see if they explain it to me."

"Very good, Marrissa. The author uses the pictures to help tell the story, and it is very important to look at the pictures for clues about the story. Today we are going to practice using pictures as clues for reading a book. I want you to look at these pictures and see if you can guess what the story is about."

Lucia held up a series of pictures and asked the students to tell her what was happening in the story. She encouraged the students as they guessed the plot and sequence of the story.

After she was satisfied that they recognized the context of the book, she told them that she was giving them a very short story—one page—and it was their job to pretend that they were the illustrators of the story. They were to draw pictures to give others clues about what the story was about. She instructed them to raise their hand if they needed any help reading the story. At the end of the lesson she had students share their pictures.

Analysis of the Lesson

Lucia's lesson had five distinct phases:

1. *The presentation*—Martin presented a story, using pictures for context clues.
2. *Structured practice*—She verified students' understanding that pictures can be used for context clues, through both her questioning and encouragement for students to comment.
3. *Guided practice*—She held up a series of pictures and asked the students to guess the plot and sequence.
4. *Application*—She gave students a one-page story and asked them to construct their own context clues through drawing pictures that matched the story.
5. *Assessment* occurred as students shared their pictures with the class members.

Lucia Martin was teaching context skills through the use of pictures. On other days she will use characterization, emotional statements, settings, and plot to do much the same. For young students, pictures are the primary agent for helping them "read" a story through surmise and implication.

Once again, Martin demonstrated direct instruction with quite a bit of flexibility both in the type of questions asked of the students and in the guided practice and application sessions. More traditional lessons using direct instruction ask very structured questions instead of encouraging students' comments, and the guided practice and application levels are more drill-oriented. The democratic classroom environment and constructivist teaching affect the way a teacher interprets and applies the direct instruction approach.

Did You Know That . . . ?

Students' sense of belonging in the school community is affected by classroom practices related to methods of instruction, teacher support, and authority/autonomy relationships between teachers and students.

- Instruction—Cooperative learning ensures students' interaction and sense of belonging.
- Teacher support—A caring and supportive relationship between teacher and student influences the student's feelings of well-being in the classroom.
- Authority/autonomy relationships—Students' feelings of autonomy influence peer relationships, motivation, and classroom behavior (Osterman, 2000, pp. 323–367).

Practice writing a direct instruction lesson plan at the grade level or subject field you are teaching.

The Comprehension Model of Teaching

The comprehension model of teaching is a close cousin of direct instruction. Its purpose is to focus students' attention on comprehension skills and help adjust reading to the content under study. The reading of fiction books and of subject field discipline texts are quite different and affect speed and intensity of concentration. In using this model, your object is to ask questions that will encourage students to perform the following tasks as they read and/or immediately following reading:

1. Identify the main idea or concept of what you have read.
2. Reconstruct what you read into your own words.
3. Summarize the content of what you have read.
4. Judge the implications of the content on future events, other genres, and other disciplines.

Finding a quiet place to study is sometimes difficult on a busy high school campus.

Suppose that a teacher was teaching about the Magna Carta as background to a study of the U.S. Constitution. The content the students were to read provided information about the Magna Carta, sometimes called the Great Charter, which was written during the reign of King John of England. King John had quarreled with the Roman Catholic Church, stolen treasures from the Church of England, lost the people's wealth in a war with France, taxed the nobles of England, and seized their land; when the nobles objected he imprisoned them. As a consequence the nobles and bishops got together and framed the Magna Carta and made King John accept it.

Before students begin to read, the teacher could suggest that they read to find out: "Why were the nobles and bishops angry with their king?" While the students are reading, the teacher should observe to detect when a student is having difficulty. Young students should be encouraged to raise their hands if they cannot read a word. When students have had sufficient time to read, discussion should begin with the initial question. During the discussion, the teacher should expect students to identify some of the causes of discord. Follow-up questions could include the following: "Summarize the events that led up to the writing of the Magna Carta" and "What were the provisions of the Great Charter?"

The discussion might conclude with the teacher asking, "How did the Magna Carta affect future laws and basic principles of government?" Other questions that could be asked are, "Could the president of the United States do the things that King John did?" and "What constitutional rights do we have that are directly related to the Magna Carta?"

> ### Teaching Hints: Comprehension Model of Teaching
> 1. Initiate silent reading with a comprehension question—"Read to find out . . ."
> 2. Monitor silent reading and help students who have problems with vocabulary.
> 3. Begin discussion with the initial question; encourage students to use their own words, not the language of the text.
> 4. Increase the complexity of the questions as the discussion progresses. Ask questions that require analysis, synthesis, and judgment using personal experiences and construction of meaning beyond the textbook.

Lucia Martin's Classroom

A small group of students was reading *Babar the King* by Jean De Brunhoff. The students were seated together in front of Martin. She began the session by asking the students to look at the pictures and see if they could guess what the story was about. (Had she not done so, the students would have been distracted by the pictures, which are numerous and colorful.) After a short discussion about what the pictures told them, she asked them to read the first page and find out: "Why are King Babar and Queen Celeste rejoicing?" When the students were ready to respond, Martin told them, "Find the sentences that tell you the answer." She then chose a student to read the sentences aloud and asked the other students whether that was correct. All responses were verified with evidence from the story.

The lesson proceeded with Martin directing the students' reading with short questions about the content. At the point in the book when controversy occurs, Martin asked the students, "How would you feel if you were the fish and frogs . . . ?" The discussion then focused on the rights of the different animals and whether those rights were respected.

The comprehension model is intended as a strategy to improve reading skills. It is used more frequently in the elementary school than in secondary schools, but it should not be limited to elementary teaching because all students at all levels need to improve comprehension, and it sharpens test-taking skills.

Practice writing a comprehension lesson plan in which students share their thinking.

The Advance Organizer Model of Teaching

The **advance organizer** at the beginning of each chapter in this text synthesizes major concepts for the chapter and transforms them into questions to be used to guide the reading of the chapter. Questions about content to be read alert readers to what they should think about as they are reading. This teaching model can be traced to the work of David Ausubel (1963), who theorized that cognitive learning will be more meaningful if (1) knowledge is presented in an organized fashion, (2) new knowledge fits into the learner's existing cognitive framework, and (3) new knowledge is relevant to the learner.

The advance organizer model has three distinct phases: (1) introduction of the organizer, (2) presentation of material for study, and (3) summarization/evaluation using the same organizer to verify understanding.

Multiple intelligences should be considered when planning the advance organizer. While some of your students will relate to abstract explanations of major concepts they will encounter, other students may need more concrete representations. A variety of tactics is always appreciated by students. As you think about this teaching model, it is important to realize that the organizer occurs at the beginning of the lesson. Many people make the mistake of thinking of it as an *advanced* organizer. It is intended solely as a means to provide structure for thinking *in advance* about cognitive concepts that are to follow.

Although some subject field textbooks are organized from simple and concrete concepts to more complex and abstract concepts, the authors rarely guide the reader with questions that help organize the information. It is for this reason that teachers need to use their pedagogical knowledge and creative instincts to assist students when they encounter subject matter that may not be meaningful to them. Let's look at several illustrations of advance organizers, other than the use of guiding questions.

Jim Sierra is concerned that his students will need to analyze some economic problems, but they have no prior experience with the content. He proceeds to write in capital letters on the chalkboard the words *SUPPLY* and *DEMAND*. Then he asks his students, "What would happen if everyone in class asked me for a new pencil?"

The students responded, "Probably you don't have enough new pencils in the classroom for everyone."

"Exactly right," replied Sierra. "Now what has that to do with supply and demand?"

After some discussion the students recognized that sometimes supply does not equal demand, and Sierra countered with, "If everyone in the school wanted new pencils, we would be faced with pencil *scarcity*. Do you know what happens when items are scarce—like the recent scarcity of gasoline?"

"Yes," students responded. "The price goes up."

"You're right again. Now suppose we consider the difference between *wants* and *needs*. Who can explain this concept?"

In this way Jim introduced key concepts and a very basic structure of the economic system to his students. His students were now "programmed" for the information that they would be reading about. At the end of the lesson Jim will use the same vocabulary and ask students what they learned about economic problems and whether the concepts he introduced helped them.

Pictures and Graphs

Sometimes pictures and graphs can be used to communicate structure for students. In Chapter 4, I used a circle graph, or concept web (Figure 4.1), to summarize the chapter. The concept web could have been presented at the beginning of the chapter to be used as an advance organizer instead of the guiding questions. I also could have drawn a circle with the caption "Teachers' Pre-knowledge." Then, dividing the circle into thirds, I could have written in each section "Needs of Students," "Subject Field Knowledge," and "Pedagogical Knowledge." This organizer could be used to introduce teachers' planning, as Figure 8.1 demonstrates.

Concrete Objects

Roger Ives was introducing geometric thinking to his students. He displayed cardboard figures on a table in the front of the classroom. He had a cube, cylinder, rectangle prism, cone, and triangle. He asked his students to name the figures and identify as many of their

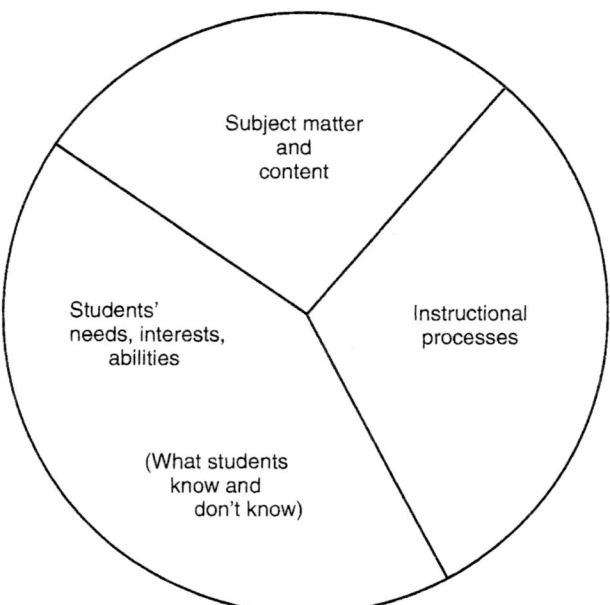

FIGURE 8.1   Teacher's Pre-knowledge
Source: J.K. Lemlech. (2001). *Curriculum and Instructional Methods for the Elementary and Middle School,* 5th ed. Upper Saddle River, NJ: Prentice Hall. Reprinted with permission.

characteristics as they could. Roger's overall objective was the development of spatial sense. After the class discussion of the figures, Roger gave the following instructions to his students:

"For the next week we're going to study two- and three-dimensional figures and geometric curves. We will work in groups, and each day your group will work with a different figure. Your tasks will be to draw the figure, construct it, describe the figure's characteristics, and define the figure. Each person in the group will try to make his or her own figure different from the others in the group. You may use graph paper, geoboards, clay, cardboard, paper, and ink. You may make symmetrical designs using pattern blocks or graph paper. At the end of the week we will share our figures and discuss their defining characteristics."

The use of the concrete figures and the initial class discussion served as the advance organizer for the teaching unit on geometric figures. Note that at the end of the week, Ives intends to have the students summarize what they learned using the geometric figures.

Teaching Hints: Advance Organizer Model of Teaching

1. Identify the purpose of the lesson.
2. Present an overarching structure to help organize new knowledge for students.
3. Present material to be read, viewed, or listened to and verify students' understanding of the organizer.
4. Use the organizer to summarize and conclude the lesson. Verify whether the advance organizer helped the students.

Using graphs, pictures, or concrete objects, write a lesson plan that begins with an advance organizer.

Cooperative Learning

Cooperative learning is another way that teachers can encourage students' interactions and sharing of expertise. By structuring the social environment of the classroom to facilitate students' communication and help-seeking behaviors, teachers stimulate students' task involvement and teach democratic behaviors. Cooperative learning groups can be categorized into two basic types:

1. *Skill-oriented cooperative learning,* in which the major purposes are to practice a skill, learn specific information, and ensure the proficiency of all group members.
2. *Inquiry-oriented cooperative learning,* in which the major purposes are group interaction, research, problem solving, and production of a group product. Inquiry-oriented group learning is discussed in depth in Chapter 9.

Both types of cooperative group learning seek to ensure the participation of all group members, who are grouped heterogeneously by student interest and choice or by teacher assignment. Typically group members are purposefully diverse in abilities, language proficiency, culture, and ethnicity. However, of greatest importance is that the group members share a common goal in their work activity, assume group responsibility, and develop group identity.

Teacher and Student Behaviors for Cooperative Learning Groups

Student Behaviors Unlike individual work or traditional grouping, cooperative groups emphasize the interdependence of group members. Participants share leadership and responsibility for the group's success or failure. There is both individual and group accountability. Emphasis is placed on the task assignment and the social skills of the group members.

Teacher Behaviors Teachers observe and monitor group work. If a group is having a problem, the teacher immediately intervenes. Most often the problem relates to misunderstanding of the work task. On other occasions, problems may be associated with group interaction. At the end of each work period, the teacher debriefs the class by asking what the group accomplished in terms of the task assignment *and* how group members worked together to accomplish their goals. To improve group work it is very important that social skills are taught and practiced.

Some social skills that need to be emphasized include the following:

- Contributing ideas and encouraging others
- Giving an opinion and compromising for group harmony
- Expediting group work through coordinating and synthesizing
- Critiquing and evaluating total group effort and accomplishments

Did You Know That . . . ?

Five characteristic elements of cooperative learning have been identified:

- Positive interdependence (We are all in the same boat!)
- Face-to-face promotive interaction (We help each other learn.)
- Individual and group accountability (Group effort is necessary to achieve our goals.)
- Interpersonal and small-group skills (Social skills are important for group success.)
- Group processing (We reflect on how well we work as a group and on substantive progress.) (Johnson & Johnson, 1999, as reported in Marzano, Pickering, & Pollock, 2001, pp. 85–86)

Advantages of Cooperative Group Learning

1. Communication and interaction are facilitated because the group is small.
2. Small groups motivate participant involvement.
3. Accepting responsibility for work tasks and for assisting others is expected.
4. Listening to others' viewpoints and sharing your own values are necessitated.
5. Negotiation and compromising are critical for group decision making.
6. Cooperative groups allow the teacher to differentiate work tasks and processes.
7. Teacher time during group work can be used for observation, listening, and diagnosing students' needs.

Disadvantages of Cooperative Group Learning

1. If students have not had experience with small-group work, time may be wasted until they learn to use the social skills needed for working with others.
2. Students accustomed to working independently may rebel and resent the responsibility of helping and contributing to others.
3. Concern may be evident that cooperative group work will lower the achievement of high-ability students. (See the section on research that follows.)
4. Concern may be expressed that academic work is sacrificed for group process social and emotional goals.
5. Aggressive, extroverted students may disrupt or take advantage of introverted, less demonstrative students.

Research Related to Cooperative Group Learning

Johnson, Johnson, Holubec, and Roy (1984) report on early research on cooperative learning:

1. For all learning tasks, including concept attainment, problem solving, retention and memory, motor learning, and decision making, cooperative groups are *at least as effective as and usually more effective than* competitive or individualistic efforts.
2. Small-group discussion promotes the development of higher cognitive strategies for problem solving than does individual reasoning.
3. Participation in cooperative groups increases the conflict of ideas, opinions, and theories and results in increased motivation to achieve and greater depth of understanding.
4. Group discussion promotes repetition of information as well as the contribution of new information, which results in greater retention.
5. Social skills, such as feedback, support, and encouragement of group members, are promoted in cooperative groups.

6. Group member diversity enriches the learning experiences of all members.

7. Group identity and "liking" for each other increases motivation to learn (pp. 15–16).

Recent Research

Johnson and Johnson (1991) reported that more frequent use of cooperative learning led students to perceive the classroom climate as "academically and personally supportive and enhancing" (p. 29). However, Anderson, Reder, and Simon (1997) warn that cooperative learning groups are misused when the learning tasks are not specific and when cooperative learning groups are used to the exclusion of independent practice and study.

Continued research by Johnson and Johnson (1996) indicates that cooperative learning produces higher achievement when problem solving, creativity, and higher-level reasoning are required. Also, the greater relevance to real-world situations affects higher achievement positively.

Grouping patterns for cooperative learning need to be varied. Johnson and Johnson (1999) recommend three types of groups: informal, formal, and base groups. *Informal groups* are ad hoc, similar to Roger Ives's use of them when students first enter his classroom and join a study group for his opening inquiry activity. *Formal groups* are used when students have a definite assignment that may last several work periods or even several weeks. Sufficient time must be considered for the formal groups to work productively. A *base group* serves as a "home" center for students to use to clarify assignments and homework and for assistance in locating resources. It is intended primarily as a support system.

Cooperative Groups Learning Models

Early cooperative learning models exhibit dichotomous learning goals. Overall, the purpose is to encourage students to learn from their peers and respect their peers. To accomplish this, all of the models group heterogeneously. Ostensibly another purpose is to discourage student competition, but several models contradict this by offering both individual and team rewards.

Three of the models are aimed at the direct instruction teaching approach. After first presenting material to be learned (phase 1) and verifying understanding through structured practice (phase 2), the teacher then divides the class into cooperative groups for guided practice (phase 3). Team members use a variety of tasks, including practice worksheets, to help each other learn. In addition, group members quiz each other to verify member proficiency.

In the Student Teams Achievement Divisions (STAD) model designed by Slavin and colleagues (1983, 1986, 1989, 1995), the teams are composed of high-, medium-, and low-ability students. The teams are carefully matched and are diverse in gender and ethnicity. The focus is on skills and facts; students take a pretest, and then after participation in cooperative learning they take another test. Points are given for individual improvement and overall team improvement.

In the Teams-Games-Tournament (TGT) model (DeVries & Slavin, 1978), cooperative practice procedures are much the same, but instead of the pretest and summative test, teams compete with each other. The teacher calls on individuals, matched by ability, from each team to compete in a "tournament" with each other. All students participate in the tournament, and points are awarded according to how well each person performed. Team points are based on the scores of the team members.

Still another model developed by Madden, Slavin, and Stevens (1986) is Cooperative Integrated Reading and Composition (CIRC). While STAD and TGT may be used at any grade level or subject field, this model was designed for upper elementary and middle school students. Teams are again composed of multiple ability levels. Students are first instructed by the teacher and then work in their groups using challenging reading materials. Students read aloud to each other, work on written responses to questions about their reading material, and may practice using vocabulary contained in the material. Groups may take practice quizzes. The sessions culminate in individual tests, and team points are rewarded based on individual scores. In general, CIRC follows a pattern of teacher direct instruction to small groups of similar-ability students, team practice, team quizzes, and individual tests.

Two other small-group teaching models (jigsaw and group investigation) will be reviewed with teaching scenarios in Chapter 9. The three models reported here all focus on skill instruction and/or the memorization of facts. They are applicable to most subjects and grade levels.

Motivation

Though cooperation is a team goal, the extrinsic motivation of earning team points defeats to some degree the development of intrinsic motivation. A major purpose of cooperative learning is to help students move from external to internal motivation. Concentration on learning tasks should bring more satisfaction to students than focusing on grades. The research verifies that cooperative group learning is more powerful in helping students retain information and skills. However, I believe that dispensing reward points undermines the principles of cooperative learning. In Chapter 9 we will study the group investigation model, which focuses on democratic processes and internal motivation for learning.

What Skills Do Students Need to Learn?

The roles of group members and the skills they need are not necessarily different from the small-group working skills discussed in Chapter 6 and those needed to participate in a class discussion. The following communication skills improve group work and discussion activities:

1. *Listening* to what others are saying. (Listening, or *auding,* is different from hearing.)
2. *Making eye contact* with the speaker; also the converse, which is making eye contact with those you are addressing.
3. *Asking for clarification* if the substance of what was said is not clear. ("Can you repeat that and give an example? How else could we say that?")
4. *Adding on* to what was said by extending the ideas and by providing examples. ("Oh, I get it, how about . . ." "I just thought about . . .")

5. *Raising questions* to facilitate thinking about the substance or issue under consideration. *Encouraging reflection* about what has been said.
   6. *Summarizing* the contributions (ideas) and *synthesizing* them so that the group is ready to present its ideas to others. ("Do we all agree that we decided . . ." "Let's think about what goes together . . .")

Sometimes it is valuable for cooperative groups to decide on the *roles* individuals will play in the group. The following roles demonstrate the preceding skills.

   1. *Initiator:* The role for this individual is to begin the discussion about the work task.
   2. *Stimulator:* This person encourages other members by commenting on good ideas and important questions. ("Joe, what do you think about that?" "Let's listen to Sally now.")
   3. *Questioner:* This individual plays the devil's advocate. ("What if . . . ?" "How else could we . . . ?" "What would happen if . . . ?")
   4. *Reflector:* "It seems that we have considered . . ." "Should we now . . . ?"
   5. *Summarizer:* "So far we have decided . . . and accomplished . . ."
   6. *Recorder:* "I've got the notes on . . . Are there any more ideas I should write down?" "Have I left anything out?"
   7. *Concluder/Synthesizer:* "OK, we're ready to go. We made four points: . . . Our decision seems to be . . . Does everyone agree?"

When students lack experience with cooperative group work, the roles give everyone a job to do. However, you do not need seven individuals for a group. The roles can be combined, and if students work well in small groups then role assignments are unnecessary; students will work out their own interactive roles in a natural manner.

Did You Know That . . . ?

> Ryan and Patrick (2001) studied 8th-grade students' perceptions of the social environment of their mathematics classroom. The dimensions of the social environment included teacher support, promoting interaction, promoting mutual respect, and promoting performance goals. Their study revealed that these four dimensions affect students' motivation and engagement. "Students' perception of being in a classroom where the teacher encouraged classmates to respect their ideas and not to laugh or make fun of them was the most important dimension of the social environment in predicting changes in academic efficacy and self-regulation of school work" (p. 355).

Specially Designed Academic Instruction in English (SDAIE)

English language learners can be assisted with a few very simple and thoughtful procedures. Lucia Martin has a number of students who are struggling to learn English. She uses some very simple procedures to help these students. When presenting a lesson she speaks slowly and distinctly. Whenever possible she uses concrete accessories to demonstrate her meaning. For example, she will use puppets, beanbag animals, flannel figures, Lego blocks, and pictures to illustrate a story or problem.

When asking questions she provides extra time for the limited English speaker to respond. She also uses facial expressions and body language to convey her thoughts and emotions. She encourages her ELL students to express themselves frequently, thereby listening to how they have interpreted the lesson and how much they comprehend. She accepts their oral contributions and does not correct them; however, she will repeat their response in her own words so that both the English language learner and others in the class will understand.

Cooperative learning groups help the ELL students and their English-speaking classmates. In group situations, students can tutor and mentor each other and develop both understanding and empathy for the individual who is struggling to learn a new language. It is often easier for students to learn from peers in small groups than in a large-group situation when the teacher is doing the talking.

Teaching Hints: SDAIE

1. Enunciate clearly and speak slowly.
2. Use props—concrete objects and pictures—to illustrate or demonstrate your lessons.
3. Provide lots of time for students to respond to your questions.
4. Accept all responses, but then repeat in your own words.
5. Use facial and body language and exaggerate emotions to express meaning.
6. At the end of the day or class period, encourage students to "tell what you learned today."

Questioning Strategies for Expository Teaching Lessons

About 80 percent of a teacher's lessons are spent asking questions; therefore, those questions need to be purposeful, appropriate to the content of the lesson, and appropriate for the students who are expected to respond. The purposes for questioning differ based on the type of lesson.

Convergent questions are used to (1) focus students' thinking, (2) verify students' knowledge and understanding of a presentation, and (3) guide students' study. Convergent questions are used most often during direct instruction and comprehension lessons. They are also used for advance organizer lessons to structure information and guide study.

Convergent questions *tend* to be highly structured and require lower levels of thinking, and are therefore considered lower-level questions.

Divergent questions are used most often to (1) stimulate thinking, (2) teach students to process information, and (3) facilitate analysis and evaluation. Divergent questions are used for problem-solving and inquiry lessons. Divergent questions *tend* to be higher-level questions and require higher levels of thinking, and are typically open-ended in structure. Examples of divergent questions will be studied in Chapter 9.

Precision Questioning

Purposeful questions elicit precisely the skill or factual knowledge you are teaching. If Lucia Martin is teaching about parallelograms, she should ask the students, "How many sides does a parallelogram have?" The skill requires the students to observe. This is a basic factual question—an important one—but it does not require higher-level thinking. However, this question sets the stage for thinking about parallelograms and is therefore vital for the learning process.

If Gerry Alred is acquainting her students with the diversity of their classmates, she might ask a student to find the country where Roberto was born. The student would then go to the map on the bulletin board and select the flag that represents Roberto's native country. Again, this question asked for basic observation of the bulletin board map and knowledge of where Roberto was born (factual data).

Now suppose that Alred was teaching about pollution problems and students have identified air, water, and noise pollution. She might ask the students, "Consider several rural and urban centers and identify which of them are troubled by all three pollutants." This would require students to demonstrate knowledge of the geographic factors that affect these areas and apply that knowledge to the identity of the rural and urban environments affected by pollution. Again, the question asks for precise information.

Convergent questions may require three thinking processes: knowledge, comprehension, and application. Knowledge questions ask for factual information; comprehension questions ask for understanding based on knowledge; application questions require both knowledge and comprehension. Alred's question required all three thinking processes.

- *Knowledge* questions usually ask students to: identify, name, define, recall, list

- *Comprehension* questions usually ask students to: explain, compare, contrast, state in your own words, classify

- *Application* questions usually ask students to: demonstrate a skill/knowledge, construct a new model, provide a new example, solve a related problem, use personal experiences relevant to the original context, mentor a peer, categorize

Clustering of Questions

Some years back, educators attempted to use teachers' questions to classify thinking skills elicited by the questions. Doing this they used Bloom's *Taxonomy of Educational Objectives: Cognitive Domain* (1956). The *Taxonomy* identified six levels of thinking processes: knowledge, comprehension, application, analysis, synthesis, and evaluation. However, in recent years there is recognition that questions should not necessarily be asked in a set order, from simple to complex, and that questions cannot necessarily be classified using a single thinking skill.

For example, let's look at one of our fictitious teachers' questions from Chapter 5. Reflecting on the September 11, 2001, terrorist attack, Jean Cantor asked her students the following questions:

1. What should the United States do?
2. Do you think the United States should retaliate? (Why?)
3. What actions should we take?
4. How do you anticipate the terrorist attack will affect our way of life?
5. What if our volunteer military force is not sufficient; would you be willing to serve if you were 18 years old?

Question 1 is an opening question that is in fact a "listing" question, but it requires knowledge, comprehension of the situation, and analysis of possible actions. It is really asking for students' feelings.

Question 2 is a yes/no question but with an underlying *why*. Again, this is in the affective domain and elicits students' values.

Question 3 requires that students recognize both possible and probable reactions to the terrorist attack. Again, students are required to use a variety of thinking skills. Students need to relate the terrorist act to real-life actions. This requires knowledge, comprehension, application, and synthesis.

Question 4 asks students to make a prediction and value judgment.

Question 5 is a commitment question; based on the discussion, students must summarize their position.

Effective questioning requires that teachers get students *involved* and *motivated*; elicit what students *know* and *understand*; and move students to higher-level thinking and processing through *analysis, valuing, synthesizing,* and *judging*. Questions are sequenced and it is a mistake to think that the only way to sequence questions is from low-level processes to high-level processes, because motivation and involvement are more likely to occur with thought-provoking questions.

Are There Some General Rules About Asking Questions?

Yes indeed. Research indicates that the following guidelines are useful:

1. Stimulate thinking with a thought-provoking question.
2. Ask precise, clear, concise questions. Don't let questions wiggle-waggle.
3. Ask purposeful questions that match your goal.
4. Remember of whom you are asking the questions—appropriateness is important.
5. Ask a variety of question types to provide a variety of thinking experiences.

Are There Some No-Nos When Asking Questions?

Of course.

1. *Leading questions* ("Don't you think that . . . ?" "Isn't it true that . . . ?") turn students off. They stop listening because they realize the question is not authentic.

2. *Yes/no questions* waste time because they need a follow-up question. Ms. Cantor's second question could have been: "Why should the U.S. retaliate or abstain from retaliation? (In her defense, she was still provoking students' involvement.)

3. *Repeating students' responses* often causes other students to stop listening to their classmates because they know the teacher will repeat the comment. But when you have students with limited English proficiency, it may be necessary to repeat responses in order to clarify what was said and to slow down the response so that students can process the information.

4. *Calling on specific students* before you ask a question may turn all other students off because they know they are "safe" and do not need to participate. It may then be necessary to remotivate with another question in order to get class participation. However, there are some extenuating circumstances. Suppose you have a very shy student who hesitates to volunteer; when you provide extra time before the question is asked, this student has time to think it over and respond. Another reason for calling on students ahead of time is to get their attention. When you have students who are not attending to the discussion, you may want to call their names out so that they will know you expect them to participate and respond.

Wait Time, Reinforcement, and Increasing Interaction

Wait Time Rowe (1974) discovered that students' participation, involvement, and interaction increased when teachers waited three to five seconds after soliciting a response before calling on a different student. Novice teachers often fear the quiet after asking a question and as a consequence hurry on to another student who they think may know the answer.

Cuing Students After waiting about five seconds for a response, it is a good idea to offer a cue. But it is important that you offer the cue to *all* students, not just those students who you think should know the answer. Rowe's earlier research (1969) revealed that teachers tend to provide cues to high-ability students but neglect to do so for lower-ability students. Cues should be focused on content-specific information.

Probes Probes are follow-up questions designed to elicit the elaboration and extension of thinking. The probe may be asked of the original respondent or used to encourage classwide in-depth thinking. Suppose that when Jean Cantor asked her students about retaliating for the terrorist bombing, a student responded: "Of course, we should retaliate." Her probe could then elicit: "Under what circumstances have countries retaliated for terrorist attacks? Cite some historical examples." Whether to focus the probe on a specific student or the class at large is the decision the teacher needs to make. It is important to recognize that some students cannot take the extra scrutiny the probe will generate.

Reinforcement Reinforcement occurs when teachers provide feedback to students. Research indicates that students' engagement rate increases when they learn whether they are right, wrong, or proceeding correctly. During a class discussion there are additional ways to reinforce thinking. Suppose a student has responded insightfully to a question and you want to be certain that all of your students recognize the significance of the response. Follow up the student's response with an additional question to the class at large: "John commented that wealthy candidates spend more money on advertising than candidates who are dependent on contributions. Should there be a limit on how much candidates may spend on advertising?" Or, ask John to repeat his response and then ask others to contribute their thoughts on the subject.

Increasing Interaction It is very important that questions and responses not be focused on several students while the rest of the class just glides along without participating. Some general rules may help you increase participation:

1. Accept all responses, without facial expression or body language.
2. Wait for additional offerings from other students, looking around the class to encourage students to talk.
3. If you need to respond, be noncommittal and nonjudgmental: "Hmmm." "OK." "Good." "Who else has a comment? "Turn to another student and say, "What do you think about that?" or, "Who can add to what Jasper said?"

Remember that your real interest is not receiving a single answer to a question, but encouraging students to listen to each other, talk to each other (not to you alone), and practice communication skills.

Discussion Strategies for Democratic Classrooms

Whole-class discussions differ greatly in democratic classrooms and autocratic classrooms. In the democratic classroom, the prime purpose is to teach students to interact with peers and to think critically. An authentic whole-class discussion has certain characteristics:

- Students share ideas, thoughts, personal experiences, and feelings.
- The discussion is a conversation among students.
- The discussion is based on evidence from research or study.
- The discussion is purposeful and progresses through natural stages:
  1. It begins with an introduction to the problem or issue for discussion.
  2. Generally there is a "problem definition" stage that leads to greater focus of the discussion.

3. The discussion may lead to further study and data gathering.
4. The discussion concludes with a decision, a summary, or perhaps a judgment.

Democratic Behavior During the Class Discussion

To encourage whole-class discussion, students need to be in a position to see each other. This may mean that chairs need to be moved into a square or circle. Conversation should move naturally around the class group, with students participating at ease. The discussion *should not* be aimed at the teacher. When a student is only addressing the teacher and expecting a response only from the teacher, there is what is called **co-action** instead of interaction.

Ideally students should not need to raise their hands to be recognized to speak, but this takes practice. Good discussions that involve the whole class do not happen initially or automatically. Discussion manners need to be taught and practiced. To help students learn the art of class discussion, there should be an evaluation at the end of the discussion. Questions such as these could be asked:

- How many participated in the discussion?
- Why is it important to listen to the person who is speaking?
- Why do speakers sometimes repeat what others have said?
- How can others recognize that you want to say something?

To participate in large-group discussion, students need to be able to see each other.

- What happens when someone monopolizes the conversation?
- What happens if small groups or pairs of classmates join in a conversation apart from the rest of the class?

The importance of listening to classmates cannot be overestimated. Until students realize the significance of this, discussions tend to be repetitious and fail to progress purposefully.

The Teacher's Role

A whole-class discussion needs a discussion leader who sets the stage and introduces the problem or issue for discussion. This can be achieved by a student leader, but most often it is the teacher's responsibility. Since interaction is of prime importance, the leader needs to ensure that everyone can see and hear each other. Eye contact is necessary to help focus on the discussion and not irrelevancies.

In a democratic classroom environment, the teacher encourages discussion often through nonverbal means, such as looking at different individuals to encourage participation, sitting down with the students versus standing over them, and even using hand gestures (such as finger to lips) directed at overly aggressive students. If the discussion is lagging and not on target, the teacher needs to stimulate the discussion through questioning tactics including probes, refocusing questions, or summative statements that help extend and expand thinking.

When the discussion is ready for closure, the teacher should call on several students to sum up and synthesize the major points accomplished by the discussion. The teacher may at this point suggest further study or research on the topic or on where the discussion has led the group.

Discussion Variations

In primary age classrooms, students participate in *unstructured* or *free* types of discussions to encourage oral speech and to learn to listen to classmates. This is usually achieved through the "sharing" time when students bring in exhibits, animals, hobby collections, and favorite books. The student often comes to the front of the class group and shares. The teacher encourages but refrains from directing or contributing to the discussion.

> After 30 minutes of small-group work in Gerry Alred's class, where the students were researching types of intolerance, she asked the students to turn their chairs so that they could see each other. Then she asked for reports from each group. Each group was to tell what they learned and accomplished, what they needed to do the next time they worked, resources they might need, and any group problems they had. (Both substantive accomplishments and group interaction were stressed.) Alred then asked the class if anyone had suggestions for the group that had just presented its report. In this manner the discussion progressed until each group had reported.

This type of discussion is *semistructured*. The students know what is expected of them, and the teacher is assessing the students' progress. This type of discussion should occur after a research/problem-solving session.

More *structured* discussion occurs when the teacher introduces a problem or an issue for discussion to accomplish specific cognitive purposes. The teacher has planned discussion questions that will move the discussion along, if necessary. The flow of the discussion is intended to help students develop concepts, process information, and recognize how their classmates are thinking about problems. This type of discussion culminates in decision making, ideas for further study, judgments, or a prediction.

Discussion Problems

Too frequently, students have had few opportunities to participate in classroom discussions. These students have been "successfully" inhibited by prior teachers and are fearful of speaking out. In this situation, aggressive students monopolize the conversation or the discussion tends to be a back-and-forth between teacher and several students.

Another cause of poor discussions may be students' lack of interest in the discussion topic. Discussion topics need to be relevant to the students' experiences and stimulating. There needs to be a purpose to be accomplished and that purpose should be apparent to the students. When students participate in planning curriculum and are aware of how the discussion topic fits what they are expected to do, topics will be meaningful and students are more likely to participate.

The Aggressive, Extroverted Talker   This individual is seldom aware that he or she is monopolizing the conversation. The trick is to help the individual gain awareness. This can be done by asking the individual to be an observer during small-group discussions or a whole-class discussion and give the group or class feedback on the quality of their discussion. At the end of the discussion time you will want to debrief the "talker" by asking the following questions:

- Did everyone get to participate in the discussion?
- Was the purpose of the discussion accomplished? If not, what inhibited or spoiled the discussion?
- What suggestions can you make to the class/group?

Another means to help the aggressive talker is to tape-record a discussion when this person is monopolizing the conversation. Then go about the debriefing process.

The Inhibited Student   Helping shy, inhibited students is much harder than dealing with aggressive students. The inhibited student is fearful—of teachers, peers, and admonishments. Confidence needs to be developed through increased time to respond and gentle encouragement to share thoughts. ("Sam, what do you think about that?" "Mary, how would you attack this problem?") Most helpful for this student is participation in a small work group that has been carefully selected with students who are unselfish and will seek out the inhibited student. Also, an individual talk with the student may reveal the problem; however, if these measures do not work, then consideration should be given to consulting the parents and other help professionals.

The English Language Learner   Class discussions are quite obviously difficult for ELL students. They do much better in small work groups, particularly if they have been placed with students who can mentor them. In a large-group discussion, it is advisable to remind other students to slow their speech down. It may be necessary, as well, to take some time to interpret the flow of conversation. Like the inhibited student, ELL students may need to be encouraged to participate, and it may be necessary at times for you to repeat what has been said so that all students understand.

Teaching with Standards

Let's look at the difference between teaching *with* standards and teaching *to* standards. Teaching *with* standards means that the diversity of the classroom, developmental needs, and the relevance and experiences of the students are considered when developing the curriculum you intend to teach.

Teaching *to* standards denotes a curriculum that is "teacher-proof" because the standards are preset; it assumes that all students are alike and that all should be held responsible for specific measurable achievement. In order to accomplish this, the standards must be written so that they are easily tested. They are behavioral standards, leave no wiggle room for curriculum differentiation, and ignore the diversity of U.S. classrooms (Hodgkinson, 2002).

Content Versus Performance Standards

Content standards focus on the subject fields and provide guidance for meaningful learning in the various disciplines. For example, the National Council for Teachers of Mathematics states that when students study data analysis and probability, they should:

- Select and use appropriate statistical methods to analyze data
- Formulate questions that can be addressed with data and collect, organize, and display relevant data to answer them (NCTM, 2000, p. 48)

When studying communication in mathematics, students should:

- Organize and consolidate their mathematical thinking through communication
- Communicate their mathematical thinking coherently and clearly to peers, teachers, and others (p. 60)

Note that these standards do not define the level of performance, specify conformity to *what* is taught, or act as a prescriptive curriculum. Instead, they serve as a guide (not a mandate) for what is important in mathematical teaching in these two content strands. Performance standards tend to focus on insignificant content because it is more easily tested.

In Roger Ives's classroom activity in this chapter, he involved students in communication of their mathematical thinking concerning the characteristics of three-dimensional figures and geometric curves. Students needed to communicate their thinking to their peers during group work and after their independent work constructing figures.

Standards do need to be considered when planning curriculum, and authentic teaching provides the means to do so whether you are using direct instruction, the comprehension model, the advance organizer model, or the suggested models in Chapter 9. The aim when working with standards is that teaching must focus on significant learning, not coverage.

Chapter Summary

In democratic classroom communities, teachers try to match content and instructional processes for relevance to the needs, abilities, and experiences of the students they teach. Expository teaching involves the presentation or demonstration of conceptual knowledge and skills, and students are asked to participate in activities that allow them to demonstrate learning through application and interaction with peers. Three teaching models that typify expository teaching strategies (direct instruction, comprehension, advance organizer) were exhibited through teaching scenarios.

Cooperative learning groups are characteristic of democratic learning communities. The advantages and disadvantages and the history of research related to cooperative learning were discussed in the chapter. The social skills identified for cooperative learning groups are needed also for successful whole-class discussions. Hints for teaching English language learners also were emphasized in the chapter.

Questioning skills and significant research on how to elicit student involvement in class discussions were linked to discussion behaviors and strategies. Discussions were characterized as a conversation among all the students rather than a back-and-forth question and response session between the teacher and a single student.

The chapter concluded with the use of standards as a means to guide teachers' curriculum planning decisions. Content and performance standards were contrasted in the discussion of teaching with standards.

Teaching Problems

1. Your students are listening to pre-Columbian music. You want the students to study the instruments constructed by Native Americans. Suggest several ways this lesson could be taught using the teaching models in this chapter.
2. Suppose a colleague asks you to observe a classroom discussion. Describe the classroom arrangement for students and teacher and take notes on the following discussion concerns:

   a. How many students actively participated? (More boys than girls, or vice-versa?)
   b. Did the students participate naturally, or did they raise their hands to be recognized?
   c. If they raised their hands, did it appear that the teacher favored some students over others?
   d. Where did the favored students sit?
   e. Where did students who were ignored sit?

f. What was the purpose of the discussion? What was the topic of the discussion? Why do you think the topic was motivating (or was of disinterest) to the students?
g. If you were to hold a conference with the teacher, what would you report to him or her about the discussion? (What conclusions did you draw after observing the discussion?)

3. Take verbatim notes on the questions asked by a colleague during a class discussion. Consider and explain the following pertinent points:
   a. Did the questions stimulate discussion?
   b. Were the questions sequenced to elicit in-depth thinking?
   c. Did the teacher call on specific students? If so, was there a recognizable pattern to whom he or she called upon? (Consider racial, ethnic, gender, and linguistic biases.)
   d. How were students encouraged to think and respond?
   e. What questioning skills did the teacher display? (Cuing, probing, refocusing?)
   f. How did the teacher accommodate English language learners or slow-responding students? (Did the teacher use SDAIE techniques?)
   g. How did the teacher take care of shy and aggressive students?

What suggestions would you make to this teacher to improve classroom discussions?

CHAPTER 9

Higher-Order Teaching Strategies

ADVANCE ORGANIZER

These questions can be used as a framework to assist you in integrating professional knowledge and understanding of the content of this chapter.

1. Why are inquiry and constructivist teaching closely linked to democratic behaviors?
2. What teaching tasks should be performed to motivate higher-order thinking by students?
3. What are the purposes of divergent open-ended questions? How do they contribute to students' inquiry?
4. How does the concept attainment model of teaching help students learn hypothesizing and discovery tactics, and what are the benefits that students derive?
5. Group investigation is the teaching model most closely identified with democratic citizenship. What aspects of this model contribute to citizenship education? How does this model differ from cooperative learning?
6. How do backward problem solving and concept webbing maps contribute to critical and creative thinking?

7. Gestures communicate meaning; why is it important for teachers to recognize and understand gestures and body language?
8. Teachers sometimes use the case study approach when there are problems with resources for students' data gathering. How does this approach help, and how can it be used to teach about the justice system?

The following INTASC issues and standards are discussed in this chapter: Numbers 1–5, 7–9.

Five inquiry-oriented teaching models are exhibited in this chapter. The purposes of these teaching strategies are contrasted with the expository models described in Chapter 8. Both teacher and student behaviors are different in these models from what is expected during expository teaching and learning. Grouping, questioning, discussion, activities, and what students produce also differ.

The Relationship of Inquiry and Constructivist Teaching

Inquiry and constructivist teaching seek to empower learners to make decisions based on their own questions, thoughts, and beliefs. For teachers, this means creating challenging classroom environments where students' ideas are respected, yet questioned by others. For students, this means expressing and sharing ideas and accepting the risk of pursuing learning even if it takes them in the wrong direction. Students need to recognize that learning can occur *even when we make mistakes,* and learning is something we do *for* ourselves; others cannot do it *to* us.

Now what does this have to do with building community, democratic behaviors, and citizenship? Earlier I said that teachers are orchestra leaders. They are also three-ring circus leaders. When students and teacher respect each other and when students experience the delight of a supportive, caring teacher, magic occurs in the classroom. You can observe in these classrooms and note that everyone is going about his or her own business. If students need resources or need to talk to a classmate, they do so in a nonintrusive way. No one misbehaves. When decisions that will affect the whole class need to be made, then the whole class is involved, asking questions and considering the consequences.

The classroom is a community that adheres to democratic values using critical thinking to achieve meaningful learning. Instead of lecturing, threatening, and demanding control, teachers "nourish" students by insisting on involvement and participation. Learning is valued in these classrooms, and teachers recognize that you do not "train" students or "drill" them; instead you motivate and challenge them.

Still another aspect of the democratic classroom is that students sometimes find themselves in the minority position, and they quickly learn that unanimity is not always possible nor desirable. **Inquiry teaching models** are intended to arouse and agitate critical-thinking processes. Students may get angry at each other when they are confronted with opposing logic, but this is a necessary part of the learning process. In a democracy there are winners and losers; yet in the end we stand united. Teachers are responsible for citizenship education, which means helping students understand and value the democratic process. Inquiry teaching models produce higher-order thinking and help teach students that there are alternative ways of thinking about any problem or situation.

Inquiry Teaching Models

In an inquiry-oriented classroom, student reflection is encouraged. For this to happen, the teacher must learn to pose interesting and motivating questions and be relaxed enough to allow time for students to mull over thoughts and ideas. Teacher and student behaviors are quite different in inquiry teaching as compared to expository teaching (Chapter 8). First of all, the teacher's main task is to raise open-ended questions that motivate students' interest. Second, it is important that students are not hurried, but are given adequate time to reflect on their personal responses. Eliciting as many responses as possible is the third task of the teacher, and this requires that you be objective and provide guidance with additional questions when necessary. Questions are used to achieve the following objectives:

1. Guide students' thought.
2. Provide structure to achieve greater depth of thought.
3. Focus on the content of the inquiry.
4. Guide students' consideration of sources of data or evidence to evaluate original ideas.

The following (true) incident is an opportunity for you to practice these objectives.

> A biology teacher assigned a major project to her students in several of her classes. Students' resources included class lecture notes, textbooks, and the Internet. She made a practice of familiarizing herself with all of the resources that students would use and she was very knowledgeable of her subject matter. She had a class rule that when using information from any resource, students needed to cite the sources they used and be sure that what they wrote was in their own words. Plagiarized work would be graded "0".
>
> When the projects were turned in she was uncomfortable with 28 of the projects (out of a total of 118), believing that the students had engaged in plagiarism.

Suppose that you are this teacher and you relate the story to your students.

1. What is the real problem here? What inquiry question should you use to interest your students? (Use a subject field of your choice.)
2. Anticipate the hypotheses (responses) the students would suggest.
3. What are some ways the students' ideas/hypotheses could be investigated? (What data should be gathered?)

4. Using the data gathered, what will students produce?
5. How will you assess your students' inquiry skills?*

The Constructivist Teaching Model

Constructivist teaching is discussed in Chapter 3, but since it is closely related to inquiry teaching it is an important consideration in a chapter that focuses on higher-order teaching strategies. (This might be a good time to review Jim Sierra's electrical energy unit from Chapter 6, which provides examples of constructivist teaching.) In constructivist teaching we rely on the use of open-ended questions to encourage students' creativity, and we provide many opportunities for hands-on activities.

> Lucia Martin asked her students: "How do rural and urban environments differ?" Martin's students are young elementary students, and she had to remind them that they live in an urban environment. After the students thought about it, they recognized that they live in a large city. With Martin's encouragement, they then were able to contrast their urban environment with a rural environment.
>
> Martin decided to provide the students with paper and crayons and suggested that they draw either a rural or urban picture of the environment. This helped make the concepts of rural and urban environments more real and concrete for the students. The drawing activity was followed with sharing and talking about their pictures and then writing stories about their pictures.
>
> On the following day, Martin brought in tools and wood. She demonstrated safe ways to use the tools and asked the students if they would like to build both rural and urban communities. The students were delighted; after forming six different groups, based on their choice of the type of community they were interested in, the students were reminded of their original question about how the environments differed.
>
> Using their own pictures and stories and books in the classroom, students began to construct farm buildings, tools, animals, factories, apartment houses, and businesses. Each work session encouraged new questions. For example, a student working on a rural environment asked, "Don't they have to have stores and other businesses in a rural environment?" Another student asked, "What about schools? Are they really small? Are they far away?" A student in an urban group asked, "Don't we need libraries and parks, and shouldn't there be schools, libraries, and parks in the rural areas?" Each set of questions led to additional research using pictures, books, and films as resources. Class discussions followed each research period.

*Data for the problem is from A. Trotter. (2002). "Plagiarism Controversy Engulfs Kansas School." *Education Week, xxi* (29): 5.

As the students learned and compared their work, Martin was integrating and teaching interdisciplinary content. Students engaged in language arts, social studies, art and construction activities, mathematics, and science. Their activities required the following:

- Group planning
- Selection of resources and materials
- Sharing conceptual understandings, pictures, stories, and new research
- Cooperative work skills as they constructed buildings and animals
- Class discussions, evaluations, new inquiry questions
- Problem solving
- Measurement skills
- Manipulative skills

Did You Know That . . . ?

American researchers visited schools in Japan to find out why Japanese students do better than American students in science after the fourth grade. They learned that the Japanese teachers all followed a similar pattern of constructivist/inquiry teaching:

1. Lessons were relevant to students' interests and experiences.
2. Students' questions and ideas were elicited.
3. Students planned their own investigations and predicted probable outcomes. Teachers assisted as needed.
4. Hands-on investigations were conducted in small groups.
5. Students discussed their work in the small group and planned their reports for whole-class discussions.
6. Findings were systematically analyzed by students and teacher.
7. Group conclusions were compared to prior predictions, discussed, and shared with the whole class. Students were encouraged to double-check their findings.
8. Conclusions were used by the teachers to sequence new lessons and students were encouraged to raise new questions (Linn, Lewis, Tsuchida, & Songer, 2000).

The Divergent Questioning Model

Throughout this chapter, open-ended questions are emphasized as gateways to inquiry and constructivist teaching. Unlike convergent questions, the divergent open-ended question is supposed to elicit a variety of responses and encourage participation and creativity. Good inquiry questions are not designed to achieve "off the wall" responses, but rather to do the following:

- Motivate ideas
- Assess students' background knowledge and experiences
- Introduce social problems and value differences
- Help students analyze and synthesize data
- Encourage decision making

Let's look at some examples of questions that raise social problems.

> More than twenty states have passed or are considering passing a law that forbids drivers to use cell phones that require taking a hand off the wheel of the car. If you were a legislator, why would you consider passing this law or voting against it?

Recognizing that you will probably elicit different responses depending on the age of your students, you can expect that students will raise questions of the rights of privacy, frequent accidents, cost of hands-free telephones, general welfare and safety, and insurance rates. This question could lead to small-group investigations of traffic regulations in your state, the number of drivers using cell phones, and the right of the state to inhibit personal liberties. Follow-up questions could narrow the field of interest to meet students' interests and needs.

> Some communities do not have freestanding pharmacies, delicatessens, dry cleaners, video stores, or opticians—just to name a few. Instead, these businesses are located in large supermarkets. What are the effects of these changes on the people who want services and on the people who were prior owners of these smaller businesses?

Project your students' responses to this question. What hypotheses would lead to an in-depth study? What data would be needed?

Practice changing these questions to accommodate your needs and your students.

Many open-ended inquiry questions are preceded by narrow, factual questions that lead to a more overarching question that requires reflective thinking and research. For example, the teacher might have had students recall small neighborhood stores that are no longer in existence:

- "Can you think of some stores you used to visit that are no longer in this community?"
- "What do you think happened to them?"
- "Where do your parents shop now?"

After a short discussion and narrowing in on the problem, the teacher might ask the more all-encompassing question: "What are the effects . . . ?"

Divergent Questions and Wait Time

Wait time assumes greater significance when you are asking open-ended questions during large-group discussions. (Review the wait time discussion in Chapter 8.) You can immediately distinguish the impulsive responder and the more reflective student who hesitates before participation. You will need to develop a strategy for encouraging the reflective student, who may be shy in addition to being reflective. For example, suppose Joan is in a hurry to offer her opinion, which may affect other students by inhibiting them or interrupting their thought processes. You might say to Joan, "That's interesting, Joan, but let's give others a chance to think through the question so that they can respond." After you have encouraged as many responses as possible, you might even return to Joan and comment, "Now that you have had more time to think it through, would you like to add to or change your original idea?" In this way you are helping Joan be more reflective and letting her know that you do value her participation.

Introverted and extroverted students do differ in the time they need to respond to questions. They differ also in other ways during small-group discussions. Nussbaum (2002) studied the approach of introverts versus extroverts during small-group argumentative discussions. He selected four introverted students and four extroverted students, grouped them homogeneously, and observed and audiotaped their discussions. He found that the introverted students' discussion was more co-constructive and creative. The extroverted students' discussion was ". . . significantly more conflict oriented." Nussbaum was uncertain whether this difference in orientation was a consequence of perceived confidence or lack of it; however, in the ordinary classroom one does not usually group students homogeneously. Since inquiry-oriented teaching tends to focus more on conflict and open-ended questions, this certainly suggests that strategies need to be used for helping the shy student participate and working on the reflectivity of the aggressive talker. (See Chapter 8.)

Now let's study some teaching models that are inquiry oriented and feature critical thinking.

The Concept Attainment Model

Gerry Alred's Classroom

Jamie said, "Ms. Alred, they're teasing me. I can't understand them."

The two other boys laughed and said, "We're practicing our Pig Latin and Jamie doesn't know it. We're only having fun with him."

"Yes, but is Jamie having fun? How does it feel when you can't understand and communicate with others? Let's see what the rest of the class thinks about it." Alred turned to the class, which had just assembled and was seated and listening to the conversation. "How many have had the experience of not understanding their parents converse?" Several of the students raised their hands and Alred called on them.

"My parents speak Russian when they don't want us to understand them."

"Mine speak Spanish, but I'm beginning to recognize some of the words even though they speak fast. Pretty soon they won't be able to fool me."

"My parents speak Japanese; I can't understand a word and it frustrates me."

Another student commented, "I don't think it's polite to carry on a conversation when others are there and they can't understand. It just isn't courteous of Ron and Jim to tease Jamie that way."

Ms. Alred looked at the three boys and said, "Well, I guess now you know what your classmates think, but interestingly enough this leads into what we were going to study today." She then turned to the chalkboard and wrote the following list:

Reading a book (No)

Listening and responding to a friend (Yes)

Participating in a debate (Yes)

Baking a cake (No)

Arguing with your parents (Yes)

Ms. Alred turned to the class and said, "I'm thinking about a couple of important concepts and I wonder if you can figure out what they are by reading my list of words on the board."

At first the students were surprised by the list and extremely quiet; then they began to throw out ideas. Ms. Alred did not insist that they raise their hands. Instead, as a student talked, she would look directly at him or her; sometimes she would say, "Wait, give me a chance to write your ideas on the board." Then another student would talk. Their ideas included *not doing things alone; talking; listening; two or more people in a group; conversation; arguing about an issue or problem.* When the students seemed to have run out of ideas, Alred said, "OK, let me give you some more clues." She wrote another list on the board:

Snowboarding

Practicing the piano

Eating lunch with friends

Lab experiment with a small group of other students

Doing homework

Alred then turned to the students and said, "Any more ideas?" The students said, "You forgot to write *yes* or *no!*"

"I didn't forget," she said. "This time you need to guess whether they are *yes* or *no*. Let's begin." She then pointed to each item and looked at the students with her chalk poised to write.

The students immediately said that the first two were *no*. But they vacillated with the next two and finally agreed that they were probably *yes*. The last one definitely elicited a *no*.

"So what do you think, do you want to change your original ideas? Do you have additional ideas?"

"I think we should definitely agree that it is *conversation*."

Another student said, "Well, maybe it really was supposed to be *communication*." Students appeared to be nodding and in agreement. No more ideas were suggested. Alred asked whether they wanted to eliminate any of their previous ideas, but no one seemed to want to do that.

"OK, you have really figured it out; I was thinking about *communication*, but I am going to add another concept; it is the concept of *interaction*. Do you know what it means? Who can give me some examples of the concept of interaction?"

Students began to give suggestions: *working and talking with others, listening and speaking with someone else, being mad or friendly with someone else, involving more than one person, communicating with others.*

"Wow, you have done great. Now see if you can tell me what *interaction* and *communication* are *not*."

The students groaned, but began to think. "It's not doing things alone." "It's not watching television or working at the computer." "Unless you are chatting with someone else on the computer." "It's not any activity you do without communicating with others at the same time."

"You've done a good job of thinking. Now tell me how the words on the board gave you clues."

One student immediately raised his hand and said, "I looked at what the words had in common." Another student added to that, "I looked at the words marked *no* to see what they had in common, and then the words marked *yes* to see how they were alike."

"You've done a good job of thinking and learning about concepts. Now let me explain why we went through this exercise. We have been studying the ways people express bias and prejudice—sometimes through humor, sometimes through written means, sometimes through graffiti, and it almost always incites hurtful reactions in others. I wanted you to think about the concepts of communication and interaction. What did you learn about these concepts from the exercise I introduced?"

The students' discussion focused on the teaching strategy that made them compare the attributes of the clues. They realized that in order to understand the concepts of communication and interaction, they also needed to understand what the concepts were *not*. Comparing and contrasting the affirmatives and negatives fostered their inquiry and helped them to think of additional examples. When Alred asked them if they understood why she inquired about their thinking process, the students quickly responded that it helped them to hear how others in the class were "cracking the code." "It's like when we see how others solve problems in math; it gives us ideas that help."

Alred used the **concept attainment** teaching model, developed by Joyce and Weil (1999). The model is derived from the work of Jerome Bruner (1966), who studied how people learn through hypothesizing and discovery tactics. Through his research, Bruner found that students derive four benefits from participating in the act of discovery:

1. An increase in intellectual potency

2. A personal shift from extrinsic to intrinsic rewards

3. Learning techniques as to how to discover/inquire
4. Recognizing that self-discovery acts as an aid to conserving memory

The process of inquiry and discovery for students is not related to invention (finding something new); however, what students learn may be new to them and it serves to build confidence in their own intellectual powers. Let's look at the phases of Alred's lesson and the concept attainment teaching model.

Phases of Concept Attainment

1. Positive and negative examples of the concept are provided on the chalkboard or through concrete representation. Each is labeled as positive or negative.

2. Students compare the attributes of the examples and are encouraged to hypothesize about the concept. The teacher writes the hypotheses on the chalkboard.

3. No confirmation of the hypotheses is given by the teacher; when students seem stumped or have run out of further ideas, the teacher writes a new list (or provides new concrete representations), but does not identify whether they are positive or negative examples.

4. Students are first asked to guess which of the new examples are positive and which are negative; then they are once again asked to provide new hypotheses or "stand pat" with the ones already identified. (They may even decide to delete some of their prior ideas.)

5. Students are asked whether they can make a statement concerning the identity of the concept.

6. The teacher confirms the statement or provides help and names the concept.

7. Students are asked to provide additional examples of both positive and negative exemplars of the concept.

8. Students are asked to share their thinking strategy during the hypothesizing phases. ("What helped you? What process did you use?")

Examples of Concrete Representation

In an art class a teacher may display works of art and label them positive or negative. The art may represent artists or periods of time or distinct types of style (such as impressionism). A literature teacher may hand out examples of specific writing genres for students to hypothesize about. A history teacher may use political cartoons for examples of historical events. A kindergarten teacher may use a flannel board with objects on it. Lucia Martin could have used her four-sided objects with a variety of shapes for a mathematics concept attainment lesson to encourage discovery concerning the characteristics of four-sided objects.

Motivation and Assessment

Though concept attainment is most often used to introduce a new abstract concept to students in a motivating style, it has been used for assessment as well. Suppose that the history teacher had been teaching students about specific historical events. Then, using the cartoons, the students are asked to demonstrate what they know through the hypothesizing stage. As another example, an elementary teacher had taught about large industrialized and multicultured cities throughout the world. The students were then given a list of worldwide cities and asked to guess the concept the teacher had in mind. Though the cities were all large urban centers, all did not represent diverse ethnic and multicultured centers.

Teaching Hints: Concept Attainment

1. Select examples (words, phrases, articles, cartoons, concrete objects) that truly represent the concept in mind. They may be synonyms of the concept.
2. Select examples that are antonyms of the concept or truly unrepresentative of the concept, because they are useful for students to contrast and sharpen their definition of the concept.
3. Remember that to understand the attributes of a concept, one must also be able to differentiate and tell what the concept is not.
4. Do not worry that students will not guess the exact concept you had in mind. If they are not close to the general idea, tell them the concept and help them see the relationship to your clues (phase 6). Then continue with phases 7 and 8.
5. If the students have expressed the idea of the concept using different language than what you had in mind, affirm their accuracy and share that there are additional ways to express the concept; you are teaching them a new vocabulary word.
6. Enjoy the teaching model; students will gain vocabulary and have a good time doing it.

The Group Investigation Model

No other model of teaching has a greater impact on students' learning and practice of democratic citizenship than the group investigation teaching model. The model helps students participate in class, school, community, and national activities. All societal decision-making activities require group participation. This teaching model requires listening, respecting diverse perspectives, compromising, negotiation, and commitment to learning through inquiry and group governance processes. It nurtures students' sense of belonging to "their" group and helps them gain a sense of empathy for others. Let's see how Jim Sierra implements the teaching model.

Jim Sierra's Classroom

The bulletin boards and the chalkboard ledge displayed a number of pictures of Los Angeles neighborhoods. Sierra directed the students' attention to the pictures and then asked his class, "What do you think we could learn about the people of

Los Angeles by visiting in different communities?" Students' responses included the following:

- "We would see people who lived in each community."
- "We would see businesses, houses, apartments, animals, and schools."
- "I don't think we could learn anything about the people by just looking at the community."
- "Maybe we could see what people like to do in the different communities by looking at play activities of kids and playgrounds."
- "Yeah, maybe even the kinds of businesses and restaurants would tell us something."

Sierra drew a data retrieval chart on the chalkboard (Figure 9.1). Sierra then told the students that they would be taking a field trip through different communities in Los Angeles, and on the trip they were to take notes about what they observed. "Before we go on the trip we will work in groups, and each group should write down expectations of what you anticipate you will observe. As you go about your discussion, consider your earlier comments. We will discuss the accuracy of those comments after our trip."

Next, Jim Sierra explained the use of the data retrieval chart and how it would be used. "We will divide into groups now to consider our expectations. When we return from our field trip, you will have an opportunity to work with your group and share your individual observations. Then each group can complete the chart, deciding on what they learned and concluded. We will then have a class discussion to share our ideas."

Sierra informed the class that they would go on the trip on Wednesday morning. (This was a Monday.) Next he organized the class into groups, and the students went to work on the first part of their assignment. After about 15 minutes, Jim called the students to order and said, "Let's discuss your expectations." The students turned their chairs around to see and hear each other and shared their groups' thoughts about the field trip. Then Jim asked the class, "Did everyone share their ideas?" The students nodded. "Were there any problems in your group that we should talk about?" The students responded "no," but they were surprised about the field trip. One group commented, "We talked about why we were really taking this trip."

Sierra explained, "*We* are studying the cultural geography of our city." Some of the students looked confused. "OK, let's play the concept game and see if that helps you." He proceeded to write a list of phrases on the board, using the concept attainment strategy:

Ways people habitually behave (Yes)
Ignorance (No)
Lacking in social qualities (No)
Shared beliefs and experiences (Yes)
Favored foods and holidays (Yes)

Sierra asked the students for their hypotheses (guesses) and then proceeded through the rest of the teaching model. His second list of unlabeled clues included disrepair and respect for surroundings (No); shared language (Yes); appreciation of the arts and learning (Yes); lack of appreciation of music, art, and schooling (No); self-discipline and manners (Yes).

The students soon realized that the concept Sierra was priming them for was *culture* and that they were supposed to be looking for signs of culture on their field trip.

What We Expect to See	What We Actually Observed
(Group Work)	(Individual Work)
What We Learned	Our Conclusions and Predictions
(Group Work)	(Group Work, Class Discussion)

FIGURE 9.1 Data Retrieval Chart

Analysis of Sierra's Group Investigation Lesson

Let's review Sierra's lesson and his anticipation of needs. He began with an open-ended question to stimulate students' inquiry: "What do you think we could learn about the people of Los Angeles by visiting different communities?" Next he elicited students' ideas. He orchestrated the students' group work by sharing a data retrieval chart for them to record their thoughts about the proposed field trip. The students were organized into groups and given a short time to discuss their ideas. He assessed their progress through a class discussion that focused first on the substantive content of their discussions and then on group processes.

From the responses concerning group processes, Sierra recognized that there was some confusion about why they were taking the trip and what they would learn. Having anticipated the possibility of this, he had prepared a concept attainment lesson to teach the concept of culture. We can assume that this lesson helped to prepare the students for what they were to take note of on the field trip.

Field Trip Classroom Management On Tuesday, Sierra talked to the students about courteous bus behavior, and he and the students decided that they would take some walking trips around some of the neighborhoods. They recognized that they needed to walk together, but in small groups following each other. Sierra told them that if he raised his hand, he would expect the students to cluster around him so that he could talk to them. He engaged the students in a discussion of courteous behavior if they met people on the street. (One student asked if she could bring a camera, and Sierra said absolutely not.) He reminded them that they would need paper or notebooks and pencils or pens for note taking and that they would "debrief" in their groups after the trip.

Phases of Group Investigation

1. Initiate the lesson with an inquiry (open-ended) question or problem.

2. Elicit students' thoughts, ideas, and hypotheses.

3. Organize students and prepare them for group work. If their ideas or hypotheses suggest that groups should choose what to work on, then groups may be organized for a precise activity. (See the example of Gerry Alred's class in Chapter 1.)

4. Have students participate in group work.

5. Hold a class discussion with group reports on the substance of their work (what was accomplished). Discuss group processes. (Did they get along cooperatively? Did everyone participate? What needs do they have?) If the inquiry activity is concluded, then this phase completes the teaching model.

6. If the inquiry activity is not completed, "recycle" (remotivate) the activity the next time the students are to work together.

After the Field Trip—What Students Observed On Thursday the students were eager to share their observations in their groups. Sierra complimented the students on their behavior and their note taking on the trip. He immediately allowed them to join their groups. The students had toured East Los Angeles, the Gardena community of Los Angeles, and the West Adams section of Los Angeles. Their discussion at the end of the group work revealed that observations in the three communities had similarities and differences. They noted small businesses, several factories, poker clubs (in the Gardena area), ethnic restaurants and markets, several supermarkets (but not as many as the students anticipated), immigration services (in East Los Angeles and in Gardena), physicians' offices, churches, synagogues, community centers, and recreational facilities (although very few in East Los Angeles). They observed people walking to businesses, schools, bus transportation, and residences, and they were aware of the social conditions of each community. Sierra had made a large copy of his data retrieval chart. As the groups shared their observations during the class discussion, he made notes on the chart.

What Students Learned It appeared to the students that in each of the three communities, there were distinct ethnic differences. (Hispanic Americans seemed to predominate in East Los Angeles; African Americans seemed to predominate in the West Adams community; Asian Americans predominated in the Gardena community.) School buildings in East Los Angeles displayed huge murals of Mexican heroes. Houses in East Los Angeles were very small and close together with fences around them, and each had pretty flower gardens. But there were also unkempt apartment buildings with no play areas, broken sidewalks, and few parks.

The West Adams community was well groomed and gardeners were evident. Large shopping centers were nearby. Students recognized that it was a somewhat affluent community. In Gardena the houses were small and apartment complexes frequent. Yards and gardens in Gardena seemed structured and neat, but did not reflect the free style of the gardens in East Los Angeles.

The students surmised that the ethnic groups they observed had not always lived in their respective communities because they saw what seemed to be "holdovers" from prior residents. For example, in East Los Angeles they called attention to the delicatessen establishments adjacent to the tortilla factories, and the synagogues and cemetery of past Jewish residents. The grandeur of the West Adams district and the age of the homes, yet the comparative youth of many of the residents, surprised the students. They realized that both African Americans and Caucasians lived in this area. In Gardena and in the West Adams area they observed a variety of ethnic restaurants and specialty markets. Gardena had distinct Korean and Japanese restaurants, churches, and many after-school learning centers, which made the students realize that the Korean and Japanese children studied their native languages and religion in the after-school centers.

Students' Conclusions

1. Ethnic groups tend to live in distinct areas of the city. (Cultural geographers refer to these as "pockets.")

2. As residents become more affluent, they move out of their original neighborhood and diversify in ways of life and where they live.

3. Surroundings, such as businesses, schools, and churches, reflect the culture and ethnicity of the residents.

4. Visiting the three communities provided many insights about the culture of Los Angeles residents.

Discussion and Insights With Sierra's guidance, the students realized that when ethnic and cultural immigrant groups move to a strange country, they tend to settle where they can feel comfortable with other members of their group for language and social assistance. As people become Americanized, they are not necessarily bound to their original community.

They studied the meaning of *ghettos* and recognized that people sometimes choose the ghetto experience for safety and service, but often as people become more affluent they discard old habits and ways of life. They noted that though the West Adams area had attracted many younger African Americans, there were still older Caucasian residents in the community. This community was more diverse ethnically, culturally, and in the age of the residents than the other two communities they visited. The students rejected the idea that nothing could be learned about people in Los Angeles through observation and visiting in the different communities.

Why did Jim choose group investigation in combination with a field trip and a concept attainment lesson? Jim recognized that *telling* the students about the people of the varied communities in Los Angeles would not be as meaningful as *seeing* (and discovering) for themselves. He prepared the students by ensuring that they understood and would focus on the concept of culture. The diversity of the city was his way of introducing the students to a study of citizenship in the United States.

How Group Investigation Differs from Cooperative Learning

The purposes of group investigation are to encourage inquiry, problem solving, and sharing diverse viewpoints. These purposes stimulate animated discussions and sometimes arguments, which need to be resolved through negotiation and compromise. Democratic processes are inherent in the participatory activity of the groups. Cooperative learning (as discussed in Chapter 8) focuses on the cooperative practice of specific skills and learning of specific information.

Individual tasks in cooperative learning are aimed at teaching other members of the group specific information or the mastery of a skill. Individual tasks during group investigation are focused primarily on research, which is then shared with group members in order to produce a group product. (In Jim Sierra's class, the group members were each responsible for their own observations, which were then shared with their groups to produce group conclusions.)

In the cooperative strategy called "jigsaw," students are assigned to a "home" group. Group members are numbered 1 through 5. Each member is given an inquiry question. All students that share a number meet to research the inquiry question. When the research is completed, students return to their home group and share the information. Then the home groups discuss what they have learned and decide on a group perspective.

Both teaching models emphasize social skills and group effort. Both require evaluative discussion that focuses on substantive progress and group processes. Teacher behav-

Divided into small groups, the students are engaged in the cooperative learning strategy of jigsaw.

ior differs slightly in group investigation because the teacher's prime responsibility is to frame stimulating questions that help focus and structure the investigation. Additional questions may be asked of individual groups if the participants need assistance. The teacher acts as a consultant during group investigation (perhaps suggesting resources), but tries to refrain from directing students as to how to proceed. Teacher observation and monitoring is vital to the success of both teaching models.

> **Teaching Hints: Classroom Management for Group Investigation**
>
> 1. Identify where each group is to work.
> 2. Verify group understanding of their task.
> 3. Be certain that you have appropriate resources for students' investigation.
> 4. Monitor group work by sitting in for a few minutes with each group.
> 5. If groups are too noisy, stop the class and ask, "Why do you think I have stopped your work?" Help the students recognize that group work does not mean they can disturb others. If one group is disturbing everyone, ask the class, "How can we help Roberto's group?" If necessary, remind the class of group work rules.
> 6. Sometimes it is necessary to change members of a group if they are unable to cooperate with each other.

Why Concepts Are Important

Lucia Martin used discussion, drawing, story writing, and construction to help her students understand and compare the concepts of *rural* and *urban environments*. Gerry Alred used the concept attainment strategy to help her students develop the concepts of *communication* and *interaction*. Jim Sierra focused on the concept of *culture* both in the use of concept attainment and through a field trip to gather data about the cultural geography of their city.

Concepts are both *names* and *categories*, and they are the ways we express ourselves and communicate with others. Sometimes the concepts we use have different meanings for different individuals, and that is why it is important to share and clarify our meanings. For young students and English language learners, it is important to stress concrete representation in order to communicate meaning. For older students who may not have language problems but are learning vocabulary oriented to particular subject field disciplines, the concepts may be abstract. Concepts such as liberty, justice, energy, quadrilaterals, and culture are examples of abstract ideas, beliefs, and categories. An example of how the meaning of a concept changes in subject fields is illustrated by the concept of role. In dramatics, role has to do with an actor's part in a performance; in political science, the concept of role has to do with leadership and power; in sociology, role may relate to values and social economic status.

Concepts not only have different meanings in subject fields and may be interpreted differently by individuals, but sometimes contextual understandings are needed. The concepts of *sequence, continuity,* and *integration* (Chapter 5) needed explanation as terms used for curriculum planning (and teacher talk). In curriculum planning, definition in the form of a generalization is often required to provide the meaning and context of a concept. In Chapter 5, Jim Sierra's unit teaching plan illustrates the contextual meaning of a concept through the use of a generalization: "Migration to the West during the period from 1820 to 1860 influenced the development and statehood of all the western and southwestern states." The generalization provides specificity to the intended meaning.

The Taba Questioning Strategy

If we place in front of a group of young students a clock, a bike, a scooter, crayons, a miniature train, and a truck, and then ask the students, "What do you see?" they will probably respond by naming the items. If we then ask the students, "Do any of these items go together?" they probably will name the bike, scooter, train, and truck. With additional urging and questioning for a means to *name* the group, the students might name them as toys; after reflection they may come up with the concept of *transportation.*

By asking appropriate questions, teachers can facilitate the process of conceptualization. The questions help students process information. The questions, of course, should be appropriate for the students with whom you are working.

Taba, a curriculum specialist in the 1960s, believed that teachers need to ask the "right" questions to promote the *formation of concepts,* which is dependent on (1) listing items, (2) grouping the items, and (3) categorizing the items (1967, p. 101). Recall that in concept attainment, the students are required to think through the attributes of items that belong together and differentiate them from those that do not fit.

Taba's second cognitive task for students was to *interpret data* through specific questions similar to those used for the formation of concepts. Again the teacher asks, "What do you see or notice about these items? Why did this happen? What does this mean?" (1967, p. 101).

Taba's third cognitive task for students was to *apply* what they have learned through the formation and interpretation processes (1967, p. 109). Suppose that instead of using the concept attainment model with his students, Sierra decided to teach the concept of culture using the Taba questioning strategy.

Jim Sierra's Classroom

When Jim Sierra recognized that students did not understand the concept of culture, he brought out a large chart with pictures on it and asked, "What are some of the ways people adorn themselves?" As the students replied, he wrote their items on the board: pins, hair colorings, toupees, ribbons, medals, neck rings, earrings, brooches, crowns, an obi, coat, face makeup, yarmulke, sailor outfit, feather on the scalp, three-cornered hat.

Next Sierra asked the students, "What belongs together?" After grouping the items, he asked the students to give a name to each group. This required students to organize the items and form more all-encompassing names or concepts for each group. The new concepts included jewelry, clothing, cosmetics, headwear, ribbons and medals, and hairpieces.

When the students had exhausted their categories, Sierra said, "Think about different people and different historical time periods. What did you notice about the people and their adornments?" Students responded that the clothing and adornments seem to relate to different groups of people with different religious beliefs and reflect different periods of history. Sierra then asked, "Why do you think this happens?" The consensus seemed to be that certain habits affect a people, and they dress and adorn themselves accordingly. Then Sierra followed up with the question, 'What do you conclude about why people adorn themselves?" After reflection, students believed that dress and adornments are affected by historical time periods, current fads, and maybe social status.

Sierra concluded his lesson by asking the students to apply both their concepts and their interpretation: "What can we say about behavior and what do you think people will say about our culture and generation?" Students responded that on their field trip, they anticipated that most of the people they would see would look alike in their dress. We dress more casually than in prior years. Dress is affected by customs and fads. People in the future will probably conclude that we don't dress up fancy—at least not very often. We are more casual and relaxed than, say, the pioneers, and our dress is less controlled by our religious beliefs or our culture.

Teaching Hints: The Taba Questioning Strategy

Concept Formation:

- What did you see? Hear? Note?
- What belongs together? On what criteria?
- How would you name these groups?

Interpretation of Data:

- What did you notice? See? Find?
- Why did so-and-so happen?
- What does this mean? What would you conclude?

> **Application:**
> - What would happen if . . . ?
> - Why do you think this would happen?
> - What would it take for so-and-so to be generally true or probably true? (Taba, 1967, pp. 92–109)

Students' Questions as Means for Critical and Creative Thinking

Backward Problem Solving and Webbing

Graphic systems such as backward problem solving and webbing (Chapter 5) encourage students to recognize connections between a *theme* (often used as another name for *concept*) and content strands. Brainstorming techniques such as backward problem solving and webbing encourage students' conceptual thinking.

> Jean Cantor asked her students, "What is one of the toughest problems that schools need to deal with today?" The students immediately responded that violence, both from their peers in the school and from outside terrorists, is probably the number one problem for schools. Cantor then asked, "What do you think are some of the causes of school violence?" Students' responses included the following: individuals who do not have many friends and feel isolated; being "out of the loop" in terms of school activities; no teacher who seems to care about you—and maybe parents who are uncaring; no opportunity to choose the classes you want to take; the feeling of being in prison because we are walled in and visitors are walled out; too many regulations—passes are needed for everything.
>
> Cantor said, "So I gather that you believe that a violence-free school is impossible without some changes in the school environment."
>
> The students nodded in agreement. One student summed it up: "A violence-free school environment should be the goal, but there need to be some changes in all schools."
>
> Cantor asked whether the students would like to conduct an investigation into some of the conditions of their own school. "If you were to do that, what would you research?" As the students framed their questions, Cantor drew a circle with the words *violence-free school* in the middle. Then with arrows pointing away from the circle, she jotted down the students' questions:
>
> - How can we increase student input in selecting and planning elective studies?
> - Why shouldn't students be more involved in selecting public service projects and studies outside of the school?
> - Why do students need a C average in all class work to participate in sports? Is this a good rule?

- Why can't students be in charge of the computer lab and library and keep it open after school hours?
- How can we make student government more attractive to all students and more powerful in setting school rules and regulations?
- Why don't we institute a club program so that everyone can be involved in an activity?
- How does our school differ from other schools? What can we learn from other schools?
- In what ways can we involve the neighborhood to help keep the school environment safe?

The students' questions were endless and well thought out. Cantor suggested that the students select questions to investigate, form small groups, and decide how to gather data.

Whole Class/Small Group

In the preceding example, Cantor worked with the students as a whole class until it was time to decide how to gather the evidence and facts that were needed. Another way she could have taught the lesson would be to move the students into small groups at the point when they were going to suggest questions for investigation. This may have resulted in greater participation and more diverse questions. After the groups suggest questions for research, the students may also desire to change groups and pursue a different interest.

Research studies such as this one provide opportunity for students to reach out into the community, learn more about district and state schooling requirements, and consider a different vision for their own education. As a result of their study and the changes they suggest, they may help educate the public outside of the school, improve the school environment, and come up with some creative suggestions for actualizing their goal of a violence-free school environment.

Teaching Hints

1. Listen attentively to the questions that students ask.
2. Build curriculum to include students' questions and interests.
3. Develop problem-solving lessons from current situations.
4. Help students gain and express meanings from the total curriculum (literature, history, visual arts, music, reading, and mathematics).
5. Surprise your students with new ideas and tasks. Provide time for students to "wonder."
6. Help students develop intrinsic motivation to make learning a lifetime excursion (Eisner, 2002).

Encouraging Creative Thinking

Jean Cantor wanted her students to learn to write short stories. The students had read a number of short stories from their literature textbook. She suggested that they review some of the stories they were familiar with and see if they could come up with a list of how the short story differs in construction from a full-length novel and what influences authors to choose specific subjects to write about.

Cantor did not intend to give the students a set of guidelines or a format for writing a short story; nor did she want to suggest topics for them to use in writing their own stories. Her purpose was not to inhibit their writing with rules or propose content for their stories; she expected the students to develop their own thoughts about how a short story might differ from a longer version and organize their own work using their own "big ideas." Her plan was a constructivist concept of how students become writers.

After students had about 30 minutes of individual (or partner) study time, she inquired about their thoughts on how short stories are constructed. She did not make a list of their responses, but she did probe their comments in an effort to guide in-depth thinking. For example, she asked, "What difficulties do you think a short story author might have? Suppose an author is writing for a magazine and is quite limited in the number of pages permitted. How will this affect the storyline? Should an author consider the audience for the story?"

The second question, concerning what influences a writer's work, encouraged an analysis of the stories they had read. Since students were allowed to work with partners or construct small groups for thinking about their assignment, it was clear that the second question really intrigued them and they tended to consult with each other. In their responses they needed to name the author, what it was about the story that "gave the author away" in terms of influences, and their conclusions. The students recognized that the environment where an author was brought up and/or presently lived often influenced the setting for the story. They commented that sexual preferences were evident. They noted that sometimes prior occupations affected the context of the story. In general, they concluded that good stories seemed to reflect an author's personal experiences.

Analysis of Cantor's Lesson

Cantor could have told the students, "Your assignment is to write a short story," or she could have given them a list of rules and characteristics of short stories and suggested a list of appropriate topics for the assignment. She did none of these things. Instead she had them develop their own conceptual understanding of how the short story differs from the traditional novel. Through the students' responses, she probed and encouraged higher-level thinking about the construction of a short story.

Too often teachers' suggestions for creative writing tell students to write about their summer vacation, what they did over the weekend, or how they felt when . . . . The consequences of this are that stories are stilted, very similar, and not very creative. Cantor created a problem-solving situation that required students to analyze what they had read and to think about the author's perspective. Ultimately the students would apply what they had learned about the construction of a short story and the need to draw upon their own experiences and knowledge to create a story.

Using Gestures to Emphasize and Communicate Meaning

All cultures (all people) use gestures to emphasize meanings. It is true, also, that some cultures use their hands to speak more than others. Teachers working with English language learners need to use more gestures than usual. Of course, we do not know whether our meaning is communicated until there is a reaction or oral communication from others. By their very nature, gestures are a form of constructivist teaching because the meaning must be constructed by the observer. Most gestures also require eye contact. The following descriptions suggest some of the possible ways to communicate through gestures. See if you can add to my list.

- *Hurry up:* quick clockwise hand circles in the air
- *Slow down:* slow counterclockwise hand circles in the air
- *Tired:* two hands held together next to face
- *Talking:* index finger and thumb clicking together
- *Quiet:* index finger to mouth or hands over ears
- *Everyone participate:* arms and hands far apart and gesturing to entire class
- *Encourage a designated person to participate:* palm up and focused on one person; eye contact also necessary
- *Stand up:* palms up and arms moving upward
- *Sit down:* palms down and arms moving downward
- *I don't know* or *I won't say!:* shoulders moving upward.
- *I can't hear:* ears cupped and pushed forward
- *Glad to meet you:* shaking hands

Note that many of these gestures can be used for classroom management. Drama teachers often suggest gestures for role-playing, and gestures are another way to teach concepts to students.

Teaching Hints

Observe your students, parents, and other teachers. Watch their hands and their eyes. What do the gestures tell you? Do the eyes communicate the same (consistent) meaning(s)? Now think about what the eyes do *not* tell you.

Using Resources for Inquiry and Problem-Solving Teaching Strategies

Resources for inquiry and problem solving are as varied as the content you are teaching. They may include pictures, artifacts, and specialized equipment for each subject (microscopes, geoboards, instruments, clothing, household utensils). Reliable sources typically include textbooks and literary sources. Simulations and games can be valuable teaching tools. The Internet provides a wide range of resources for students' research. These tools will be discussed in Chapter 12.

As you plan inquiry activities, make a list of resources for your students to use, and don't forget "people" resources, such as neighborhood specialists, the librarian, parents and other teachers, and students who have special talents. Students can develop their own resources through observation, writing questionnaires, and interviewing knowledgeable others.

The Case Study Approach

The resources students need are sometimes unavailable, too bounteous for students to select what they need, or too difficult for them. When this occurs, teachers may choose to develop their own case study materials for students to use in an investigation. This approach assists the teacher in reducing both the amount of data and the time it would take for students to gather their own data. However, case study materials need to be appropriate for the students you teach in terms of reading and vocabulary level, concept load, and specialized skills such as reading graphs, maps, and charts.

Secondary Education Case Studies   In Jean Cantor's literature class, the students were reading current biographies and autobiographies of important people in American life. Cantor's purposes were for students to (1) develop an appreciation of the biography and autobiography as a reference tool; (2) differentiate between the styles of biography and fiction; and (3) recognize the significance of biography as a means to authenticate historical information.

Case studies may be about current or fictional issues and problems. Since Cantor chose to integrate her literature and history coursework, she chose historical contexts for a case study of biography versus fiction. She chose four rather different books, and in each of them specific chapters for the students to read. The books were David McCullough's biography *John Adams;* Robert A. Caro's biography of Lyndon Johnson, *Master of the Senate;* Katharine Graham's autobiography, *Personal History;* and Margaret Truman's portrait of White House wives, *First Ladies.* Her chapter choices focused on dilemmas that affected Adams, Johnson, Graham, and several wives of presidents.

Elementary Education Case Studies   Case studies are also appropriate for young students. In fact, the wide diversity of reading levels in the elementary school emphasizes the importance of case study resources appropriate for the learners involved. In an elementary school in Los Angeles, some fourth-grade students were involved in a playground dispute that culminated in destruction of lunchroom and play equipment. The problem was serious enough for the teacher whose students participated to conduct personal interviews with the students and ask the students to write out their own versions of (1) What happened? (2) Who was involved? and (3) Why do you think this occurred? The interviews were taped and the written versions were duplicated.

Very little motivation was needed for this teacher to implement the case study approach, because the students all knew it was a classroom problem. The students were divided into groups and provided with tape recordings and personal statements. Obviously some of the "defendants" were in each of the groups. In this case the teacher did not ask the students to define the problem or state hypotheses at the beginning of the inquiry. Instead she told them that they were on a "fact-finding mission" to clarify what happened, what caused it to happen, and how the problem could be avoided in the future. She suggested that each group should decide on how to use their data, take notes, discuss, come to some conclusions, and prepare for a class discussion.

> **Teaching Hints: The Case Study Approach**
>
> 1. Choose the problem for study in the form of an inquiry question.
> 2. Ask students to hypothesize about the problem.
> 3. Provide data for the students to use; clarify terms, issues, and students' questions.
> 4. Have students work individually or in groups to analyze data.
> 5. Hold a class discussion that focuses on analysis. (What happened? Why did it happen? What are the consequences? What conclusions and/or inferences can we draw?)

The case study approach may be used formally with actual "cases" such as Supreme Court controversies, and moot courts in the classroom will help students understand the justice system. This approach can also be informal, as in the elementary school conflict situation or Jean Cantor's literature and history case. The decision for using this approach should be based on resource and data needs and availability. Case studies are considered open-ended because students make the decisions when their research concludes. For additional information on case studies, see Lemlech (2002).

Chapter Summary

Inquiry and constructivist teaching are contrasted with expository teaching models (Chapter 8) and linked to creating a classroom community with democratic citizenship responsibilities and behaviors. Teaching strategies associated with inquiry are facilitated by open-ended questions, reflective responsive time, and social interaction. Teaching episodes in this chapter demonstrate concept attainment, group investigation, the Taba questioning strategy, backward problem solving, and the case study approach.

Teaching Problems

1. Your students are studying their senses. You want them to recognize that we have five senses that affect our perceptions. You have decided on a concept attainment strategy. Your first set of examples includes the following:

    lyrical (Yes)
    lissome (Yes)
    bedraggled (No)
    aroma (Yes)
    personally (No)
    piquant (Yes)
    grim (No)
    nearby (No)
    gaze (Yes)

    Your task is to create the second list of clues, which will *not* be labeled *yes* or *no*. Develop your second list using the five senses and the "distractors." If you try this lesson with your students, see if they recognize the five senses and can list positive and negative attributes for examples.

2. Create a concept web appropriate to your grade level and subject field. Refer to Chapter 6 and the section on backward problem solving in this chapter for help. See if you can use any of the following choices for your concept web: *matter, humans, transportation, the planet*.

3. Write a sample lesson plan at your grade level and subject field using concrete representations for a concept attainment lesson.

4. You are teaching an advanced placement class in physics, history, economics, or calculus. Write an inquiry question to motivate students' thinking and follow-up questions after anticipating their responses.

5. You are teaching a class in the arts (visual, performing, music, dance, drama). Write an inquiry question to motivate group investigation. Complete the lesson plan, indicating the resources students will use and what you anticipate will be the students' products.

6. Use the Taba questions for concept formation, interpretation, and application. Refer to Jim Sierra's lesson in which he used Taba's cognitive questions.

7. Create a data retrieval chart to be used in a group investigation lesson. Consider the topic of energy and the ensuing problems or possible solutions for urban centers, including fuel, population growth, carcinogens, conservation, efficiency, alternative sources of energy, and architecture.

PART 5

GUIDING AND ASSESSING STUDENTS' PERFORMANCE

Chapter 10 looks at the ways teachers can find out how students are progressing and how well their own teaching was understood. Monitoring is a means to obtain instant feedback on both teaching and learning. It is a means to guide students and meet individual needs. Discussed are ways for students to help each other as partners and coaches, ways to reinforce students' progress, and how to share with parents or guardians during a parent-teacher conference. Chapter 11 concentrates on how assessment can inform instruction. Assessment is defined and discussion highlights how to assess students' ways of thinking, their content knowledge, and communication skills. Rubrics are demonstrated and both formal and informal means of testing are discussed.

CHAPTER 10

Informing Instruction Through Monitoring Students' Performance

ADVANCE ORGANIZER

These questions can be used as a framework to assist you in integrating professional knowledge and understanding of the content of this chapter.

1. What should teachers look for when monitoring student performance?
2. What data do students contribute to assist teachers' monitoring?
3. What should teachers look for when monitoring English language learners?
4. What should teachers look for when monitoring critical-thinking skills?
5. How does monitoring individual skill practice differ from monitoring small-group work?
6. How should a teacher plan for a parent conference?
7. Why should teachers consider three-way student, parent, and teacher conferences?

 The following INTASC issues and standards are discussed in this chapter: Numbers 1–4, 6–8.

Monitoring students' performance means to "oversee" and guide their work. By doing so, teachers not only demonstrate that they are anxious to provide help to their students, but also determine whether their own teaching performance was effective. A number of ways to assist students are provided in the chapter, as well as suggestions of factors to look for. The chapter also provides information on planning for parent conferences and parent-student-teacher conferences.

The students in Roger Ives's biology class have just been given a group work assignment.* They are to prepare pro and con positions for a classroom debate on genetic literacy. Students will need to engage in research to determine the reality and implications of genetic issues: Should everyone undergo DNA testing? Should everyone have access to genetic information (health organizations, employers, insurance companies)? Genetic information could lead to "designer babies"; should genetic engineering be allowed?

Marci raised her hand: "Mr. Ives, when we do group work, how do you know who is doing the group work and whether everyone does his share? Do we all get the same grade?"

Mr. Ives responded, "That is a very good question, and it tells me that I have not communicated to you how you and your classmates demonstrate what you are learning and, in addition, what I am looking for." Ives went to the board and wrote down the ways he monitors students' work. Then he continued, "So you see, Marci, that I am quite aware of the contribution of each individual even when you work in groups. Though you do get group credit, you also are graded individually. The purpose of group work is to share ideas to enrich and diversify what you learn and to provide a more active learning experience."

Mr. Ives's notes on the board will be used to discuss how teachers can monitor and guide students' work. Marci's concern about assessment is frequently the concern of both students and parents, who sometimes feel that the individual is sacrificed for the good of the larger group. Monitoring and assessment of students' work can occur whether students are working individually or with others, as the rest of the chapter will indicate.

---

*Lesson content suggested by J. Franklin, "Promises and Perils: How Genetic Literacy Will Affect Students' Lives." *Curriculum Update* (2002, Summer)

Teacher Responsibility for Student Performance

During the nationalist period of U.S. history (1776–1876), schoolmasters were required to sign contracts with the school trustees that stipulated the following:

- The number of students they would teach
- The number of days of required schooling
- That students would be taught as much as they were capable of learning
- That a progress report for each student would be submitted at the end of the term (Lemlech, 2002)

The accountability movement and teachers' responsibility for assessment can be traced to this period of U.S. history.

Experienced teachers today recognize that when their students do poorly, it is a sign that their teaching was ineffective. The actual adage is, "When students fail, teachers have failed." The only means to prevent student failure and to obtain feedback on your own teaching is to closely monitor and assess students' on-task performance.

Responsibility for performance is not limited to the classroom. When several members of a professional sports team get hurt, the question is always raised as to whether the training program was adequate. Baseball pitchers are particularly vulnerable to game "overuse," and coaches are considered at fault if a pitcher is injured. Whenever children participate in organized sports programs, their coaches (who tend to be parents) are responsible for preparing the children with appropriate warm-up and cool-down exercises. So it is not surprising that the public insists on teacher responsibility for student performance.

What Is Monitoring?

When teachers **monitor** their classrooms, they are basically engaging in purposeful observation of the class to detect problems in teaching, student practice or application, and general behavior. The teacher may gather data about their classroom environment, the tasks students are engaged in, the appropriateness of subject field content, or students' interaction. An effective teacher may absorb information related to all four commonplaces of instruction; however, purposeful observation typically focuses on one of the four components.

Mr. Ives's class is preparing for a debate, and he will be sitting in with the different groups to see what resources they select, what Web sites they visit, how discussion progresses within each group, how well students interact (leadership within the group, contribution of all members, problems with content, problems confronted by English language learners), and what debate positions they choose to take. He will be open to group questions, and while sitting in with a group he will also eyeball the rest of the class to perceive any problems that may occur and anticipate which group he needs to visit next.

Did You Know That . . . ?

Most teachers monitor students' understanding of lessons—unconsciously! When asked why they deviated from their lesson plans or retaught a lesson with a different focus, they respond, "Something just told me I needed to do that." In actuality, the teachers are reading students' expressions, body movements, wiggles, and eyes (Pensavalle, 2002).

Controlling the Classroom Environment

As Mr. Ives strolls about his classroom, he notes the placement and space for each group and their access to resources. Social cognitive theorists believe that the knowledge and skills students learn depend on the environment in which learning takes place (Langer, 2001). For this reason, Ives wants an easygoing and comfortable class environment. He knows that if groups are too crowded, students won't be able to work. He worries about talking that is too loud and may interfere with other groups' discussions. He likes to limit group work to five students in order to facilitate discussion and group work assignments. If students are engaging in large-scale productions such as making models or experimenting, he may suggest that a group work outside the classroom on the playground or in the hallway; however, this increases his supervisory problems because he too will need to leave the classroom at times to visit the absent group.

Ives carries a large yellow pad with him as he observes, and he is constantly taking notes about what he sees and hears. If groups are too close together, he suggests that they move, or he waits until evaluation and asks students for suggestions on how conditions can be improved. He has numbered each group and listed the members of each group, since group work will continue for more than one class period. As he visits each group, he notes what each person is doing and whether he or she is making a positive contribution to the group. Sometimes he jots down a question to ask a specific student.

Individual work often requires greater monitoring efforts because of the individual attention required. Teachers need to develop a system whereby students raise their hand or give some visual signal when they require teacher help. As you tour your classroom giving advice and assistance, you may discover misunderstandings by more than one student. When this occurs, you need to either (1) stop the group as a whole and engage in reteaching or refocusing, or (2) if the misunderstanding is shared by just a small group of students, engage in small-group teaching for these students. It is wise to take notes on who is having difficulty and the nature of the problem. The monitoring of individual work provides opportunity for guidance focused on individual needs.

> **Teaching Hints: Monitoring Individual Skill Practice**
>
> 1. Observe students' expressions and work behaviors.
> 2. Remind students to seek help, if needed, by raising a hand or giving another visual signal for teacher assistance.
> 3. Assure students that there are a variety of ways to perform the task.
> 4. Walk around the classroom and ask individual students to explain their work.
> 5. Reteach skills, as needed.
> 6. Record notes concerning individual needs.

Encouraging Complex Thinking Skills

To encourage students' thinking beyond the written page, beyond fundamental literacy skills, and beyond the workbook, there needs to be opportunity for students to pursue interests and ideas in depth. Students need open-ended questions and tasks and small work groups to share thoughts and plans with their classmates. Roger Ives's plan for a class debate provides common curriculum content for all students, with opportunity for the students to select their own resources, express individual viewpoints, and choose the points they want to emphasize. Students can begin their research and thinking at any starting point. Group members may begin by discussing and arguing among themselves before dividing up the inquiry tasks, or by assigning the questions to individuals and discussing assumptions and critical points after data have been collected. In essence, Ives's assignment was designed to *differentiate* instruction by allowing a great deal of student autonomy.

Monitoring English Language Learners and Students with Special Needs

Time used for monitoring students' work performance provides ideal moments for assisting ELL students, students considered at risk, and any other student with a special need. Whether students are working individually or in group situations, it is possible to go one-on-one with a student and develop the special relationship needed to encourage the student's performance, suggest instructional approaches, and really focus on individual needs.

> **Teaching Hints: Monitoring English Language Learners**
>
> 1. Verify that the student is participating in planning and discussion.
> 2. Verify that the student is comprehending group tasks.
> 3. Does the student need a buddy to provide assistance?

> 4. Does the student need lesson content introduced in his or her native language?
> 5. Is the student able to perform tasks in English, or should the student use native language skills?

The extra attention given to individual students translates into better teacher-student relationships and higher achievement. Once this relationship is developed, the student will confide in the teacher and provide significant feedback concerning instructional needs. When an ELL student or student with a special need is working in a small group, you need to know whether he or she is able to fulfill work tasks, has a peer partner to assist, needs different resources, and is accepted by the rest of the group.

If you are fluent in the native language of your ELL students, it may be beneficial to provide an overview of content in the native language and then provide the substance of the lesson in English. Of course, this is appropriate only if you have a number of students with the same language background.

The Individuals with Disabilities Education Act (IDEA) provides extra funds to states to help care for students with special needs. According to the National Center for Education Statistics, 45.7 percent of the 6.2 million students in special education have specific learning disabilities. The remaining population have physical disabilities. The special education population has grown considerably in the last fifteen years. Some educators believe this is a consequence of better means to identify children with learning problems. But some legislators are convinced that the reason the population has increased so dramatically is that teachers may have a harder time teaching these children, and so they try to rid themselves of problems by placing these children in special education. Since 1986, funds are included for infants and toddlers who attend preschool classes in the public schools. Presently Congress is considering putting a cap on the amount of funds schools receive.

Monitoring Each Student's Contribution to Group Assignments

Teachers can use a number of generic techniques to verify and check on students' participation, as well as specific subject field techniques to check content knowledge. The debate planned by Roger Ives is clearly an inquiry-oriented assignment. The students do not know whether they will be arguing the pro or con side of the argument, but they also need to recognize that in order to prepare for a debate, it is necessary to anticipate what your opponent(s) will retort, so it is important to prepare for both the pro and con.

The following examples will illustrate.

1. Students may be asked to jot down their pro and con ideas, with their resources cited, on 3 × 5 cards. Mr. Ives can then inspect the cards. During the actual debate, students can use their 3 × 5 cards as prompts for the points they want to make.

2. Students' choices for resources for each question can be turned in so that Ives can check the pattern of thinking. When using the Internet, students may be asked to list

the sites they visit. Again, this will illustrate how the student is pursuing research about the topic.

3. When Ives visits each group, he can ask questions of individuals or engage the whole group in discussion to monitor student engagement.

4. Students can be asked to keep a journal in which they write down what they did each day to contribute to the group project. The journal may be included in the student's portfolio.

5. Group work typically ends with a whole-class discussion. Students' contributions to the discussion will provide insight into their work. When students participate in the discussion, they can be asked to cite their resources.

To monitor students' critical thinking, Ives needs to listen and observe students' participation using the skills listed in Figure 10.1.

Ives can use Figure 10.1 as a checklist to monitor whether students are participating and contributing to their group. He will be able to ascertain whether specific students are focusing on the problem or coasting on others' work. The checklist will assist Ives when he engages in formal assessment of each student's work.

Providing Guided Practice and Social Interaction

The purpose of **guided practice** is to verify students' understanding of the skill presented during direct instruction. This requires the teacher to view each student's performance and offer suggestions if students are having difficulty. It is the time when you will be able to

---

Names of Students

- Defining the problem: _____
- Raising questions about the problem: _____
- Suggesting areas for investigation: _____
- Posing hypotheses: _____
- Suggesting possible resources and means to use them:_____
- Gathering data: _____
- Comparing and contrasting data: _____
- Analyzing data for relevance and accuracy:_____
- Synthesizing and generalizing about the data: _____
- Making inferences and theorizing based on the interpretation: _____

FIGURE 10.1 Checklist for Monitoring Critical-Thinking Skills

ensure that you taught what you intended—and if you did not, to reteach. Obviously, monitoring students' performance is critical to the process of direct instruction.

As you tour the classroom during the guided practice segment, ask students to explain what they are doing. Sometimes you will be rudely awakened to the fact that students tend to imitate your performance with little or no understanding. In mathematics, students frequently attempt to follow a specific process without recognizing that what they are doing makes no sense. Thus it is valuable to provide time for students to demonstrate unique, individual means for solving problems and to emphasize that there is more than one way to achieve the end result.

Social interaction requires a different perspective for monitoring students' performance. Not only are you attempting to gather information about what students know, but you are also checking on students' ability to communicate and work cooperatively with peers. A scenario in a fifth-grade classroom reveals what a teacher learned while monitoring group work.

> Brad was perpetually in trouble. He was a show-off, interrupted others' work, and seemed to need attention constantly. When he was supposed to be working with a small group of students, the other students in the group ignored him. As a consequence, he wandered around the classroom. His teacher confronted him and realized that he was very unhappy because his group gave him no responsibilities: "I've got nothing to do and they don't want me in their group."
>
> The teacher went over and talked to the group and told them that Brad was an expert photographer and perhaps they should ask him to take some pictures for their group report. The group agreed, and the next day they talked to Brad (for the first time) and asked him to take on that responsibility. Brad was given permission to bring his camera to school, and he began to take pictures on the playground and in the cafeteria, the principal's office, the gymnasium, and the library. Then he wrote captions for the pictures, attended group meetings, and discussed his pictures and how they would fit in the group report. He became a "model citizen."

Brad's problems in the classroom did not disappear entirely, but his behavior certainly improved. His teacher's insight about genuine responsibility paid dividends. Brad gained respect from his peers and learned that cooperative work with classmates requires everyone to share responsibility and work toward a common, accepted goal.

Monitoring small-group work often reveals students' misconceptions and lack of focus on significant ideas. By listening to students during group project planning, you can alleviate the problems of going off in the wrong direction, wandering from the topic or assignment, and misunderstanding. Simple questions to help the group refocus their thinking will often get them back on track and save you and the students much aggravation.

Teachers can learn a great deal about their students while monitoring small-group work sessions. Partner and three-person groups also reveal significant information about student learning and ability to work cooperatively with others.

# Did You Know That . . . ?

Langer (2001) studied middle and high school students enrolled in English language arts programs in four states and eighty-eight classrooms over a two-year period. Six factors differentiated more-successful classrooms from less-successful classrooms: (1) Skills and knowledge were taught in a variety of lessons and contexts; (2) tests were used to inform curriculum and instruction; (3) to ensure coherence, teachers integrated content and structure of lessons; (4) teachers emphasized thinking and doing; (5) teachers encouraged generative learning; and (6) collaborative and shared cognition were encouraged in the classroom organization (p. 876).

Partner Work and Coaching

Both practice and application tasks are often enhanced by pairing students to work together. Partners may be selected by students or by teachers for specific purposes. For example, the needs of English language learners may require that a student with greater language proficiency work with a student who is struggling to learn the language. A student who is more creative may motivate a student who fears taking risks. However, it is important that each student in the partnership has something to offer the other student. The student who tends not to take risks may be extremely conscientious and consistent, while the creative student tends to jump from one idea to another. As partners these two students may balance each other and perform better.

Partners contribute to each other when engaging in science investigations.

Similar to grouping students, partners should be rotated so that students do not become overly dependent on one person. Partner choices should be situation specific. In language arts, partners may help each other with creative writing ideas; in science, partners may contribute to recording experiment observations; in mathematics, partners may suggest different processes for solving problems.

In an advanced placement senior physics class at Oak Park High School (California), the teacher, Dave Nelson, allowed students to choose a partner or group of up to four students to create a roller coaster. The assignment had specific dimensions and constraints and was complex enough to assure that students working together would be challenged. Students depended on each other to obtain supplies, review the research principles of movement, and construct the actual three-dimensional electric roller coaster to meet specific criteria. Students self-tested the roller coaster and then demonstrated the project in class. During the actual construction stage, students were encouraged to consult with the teacher when problems were encountered. Teacher monitoring of student work was limited to students' consultations with the teacher and questions asked by the teacher during consultations and presentations.*

Did You Know That . . . ?

A study by the University of Minnesota Center for Adolescent Health and Development reported by the director Robert Blum that school "connectedness" is influenced by the following:

1. Well-managed classrooms with opportunities for extracurricular activities
2. Empathetic and consistent teachers who allow students to make decisions
3. Comprehensive health care programs that include physical and health education, nutritious meal programs, and counseling (Bowman, 2002b)

Communities of Learners

Assignments such as Dave Nelson's help build communities of learners. Students learn to share knowledge and skills and to build common understandings and language related to the field of study. Most important, they learn to trust one another and develop a cooperative structure for interacting with others.

When students are encouraged to work and share ideas with peers, it helps to create an environment that values learning, relaxes students, and makes the classroom a comfortable place to be. Simone (2001) describes how she encourages students to analyze the writing process. While reading aloud to her students, she stops at intervals and asks them to consider the meaning of the author's statements. Then she tells her students to turn to a neighbor and brainstorm their insights. Partners are casually arranged, and after a short

---

*Content contributed by Dave Nelson, Science Department Chair at Oak Park High School, Oak Park, California.

period of time Simone asks them to share their thoughts. She monitors the students' listening skills through their understanding of the story, their thinking skills from their insights about the author's use of writing devices, and their interactions with peers through the discussion that follows.

Monitoring students' performance should not imply behavioral control. Instead it should have the connotation of facilitating students' performance. The monitoring process may be formal, as in checking understanding during direct instruction, or informal, where students come to you for consultation and guidance or in the process of visiting groups during group research and planning tasks.

Teaching Hints: Monitoring Partner and Three-Person Teams

1. Verify that each partner has something to contribute to the team so that each may lead at some time during the partnership.
2. Verify that partner interactions are cooperative, with each partner contributing effort.
3. Verify that partners offer advice and ideas and share insights with each other.
4. Unless there is dissension between partners, monitoring should occur with all members of the partnership together.

Reinforcing Students' Progress

The significant aspect of monitoring students' performance is the opportunity it gives you to gain insight concerning students' needs. Monitoring becomes the gateway to differentiation of instruction.

> Lucia Martin was having her students do addition problems and manipulate ice cream sticks to help them solve single-digit problems. As she walked around and observed, she noted that some students moved the sticks in groups from one problem to another when the numeral was the same, while others needed to count them out one by one in order to set them up for the new problem. She realized that these students, at the preoperational level, lacked the concept of reversibility (Chapter 3) and would need more practice with concrete objects. But other students were far advanced, and for them the problems were equivalent to busywork and not productive learning. She realized that for students to have continuous progress, she needed to group her students in mathematics to challenge some of the children, while others would need more experience with concrete objects.

Parents should not be expected to be teachers.

By providing individual assistance, teachers are able to guide students' work.

Homework

Homework assignments are another way that teachers can reinforce what they are teaching in class. Homework should not be assigned to keep students busy, to involve parents in the teaching process, or even to practice a skill. Homework assignments should be at the application level so that students will work independently to apply what they have learned in school at a higher level of understanding and in a unique way.

The criteria for Mr. Nelson's roller coaster assignment required that students apply their experience and knowledge of physics in order to construct a roller coaster that would carry a marble to the top of the roller coaster and include an 8-inch-diameter loop and a 2-inch horizontal jump. Additional constraints were built into the assignment. This project was certainly beyond testing students' knowledge and comprehension of physics; complex thinking skills were required.

Monitoring and Feedback for Homework

Perhaps one of the biggest causes of student dissatisfaction with their teachers relates to correction and feedback on homework assignments. Too often students bring their work to class, hand it in, and never hear anything more about it. If teachers believe that homework has a purpose, then surely it must be examined and discussed with the students. Discussion of homework provides a means for students to share unique ways to accomplish goals, innovations, and sometimes old skills that their parents may have demonstrated.

For teachers, homework is a means to discover whether students own proper tools and work space at home to accomplish home studies. It is sometimes surprising that so many students have no space of their own for studying, no dictionaries or other print materials, no computers, no typewriters. Access to public libraries may be limited to the parent's ability to drive the child, and parents often work and sometimes do not have an automobile. Students frequently depend on the school library and computer lab, and too often these resources are unavailable after school and on the weekends. Clearly our schools need to do better to provide equal access for all students to learn.

Most important for teachers is the feedback homework provides on whether students really understood what was taught. For this reason, application assignments are extremely important. It is one thing for students to respond in class with precisely what was taught and another thing to use what was taught in a creative and different way.

Though some teachers have routinized the collection of homework, others use it as a means to motivate the class period. Beginning with the homework assignment, teachers can initiate a class discussion in which students share what they did. Some teachers have students form small three-person teams and critique each other's work. Perhaps the most important point is that homework can be the jumping-off place for beginning the next lesson, and students can contribute how the prior assignment links with what is presently being taught.

Did You Know That . . . ?

> Emmer and Gerwels (2002) studied cooperative learning practices in elementary classrooms. They observed student engagement, student interaction and cooperation, and individual and/or group accountability. They found that teachers who were most successful actively monitored group work and provided assistance and feedback. They also noted that groups do better if their group tasks involve manipulative materials.

Behavioral Monitoring

Suppose you have a student who disturbs the class frequently with verbal outbursts. The student is aware that this is unacceptable, provokes the teacher's wrath, and annoys other students. After numerous conferences with the student and parents, you decide on a self-monitoring plan in which the student keeps track of the number of times she is admonished either verbally or by gestures to control the outbursts. You explain a simple graphing technique for the student to use, with numbers on one side of the graph representing the number of reminders and days of the week at the bottom of the graph. The object is for the student to try to decrease the "reminders" as the week progresses. Such a technique may also prove to be a monitoring device that enables the teacher to determine whether on certain days the student has more difficulty than on other days, thereby contributing information that may determine the cause of the behavior. Figure 10.2 depicts a histogram that the student may be taught to draw. The student is responsible for keeping track of her own behavior and for sharing the histogram with her teacher and parents. This strategy is often effective in curbing problem behaviors.

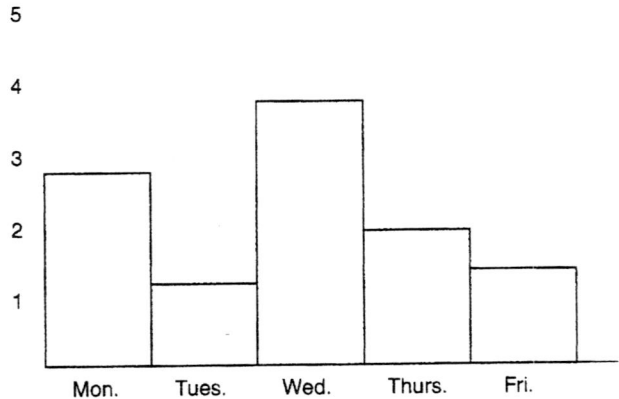

FIGURE 10.2 Teacher "Reminders"
Source: J. K. Lemlech. (2000). *Curriculum and Instructional Methods for the Elementary and Middle School*, 5th ed. Upper Saddle River, NJ: Prentice Hall. Reprinted with permission.

Sharing Student Work with Parents

Telephone calls are a wonderful means to share good news. Calling parents to report that their son or daughter did something extraordinary or unique *for them* is a wonderful treat for parents. The call does not have to report A+ grades, but it should report progress in academics and/or behavior, such as promptness and diligence with work tasks.

If, however, students' work requires parental concern, it is far better to meet with the parents personally. To arrange this you might want to write a note or have the school secretary call to set the appointment. You do not want to get into a sustained telephone conversation when there are troubling aspects of school work behavior to discuss.

Notes to parents should be carefully constructed, whether communicating good news or the need for a conference. It is wise to edit your notes by reading them aloud to yourself to verify that they say what you want and communicate clearly. If you have a teaching buddy, it is always a good idea to have someone else read the note before you send it home. Figure 10.3 provides an example of a request for a parent conference.

The note does not say precisely what the problem is about, but it is clear that the teacher expects parents to comply with the request. In some schools there may be formal conference request forms for teachers to use. It is wise not to say too much in the note; instead hold off for the conference. You do not want to antagonize parents or put them on the defensive as they contemplate the meeting with you.

Parent-Teacher Conferences

The conference should be treated as a personal conversation between you and the parent. To facilitate communication, there are some basic, commonsense ways to initiate discussion.

1. You and the parent should sit either side by side or across from each other at the same level. (Do not be seated at your desk.)

> September 30, 2004
>
> Dear Mr. and Mrs. Romano:
>
> I have been working with your son, Jesse, for the last several weeks to help him improve both his homework and in-class assignments. I think it would help Jesse if we met to plan consistent assistance for him. I would appreciate it if you would call the school secretary and arrange a time for us to meet together. I am available to meet with you after school any day during the first week of October.
>
> Sincerely,
>
> Jim Sierra

FIGURE 10.3   Parent Conference Request

2. Remember that it is as important to *listen* to the parent as it is to *talk*. True communication occurs when you talk *with* someone, not *to* someone.

3. Speak in an adult tone and use adult language. Avoid professional jargon and avoid speaking as if you were talking to children.

4. Remember that parents may be defensive concerning their children's behavior. They should respond as the child's advocate.

5. Take special care not to use stereotypical ideas ("boys will be boys").

6. Begin the conversation by greeting the parent and engaging in some small talk to develop a "comfort" level and rapport before getting down to the issues involved.

7. Gather appropriate data for the conference. This means accumulating the student's work samples and any evidence that you have.

> Mrs. Romano has come to school to meet with Jim Sierra. She has rarely come to school to meet with a teacher; however she does attend "back to school" nights. She appears somewhat apprehensive and Jim wants to put her at ease. He motions for her to sit at a round table where six students normally sit, and he joins her. They are sitting side by side with their chairs pulled slightly apart for comfortable conversation. Jim has a pile of student work near him to use during the conference.

The conference between Mrs. Romano and Jim Sierra followed a typical strategy (Table 10.1):

1. Get acquainted and comfortable. Try to put the parent at ease.

2. State the purpose of the conference.

3. Ask questions to obtain information from the parent. Remember that the parent knows the child far better than you do.

TABLE 10.1 Conference Between Mrs. Romano and Mr. Sierra

Conversation	Interpretation
Sierra: Thank you for coming into talk with me, Mrs. Romano. I am pleased to see you again. You are looking well; how is Mr. Romano?	Courteous greeting.
Mrs. Romano: He is fine, thank you for asking. My husband and I were very concerned about Jesse's school work when we received your note. Has Jesse been misbehaving?	Parent wants to get to the purpose for the visit.
Sierra: It is not that Jesse really misbehaves, but he is not as attentive as he needs to be, and I thought perhaps that you could help me.	Teacher wants to be tactful and not upset the parent.
Mrs. Romano: What is Jesse doing?	Parent is asking for specifics.
Sierra: My concern is more on what he is not doing. His homework is usually late or not done at all. In class he doesn't always listen, he tends to wander about the room, and he has difficulty settling down and accomplishing work tasks. I wondered about his health and whether he displays any of these behaviors at home.	Teacher has decided to lay it out and tell the parent exactly what is happening. He raises the question about the child's health.
Mrs. Romano: I think his health is OK, though he hasn't seen a doctor recently. Sports are very important to Jesse. He is on a soccer team sponsored by the American Youth Soccer Organization. He has practice usually just one afternoon a week and a game on the weekend.	Parent shares information about child's personal interests.
Sierra: What other activities does Jesse engage in?	Teacher recognizes that soccer could not be the only distraction.
Mrs. Romano: Well, he likes to get together with his friends. They ride bikes and "mess around," as Jesse describes it. He watches a little bit of TV in the evenings.	Parent opens up and mentions other activities.
Sierra: When does he do his homework?	Teacher raises the relevant question.
Mrs. Romano: I ask him every day if he has homework. Usually he says he has taken care of it. Sometimes he asks for help.	Parent responds hesitantly.
Sierra: Does he tell you about what he is studying at school?	Teacher seeks more information.
Mrs. Romano: Not usually. Sometimes he talks about science experiments. He hasn't told us that he doesn't finish his work or that it is difficult for him.	Parent shares additional information.

(continued)

CHAPTER 10 Informing Instruction Through Monitoring Students' Performance

Conversation	Interpretation
Sierra: Mrs. Romano, let's look at some of Jesse's assignments and what he has accomplished. (He displays some math work, writing portfolio, art, social studies, and a science project. He then explains each piece of work and what should be there.) It is obvious that Jesse excels in science, but he neglects his other work. One of his problems seems to be that he doesn't listen when assignments are explained. Do you notice whether Jesse listens to directions at home?	Teacher displays actual evidence to convince parent of the problem. Teacher recognizes student's strong subject and then acknowledges a behavioral problem as he raises a behavioral question.
Mrs. Romano: Well, I just thought it was natural for boys his age to pay little attention to their mothers. I think he listens to his father better.	Mother excuses child using stereotyped behavior explanation.
Sierra: Mrs. Romano, I don't really think this is a gender problem. Let's see if we can problem-solve and find a way to help Jesse. First off, I think it would be a good idea to have a doctor check Jesse to see that his health is fine. If you would like, I probably can get vision and hearing tests done here at school.	Teacher suggests further inquiry.
Mrs. Romano: I will take him to our doctor, but I would appreciate the vision and hearing tests done here at school, if possible. What else should I do?	Mother accepts the teacher's offer and assumes some personal responsibility.
Sierra: Ask Jesse to show you his homework assignment every day. See if he understands the assignment and insist that he sit down and work on it. Then inspect his work for completeness and responsiveness to the assignment. Talk to him about his work at school, but do not bawl him out; just find out his perception of how well he is doing. Call me about what you have learned and also his doctor's report. Then let's plan another conference in about two weeks and ask Jesse to attend. Do you think that would be a good idea?	Teacher suggests parental guidance and oversight of student's work. Teacher provides a concluding plan and asks for parent agreement.
Mrs. Romano: Yes, I do. Jesse obviously is not taking his schoolwork seriously and it would be a good idea if we talked with him together. I will ask his father to attend also.	Parent commitment is obtained.
Sierra: Mrs. Romano, thank you for your promptness in responding to this problem. Let's see if between the two of us we can make some real progress, and I will look into checking out the vision and hearing tests with our school nurse. I look forward to hearing from you. (Teacher and parent shake hands, and parent leaves.)	Conference is concluded. Commitment and joint efforts are confirmed.

4. Use the student's work as evidence of accomplishments or needs for improvement. Interpret the work assignments and test scores.
5. Listen and respond to parents' questions and comments.
6. Develop a plan with the parent to assist the student.
7. Share decision making with the parent and plan a future meeting if necessary.
8. Thank the parent for attending the conference.

Unplanned Conferences

Sometimes parents show up at the classroom door because they are angry or upset about something they think happened in the classroom or because of problems in the home. It is wise to sit down with them and "hear them out." An unplanned conference is not remarkably different from a planned one, except that you need to begin by calming the parent and demonstrating that you, as well as the parent, are the child's advocate.

Teaching Hints: Unplanned Conferences

1. Sit down with the parent/guardian and get comfortable.
2. Ask the parent to explain what is troubling him or her. Give enough time for the parent to vent anger or frustration. (Do not respond defensively.)
3. Ask questions, listen carefully, and gather information.
4. If the parent asks questions, respond in a neutral manner without anger or professional jargon.
5. If the student is having a problem and you are aware of it, share what you are doing about it. If you are unaware of the problem, ask the parent for suggestions.
6. Develop an action plan with the parent; share decision making and responsibility.
7. Summarize goals and plans and obtain commitment for another conference at a future date to share accomplishments and needs.

Whether conferences are planned or unplanned, remember that both you and the parent have a stake in the outcome. You both want the student to do well and both of you should be the child's advocate.

Teacher-Parent-Student Conferences

The three-way conference occurs most often with secondary students because it is somewhat awkward for a parent to confer with a teacher without student resentment; however, elementary students also may profit from the interaction of parent and teacher. The purposes of the three-way conference are to communicate learning progress, share information about student effort, and gain information to improve teaching. A good technique for beginning the conference is to ask the student to share his or her perception of learning progress. To do this, the student should gather work papers, projects, and tests—just as the teacher would do—and explain them to the parent. If additional explanation is needed, the teacher should add on to what the student is communicating.

All three parties at the conference should share their perceptions of student effort. If they agree that effort needs to improve, a plan for improvement should be made with all three in agreement. The conference should close with set goals and actions and perhaps a target date for another conference.

The advantages of including the student at the conference are as follows: (1) The student hears what both parent and teacher say and is free to respond. (2) Nothing is hidden from the student or the parent. (3) The student's effort is the bottom line, and the student helps to set future goals. (4) The student recognizes that both teacher and parent are acting on his or her behalf and working cooperatively and respectfully together.

Chapter Summary

Monitoring students' work helps teachers learn about their own teaching effectiveness. Through monitoring, teachers learn about (1) student misunderstandings, (2) students' social skills, (3) appropriateness of subject field content, (4) classroom behavior, (5) classroom environment, and (6) students' thinking skills.

Teachers can use a variety of means to gather information about students' learning, including observation, individual conferences, portfolios, student-made exhibits, journals, note taking, discussions, homework, and social interactions. This information helps teachers differentiate the instructional program. Parent conferences are another source of information, and conferences should be carefully planned and include exhibits of students' work.

Teaching Problems

1. A new Latina fifth-grade child has entered your classroom midsemester. You introduce her to the class and explain the work assignment. The child appears very shy, so you do not question her, but you take her over to a small work group and suggest that she join the group. Later as you monitor the class, you notice that she is sitting still but does not appear to be working. Suggest ways to find out about the child's skills without embarrassing her.
2. A middle school parent has barged into your classroom after school and begins to rant about how you have mistreated her son. Describe how you will handle this situation. (You do not recall doing anything unusual affecting the boy.)
3. In your high school English class, several students complain that "they do all the work" and others in their group get credit without contributing to the group project. What are some things you can do about this?
4. You have given a student a D grade on his midsemester report card. This means that the student will not be able to participate on the soccer team. The student and his parents are furious with you. Although you could have given the student a C−, you chose not to do so to focus on the need for the student to exert more effort. Now the parents and the student want a conference with you, and they want you to change the grade. How will you prove to the parents that the student deserved the low grade, and how will you deal with the three-way conference?
5. When you look at Figure 10.2, what questions come to mind? What would you want to investigate? Would you question the parents?

CHAPTER 11

Informing Instruction Through Assessment

ADVANCE ORGANIZER

These questions can be used as a framework to assist you in integrating professional knowledge and understanding of the content of this chapter.

1. How does assessment help teachers improve students' learning and their own teaching?
2. What tools can teachers use to assess and gather appropriate evidence of students' learning?
3. How do rubrics enhance students' work and provide means for teachers' judgment?
4. What are the opposing concerns regarding the use of standards for planning curriculum and instructional activities?
5. What are the advantages of teacher-made tests, and what types of tests are used?
6. What do standardized tests tell us about students' performance?
7. Though grading is a teacher responsibility, why does it tell us so little about student performance?
8. What problems do English language learners have with tests, and how can teachers help alleviate some of those problems?

CHAPTER 11 Informing Instruction Through Assessment   239

 The following INTASC issues and standards are discussed in this chapter: Numbers 1–3, 7–9.

Assessment is an ongoing process, and there are a variety of ways to assess students' learning. This chapter identifies formal, informal, and product-producing means for determining how students are doing in the classroom. But assessment not only tells us how well students are doing, it also informs teachers how well they are doing. Examples of standardized, formal, and teacher-made tests are given. Several rubrics are provided at elementary, middle school, and high school levels as examples of how to set criteria for student performance. In addition, student portfolio assessment is described.

What Is Assessment?

When Jim Sierra met with Jesse's mother, Mrs. Romano, he had prepared exhibits or samples of Jesse's class work and homework. The exhibits told the story of how well Jesse was performing in the different subject fields. In addition to the display of Jesse's work, Mr. Sierra had his own impressions based on Jesse's participation in oral discussions, project participation, pattern of effort, and interaction with others. These "impressions" were subjective based on Mr. Sierra's professional experience and understanding of Jesse's developmental level. The concrete work materials data, testing data, and Mr. Sierra's subjective data form the basis for assessment of Jesse's performance.

Assessment is not determined by a single piece of evidence, such as standardized tests or teacher-made tests. Assessment is the gathering of many types of student work in order to gain insight about the student's performance. Using a variety of data the teacher is then in a position to make a judgment about the student, which may culminate in a grade for performance.

Authentic Assessment

Authentic assessment involves gathering natural evidence related to real-life experiences. It is considered natural because it involves the everyday tasks and activities that students are performing. The tasks are constructivist in nature because students are developing meanings as they go about their work activities. So if young students are studying simple magnets, they might experiment with objects to find out what magnets will attract. When they begin to recognize the category of objects that magnets attract and can state a generalization, we know they have constructed meaning through their own experience. If they have the opportunity to build electromagnets, they will have constructed natural (and authentic) evidence of that experience.

Dave Nelson's roller coaster activity for senior high school students is considered natural evidence of students' understanding of the laws of physics; it is constructivist because students are gaining meaning as they work toward satisfying the criteria of the task. To judge the students' learning, Nelson will use the criteria to evaluate how well the students performed what was expected.

When teachers write learning objectives, goals, or purposes for instruction, the learning activity must be designed to accomplish the desired objective (purpose, goal). So if Jean Cantor expects her students to learn to write poetry, she needs to teach about poetic forms and then ask her students to select a specific form and write a poem that exemplifies their selection. The written poem is considered evidence of the student's understanding of poetic forms and can be a piece of what is to be used for authentic assessment.

Table 11.1 identifies the three types of assessment and when they are performed.

Assessing Students' Ideas and Ways of Thinking

Working in a democratic classroom community affects students' ideas and ways of thinking. A classroom community that encourages students to take risks by expressing their ideas and thinking processes will accomplish different goals from those of a classroom that is strictly controlled, where students are expected to respond only when they are specifically questioned by the teacher. The cultural environment of the democratic classroom community encourages social interaction and solicits diverse perspectives and independent thought.

The culture of the classroom either encourages students to reflect on their classmates' ideas or rewards students for immediate responses in a stimulus-response fashion. The former classroom environment helps students construct their own understandings, while the latter encourages competition to be the first to respond. Shepard (2000) describes the effects of constructivist learning theories as (1) developing intellectual abilities in a social and cultural environment; (2) learning and thinking that involve metacognition; and (3) using prior knowledge and cultural perspectives to help shape new learning (p. 8).

TABLE 11.1 Assessment Informs Instruction

When Performed	Purpose
Prior to instruction	*Diagnostic:* To find out what students know; determine past experience. Is your planning appropriate for students' needs?
During instruction	*Ongoing, Formative:* Feedback through monitoring means. Progress information. Are you teaching appropriate knowledge? Are students learning what you expect? Do you need to modify your plans?
After instruction	*Summative:* To review the learning process. Are students ready to move on? How much have they learned? Are you satisfied with what they have learned and your own teaching? Can you evaluate individual students' progress?

A prime means to assess students' ability to think independently and engage in higher-order thinking processes is to pose a problem that elicits conflicting viewpoints. Most subject fields will be fruitful for selecting an argumentative question, but to provide you with an example of a teaching controversy, think about the following question: *What is the best way to teach English to English language learners?* Try out this question with your classmates and teaching colleagues and jot down the critical-thinking processes that are required to argue the different perspectives. Compare your list with Figure 10.1's checklist for critical thinking.

Teaching Hints: Assessing Students' Ideas and Thinking Processes

1. Through discussion, debate, or written materials, pose an issue with conflicting perspectives. (*Example:* Why was the involvement of Americans in the Vietnam War necessary or unnecessary?)

2. Do your students raise significant issues?

3. Do your students listen to opposing viewpoints and respond rationally with their own thoughts?

4. Do students offer evidence to support their ideas and thinking?

5. Can students analyze, synthesize, and generalize about the conflicting perspectives and the evidence?

When trying out a provocative question with your students, if you discover that they are unable to define the problem (identify the conflicting and significant issues), raise questions, pose hypotheses, analyze the different arguments, and interpret the varied perspectives, then you know that they have not had experience participating in critical thinking, and the process needs to be modeled and practiced. Yeh (2001) notes that since state-mandated tests are supposed to improve students' learning, test items should include questions that test students' ability to engage in critical thinking. He believes that the best way to improve students' higher-order thinking is to have them participate in argumentative discussions and debates.

Did You Know That . . . ?

In a study of English language learners, Thomas and Collier, researchers at George Mason University, used a longitudinal approach to study special programs (bilingual and mainstream) for students to learn English when they first entered school. They concluded that submersion programs deter student motivation to learn, and these students do not do as well on standardized tests as students who began school in bilingual education classes and then transferred to mainstream classrooms (Zehr, 2002).

During rehearsal of a play based on the study of Buddhism, the teacher is able to ascertain students' understanding.

Assessing Students' Content Knowledge and Understanding

As stated earlier in the text, curriculum (subject field content) and instruction plus learning activity (the delivery system) are two sides of the same coin. The instructional process and the learning activity must match the instructional (content) goal. Whatever you want students to learn must somehow be incorporated into the learning experiences (activities and work tasks). If activities are not consonant with the goal of the lesson, then students' performance will be irrelevant. Whatever students produce, they should be able to explain, and their explanation should describe the lesson in their own words.

Suppose I wanted to test your understanding of the preceding paragraph. One way would be to ask you to draw a figure depicting the relationship of curriculum content, instructional processes, and learning experiences. Then I would ask you to write a couple of sentences about your figure to explain it to someone else.

 Did You Know That . . . ?

Popham (2003) describes five attributes of "instructionally beneficial data":

1. *Significant* data provides information that is focused on your curriculum goal. It is not focused on low-level knowledge.
2. *Teachability* requires that the test measures what is reasonable for teachers to teach and does not require special intelligences for students to comprehend.

3. *Describability* means that the test is related to specific content targets that are easily defined.
4. *Reportability* requires that any test students are required to take provides specific information to the teacher in order for the teacher to know what was successfully taught and what was not.
5. *Nonintrusiveness* relates to the time factor. The test should not take so long to administer that instructional time is usurped.

Let's revisit the classroom of Gerry Alred, whose students were studying civil rights. Each group had the option of selecting a topic for research. One of the groups chose the topic of bullying on school playgrounds. They were required to gather evidence that this is a real issue that affects civil rights. They would need to present their evidence to the class as a whole. Alred's problem would be to assess students' knowledge and understanding of civil rights as it affected students who were subjected to bullying.

- She would look for specific evidence that displayed the emotions and feelings of students who were hurt by bullies.
- She would expect her students to identify bullying behaviors and how these behaviors infringe on the rights of others.
- She would expect the students to document the frequency of bullying behaviors in their own school as well as look at research that describes incidents in other schools.
- She would look at the learning resources students used to gather their evidence.

Group investigation was the instructional strategy used for the research activity, and each group had a similar learning experience activity, but with different topics. The curriculum content was focused on civil rights. The learning activities included research, identifying specific information on how bullying behaviors affected the civil rights of others, documenting research, writing a report, and presenting the report and figures to the class. Alred's curriculum goal was supported by the indicators of learning that would be produced by the class and the higher-order thinking required by the tasks.

Now let's look at a primary classroom involved in block play.

The students are building a miniature city. They are working in pairs or triads. Students are constructing apartment houses, a bank, bridge, market, hospital, police station, fire station, and office building. The teacher is circulating, listening to the students as they interact and make decisions concerning which blocks to use and how many will be needed for their construction. The teacher approaches the three students building an apartment house. She asks them questions:

- How many apartments will there be in your building?
- How many blocks will you need for each apartment?
- Why did you choose long blocks and square ones?
- How many of each will you need?
- I notice that your apartment house is quite long and has a single floor. What if you were going to build a tall apartment with two floors instead of a single-story building? Would you need the same number of blocks and the same amount of space?
- Suppose that you were going to increase the height of your apartment house. How would it affect the number of blocks you will need?

The teacher is integrating mathematics and social studies. The students' thinking skills are being judged by their counting of blocks, their decisions about which blocks to use, and their ability to figure out how changing the structure of the building may affect space and the number of blocks to be used. Later the students will be asked to tell the class about their building and how its structure affects the city. The teacher will assess their oral explanations.

An art class has just concluded a study of impressionist painters. They are asked to create their own paintings simulating impressionism. Though they are not expected to create master works of art, their paintings should depict key elements to be found in the work of an impressionist painter. As students explain their work, they will be expected to call attention to these elements and write an accompanying paragraph about their work. Both the painting and the paragraph will be placed in the student's portfolio.

TABLE 11.2 Assessing Impressionist Paintings

Elements	Yes	No	Comments
Painting focuses on nature; emphasis on form, color, design			
Patches of color visible			
Use of complementary colors			
Brush strokes visible			
Details of objects ignored			
Sunlight appears to focus and brighten subject			

Assessment in each of these three examples is an ongoing process. The teachers are both monitoring students' work and assessing their performance. The teachers are observing, listening, and asking questions. Table 11.2 provides an example of a content-focused assessment of students' paintings. Note that the quality of the painting is not assessed—only the inclusion of the elements of impressionism.

Content assessment often focuses on the reports or projects that students produce. Karen Adazzio is integrating science, technology, and society. She is performing a summative assessment of her students' understanding of global and societal effects of weather and climatic conditions.

> Suppose you lived in (1) New Zealand or (2) Scotland.
> 1. How would time, terrain, and seasons differ from those where you live now?
> 2. How would the differences affect ways of life such as basic needs?
> 3. In what ways would societal effects be evident? Consider occupations, tourism, agriculture, exports and imports, and animal life.
> 4. If your family were to relocate, which area of the world would you prefer and why?
>
> You may respond through drawing, graphing, writing, or a combination.

Note that the teacher is providing a means for students to use multiple intelligences and preferred ways of responding.

Assessing Students' Communication Skills

Communication is an active process. Oral communication requires the participation of more than one person. Active participation requires speakers and listeners who interact with each other. Communication also occurs through reading and writing in the content fields. Since language has no conceptual content, it must be assessed through content in the different disciplines. Many communication skills can be assessed only by listening to students as they participate in class discussions, small-group work conversations, ad-lib public speaking, teacher-student conferences, and sharing-type activities. Let's examine some other communication experiences that provide assessment data for teachers.

Speaking Experiences *Storytelling* occurs in primary classrooms where students tell their friends about an experience or a book they have read. Teachers can assess the student's ability to communicate the beginning, development, and conclusion of the story. Is the student able to sequence the events of the story? Does the student tell the story precisely as it is, make inferences, discuss characters and characterizations? Is the student able to motivate interest in the story and respond to classmates' questions?

In upper elementary, middle school, and high school classrooms, storytelling occurs when students give book reports to the class as a whole. The teacher may be assessing the critique that is provided by the student. Is it insightful and reasonable? Is the book compared to others the author has written or to other authors? Does the student refer to writing devices, descriptions, and the author's personal experiences that may have contributed to the book? Does the student communicate the context, period of time, and appropriateness to current events? How well does the student respond to classmates' questions?

Writing Skills Writing skills can be assessed in a variety of ways, each of which depends on the purpose of the activity. For example, if a student is working on a class or school newspaper and is reporting an event, then the assessment should focus on how well the student generates interest, reports what happened, and writes appropriately for the audience who will read the newspaper.

For term papers and project reports, early drafts, outlines, and notes can be assessed. Organizational skills can be evaluated—is the paper focused on the subject? Conceptual understanding can be evaluated—were appropriate resources used? Vocabulary and writing mechanics can be assessed—did the student include subheads, time-lines, captions? Did the student do a good job of proofreading?

Suppose students are writing an original story or play. You may set criteria with your students' help so that they know what elements should be tended to in their creative work. In Jean Cantor's class, she and her students identified the following literary elements that needed to be emphasized in their stories or evaluated in the literature they read:

1. Setting—Where are the events in the story happening?

2. Plot—What is the storyline about?

3. Problem—Is there an underlying problem that confronts the characters?

4. Characterization—Is each character identifiable as a distinct personality?

5. Literary style—How do you or the author maintain interest? How would you characterize the style of writing?

These elements could be used on a check sheet to monitor students' work or to judge the work for grading purposes. If students are to evaluate literature that they have read, the elements may be used for the actual assignment. Literary elements such as these can be turned into a rubric to guide students' work.

What Teachers Learn

Assessment helps teachers find out whether they have a community of learners—are the students on task? Are the students interacting productively with their classmates? Do students ask relevant questions of each other and the teacher? Do they choose appropriate resources? Are they attuned to use teacher "hints" to improve their performance?

Teachers learn about what they have taught and what they need to teach by the feedback they get during these monitoring/assessment processes. Do students demonstrate prior knowledge that helps them in their current task? When talking to the students, do responses indicate that students are missing significant content knowledge? What is the next step in teaching the students? (What needs to be taught tomorrow?) Do students have the skills needed to complete their performance? (Do students need organizational skills, research skills, graphing?)

Both teachers and students need to evaluate their own work. Teachers evaluate whether they have taught what they intended and what students need, and students evaluate their work based on the criteria by which it will be judged. Realistic self-assessment is extremely important in the learning process. Self-assessment requires that the individual (teacher and student) take responsibility for his or her own learning. Writers proofread their own work by reading aloud and determining whether they have written what was intended, whether tenses are correct and words appropriate. Teachers self-assess by finding out whether students are producing what was intended and can explain their work. Students use criteria for the activity to assess whether their projects meet the preset goals and standards.

Student Portfolios

Portfolios originated in the art world for artists to display their work to prospective buyers and art gallery owners. Other professionals liked the idea, and soon public relations specialists and advertising "idea" folks were showing specimens of what they had accomplished. Today one can walk into almost any professional office or business and see a display that represents the "handiwork" of the owner.

Students' portfolios should convey the learning process. The portfolio represents the best evidence of the student's performance and progress in the classroom. When asked to do research or write a report on a specific topic, the portfolio should show the student's outline, research sources, notes that were taken, drafts of the report, and the final product. Each specimen in the portfolio should be accompanied by an explanation in the form of a caption or paragraph about it. A self-critique of important work should be included. The critique represents the reflective process in which the student analyzes the work and determines in what ways it meets the criteria, what could be improved, problems involved during the research process, what really went well, and why the student feels proud of the effort.

Teaching Hints: Portfolio Assessment

Portfolios may contain evidence of the following:

- Research processes
- The writing process
- Creative work (story writing, artwork, poems)
- Experiments, projects, reports, diaries, journals, records, and logs

> Each exhibit should be accompanied by an explanation and critique. The critique may be written or audiotaped. It is a good idea to include a table of contents at the beginning of the portfolio, and a preface by the student may be included. Portfolios may be assessed for a variety of elements:
>
> - Subject matter skills, depth of understanding
> - Use of technology (media productions, technology tools)
> - Developmental processes as indicated by outlines, notes, drafts, and final report on the writing and editing process or artwork production
> - Indicators of social responsibility, interaction with peers
> - Overall organization of the portfolio
> - Self-assessment, reflectiveness

For elementary students there can be portfolios in every subject field, or a single portfolio may contain work from several subjects. Portfolios for secondary students are single-subject-field oriented unless subjects are integrated, such as life sciences, English language arts, and social studies.

The process for producing the portfolio is the same at all levels. What is to be emphasized is the growth process. When the content of a report is to be evaluated, not only should the criteria set by teacher and students be used, but other criteria such as relevancy, clarity, organization, originality, and interest may be factors to assess. It is important to remember that the portfolio represents what students *can do;* it is not intended to demonstrate students' failures. Both student and teacher should focus on the link between performance and learning.

Rubrics

Rubrics identify the expectations that you and your students set for a given learning activity. The rubric may be written by the teacher alone as a set of criteria statements for a project, or it may be jointly developed by teacher and students. Rubrics can be in the form of a checklist or a system for grading a particular project. A rubric used for grading typically identifies outstanding performance as compared to good, average, and poor performance. Some rubrics use point systems to differentiate acceptable from mediocre or unacceptable performance. Physics teacher Dave Nelson gave his students a list of requirements for building the roller coaster. The requirements served as the criteria statements. He also identified how he would grade the projects. Mr. Nelson's project serves as an example of a content-oriented rubric. A partial list of his requirements and grading criteria follows.

Dave Nelson's Marble Roller Coaster Requirements

1. The ride must last at least 15 seconds, excluding conveyance to the top.
2. There must be one 8-inch-diameter loop followed by a 2-inch horizontal jump.

3. It must be made of a track that is no more than a half-circle in cross-section.
4. The marble must remain on the track except for the horizontal jump.
5. There must be an electrical conveyance with an on/off switch to get from the bottom to the top.

A partial list of his basis for grading included:

- 50 points for successful completion
- 25 points for the submission of a scaled 3-D model of the roller coaster
- 25 points for determination of values with explanations and calculations:

  Coefficient of friction for the track
  Loss of frictional heat energy during the ride
  Potential energy of the marble at the top of the ride
  Kinetic energy of the marble at the bottom of the ride
  Unaccounted energy loss during the ride

Nelson also included bonus points for an efficient design, sturdy construction, and decoration. Students evaluated their roller coasters using the requirements (criteria statements) and the point system that would be used for grading the project.

Printed with Dave Nelson's permission.

Rubrics can be very simply designed to identify significant concepts in a subject field or may focus on specific skills. The rubric in Figure 11.1 was designed to help students engaged in creative writing. Figure 11.2 demonstrates the use of a rubric for assessing primary students' classification skills; and Table 11.3 is an example of a rubric used for assessing group work projects.

Did You Know That . . . ?

In the teaching of world geography, it appears that teachers fail to teach the reasons why the cultural behavior of other people differ. Instead they are reinforcing misconceptions about other cultures. The National Assessment of Educational Progress in 2001 indicated that fourth- and eighth-graders scored only at the Basic level, and only one-fourth of twelfth-graders were proficient in geography (Holloway, 2002).

Standards and the School Curriculum

What should students know and be able to do? This question has stimulated one of the most temper-laden controversies among educators and the lay public. In 1992 the National Council on Education Standards and Testing charged that U.S. schools were teaching low-level curriculum content and had low expectations for student performance. Those who favor content and performance standards believe that setting standards will reform our

Excellent	Good	Average	Improvement Needed
Opening sentence creative and motivating	Opening sentence sets context of story	Opening sentence somewhat creative	Organization of storyline needs revision
Distinct development and appropriate conclusion of storyline	Storyline exhibits beginning, middle, and end	Storyline not fully developed	
Personalities of characters provide behavioral clues	Characterization partially developed	Personalities of characters not totally developed	Ideas need to be clearly communicated
Language usage appropriate, descriptive, purposeful	Language usage appropriate but figurative language lacking	Some repetitive use of words	
Mechanics of writing well executed	Several mechanical writing errors	Some errors evident in mechanics of writing	Errors in mechanics of writing (punctuation, spelling, run-on sentences)
Self-editing apparent	Some self-editing needed		Self-editing needed

FIGURE 11.1 Rubric for Assessing Creative Writing Skills

Superior	Average	Poor
1. Given an assortment of rocks, the student groups the rocks by *texture* and then regroups the rocks by *size*.	1. Given an assortment of rocks, the student decides on a single classifying system.	1. Given an assortment of rocks, the student attempts to sort them but makes errors in classifying the rocks.
2. Student can explain own thinking process and characteristics of the two categories used for classifying the rocks.	2. Student can explain own thinking process and characteristic of single category selected for classification.	2. Student fails to describe a system for sorting the rocks.

FIGURE 11.2 Rubric for Assessing Classification Skills

TABLE 11.3 Rubric for Assessing Project Work

	Excellent	Satisfactory	Needs Improvement
Content	Detailed, in-depth, clearly expressed ideas	Some depth, somewhat clear	Lacks depth, unclear
Organization	Clear: introduction, development, conclusions	Somewhat organized, conclusions need to follow from content	Lack of organization; beginning, middle, and end confused
Creative use of resources	Variety of texts and technology; well-documented, interesting	Some variety of resources, better documentation needed	Few resources, lack of documentation
Group interaction	Good communication among members, cooperative work, all accept responsibility, good use of time, motivated	Some group problems with participation, adequate use of time	Limited participation, group problems, unmotivated, poor use of time
Mechanics of writing	Carefully edited for spelling and grammar, well written	Some errors in written expression	Lacks clarity and editing for errors

Source: J.K. Lemlech. (2000). *Curriculum and Instructional Methods for the Elementary and Middle School,* 5th ed. Upper Saddle River, NJ: Prentice Hall. Reprinted with permission.

schools by defining precisely what ought to be taught, and that standardized tests should be closely aligned to those standards.

Proponents of standards, including Gandal and Vranek (2001), believe that if the standard cannot be measured, then it is imprecise, too all-encompassing, and fails to give teachers necessary guidance for teaching. These authors state that "well devised and implemented academic standards and tests, and the accountability provisions tied to them, can change the nature of teaching and learning" (p. 9).

That is just what opponents of standards fear. Opponents of standards believe that the standards are another form of behaviorism and result in treating students as objects and passive receptacles to be filled and then evaluated. When standards are set by forces outside the local community and school, there is the danger of ignoring the needs and interests of the school population.

Alfie Kohn, a leading critic of standards, differentiates between *outcome* standards and *content* standards. Outcome standards, he notes, are "confusing harder with better" (1999, p. 68). Content standards focus on what students should learn in the various subject field disciplines. Kohn (2001) suggests four criteria to judge the harm caused by sets of standards or frameworks:

1. *Specificity:* Those who believe that a given curriculum should be "teacher-proof" assume that teachers are incapable of defining their own curriculum; they want standards (such as facts and skills) to be so specific that teachers cannot foul it up. Specificity also requires a great number of standards, which forces teachers to "cover" the material instead of teaching in-depth studies.

2. *Quantifiability:* Standards that do not lend themselves to measurement are not considered appropriate by proponents of standards. Therefore, standards cannot focus on student appreciation of artwork, enjoyment of reading, creative experimentation, or intellectual exploration because of the difficulty of assessment.

3. *Uniformity:* An example of this criterion is a statement by Gandal and Vranek (2001, p. 7): "Students, teachers, and parents need a clear idea of what students should learn each year, and those goals should be reasonable, rigorous, and *the same for all children*" (italics added). So forget about meeting individual needs, multiple intelligences, and cultural responsiveness.

4. *Mandates:* Kohn (2001) defines this criterion as a "teach this or else" (p. 38) dictum. Teachers are bullied by the tests they are forced to administer and as a consequence they will teach to the test. Again this forces "coverage" rather than pursuing students' interests and focusing on content-based in-depth teaching. (Proponents advocate *alignment* of teaching and standards.)

Content-Based Standards

Many of the discipline-based professional organizations have identified what they consider significant **content standards.** These standards, written by experts in their chosen fields, represent the conceptual understandings that should be explored by students in the various subject field disciplines. Some of these standards will be used as examples.

English Language Arts   The National Council for Teachers of English and the International Reading Association expect students to *learn to read and write for different purposes.* The standards also encourage teachers to integrate these purposes across subject fields and to use a variety of subject field texts and literature books for students to test their reading skills. Students soon learn that it takes longer and requires more concentration to read a science text than it does to read a novel. Teachers recognize that students need different skills for writing a book report and writing a science experiment report. These skills and the organization of them need to be taught.

Writing a Book Report

1. Describe the *setting* of the story. (Where does it take place?)

2. Summarize the *plot* or *theme* of the story.

3. How does the author hold your interest? Is there a *problem* or *struggle* confronting the characters in the story? Identify it.

4. Do you identify with any of the characters? Are the characters convincing? Does the *characterization* change as you progress through the story, or is characterization consistent throughout the story? Provide examples.

5. Describe the author's literary style. For example, are chapters organized to follow each other consistently, or is each chapter focused on a single character?

Writing a Science Experiment Report

1. Identify your inquiry problem. (What do you want to find out?)

2. Identify your questions or hypotheses that guide your inquiry.

3. Describe your procedures. (How did you go about experimenting? What did you do first, second, . . . ?)

4. Include your recording notes and the period of time involved in the experiment.

5. How did you or can you test the results of your experiment?

6. What conclusions did you make? Explain how your conclusions are consistent or inconsistent with your hypotheses. Do the conclusions provide answers to your questions?

7. What recommendations for follow-up experiments can you make?

Both of these assignments require writing, but the nature of the writing is quite different, as was the reading assignment prior to the reports. Yet both assignments fulfill the standard set by the two professional organizations.

Mathematics The National Council of Teachers of Mathematics was one of the first professional organizations to set standards for student performance. It identified significant *strands* for mathematics education and then organized standards for each of the strands. The strands were not organized for specific grade levels, but are to be integrated throughout the math program.

> Lucia Martin's students were comparing and classifying geometric figures. The standard suggests that students should analyze characteristics and properties of two- and three-dimensional geometric shapes. She began the lesson with wood figures on the chalkboard ledge and above each figure she wrote either "yes" or "no" for the beginning of a concept attainment lesson. The concept was two- and three-dimensional geometric shapes. For students to prove their understanding of these shapes, they needed to provide examples and nonexamples of the shapes in their classroom. (The broom is a nonexample; the textbook is an example of a rectangle; the figurine is a nonexample; the water bottle is a nonexample; the rug is an example of a flat figure, but not three-dimensional; the clock is an example of a circle.)

> After the concept attainment lesson, Martin told the students that they would have an opportunity to work at several learning centers with geometric shapes. At the centers they would sort shapes by size, items that would roll, and items that were curved. At another center they would have an opportunity to work with play dough and create three-dimensional shapes; at a third center, they could make a geometric design with tiles (a tessellation) using a single shape or a variety of shapes. Later students would share their designs and talk about them.

Martin's lesson provided for oral language participation and manipulative activities that included satisfying students' multiple intelligences.

Science *Benchmarks for Science Literacy* (Project 2061) was the work of 150 teachers and administrators who accepted the challenge to create a document that would guide science, mathematics, and technology teaching in grades K–12. The document they produced was an attempt to limit coverage of these areas of the curriculum but select sophisticated ideas that would link the subject fields including the arts and humanities and vocational subjects. The goals or standards are broad-based and can lead to a wide variety of learning experiences. For example, the study of learning identifies the following goal:

> Learning means using what one already knows to make sense out of new experiences or information, not just storing the new information in one's head.

> Karen Adazzio posed the following problem to her students: *"We frequently see five-day forecasts of the temperature and weather conditions on television. How do meteorologists study weather conditions and make those predictions?"*
> After giving the students time to think about it, they began to offer ideas based on their past experiences and knowledge. Contributions included the following: *"They study wind movements."* Another student suggested, *"Air masses." "Rotation of the earth,"* said another student. *"I think they study cold and warm fronts; temperatures and hurricanes and tornadoes."*
> Next Adazzio asked, *"What instruments would you need to predict the weather?"* The students scurried to their science books and came up with a list of instruments. After recording their list on the board, Adazzio asked the class if they would like to make some weather instruments, diagram their findings, and study weather maps. Students would need to figure out what materials they would need, develop a plan for constructing the instruments (anemometer, barometer, thermometer, weathervane, hygrometer, rain gauge), and learn how to read weather maps. Ultimately students would learn about the U.S. Weather Service, investigate human-made weather, develop weather-keeping records, and compare climates in different areas of the world.

Adazzio was building on what students already knew about weather and climate and motivating them to build on that knowledge. Students worked in small groups; the instructional strategy was group investigation. The standard or goal was broad and allowed Adazzio to select the topic and her instructional strategy. Students would learn that their existing knowledge formed the basis for learning new skills and understandings. Assessment would be based on what they learned, how they learned it, and what they produced.

Did You Know That . . . ?

In a small K–12 unified school district in northern California, Barranti (2001) questioned how the requirement to implement content standards affected the instructional program of elementary classrooms (K–6). The standards included English language arts, mathematics, science, and history. The district was 82 percent minority. Staff development for the teachers was mandatory prior to adoption of each subject's content standards.

Affected by the implementation of content standards were report cards, progress reports, retention decisions, parent conferences, assessment activities and tasks, and grading. Both instructional time and instructional strategies were affected by the standards. Reporting requirements took more time, and preparing for standardized testing caused major changes in the use of instructional time.

The researcher concluded that positive effects of implementation included consistent curriculum from school to school and class to class, more demanding review of student work, more work on specific knowledge and skills, and greater coverage of content. The negative effects included greater focus on standardized testing, more time spent on lesson planning, less time spent on subjects not included in the content standards (music, art, physical education, and social studies), and limitation of instructional strategies. In the words of one teacher, "Things are slighted that aren't tested."

Teacher-Made Tests

Teachers have a wide array of choices when it comes to testing their students. You know what you have taught and what you expected from your students. If you have done a good monitoring job, then you have adapted and modified both what you taught and how you taught it, and you have a very good idea what your students have learned. In addition, if you are a constructivist teacher, then your students have produced a number of projects that demonstrate their learning progress. If students are keeping a portfolio, you should have evidence of the learning process and its progression.

Teacher-made tests are "reality-based" because they are targeted at specific students, specific contexts of what was taught, and particular processes. Karen Adazzio's weather instruments will demonstrate students' research and practical understanding of how the instruments are used. Dave Nelson's marble roller coaster project will demonstrate students' understanding of heat energy, laws of motion, and kinetic energy. These are concrete examples of students' knowledge and understanding without use of paper-and-pencil tests.

But paper-and-pencil tests are as necessary in the classroom as practical projects. One of the first things to remember in the construction of tests is that teacher time is spent either in the making of the test or in the grading of the test! Objective tests (multiple-choice, true/false, fill-in) take longer to construct than to grade; essay tests are easily framed, but take much longer to judge.

True/False and Yes/No Tests

Relatively easy to write, the true/false or yes/no test can include many questions, thereby increasing the comprehensiveness of the examination. The trick in designing this test is to make sure that the questions are not all low-level fact questions. Still another problem is that the test probably does not match the teaching strategy you used to teach the content you are testing. In writing the true/false or yes/no question, it is important to convey a single idea that is not ambiguous and confusing because it *may* be true under certain circumstances and untrue under other circumstances.

Sample Question: Barometers measure atmospheric pressure. When air pressure decreases, the barometer level falls; when air pressure increases, the barometer level rises. (Answer: True or Yes)

English language learners may have difficulty with this type of test because it is so dependent on vocabulary comprehension. It is important to ensure that questions do not become "reading" tests rather than concept/content tests.

Multiple-Choice Tests

More difficult to write, the multiple-choice test depends on logical choices and students must be instructed to select the best answer.

Sample Question: High and low air pressure provide weather information. Pressure is measured using:

  a. A weather vane
  b. An aneroid barometer (Correct)
  c. An anemometer

Sample Question: If you have a rash and a high temperature, you should ask for advice from:

  a. A schoolmate who had a similar problem
  b. A relative who studied health problems
  c. A health professional, such as a doctor or nurse

Objective tests need to be carefully written to ensure that they are appropriate for the grade level of the students as well as appropriate to the content that was taught.

Essay Tests

Essay tests give students the opportunity to express their knowledge and ideas in depth. As a consequence, students need time to plan and outline what they will write. Essay examinations require more class time than the typical objective test. Essay questions need to be well framed, clearly written, and focused on significant content. Before setting students to work on the examination, it is a good idea to verify their understanding of the question and remind them to plan and outline their ideas before starting to write.

Again, special care should be given to English language learners, who will need more time to write an essay exam. You may want to consider allowing these students to audiotape their responses or express their thoughts in their native language. This of course assumes that you are fluent in the student's native language.

Sample Question: (1) How do meteorologists predict weather, and (2) what factors affect yearly temperatures in the United States? Explain the means that meteorologists use and the controlling factors affecting climate in different parts of the United States.

Discussion: This is a two-part question; each could have been asked separately. However, it is clearly written and the second sentence tells students specifically what they must do in responding. This question would be appropriate for upper elementary or middle school students. To make the question even more specific, the teacher could have identified specific areas of the United States for students to concentrate their efforts.

Sample Question: Labor unions began to organize early in the twentieth century. What motivated workers to organize into unions? Who were influential in the labor movement and what problems did unions encounter?

Discussion: This is a very open-ended question that encourages individual thoughts and attitudes as well as an in-depth response. Students may answer using knowledge of U.S. history, world history, and governmental regulations. The question is appropriate for middle and high school students.

Standardized Tests

Standardized tests are norm-referenced, which means that a student's performance on the test can be compared with the performance of other students. So a student in New York City can be compared with a student at the same grade level in North Carolina. The problems associated with standardized tests upset many educators and parents. These will be briefly discussed.

1. In general, the test depends on the student's reading skills, so a student who has low achievement in reading will naturally do poorly on the standardized test because it is so difficult to control for reading skills.

2. If the test has not been normed with minority populations, minority students may have a harder time on the test than the normed population, primarily because the content of the test may be related to sociocultural factors and not indicative of the performance of minority children.

3. Standardized tests rarely reflect the content the teacher has taught. Even in conjunction with state-mandated standards, the test seldom corresponds with the teacher's curriculum.

4. Standardized tests measure low-level knowledge. Students must respond with a single correct answer without being able to justify their response with multiple ways of arriving at the answer. Students are not asked to demonstrate critical thinking or ability to synthesize information. Problem solving is not valued; thus students in inquiry-oriented classrooms will find that the test is interested only in basic skill information that can be bubbled onto the answer sheet.

Wassermann (2001) thoughtfully discusses the standardized testing movement by commenting on society's need for "certainty," which has led to reliance on test scores. She comments that scientists recognize that for most problems they tackle, there are no single correct answers and often a lot of discrepant information. For teachers, the scores on these tests are not helpful in knowing what to teach or in finding out what students really can do.

Wassermann highlights the work of secondary teachers in Coquitlam, British Columbia, who decided to write a profile of what they considered important to stress in teaching and learning. Their *Profiles of Student Behaviors* involved intellectual development, skills, and attitudes. The following list briefly summarizes Wassermann's discussion of the profiles developed by these teachers (2001, pp. 38–40), which represent what has been discussed in this book as a true learning community.

1. *Thinking ability.* Students recognize significant issues when presented with topics or problems. They listen to and respect the ideas and thoughts of their classmates. They can differentiate between opinions, facts, and assumptions. They willingly consider conflicting evidence and weigh new ideas with their own beliefs. They support their ideas with evidence and can interpret data. They are willing to take risks in their own production of creative work.

2. *Skills.* Students are able to communicate both orally and in writing their own thoughts, and they do so with clarity, attention to the conventions of writing and speaking, and the use of evidence and examples as needed. Students can do research, gather data, keep records, and depict their findings in varied ways. Students listen to the thoughts of their classmates, and in group discussions they respond respectfully and thoughtfully.

3. *Attitudes.* Students are sociocentric. They are strong individually concerning their own abilities and beliefs, but accepting of their classmates' abilities and beliefs. They can deal with uncertainty and ambiguity and recognize both societal and global problems and issues. They are willing and able to evaluate their own work and not afraid to admit when they need help. They are learners in a learning community.

Fear of Tests

Many students do poorly on tests because of nervousness and frustration. Slow and poor readers have difficulty, particularly with timed tests. Others have panic attacks thinking about taking a test. It is important to communicate the purpose of the test to students and to reassure them that the test is not the only criterion used to evaluate their work. To do this you need to have examples of these students' "good" work and let them know how proud you are of them. Because the springtime standardized testing week has become such a fearsome time for many families, in some communities parents are opting out and purposely keeping their children at home. This is an option that parents can exercise, but if you are able to communicate with students and help them cope with their fears, many will perform better and not be as upset.

Judging and Grading

Judging students' work is typically considered a subjective responsibility; however, with the use of rubrics subjectivity is diminished. For example, suppose you were to be evaluated for your use of cooperative learning. Accepted by the education community, cooperative learning associates teacher and student behaviors with the teaching strategy:

- Students work cooperatively with each other in a small group.
- Each student has a work task to contribute to the group assignment.
- All students in the group are "on task."
- The teacher has motivated the group assignment.
- The teacher actively monitors each group's progress by listening to the students at work, making suggestions as needed, and moving from group to group.

Someone observing your use of this strategy could take notes or record on a check sheet the characteristics of cooperative learning. The person could then judge the quality of your performance.

Recall that rubrics are criteria statements. If you were judging your students' writing progress, you and your students could decide on the basis for evaluating the quality and progress of writing. Your rubric for an informational paragraph could include the following criteria: (1) opening sentence is clear and captures interest; (2) significant issues are identified; (3) mechanics of the writing are perfect; (4) paragraph development includes information concerning who, when, and where; and (5) the closing sentence is meaningful and sums up and concludes the paragraph. You should judge the changes from first draft to final product. The progress from draft to final copy serves as part of the evidence. Deviation from the rubric criteria should be used to coach the student.

Recall Dave Nelson's criteria for the marble roller coaster. Not only did he list criteria, but he gave the students a point system for how he would evaluate their projects. His point system would be used for grading purposes. The advantage of using both criteria and the

Students help each other by making suggestions, sharing ideas, and correcting mistakes.

point system is that students will know why they received a certain grade and what they need to do to improve their projects.

Grading by itself communicates no useful information. Neither student nor parent can know what makes up a satisfactory or superior performance. If a teacher believes that all grades should follow the "normal" bell curve even though the makeup of the class is above average, it will mean that some students will have to receive C grades or less, even though their scores are above average.

In some schools, standards of performance are identified; instead of receiving grades, students are judged based on their performance of the standard. For example, suppose you and your colleagues think it is important to assess students' critical thinking and participation in class discussions. You have set the following standards for performance:

- After listening to (or reading about) an issue with conflicting perspectives, the student raises significant questions pertaining to the issues.
- The student listens actively to classmates' opinions and ideas and responds clearly.
- The student offers evidence to support his or her own ideas and thinking.
- The student analyzes, synthesizes, and generalizes about conflicting perspectives and the evidence.

You and your colleagues would then develop a "value key" for assessing students using these standards. For each standard there are four areas for check marks:

1. Student does not participate.

2. Student participates but responses lack clarity.

3. Student actively participates and demonstrates understanding of issues.
4. Student actively participates, uses prior knowledge and experience, consistently provides evidence of conflicting viewpoints and issues, and exceeds expectations.

Judging and Grading English Language Learners

This value key certainly would be a biased means to measure the contribution of ELL students. As indicated in Chapter 10, observation and individual conferences will be the best technique for verifying how well the student is doing. Alternative assessment means must be used to gather data both for teaching the ELL student and for verifying what the student can do. One must observe the student's use of manipulative materials, search for resources, study skills, ability to communicate in the small group with peers, progress in learning English, and the products the student produces. The student needs to be graded based on his or her own level of progress, but not in relationship to expectations for other students.

Teaching Hints: English Language Learners

1. Allow students to respond to test questions without penalizing them for their use of English.
2. Whenever possible, allow the ELL student to use a variety of tools (visual aids, manipulative materials) when engaging in project work.
3. Assist the ELL student in understanding questions, concepts, and issues through the use of repetitious vocabulary.

Chapter Summary

Assessment needs to be an ongoing process to improve learning. Finding out what students know and can do is vital for teachers to plan appropriate curriculum and instructional activities. Assessment is accomplished using a variety of techniques: observation, whole-class discussions, small-group interaction, project work, research activities, writing samples, arts activities, and teacher-made and standardized tests.

Work samples, student interaction, and test information are considered the "evidence" of students' performance. Using the evidence, the teacher adds subjective judgment based on professional experience, knowledge of individual differences, and developmental levels. Teachers learn much about their own teaching effectiveness when they study their students' performance. Both teachers and students need to reflect on, evaluate, and critique their own work performances, and both teachers and students may use portfolios to help accomplish this. Rubrics are a means for identifying whether expectations for performance are met. The rubric may be in the form of a checklist or rating scale.

The use of standards for selecting curriculum and instructional experiences is a controversial issue. Conflicting opinions concerning their use are discussed in this chapter, as well as examples of how teachers can use content standards to improve learning. Teacher-made tests and standardized tests are discussed, with examples of both objective and subjective teacher-made tests. Research concerning problems for English language learners when tested are cited, and suggestions for helping them are identified through teaching hints. Controversial perspectives concerning standardized tests are featured. The chapter concludes with a discussion of teachers' needs to judge and grade students' work.

Teaching Problems

1. You are teaching a fifth-, eighth-, or tenth-grade class and using the theme of *systems*. As a fifth- or eighth-grade teacher you are integrating curriculum. As a tenth-grade teacher you will use interdisciplinary content. (a) Identify a research project for your students. (b) Determine what subject fields will be involved. (c) Using Table 11.1, describe how you will diagnose students' pre-knowledge, formative progress, and summative understandings.
2. A music teacher wants to know if his students can differentiate tempo among a variety of musical compositions. Suggest several ways the teacher can assess students' capability and understanding. Identify what the teacher will learn from each of the assessment means that you suggest.
3. Primary-age students are working in small cooperative groups. Students are using manipulative materials to build a farm, a large market, or a train station. Describe what the teacher can learn about the students by visiting with each group. For each factor that you identify, suggest a follow-up instructional lesson.

Multiple Choice

For each multiple-choice question, select the likeliest description for each concept. Answers are given in Appendix A.

4. Rubric:
   a. Criteria requirements for a piece of work or a project
   b. A system for judging the quality of students' work
   c. A means to identify work for a portfolio

5. Grading:
   a. Provides information to teachers to plan future lessons
   b. Communicates to parents students' standing in the class
   c. An abstract symbol used to describe students' work habits and skills
6. Standardized test:
   a. Aligns what teachers teach with what is tested
   b. A system to compare students' work with other students in different regions of the country
   c. A system to allow test writers to design the curriculum
7. Monitoring:
   a. A means for teachers to snoop in the classroom to verify what students are doing
   b. A means to observe, listen, and refocus students' work to determine what students know and need to learn
   c. A system to make teachers look busy while students are involved in busywork
8. Content standards:
   a. A means for the lay public to define the curriculum that teachers are to teach
   b. A curriculum that is the same all over the country and does not differentiate students' needs
   c. A uniform system designed with the idea that "one size fits all"
   d. Identify significant content to be taught in each subject field
9. Assessment:
   a. Formal and informal means to gather information about students' learning and

work products; tests, work products, and conferences are used for evidence
   b. A means to judge the quality of students' work
   c. A system of evaluation
10. Authentic assessment:
   a. Focuses on real-life relevant activities and work products, giving students opportunity to choose work tasks to demonstrate understanding
   b. Manipulative materials are often chosen for students to use in learning
   c. Tests are aligned with learning tasks to achieve authenticity
11. Judging:
   a. May be based on subjective or objective means to determine how students are performing and learning; does not necessarily lead to grading
   b. Uses a variety of techniques and evidence to make decisions concerning the quality of students' work
   c. May be based solely on accomplishment of set standards
12. Portfolio:
   a. A collection of student work that is self-evaluated and critiqued using evidence from rubrics and other sources
   b. Teacher-selected work products collected to demonstrate students' work to parents
   c. A progression of students' authentic work demonstrating phases of learning, containing self-evaluation, critiques, and reflections based on evidence

PART 6

TECHNOLOGY AND PROFESSIONAL PROBLEM SOLVING

Chapter 12 reviews the ways that technology can integrate teaching and learning. Technology can be used to assist in the differentiation of instruction. Both project-based learning and problem-based learning are explained. Using technology the teacher can reinforce skills, support and motivate lessons, conduct assessment, communicate with students and parents, and save professional time in organizing, planning instruction, and record keeping. Chapter 13 concentrates on the problems and concerns of the new teacher. The focus is on whom to ask for help and in what ways peers, mentors, administrators, and professional organizations can provide assistance. Teachers' professional portfolios are discussed. National Board Certification procedures, the balance necessary between personal and professional responsibilities, and professional ethics are all considered in this chapter.

CHAPTER 12

Integration of Technology for Teaching and Learning

ADVANCE ORGANIZER

These questions can be used as a framework to assist you in integrating professional knowledge and understanding of the content of this chapter.

1. How can the Internet be used for student learning and to differentiate instruction?
2. Why is questioning so important when using technology for research purposes?
3. Under what circumstances would you use project-based learning and problem-based learning?
4. How can technology be used to support lessons? What organizing and planning problems should be anticipated?
5. How can you use technology as a personal and professional communication tool?

The principal author for this chapter is Hillary H. Hertzog, Assistant Professor of Education at California State University, Northridge.

 The following INTASC issues and standards are discussed in this chapter: Numbers: 1–3, 4, 7, 9, 10.

The use of technology in classrooms is now considered a standard component of the curriculum. However, teachers still debate how best to use technology, especially when there is limited access. This chapter describes uses of technology for Internet-based research and activities; for learning and problem solving; as a student tool for organizing, manipulating, and showing data; and as a teacher tool for presenting content and concepts to learners. In addition, technology is considered as a communication tool for interacting with the community. The greatest hazard to integrating technology into your classroom is the possibility that it will not work successfully. Unless you learn to create a contingency plan, you may become frustrated with planned lessons that can't be enacted. Learning to plan and manage technology is described as a critical component to learning how to use it in the classroom.

Can you remember when there weren't computers in offices, banks, markets (bar code readers *are* computer technology), and even schools? Computers are actually a relatively new "invention" for modern society, but they are changing the way people work and we are just beginning to understand how they change the way people think about learning (Jonassen, 2002). Computers are only one form of technology. Even an overhead projector is considered a form of technology. But computers significantly influence how we work and learn and what resources we have available to us. The purpose of this chapter is to explore how computers can be used as an important part of the teaching and learning process.

Computer technology has been in schools since the 1970s, when computer-assisted instruction (CAI) was introduced as a way of moving worksheets from an independent activity to an interactive activity with the computer giving feedback about the accuracy of learners' answers. This approach to using computers provided what was called *drill and practice* and was helpful in getting someone to practice skills such as addition, subtraction, and identifying correctly spelled words. As an understanding of how to program computers increased, tutorials became popular. A tutorial monitored student responses and, by accepting a correct answer or branching after an incorrect answer, the computer could help the learner think about the next level of learning. Simple simulations like Oregon Trail also became popular.

Researchers studied whether computers could influence learning by measuring student achievement. Results of those studies were inconclusive. There was no question that motivation due to the newness of computers and their ability to provide immediate positive feedback increased. But researchers did question whether that motivation could be sustained over time; for every study that showed increased learning, there was another that showed no increase (Becker, 1992).

Computer technology continued to improve. Fortunately, teachers and researchers, especially in the area of cognitive psychology, continued to search for ways to incorporate this increasingly powerful tool into the teaching process and to discover how it influenced learning. With the increased capacity of the Internet and the development of powerful tool programs such as word processing, publishing, and spreadsheet programs, teachers are thinking differently about how technology influences the learning process. Instead of learning *from* computers, there is an increased emphasis on learning *with* computers. (Jonassen, 2002). Recognition of the importance of teachers learning how to use technology effectively with students resulted in the recent drafting of national technology standards for teachers by the International Society for Technology in Education. Those standards cover six domains:

1. Technology Operations and Concepts
2. Planning and Designing Learning Environments and Experiences
3. Teaching, Learning, and the Curriculum
4. Assessment and Evaluation
5. Productivity and Professional Practice
6. Social, Ethical, Legal, and Human Issues

This chapter will help you understand how computers, peripherals (related hardware), and software can help you enhance your teaching and the curriculum your students experience. Classroom management of technology also will be considered.

Did You Know That . . . ?

> The U.S. West Foundation in partnership with the National Education Association has helped to foster the integration of technology in fourteen midwestern states. In partnership with local universities, 50,000 teachers received professional training and 4,200 laptops were distributed. The network of teachers became a community of learners as teachers exchanged information, teaching units, and curriculum ideas. The U.S. West Foundation can be contacted at www.uswf.org/edrfp.htm (Schwab and Foa, 2001).

Computer Technology for Student Learning

Jim Sierra wants his students to do a social studies project as part of the unit on westward expansion in his fifth-grade classroom. He knows that the textbook gives some basic information about how westward expansion happened and where settlers went, but he feels that the information doesn't help the students think about the difficulties that settlers faced or understand the problem solving that they engaged in as pioneers. The school where Mr. Sierra teaches has Internet access set up in the library. There are six computers and printers that his class can use. He schedules three one-hour periods in the center for his class. He then decides to search for relevant Web sites where his students can access information. He creates a word-processing document and lists a couple of guiding questions at the top of the page. Then he pastes the seven site addresses on the remainder of the page and leaves a couple of blank lines at the bottom for students to add their own site addresses. Before the class leaves for the first session in the library, he assigns the students to groups, and the class discusses how they can record the information they find. They decide that they might be able to print out information from the first couple of Web sites and have some of the team members begin to look at the quality of the data. The other team members will go to the remaining Web sites and copy and paste information into other word-processing documents that they can take back to the classroom computer and print out. A couple of kids decide that they could take the disks home for their group and print from their home computer that night. Sierra tells them that he will make extra copies on the copier at school the next day at recess. The class heads for the media center.

Should Mr. Sierra have identified Web addresses for his students?

Researching information using technology can be effective if the teacher considers the intended purpose of the research experience and guides the students to ask effective questions and use effective research skills. Helping students learn to ask significant questions is important because Mr. Sierra believes that the students have to sort through more information than they can possibly use. McKenzie (2000) calls use of the Internet for accessing information "the information gold rush" and suggests that the most important skill in learning to use technology for research purposes is to learn to ask the right questions to direct decision making concerning what is relevant information and what is not. The teacher can assist in that process by preselecting the sites, which requires that the teacher anticipates what questions students might ask and has time to evaluate whether those questions can be appropriately answered. Of course, preselection of sites also allows the teacher to identify sites that give misinformation or that mask themselves as an informational site, yet may serve another purpose such as advertising or persuasion.

Web sites should also be evaluated for their ease of navigation. Being able to move around through a Web site, find the information you are looking for, and remember where you are in the site and how to get back to previous parts of the site you have already visited are important components of Web site design. Several sources can be used for evaluating a Web site, including the following:

- ED's Oasis: www.classroom.com/edsoasis/guide2.html
- Kathy Schrock's Guide for Educators: school.discovery.com/schrockguide/eval.html
- Purdue University—Evaluation of Internet Information: thorplus.lib.purdue.edu/~techman/eval.html

Technology labs are busy and popular places in schools.

Evaluation of Web sites should be the first step in Internet-based research.

Technology-based research can take place either by "mining" the Internet or by using data-based software such as electronic encyclopedias and almanacs. In both cases, it is important that students understand the ethics of using data from sites or programs, and that they know what is considered to be plagiarism. Much of what is on the Internet is for public access, but some is copyrighted. Copyright statements will appear on a site, but if there is any confusion the owner of the site should be contacted. In addition, plagiarism of writing that appears on the Internet is increasing because of the ease of copying text. It is important to teach students what plagiarism is and to model for them how to use the text from a Web site and weave it into their own writing. (See www.lccc.cc.wy.us/library/wwwresource/plagerism.asp for resources about plagiarism.) It is also important that students know how to appropriately cite programs and sites where they access information. (See www.bedfordstmartins.com/online/citex.html for examples of how to cite Internet-based resources.)

A *WebQuest* is a type of Internet-based activity that directs learners to sites where information about a given topic can be researched. The WebQuest concept was designed in 1995 by Bernie Dodge and Tom March. According to Dodge and March (2003), the WebQuest is inquiry-oriented and saves class time because students do not need to conduct the whole search on their own, yet the thinking process is designed to support student analysis, synthesis, and evaluation. WebQuests can be structured to cover a wide variety of topics. To create a WebQuest, Dodge recommends that you follow a sequence of design steps: selecting an appropriate topic, selecting a design, deciding how learners will be evaluated, designing the process, and polishing the product. Examples of "design patterns" can be seen at Dodge's Web site at webquest.sdsu.edu/designpatterns/all.htm.

You can find a huge number of WebQuests on the Internet—just do a search and you'll see how many there are! How do you evaluate their quality? Perhaps the best approach is to consider the concept and purpose of research as a higher-level-thinking activity. Research, whether it is technology-based or book-driven, relies on the questioning ability of the researcher. Questions must be formulated for testing hypotheses; they drive the evaluative process and serve as guiding tools for decision making about what the next step in any research project should be. When evaluating a WebQuest for its potential learning effect on learners, it is important to judge what kinds of questions the learners are encouraged to create, study, and test. A poor WebQuest will minimize the kinds of questions the learner asks. It will ask questions for the learner and provide structure for finding the answers to those questions. It will minimize the questioning-thinking process for the learner. According to McKenzie (2000), the learner's thinking process has been "prepackaged" and the search reduced in scope. Enact a WebQuest yourself before sending students to complete it. Be sure that it doesn't represent oversimplified Internet searching without significant questioning conducted by the learners!

Teaching Hints: Choosing Web Sites

Consider the following questions before choosing Web sites for students to use:

1. What is the curriculum-related purpose of the activity?
2. Does the Internet enhance the activity? In what ways will it be used?
   a. to practice information-seeking skills
   b. to become informed about a topic of inquiry or answer a question
   c. to review multiple perspectives concerning an issue
   d. to solve authentic problems
3. How will students use online resources?
4. Do my students have the necessary skills in data analysis and information synthesis?
5. Do I have the necessary time and support for the activity?

Courtesy Coulter, Feldman, & Conold (2000).

Using technology to add to students' resources for research projects needs to be well planned and developed to incorporate teaching students how to ask the right questions, evaluate where they are gathering data from, and avoid falling into unethical situations such as plagiarism and inadequate citing of resources.

Did You Know That . . . ?

The address of an Internet site, especially the last three letters of the domain name, can give you a hint about the kind of information housed on the site.

- memory.loc.gov: A URL that ends in .gov is owned by the government.
- jefferson.village.virginia.edu: A URL that ends in .edu is owned by an educational institution. Remember that some schools have beliefs that may influence the information put on the site.
- www.pbs.org: A URL that ends in .org is usually a nonprofit organization. Some are more unbiased than others, but you must always investigate who is in charge of the organization.
- www.snowcrest.net: A URL that ends in .net is a network address. It can be operated by a nonprofit group, a for-profit group, or an individual.
- www.americanwest.com: A URL that ends in .com is usually a for-profit group attempting to make money.

In all cases, you need to investigate who runs the site and evaluate information on the site as being factual or biased before having students use it as research data.

Using Technology to Differentiate Instruction: Computer-Based Learning (CBL)

Jim Sierra has several students who are above grade level in math and several who are below grade level. His math textbook gives suggestions for enrichment and reteaching, but his biggest challenge is to find differentiated activities for students to do. Following directed lessons in math, as students move through structured practice, he has some students going to classroom computers with a folder in hand. The students look in the folder for a data sheet that tells them the last lesson they finished in a particular software program, open the program, and begin working. At one computer, a student is reviewing decimals because of poor performance on a quiz by using Math Workshop by Broderbund. At another computer, a student is working ahead to understand more complicated aspects of geometry than those in the textbook by using Geometry World by Cognitive Technologies.

Mr. Sierra is using different software programs to meet the needs of his students. He can choose from several types of software programs:

- Drill-and-practice software that allows students to practice a skill and receive immediate feedback about correctness
- Tutorials that provide information about concepts or skills, provide feedback, and assess proficiency with the concept
- Instructional games that imbed practice with skills in gamelike situations
- Simulations that reflect real or imaginative situations
- Problem-solving programs that are designed to have the student apply problem-solving strategies to real or imaginative situations

The decision of when to use these various type of software should be determined by the quality of the software program and the perceived learning benefits for the student. Several sources for evaluation criteria are available to the teacher. An example of a checklist of evaluation criteria is at Children's Software Review, www.childrenssoftware.com/rating.html#inst. You can also use Internet-based database tools to search libraries of evaluations that others have done. An example can be found at the California Learning Resource Network, www.clrn.org. Criteria for evaluating software usually include elements that examine the design and pedagogical soundness of the program, appropriateness of

Computers provide a means of differentiating instruction for students.

the content, user flexibility associated with working the program, and technological features that make the program easy to use (Roblyer, 2003). Many programs track students' progress. Look for programs that will report performance. Have students note this in a computer folder and keep track of how they progress through a software program. It will usually take a student several sessions to complete a topic-focused component of a program.

The Thinking Connection—Problem Solving, Project-Based Learning, and Problem-Based Learning

Though many experienced teachers are familiar with using computers for drill and practice, tutorials, or simulations, it is also important to understand how some newer applications of computers are intended to develop learners' problem-solving skills. Problem solving is addressed in a variety of ways using both software and Internet-based activities. **Problem-based learning** has three main characteristics. First, it motivates students to be involved in the problem. Second, it organizes curriculum around the problem, allowing student learning to be relevant. Finally, it creates a learning environment in which the teacher coaches and guides student inquiry (Torp & Sage, 1998). Problem-solving software engages learners in the kinds of problem solving that are considered constructivist and inquiry-oriented.

There are two kinds of problem-solving software. Programs are intended to engage learners in thinking processes such as metacognition, observing, recalling information, sequencing, analyzing, finding and organizing information, inferring, predicting outcomes, making analogies, and formulating ideas (Roblyer, 2003). The first type is specific to a content area. Many math-based programs involve problem solving. For example, the Geometric Supposer by Sunburst allows learners to draw geometric shapes and manipulate them while solving problems. The second type of software is content-free. One of the most popular of those programs is called Factory, in which the learner has to problem-solve what sequence of machines must be organized to create a product. Sequential and spatial thinking are required. Students can develop and practice problem-solving skills in a computer-based environment.

In problem-based learning the teacher usually presents the problem to the students. The problem must require students to decide what is important and brainstorm what information they need to gather and apply, and it must leave resolution of the problem as an open-ended experience that could be solved in many ways. Many problem-based learning situations are now being created that can be approached with technology. The Center for Problem-Based Learning provides an excellent Web site describing what it is and showing examples of problem-based learning: www.imsa.edu/team/cpbl/problem.html. Another site with background information about problem-based learning is the SCORE project in California for History/Social Science (www.score.kiz.ca.us). The stages of the problem-based learning cycle are as follows: Stage 1, encountering and defining the problem; Stage 2, accessing, evaluating, and utilizing information; and Stage 3, synthesis and performance.

Project-based learning engages learners in producing a product. Projects should have depth, take time to complete, and be complex. Project-based learning results in the creation of an artifact at the end of the project. Projects can be created with productivity software such as presentation, word processing, desktop publishing, or spreadsheet programs. A well-constructed project requires different types of problem solving for the project to be completed. Project-based learning is usually interdisciplinary and is completed cooperatively by groups of learners. Dave Nelson's physics assignment to make a roller coaster is an example of project-based learning without the use of technology.

Many project-based learning initiatives are currently underway that integrate the use of technology. The largest educational technology organization, the International Society for Technology in Education, is gathering information on and examples of project-based learning (www.iste.org/research/roadahead/pbl.cfm). Several initiatives have Web sites where project-based learning is described and ideas are located. The Challenge 2000 Multimedia Project (pblmm.k12.ca.us) has resources that describe project-based learning and how it differs from problem-based learning. The site shows multimedia projects completed by different grade levels. The Buck Institute for Education also describes project based learning in its handbook (www.bie.org/pbl/pblhandbook/index.php) and shares examples of project-based units (www.bie.org/pbl/resources/examples.php#ss). Along with other groups, these initiatives are examining the learning benefits of having students solve problems together as they create projects using technology.

Implementing either project-based learning or problem-based learning requires a change from traditional instruction. Because students are expected to be more self-guided, criteria in the form of rubrics are often used and students will know how they will be graded. Students also need to learn how to work as part of a group, since all of these experiences require cooperation. The teacher is challenged to change the teaching style from directing student learning to facilitating student learning. Finally, teachers will need to manage the use of technology by students so that access is not an issue. Learner outcomes will include an increased ability to think about how to use technology as a resource, ability to apply higher-level thinking to problem situations, and increased motivation for learning.

Technology as a Student Tool

Jean Cantor likes to use computer software to meet the individual needs of her eleventh-grade students; to do this she includes technology-based projects in her curriculum units. She finds that including such projects motivates her students to produce quality work because they will be sharing it via technology within the class and with other classes. In fact, Ms. Cantor looks for projects that allow her students to put their work on the class Web site so that other classes can access the work. Cantor's class is completing a project in which students are writing poetry anthologies and publishing them on the Web site. They are also publishing a hard copy of the anthology that will be placed in the school library and sent out to local doctors' and dentists' offices to be displayed in their waiting rooms. Ms. Cantor believes that this use of technology motivates her students to write more and better because they have an audience for their writing.

While computers have been integrated into classrooms for years with the idea that they could increase learning, the use of software tools such as word processing, desktop publishing, multimedia and presentation software, databases, and spreadsheets has been a more recent addition to computer-based curriculum projects in classrooms. These kinds of programs offer many benefits in the classroom and are necessary for students to learn, since they will play an important role in adult work environments.

Did You Know That . . . ?

> Lou, Abrami, and d'Apollonia (2001) synthesized research on individual computer work and small-group computer work in a study that involved 11,317 learners. They found that the social context of using computer technology in a small group resulted in substantially better projects and greater learning than when students used computer technology individually.

Writing: Word Processing and Desktop Publishing

There are two distinct ways that word processing and desktop publishing tools can enhance learning for students. When included as part of writing process instruction, *word processing software* is recognized as a convenient tool for editing and publishing material. Computers allow students to create polished-looking products for sharing publicly. However, the most powerful use of word processing may be for use as a revision tool. Because word processing allows the author to move text around, highlight text with color, and even strike through text, the word processor becomes a tool that can make the revision process more visual to the author and convenient for cutting and pasting various attempts at revision. Using the word processor as a revision tool must be taught to learners, so it is important to combine the use of word processing by the students with modeling by the teacher.

Word processing requires that the author learn keyboarding skills. Keyboarding is essentially a psychomotor skill, and the teaching of keyboarding should be considered such a skill. It is not uncommon for schools to send students to computer labs for an intensive three-week "unit" to learn to keyboard using popular programs such as Mavis Bacon's Teaching Typing or Typing Tutor, but sometimes teachers then forget to provide for practice time. Psychomotor skills decrease over time if not practiced, so time spent on intensive practice without short practice intervals is essentially worthless.

Desktop publishing software formats word-processed information into a particular kind of document. Desktop publishing provides the author an opportunity to easily include titles, subtitles, columns, and graphics. Many word-processing programs such as Corel WordPerfect and Microsoft Word have desktop publishing capabilities, or you can use a separate publishing program that can integrate documents word-processed with another program. Desktop publishing aligns itself with many curriculum-based projects in different subject areas such as newsletters, posters, flyers, brochures, anthologies of student work, invitations, and calendars.

Organizing Data: Spreadsheets and Databases

Spreadsheets and databases can be used in the curriculum to organize data. *Spreadsheets* can be programmed to perform mathematical calculations on numerical data, organize that data, and produce a variety of graphs. Data is organized in individual cells and can be changed or added to as needed. Databases organize categorical information by fields and can be used to sort information, organize data, or analyze patterns of data. In databases, you can add fields at any time without changing previously entered data.

Spreadsheets offer many advantages to calculating numbers on a calculator. Most programs will calculate and compare numbers stored in the program through the use of formulas that are programmed in for data sets. These data sets can be saved and added to at any time, automatically changing the calculations. This is the basic premise of the electronic gradebook programs that are becoming popular with teachers. Spreadsheets also allow you to copy data to other cells of the spreadsheet. This means that you can add data, create new spreadsheets for showing related data sets, or make subcomponents of larger spreadsheets. Spreadsheets can be used to add a mathematical component to curriculum-based units in other subject areas for portraying numerical data. In science, they can be used for such projects as charting weather or astrological data, recording results in experiments, and tracking data. In social studies, spreadsheets can record and manipulate numerical data, such as demographic changes in a community by population, socioeconomic status, or ethnicity over time.

Spreadsheets may be a component of more complex tool packages such as Microsoft Works or ClarisWorks. Those kinds of programs tend to make it easy to move the numerical data between a word-processed report and a database. Spreadsheets can also be used as a stand-alone program. Most spreadsheets now have the ability to insert graphs into word-processed documents or multimedia presentations. One spreadsheet called Cruncher has actually been created for an early elementary audience. It has a very easy-to-use and colorful interface that is attractive to young children. However, it still maintains the basic mathematical functions that all spreadsheets have in common.

Databases are programs that allow you to store, organize, and manipulate both text and numerical data. Database programs create files and store data in a location called a *field*. Databases allow you to change information, sort information alphabetically or numerically, search for specific key terms or conditions, and retrieve reports. Database files also can be merged together with word-processed documents to create reports. Use of databases can teach students research, study, and organization skills; how to use data to create pictures; and how to pose and test hypotheses and search for research information (Roblyer, 2003).

Building a database is a difficult task. When students are learning about databases, you will want to specify what categories of data they are supposed to enter. As students become more skilled at understanding what kinds of data can be recorded and manipulated in a database, they will be ready to add some additional categories. Eventually, they may be able to create database categories of their own and then perform the necessary research.

Using Graphics: Multimedia and Presentation Software

Multimedia is one of the fastest-growing components of technology. The media can be still pictures, sound, video, animation, and/or text that are combined to create a presentation. Due to recent advances in memory storage and digital media, current computers can come with digital movie editing capabilities that even young children can use. Multimedia can enhance classroom curriculum by providing motivation, flexibility in expression, development of creative and critical-thinking skills, and improved writing and process skills.

Having students create multimedia in the classroom for a curriculum-related project requires significant planning. Students need to determine how the multimedia project will operate, first storyboarding what the audience will see and experience. Plans need to consider such topics as learner control, use of color, graphics, animation, audio, and video. The construction of multimedia also takes up a large amount of memory, so it is essential that the teacher think about how projects will be saved. For audio, video, or animation, even a large-capacity Zip disk will probably not be enough of a storage device. "Burning" a CD with a CD burner hooked up to the computer as a peripheral device is the most common choice for saving multimedia presentations. These devices make a CD that stores data files, much the same way that music CDs are produced. In addition, the teacher will need to consider how the project will be shared. If it is to be shared with a large group, then the use of a liquid crystal display (LCD) projector is recommended. Otherwise, the presentation will be visible only on a small computer screen.

Having students use technology as an authoring tool for representing writing, showing data, manipulating data, and thinking about the relationship between different types of data adds a noteworthy depth to curriculum units and projects. Students learn to be problem solvers, be creative, and work cooperatively, and are motivated to show their best work. Organizing for this level of work in the classroom takes careful planning, with a system for keeping learners accountable for daily progress and expectations for quality of work clearly defined.

Technology as a Teaching Tool

> Jim Sierra has traditional materials for his westward expansion unit—the social studies textbook and a couple of historical fiction books that he will read after lunch. He has some projects for the students to do—they'll make covered wagons and determine what items should go into it. They will also make a map that shows the two most popular routes for going west. But Mr. Sierra also knows how to use technology to access additional materials that are on the Internet and how to use software tools to share those materials with his students. He will be showing a multimedia slide show of artwork that depicts the journeys of the pioneers in their covered wagons as they traveled west. These should help the students visualize what life must have been like for the early pioneers. He accessed these pictures from the Internet by looking for pictures that were not copyrighted. In addition, Sierra has access to the original journals of people who traveled west from the U.S. Library of Congress Rare Books Collection. He has compiled those journals into word-processing documents. After compiling five journals, he has enough for cooperative learning groups to each follow the journey of a different family and document the path the family took and the problems that had to be overcome. In addition, Mr. Sierra accessed maps on the Internet that will help the students trace the route the settlers took. He plans to initiate the unit with these activities to build motivation for learning the historical content planned for the unit.

Technology as a Support Tool

When you think about how technology can be used to augment a lesson, you should consider how technology gives you additional materials, how you can use various software tools during a lesson to model a skill or present a concept, and how technology may be used to record data created during a lesson. In planning to use technology in the delivery of a lesson, both the goals of the lesson and parts of that lesson should be considered during the planning process.

All lessons have some type of introduction intended to motivate a learning experience and some type of culminating event that brings the lesson to a close. Using the direct instruction teaching model, the teacher uses the motivation phase to assist students to think about the topic to be studied and stimulate prior knowledge about the topic. The lesson is directed through a study of the topic and structured and guided practice with that topic. At the midpoint of the lesson, students are asked to apply what they have learned. The lesson ends with the teacher reinforcing the lesson by asking students to think about what they have learned, and perhaps defining it in such a way that the students will remember what was learned.

Some lessons are more inquiry-based and student-driven. These lessons also need to begin with some type of motivation, but the motivation is intended to cause inquiry to happen. The group investigation teaching model may be used for problem solving. The learning activity becomes an investigation generated during the motivation phase of the lesson, and the culmination may be an application of what was learned during inquiry.

Whether you want to teach a directed lesson or an inquiry-based lesson, technology can be used to augment the phases of the lesson. You can use the computer to generate materials that might not have been otherwise accessible. For example, you can increase the amount of data available during a lesson, manipulate the data in a lesson, gather evidence of practice, and use the computer for a culmination activity. Some examples for language arts and science are given in Table 12.1. Using technology to teach a lesson requires you to have some way of making the computer screen visible to the class. Of course, having an LCD projector in the classroom or lab is the easiest, but it is also possible to hook up a video monitor to a computer so the class can view the display as if it were on a television. A visit to your local computer hardware store will help you purchase the inexpensive cables for accomplishing this. It is important to understand the purpose of the technology and to plan for supporting the lesson objectives. If using the computer during a lesson doesn't purposefully make the lesson better, don't use the technology!

Technology as an Assessment Tool

Technology can be used for creating and recording assessments and organizing and analyzing assessment data. Assessment can be either performed, organized, and analyzed by the teacher or engaged in as a joint enterprise by teachers and students. There are many web sites on the Internet that will assist you in developing rubrics. For example, the RubiStar site (rubistar.4teachers.org) provides ready-made rubrics or will assist you in developing your own. Electronic portfolios provide examples of how performance-based data can be organized and analyzed to assist the teaching and learning process. Some Web sites link to the wide variety of portfolio assessment resources available on the Internet. An

TABLE 12.1 Using Technology to Augment Lessons

	Directed Lesson	**Inquiry-Based Lesson**
Language arts (examples do not follow one lesson goal)	Motivation/introduction Ideas • Use an Internet site that shows a project the class can complete (example: online class poetry contest). • Show published samples of work created in previous lessons. Learning activity ideas • Model, using a word processor, how an author thinks about the writing process (example: how to write a good lead) by writing in front of the class. • Have work samples available to examine (example: work that needs revision or editing) and correct. • Print out stories or poems from the Internet to compare with the story in the textbook (example: fables). Culmination ideas • Create examples of the topic/concept learned and print for dissemination. • Show student work samples (save as computer files, take digital pictures and show on screen).	Motivation/introduction Ideas • Give a multimedia slide show of pictures captured from the Internet to stimulate student questions. • Introduce a project from an educational Internet site that promotes projects (example: Global Schoolhouse www.globalschoolnet.org/GSH/index.html). Learning activity ideas • Create word-processed list of URLs students may use for research; demonstrate how to link. • Provide multimedia slide show template for groups to share product. Culmination ideas • Create/provide rubric for peer assessment of group projects (example: RubiStar, rubistar.4teachers.org).
Science (examples do not follow one lesson goal)	Motivation/introduction ideas • Show a Web site with recently collected data (example: USGS National Earthquake Information Center data on the most recent earthquakes, neic.usgs.gov/neis/bulletin). • Offer CD-ROM encyclopedia information about the science topic to stimulate what students already know about it.	Motivation/introduction ideas • Show a live webcam to stimulate student questions (example: www.montereybayaquarium.com). Learning activity ideas • Have students collect experiment data on a spreadsheet. Transfer the data to a multimedia slide show for analysis.

(continued)

TABLE 12.1 Using Technology to Augment Lessons *(continued)*

Directed Lesson	Inquiry-Based Lesson
Learning activity ideas • Download information from a Web site that is not available in textbooks for the lesson (example: microgravity-related information from NASA, microgravity.nasa.gov/oeK-12.html). Culmination ideas • Create (with students) a summary of what was learned from the lesson—add graphics, distribute to parents, or post on class Web site.	Culmination ideas • Prepare a "scientific proceedings" book of cooperative learning group investigations and publish it for parents.

example is the Web site of Dr. Helen Barrett (electronicportfolios.com/portfolios/bookmarks.html). Many electronic grading programs are also available for download; for example, see the many listed at the DMOZ Open Directory Project (dmoz.org/Computers/Software/Educational/Teachers_Help/Gradebooks).

Technology as a Communication Tool

Technology can enhance your ability to communicate with families and the community. Beyond the traditional use of word processing to publish professional-looking letters, consider using word-processing or desktop publishing programs to create certificates, brochures, bulletin board components, postcards, and even business cards. Professional-looking correspondence is always perceived as more important to the audience who receives it!

Probably the fastest-growing use of technology-based communication is the development of the classroom home page. Many free programs (such as Netscape Composer) are available to help you build a home page. You can also find tutorials on the Internet that will lead you through the process of building a home page. Consider the following questions when constructing a classroom home page (Leu & Leu, 2000):

- Do you want a location where parents and others can send your class e-mail?
- Do you want a location where students can post their work? How will you organize it?—by subject area or date?
- Do you want a location where due dates for major assignments are posted?
- Do you want a location of organizing links to sites for different class units and assignments?
- Do you want a location where students can publish a classroom newsletter?

Did You Know That . . . ?

You can find sites on the Internet that will help you with ideas to build a class Web site:

- Education World: www.educationworld.com/a_tech/techtorial/techtorial013.shtml
- MySchoolOnline: www.myschoolonline.com/golocal/
- Basics of K–12 Site Design: www.pekin.net/pekin108/webmasters/class2/tips1.html

Here is a bibliography of links to help you make a Web site:

- Web Page Development Resources: www.orangeusd.k12.ca.us/resourcetools/pagedevelopment.htm

You can also see lots of examples of class Web sites:

- Find a Site: www.myschoolonline.com/golocal/map/
- Best Site Showcase: www.myschoolonline.com/article/0,1120,31-15942,00.html
- www.myschoolonline.com
- First Grade Friends: www.mrsperkins.com
- Ms. Clark's Class: www.hollyclark.com

Organizing and Planning for Technology

There is nothing worse than planning for technology in your lesson and having it fail when you are standing in front of the students! You can avoid that nightmare by planning appropriately for the use of technology in the classroom. There are several important considerations—what the technology will be used for, what resources will be technology-based, how students will be grouped to use technology, what product will be created with technology, and what types of technology will be used. Consider the following topics and questions:

- *Needs:* What are the technology needs of the lesson? Can they be adjusted if the technology is unavailable?
- *Access:* What level of technology is accessible? Is there a lab? Are there classroom computers? Does available technology have needed software? If Internet access is needed, is it available? What kind of viewing system is available?
- *Grouping:* How much technology is needed? Can differentiation in grouping patterns be used if necessary?
- *Activity:* How does technology support learning in the lesson? What kind of product is being produced?

After answering these questions, you need to create a technology management plan. This plan should include a contingency plan for the possible failure of technology. Access to functioning hardware and availability of needed software applications are two major factors to consider. When developing a technology management plan, think down to the next lower level of technology access that you have, and have a backup plan. See Table 12.2 for examples of backup plans.

TABLE 12.2 Examples of Technology Contingencies

Planned Technology Access	Problem	Technology Backup (create before the lesson)
Have Internet access in lab or classroom for groups to look at Web sites	Internet is down	Save a copy of the Web site on the teacher's computer or a CD
Have Internet access in lab for individual students or cooperative groups to use	Internet is down	Create CDs for groups; use a different Web site for each group if needed
Use word processing software for modeling writing	Instructor's computer is not working; projection is not possible	Use chart paper for modeling
Use word processing software for examining work completed at individual computers	Instructor's computer is not working; projection is not possible	Print out the work from individual computers and share with the whole class or trade with individuals
Use word processing software in the lab to compose/revise/edit/publish writing	Lab is not available; only a few computers in the classroom	Use word processing software only to edit/publish
Use spreadsheets for individuals or groups to collect data	Not enough computers with software available	Print spreadsheets with appropriate fields identified so that data collection can be done by hand if needed
Use spreadsheets for analyzing data, including graph construction	Not enough computers with software available	Have calculators and graph paper available for construction by hand if needed
Show multimedia slide show of pictures	Instructor's computer is not working; projection is not possible	Print selected slides ahead of time as transparencies in a laser printer; use on an overhead projector
Individual or group construction of multimedia presentation	Instructor's computer is not working; projection is not possible	Have a template prepared so that the whole class can add to the copy on instructor's computer only

Chapter Summary

Technology is becoming an important part of the classroom curriculum and instructional process. Powerful computers and their peripherals, along with more complex software applications that are easy to use, make it easier to incorporate the use of technology in ways that promote student learning. The expansive amount of information available on the Internet and CD-ROM can be used by students for researching data beyond books. There is easier access to graphic data such as pictures and maps. In addition, students can use technology to learn content, concepts, and skills in a differentiated way with computer-based learning (CBL). Students can also use technology to engage in highly motivating problem-solving activities, project-based learning, and problem-based learning.

Technology also can be used by students as a powerful productivity tool. Word processing and desktop publishing can impact student writing and publishing. Professional-looking products can motivate students to apply their writing skills more seriously. Students also can use spreadsheets and databases to organize data for reporting or analysis.

Technology has also become a powerful teaching tool. Technology can be used to augment directed and inquiry-based lessons by providing additional material that can be shared in efficient ways. Technology is quickly becoming an important communication tool because both schools and families have more consistent access to the Internet. This has resulted in a significant increase in class Web sites.

Whether for student or teacher use, it is important to organize for technology. Lesson planning needs to include contingency plans for how to complete lesson activities if the available technology fails. Contingency planning needs to happen before the lesson, so that valuable learning time is not lost.

Technology is considered such an important skill that the largest teacher organization that promotes the use of technology recently published technology standards for teachers. All teachers need to become competent in the use of technology for supporting curriculum development and learning.

Teaching Problems

1. What are the advantages and disadvantages of preselecting Web sites for student research?
2. Plan a lesson that demonstrates how computer technology can be used to accommodate diverse learners by differentiating instruction.
3. Contrast project-based learning and problem-based learning by planning two learning experiences in a subject field of your choice.
4. What is the value of using the Internet to communicate with colleagues and students' parents?
5. Create a project that requires students to use multimedia and presentation software.
6. Contrast use of technology for a direct instruction lesson and a group investigation lesson. Provide an example of each.

Chapter 13

Growing as a Professional

ADVANCE ORGANIZER

These questions can be used as a framework to assist you in integrating professional knowledge and understanding of the content of this chapter.

1. Why is it advantageous to develop peer relationships?
2. How can teachers coach each other?
3. When novice teachers need help, whom should they ask?
4. What professional problems do new teachers encounter and what are some ways to alleviate them?
5. Why should new teachers get involved in professional organizations?
6. How is National Board Certification accomplished?
7. What should portfolios contain and how should they be evaluated?
8. Ethical professional behavior is respected by colleagues, parents, and students. What should teachers remember?

 The following INTASC issues and standards are discussed in this chapter: Numbers 2, 3, 6, 8–10.

The theme of this chapter is to help beginning teachers solve typical professional problems that occur naturally in the early days of teaching. Consideration is given to (1) the development of collegial relationships with peers, (2) how colleagues can help each other, (3) whom to ask for help, (4) whether to get involved with professional associations, (5) the development of professional portfolios, and (6) ethical questions and behaviors.

Interpersonal Relationships with Peers, Mentors, and Administrators

The school had a population of 900 students in a low-income area of a San Fernando Valley (California) community. Four new teachers who had just completed student teaching were hired. After viewing their classrooms and scrambling for supplies, books, and equipment—of which there was little—they arranged their furniture and tried to steady themselves for their first "on their own" teaching experience. At the end of the first week they each received a note from the principal that she would like to meet with them as a group on Monday afternoons when school was dismissed.

The four teachers had no time to get acquainted; each was busy paddling upstream in a strange environment. They met in the principal's office, the principal was a kind, extremely busy, but conscientious administrator. "What problems are you having?" she asked. The problems were so numerous and overwhelming that the four teachers were speechless. They were also afraid to admit any weaknesses, lest they be considered incompetent.

The principal, not to be deterred, began talking about classroom environments, school rules, and management problems. She told the teachers that they were always welcome to come to her for assistance, and that she would be visiting their classrooms. The Monday meetings were to occur every other week and they should feel free to discuss their problems.

After the meeting the four teachers felt compelled to get together and discuss the Monday meetings. They decided that each would take a turn at raising a question or problem to accommodate the principal's need to help them. But another outcome of the meeting was that the four teachers were drawn together and began to rely on each other for advice.

How Can Peers Help Each Other?

Note: In this chapter it is assumed that you are about to complete your student teaching or are an intern teacher, an emergency credentialed teacher, or a probationary teacher.

During that first year of teaching the four new teachers from the opening vignette first began consulting each other on tacit understandings that they were unclear about: "Must we keep our students in line when walking to and from the playground?" "Why does it appear that I have all the problem kids and the other fourth-grade teachers have all the good kids?" "I really can't teach music; do I dare ask the principal about it, since she used to be a music teacher?" "Should I send kids who are misbehaving to the office?" "Do I dare miss the faculty meeting?"

As the year progressed and the teachers began to consider the questions they prepared for their Monday meetings, their attitudes toward and questions for each other changed. Their concerns about the school culture and relationships with other teachers were less worrisome, and they began to ask each other for pedagogical opinions.

Middle and high school teachers face similar indoctrination problems. The tacit understandings that exist within every school are rarely shared. The "egg-crate" structure that inhibits teacher interaction and promotes isolation still exists in the majority of schools today. But in schools with teaming and block structures, teachers find strength and professionalization through communication with their peers.

Advantages of Peer Relationships

The four teachers in the opening vignette derived emotional comfort from their interactions and decision to "make their principal happy" by bringing up teaching problems. As the semester progressed the teachers developed friendship and a caring relationship. They lent each other teaching supplies and materials. They began to ask each other for assistance and ideas for lessons, and this led to talking about the lessons afterward. They would spend time talking about what worked, what didn't, and what alternatives they could have tried. As a consequence they learned to reflect on their own lessons and their friends' lessons. Talking about teaching helped improve their teaching. They were learning from each other in ways that they could not learn from more experienced teachers who did not share the same problems.

These young teachers had discovered a form of professional development that research indicates really works in improving school culture, classroom environment, student success, and pedagogy (Lemlech, Hertzog, & Hackl, 1994). Takenaga-Taga (1999) related another example of how science teachers at a Los Angeles science, math, and technology magnet school formed a network to make curriculum decisions. The network meetings were used to share plans, reflect on instructional changes, and bring in experts as resource people. Takenaga-Taga reported that the meetings made the teachers feel empowered and optimistic about the changes in their own teaching and the contributions they were making to the school.

Time—The Inhibitor of Professional Development

Time for teachers to plan lessons, interact with other teachers, visit demonstration lessons in other schools, coach peers, observe, advise, and visit within the same school—all of these significant acts require not only personal commitment and administrative support and encouragement, but sometimes district approval. As a consequence it often seems that there are built-in constraints that defy the impetus for professional development. Yet these are the very activities that reap quality improvement in teaching performance. How is the constraint of time overcome?

1. *Banked time:* By teaching an extra 15–20 minutes four days per week, teachers free themselves for an hour of staff development or team meetings on the fifth day of the week. The extra teaching time can be arranged before or after the normal school day or subtracted from an hour of lunch time.

2. *Teaming:* Three-person teams can be created so that two members of the team work with all three of the classes and the third member has free time for observation within the school or with the team partners.

3. *Substitute time:* Using staff development funds, substitute teachers can be employed to free up teachers for planning conferences, observing, and networking.

4. *Outside funding:* Businesses in the local community have been funding professional development time for teachers. Funds are used for travel expenses, substitute pay, expert pay, and after-school or Saturday compensation. Ohio, New York, Minnesota, Washington, and California have been prominent in programs to improve professional development.

Program Quality Review in California

In the early 1990s California implemented a process to improve professional development in elementary schools that would be comparable to the secondary accreditation process. The program has changed considerably through the years, but the basic premise remains the same. When a school is under review, two consultants are selected from outside the school district to be "critical friends" of the school faculty. One consultant is expert on facilitating the "change" process; the other consultant is expert in the selected subject field that will be the focus of improvement (Encinas, 2001).

The school faculty decides on several essential questions that will be used to determine whether there is evidence of student performance that indicates improvement in teaching processes. A leadership team at the school is selected to help focus the process and determine the scope of the school's improvement plan. Each school under review may select different subject fields to direct their inquiry. Typically the process begins with peer observations. Teachers are prepared with ways to observe and what to observe as they visit in other classrooms. In general the teachers do not observe at their own grade level. Teachers are released for 70 minutes for observation. One teacher stated, "This was a good experience for all of us to see each other teach. We got a chance to see our peers as professionals in action" (Encinas, 2001, p. 142).

Encinas commented that the observation process helped to develop an esprit de corps and collegial relationships among the faculty. Another teacher remarked, We have no common preparation times. The only time we did any sharing was when we did the peer observation. It allowed us to see what the teachers are doing and the students are producing. It gave us a chance to evaluate what we were seeing. Teachers liked what they saw at the different levels. Everyone volunteered to do this" (p. 142).

In the school that Encinas studied, two curriculum areas were selected—English language arts and mathematics. She concluded that the quality review process depends on the leadership team for expertise in knowledge of state frameworks and standards, and that the makeup of the team should include both experienced and newly trained teachers. The consultants' role also was crucial to the process because they must be capable of analyzing the school process and documents and must serve as coaches, cheerleaders, and communicators.

Students' performance and school improvement are enhanced when teachers have the opportunity to work with their peers and develop relationships that allow them to learn from each other and critique each other in a collegial manner. Teachers at all levels (K–12) need to break out of the "egg crate" that has confined them and have the opportunity to develop professional relationships, similar to other professional groups.

Did You Know That . . . ?

> Routman (2002) believes that teachers need to engage in professional conversations in order to create meaningful and lasting changes in teaching and learning. Professional development without time for professional dialogue is a waste of time. Professional conversations help teachers weigh one instructional method over another and reflect on how theory and research inform teaching.

Collegial Relationships

Collegial relationships do not develop overnight, nor are they developed because you teach at the same school or even next door to another teacher. Teachers find it quite natural to lend supplies to each other, suggest resources, and provide general assistance to each other—but these are everyday kind of "helping" behaviors, the same sort of behavior you would proffer to the neighbor across the street.

Collegial relationships require that you open up (instead of covering up) your personal beliefs about teaching, recognize that it's okay to make mistakes and not know everything, and be willing to accept another's expertise. (We can't all be experts at everything!)

Colleagues study teaching together by engaging in reflective problem solving. This entails relating what you did and when you did it and how the students reacted. When colleagues observe each other (Figure 13.1) or use video to record lessons, it is much easier to ponder alternative means of conducting a lesson. Reflection, or using metacognitive skills, not only can improve students' performance, but also certainly helps improve teachers' use of teaching strategies. Lemlech and Kaplan (1990) have defined **collegiality** as follows:

> The establishment of a professional relationship for the purpose of service and accommodation through the mutual exchange of perceptions and expertise.

Figure 13.2 identifies the colleague's analysis of the observations and suggestions to be communicated. The postconference should stimulate reflection and demonstrate courteous professional conduct.

> ***Problem/concern:*** Do my questions motivate discussion? How many students respond and discuss?
>
> ***Overview of lesson:*** I will lead a whole-class discussion by asking questions to elicit students' discussion.
>
> ***Focus of observation:*** Appropriateness of teacher's questions; students' participation (how many? all over the classroom? girls and boys?)
>
> ***Notes:*** Teacher's questions verbatim; students' responses abridged

FIGURE 13.1 Informal Peer Observation—Initial Conference

Coaching

The best coaches for teachers are other teachers, because peer partners are able to relate to common teaching problems. When learning a new teaching model you need a partner to observe your performance to see if you are really being "true" to the model. Teachers always adapt and modify teaching models or strategies to fit their students' needs; however, when learning a new way of teaching you need to recognize that the benefits or purposes of the teaching model will be subverted if you do not carry out the model as it is intended.

For example, suppose you are learning to use the concept attainment model of teaching (Chapter 9) and you ask your students for their "guesses or hypotheses" about the concept, but instead of accepting all students' responses you cut off some of the students' suggestions because you think they are too far-fetched. After giving students more clues to help them confirm their ideas, you find that practically no students are willing to speak

> **Analysis of Notes:**
>
> 1. Students sitting closest to you tended to participate more than the rest of the class.
>
> 2. No difference between boys' and girls' participation.
>
> 3. Your questions seemed relevant and motivating, but perhaps you didn't look around enough at students to encourage more participation.
>
> **Suggestions:**
>
> 1. How about having students move their chairs so that they can all see each other during the discussion?
>
> 2. Provide more "wait" time after you ask questions to encourage more discussion.
>
> 3. Try some nonverbal gestures to encourage participation.

FIGURE 13.2 Informal Peer Postconference Form

out. The reason is quite clear. Students are afraid of risk taking because you did not allow all of the initial suggestions. A good coach would have detected this and realized that you were giving miscues to the students by rejecting some of their ideas. Even if you had reflected on how you did during the lesson, it is very likely you would not have realized what went wrong without your partner's help.

> **Teaching Hints: Coaching**
>
> Lemlech, Hertzog, and Pensavalle (1998) recommend the following strategy for coaching a peer partner:
>
> 1. Talk to each other about a very specific teaching problem, situation, or concern.
> 2. Decide together how an observation can occur (actual or video).
> 3. Decide what aspect of a lesson should be the focus of the observation.
> 4. Decide whether notes are to be taken or a check sheet created. If a check sheet will be used, create it together.
> 5. Have the observing partner share the notes or check sheet so that both teachers can analyze the focus of the observation.
> 6. Agree that the observing partner will not provide feedback on any other aspect of the lesson—unless the teaching partner requests additional information.

Teacher-Mentor Relationships

Teacher-mentor programs have been developed in many school districts to help novice teachers. The mentor is released for a set number of hours each month to visit with the novice teacher. In general the mentor is supposed to give advice on classroom management, planning lessons, and assessment. The mentor usually observes the inexperienced teacher and provides critique and advice. Some mentors do demonstration lessons in areas of need for the teacher.

Mentors are selected on the basis of their experience, expertise, and leadership ability. However, a number of problems have arisen in mentorship programs. First is the problem of communication. The mentor is often from a different school, perhaps older, and inexperienced with how to teach and relate to adults versus children. Teachers who are being mentored do not like to reveal their needs and shortcomings to the mentor because they fear the likelihood that the mentor will report to the principal or their district supervisor. Hertzog (2002) verified in a study of the problems and needs of novice teachers that mentors are seldom asked for help in comparison to other new teachers, partner teachers, or grade-level chair people.

Unlike collegial relationships with a peer, the mentor is perceived as a superior with power. The culture of the relationship is uneasy and the teacher often feels that he or she is back in student teaching. Because mentors are not given enough hours to spend in the classrooms in a helping role, they see their teachers infrequently and so are viewed as strangers in the classroom environment.

Mentors who work in the same school often have a better relationship with those they tutor. They understand the culture of the school and the new teacher's problems of adjustment. There is often more time to visit and talk before and after school or during lunchtime. Successful mentors learn to spend time exchanging teaching anecdotes and encouraging the novice teacher to take risks with new teaching strategies. Most important is for the mentor to be an advocate for the new teacher and assure the teacher that reports on the mentoring process are not given to the principal of the school.

Relationships with Administrators

The principal is critical in setting the tone of the school. Principals with "open door" policies encourage faculty to drop in and chat. In this way the principal learns what individual teachers are experiencing, their problems, and how the school is functioning. The social atmosphere of the school is also important. Encouraging teachers to be on a first-name basis with each other and with their principal helps generate a relaxed atmosphere. However, in front of the public more respectful greetings are appropriate.

Although all administrators are supposed to be instructional leaders as well as managers, some have not had current experience in learning teaching models and the variety of teaching strategies needed for diversely populated classrooms. In many professional development classes and projects, principals are asked to attend along with the teachers so that they can help teachers succeed when practicing what they are learning.

New teachers can expect that their administrator will use a variety of techniques to verify that things are going well in the classroom. *Walk-throughs* are informal means that administrators use to just drop in, wave a greeting, sometimes walk around the classroom, and then leave.

More formal techniques should be used to monitor instruction, student learning, and classroom management. These techniques come under a variety of headings, such as **clinical supervision.** Formal observations are preceded by a preconference (much like peer coaching) to find out what the teacher intends to accomplish, how it will be taught, what students will be doing, and how the teacher will assess learning. Observation notes should be given to the teacher, who frequently is asked to analyze the notes for personal insights. This is followed by a formal conference to discuss the observation. Most school districts (and states) require several formal observations each school year.

It is wise for the teacher to be explicit in the teaching plan delivered at the preconference so that there is no misunderstanding concerning the teaching strategy and the rationale for using it. This is particularly true if you feel that the administrator may not be familiar with the instructional strategy.

If you have deviated from your proposed lesson plan during the observation, you should explain at the postconference why you did this. Perhaps you observed that students were misunderstanding the concept you were teaching or perhaps a student brought up a question that you thought was particularly meaningful. These are valid reasons for adapting your lesson to the situation or modifying your lesson plan to accommodate students' needs and should be communicated to the observer.

Obtaining Help, Support, Assistance: Typical Beginning Teacher Problems

During student teaching, internships, and alternative emergency programs there are a variety of sources for help. Student teachers have a (master) classroom teacher, college coordinator and/or methods instructor, and program director. Interns and emergency credentialed teachers should have a college coordinator who is usually the methods instructor, and perhaps a school-based mentor for assistance. The problems for most novices are (1) fear of asking for help, (2) confusion about whom to ask for help, and (3) bewilderment as to the nature of the problem in order to request assistance.

Individuals who go through a college preparation program and student teaching have class time with an instructor and their student teacher peers as well as the assigned classroom teacher—so there are plenty of individuals with whom to share their concerns. But individuals who are plunked in a classroom and expected to carry out an academic program without appropriate preparation need help! In this section we will look at the nature of the problems and concerns of first-year teachers.

Problems of novice teachers, not necessarily in order of frequency, include lesson and unit planning, time management, student diversity, behavior problems, small-group teaching, instructional strategies, relationships with more experienced teachers, and school policies. Though most of these problems have been the focus of other chapters, the perspective here is what the inexperienced teacher must do to obtain assistance with these problems.

Lesson and Unit Planning

Most school districts have teaching guides that suggest units of study in subject fields and in grade levels. State frameworks are available in most states in each subject field and these, too, suggest appropriate units. For example, in science, "systems" is an appropriate theme for all grade levels.

- Grades K–3: Teachers might focus on how organisms interact in ecosystems, after first determining that students know what an ecosystem is.

- Grades 3–6: Teachers might consider teaching how energy flows within the ecosystem.

- Grades 6–9: Teachers could focus on how ecosystems change.

- Grades 9–12: Teachers might ask about the responsibilities of people toward ecosystems.*

At the secondary level, department chairpersons usually have course outlines for new teachers to review; at the elementary level, grade-level chairs should be of assistance. It is normal for new teachers to ask about these documents and to find out what other teachers are doing at the same level and for the same subject. Team with another new teacher to ask for assistance, or ask the teacher next door.

---

*Suggestions stated in the *Science Framework for California Public Schools K–12*.

Time Management

Time turns the wheel and runs the classroom. Lessons need to fit into available time. Young students have shorter attention spans than older students. Procedures needed in lessons control the work time. For example, an art lesson requires certain materials that need to be set up. The lesson time must consider how long it will take to clean up. Manipulative activities require setup and cleanup time. Movement to learning centers or use of computers requires time consideration. Small-group work requires movement time, discussion time, and evaluation time (as do all lessons). See Chapters 4–8 for additional help.

Unit planning requires an estimate of how many days or weeks will be needed for students to engage in projects and work tasks to study unit content in depth. While lesson planning has to do with the daily allotment of time to a given concept, units require long-term planning.

When you consider your daily lesson plans, always plan *more* than you think can be handled in a class period. As you become experienced with the content and more knowledgeable about your students, you will be able to plan more exactly. Another trick of substitute teachers and more experienced teachers is to plan what is often called "sponge" activities. These activities should be significant content experiences that can be used when a group of students or the whole class finishes work tasks faster than anticipated. Chapters 6 and 7 should be helpful for review.

Student Diversity

Student diversity is another component of planning. To be considered here are the diverse needs of students of varied ability levels, speaking a variety of languages with English as a second language, and students whose interests and ways of learning (multiple intelligences) are different and perhaps unique. Lessons need to be planned that consider the diversity of the classroom; you can do this by differentiating what groups of students focus on (content), how you teach (process), what students are to produce (products), and the environment of the classroom.

For English language learners you may need to consider peer partners, more manipulative and concrete materials, your personal expressions, greater clarity of instructions, cooperative learning, and perhaps repetition. If you are teaching abstract concepts such as freedom, systems, or imaginative genre, then your teaching strategies need to be carefully thought out. An advance organizer and the concept attainment models should be helpful. Chapters 8 and 9 are appropriate for review.

Behavior Problems

Behavior problems are caused by a variety of factors that may include the environment of your classroom, personal problems of students, social interaction problems of students, and instructional planning that lacks motivation or does not provide for student diversity (language, giftedness, learning styles). As a consequence, students may act out and behave in antisocial ways. Sometimes new teachers find that they have been loaded down with too many students who have emotional and social problems. Review Chapters 5 and 6 for some helpful ideas.

In addition, consider discussing the problem with a partner teacher, a mentor, or a more experienced teacher. Take time to keep an anecdotal record on individuals who are having problems. Analyze your notes and see if you can find a common pattern. Go back to your lesson plans and see if you are challenging your students and providing interesting things to engage them. Reflect on how you respond to these students who misbehave. Have you tried individual, private conferences to discuss the problem with the student? Do you need a parent conference to obtain insight on home patterns? Do you suspect a health-related problem? Try to remember that most behavior problems are a consequence of the classroom environment and instruction. Instead of thinking about Bobby as a behavioral problem, say to yourself that Bobby is a boy with problems, and you need to discover how to help him solve them.

Small-Group Teaching

Small-group teaching is appropriate for K–12. The following are some of the reasons why novice teachers have problems when students work in small groups:

1. Students may not have had enough experience working in small peer groups. If this is so, the answer is *practice*.

2. If movement to the small group is too noisy, it may be because time was not given for each group to move separately. Never have the whole class move at the same time! Also, be certain that each group knows precisely where in the classroom they are to work.

3. If groups are not working productively, it may be that they did not understand what their work task involves. They need to be "refocused." Before sending them to the small group, verify understanding.

4. If problems develop suddenly while students are working, stop the whole class, find out what the trouble is, and reteach or clarify instructions if needed. Monitor group work closely; circulate constantly.

5. Do not forget to evaluate both what was accomplished and cooperative work patterns for each group.

Chapters 4–9 deal with problems associated with small-group teaching.

Did You Know That . . . ?

Both new teachers and veteran teachers profit from a school environment that encourages collaboration across experience levels. Johnson and Kardos (2002) also recommend on-site and on-time professional development in which a new teacher can ask for help from a small team of colleagues on short notice.

Instructional Strategies

It is difficult for novice teachers to take risks because of fear that if students act up, classroom control will slip and who knows who will walk in the door! But the real risk is in not trying new ideas and finding yourself stagnating in the classroom with students who are bored silly. Hamburger sandwiches may be a treat on Monday, but if you have to eat the same lunch five days a week, it is no longer a treat. Therefore, it is extremely important that you vary what you do and how you do it.

If possible, experiment with a peer observing, or at least talk it over with a friend, then try it and tell your students that you are experimenting with some new teaching strategies and you want their opinion about what they learned, and whether they would like to try it again. Students will be more receptive and understanding when you share your concerns about teaching in a new way. What you are really doing is telling them that they are important to you and giving them some responsibility to share their feelings. A new teacher told me about the following incident:

> A middle school teacher brought a tape recorder to her history class and played music from the 1950s, 1960s, and 1970s. She told her class that she wanted them to think about what the music communicated, the historical time period, and the social culture represented by the music. She played six different pieces, three of which were:
>
> "Truth Don Die"
>
> "Raggle Taggle Gypsy"
>
> "I Want To Hold Your Hand"
>
> The titles of the songs were obvious from the music, and after the students listened she had them break into small groups and discuss the songs using the questions she had asked at the beginning of the lesson. Later, after group discussion, she asked them to evaluate the lesson: "What can we learn about history by listening to music from different periods of time?" Then she asked them, "Do you think this is an appropriate way to study history? Did you enjoy today's class?"

The students recognized that music emanates from culture and is indicative of how people feel at particular times and under certain circumstances. They told her that the lesson was a success, but the novice teacher had been scared to death trying it out. (She is no longer afraid to experiment with new ideas.)

Relationships with More Experienced Teachers

Novice teachers often fear interactions with experienced teachers because they don't want to appear stupid or have it reflect on their prior education and practice. What one forgets is that experienced teachers remember what their first teaching experience was like. Most experienced teachers want to help you, but do not want to impose their beliefs and experiences on you.

In most cases you need to initiate the interaction. You may find it more comfortable to seek assistance from a teacher with just slightly more experience in the same school.

Also, it is a good idea to keep in touch with your prior classmates even though they teach in different schools and districts. Sharing problems and frustrations helps you reflect on appropriate actions. You need to recognize that there are two types of reflection. First, there is reflection as you are teaching and observing your students and you recognize that something is awry, as a consequence you perceive the need to make some changes in your plans. Schon (1983) calls this *reflection in action*. The second type of reflection occurs after the lesson, when you recognize that you had alternative ways of teaching and perhaps better ways than what you implemented. Schon calls this *reflection on action*. Both types of reflection are important, but the second type—after the fact—may be more beneficial when you reflect with a colleague.

School Policies and Procedures

Hopefully, before you accepted the position at your school you asked a lot of questions of the district personnel officer and the school principal. Some things that novice teachers need to know are as follows: What kind of support and assistance will be available? Does the school have a specific instructional policy and a discipline policy? If the school's instructional policy and discipline policy do not agree with your beliefs and philosophy of teaching, then you need to select a different school and/or perhaps a different school district.

Many school policies and procedures are difficult to learn about until you are directly involved at the school. The following are examples of new teachers' problems.

- You have planned a video lesson, but you failed to find out if a VCR and monitor were available for the day of your lesson. Is it necessary to sign up for equipment, and if so, how far in advance must you do so?

- You have just discovered that a music teacher comes once a week to your classroom, but she has been scheduled during your mathematics time. Can the schedule be changed? Why were you not consulted?

- You want to send a group of students to the library for research. May you do so?

- During fire drills or emergency situations, is there a specific place where you should take your class? What procedures are involved?

- What do the different bells tell you about school procedures?

- When it rains, are there specific school policies that affect recess and lunch time?

- There is block scheduling at your school that affects the daily schedule. What happens when you have students who are involved in a special program during first period? Will these students be leaving your classroom every week during the first period?

- One of your eleventh-grade students got hurt over the weekend and comes to class on crutches. Are there special procedures or a policy that affects allowing this student in class without first clearing it with the school health officer? Also, suppose the student tells you that he needs to go have physical therapy and his mother will pick him up at a specific time; do you need a note? Should the student wait in the office? What is your responsibility for the safety of this student?

These kinds of questions affect your composure and comfort in the school environment. You can't find the answers on a procedure sheet handed to you the day before school begins. You need to learn the "hidden" rules and procedures quickly, and the only way to do so is to ask other teachers, the school secretary, and your school-based adviser (if you have one). It is your responsibility to anticipate many of these questions and find out what policies will affect your life at the school.

Whom Can I Ask for Help?

Throughout this section suggestions have been made concerning your need for someone to turn to for assistance. You need to be the judge as to the type of help you need and who will be the best person for support. This section will review some of the options to consider.

Another Beginning Teacher

Consult another beginning teacher (first or second year of teaching) and develop collegial relations so that you can both observe each other, obtain critique and feedback, ask advice, and share problems and frustrations.

Teacher-Mentor

It will make a difference whether a mentor is at your own school or another one in terms of what you want to ask. Procedure and policy questions can be answered only if the person is at your own school. Find out how often this person will come to see you and what type of assistance will be offered. Classroom management and instructional help should be in the domain of this person.

College Adviser

Your college supervisor/coordinator typically welcomes calls from prior students and is usually available to come out and offer advice on management, behavior, and instructional problems.

Experienced Grade-Level or Content-Area Teacher

This is a person at your school who should be able to tell you about the scope and sequence of the curriculum at your school. Course outlines and unit plans may be available. If at all possible, choose an experienced teacher whose teaching style and ideology are similar to yours. If you are an innovative, informal type of teacher, you do not want advice from a traditional and formal teacher.

Department or Grade-Level Chairperson

School policies, content-area information, general instructional assistance, resources, course outlines, and the role of district and state frameworks should all be available from the department or grade-level chairperson.

Principal or Assistant Principal

Seek advice from your principal or assistant principal on significant information, such as district workshops and study groups. If you have not had a mentor or adviser assigned to give you some support, ask the principal or assistant principal about this. If the person assigned to you is never available, ask about it. Do not expect help on lesson plans, management of time, and simple instructional problems. Try not to discuss personal matters; save this for your colleague!

Did You Know That . . . ?

> "Tests are thermometers, not cures." Meier (2002, p. 198) tells us that we need to rely on observation and assessments by teachers who know their students, the community, and the family. She believes that we need some standards, but *not* standardization.

Additional Resources

Suppose you have a student who you suspect is being abused. It is your responsibility to report this. You may begin the process of obtaining help by first going to your school nurse or social worker. The next step is the school principal. Be prepared with evidence, notes, or a list of reasons why you suspect a problem.

Suppose that you recognize that a student is malnourished, does not have a lunch, and appears not to have had breakfast. Again, seek out a social worker or health provider if available. If not, check with your department chair or grade-level chair about school procedures. Community agencies are sometimes enlisted for aid to families. Local universities sometimes provide medical assistance when needed.

For students who need special help because of dyslexia, other physical problems, or language needs, consult with the school counselor if one is available. Otherwise begin with your department chair or grade-level chair, then head for the school office to see your assistant principal or principal. District and state funds are often available for additional assistance for these students. Many school districts even employ, on a consultant basis, registered physical therapists to provide advice, physical training, and assistance in planning the Individualized Education Program (IEP) for students with special needs.

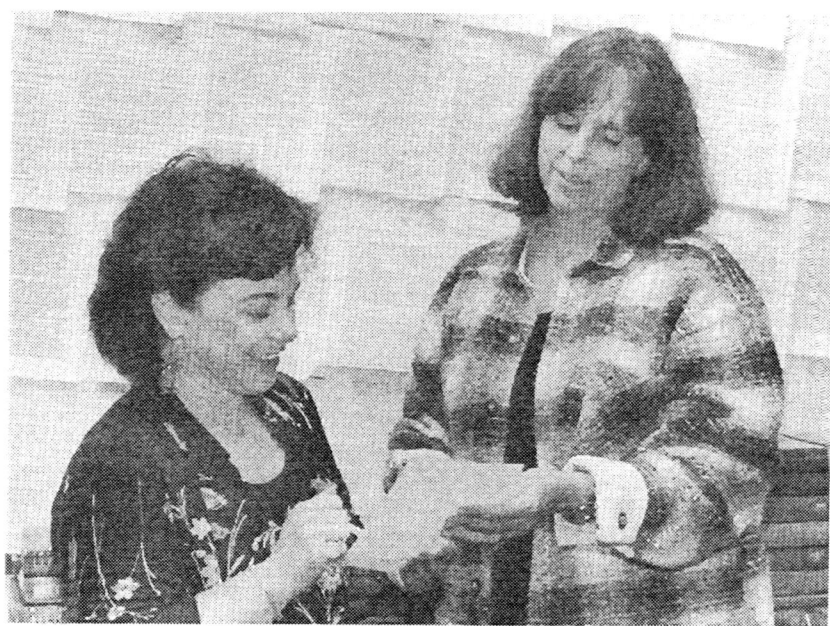

Professional problems need to be discussed with a trusted colleague, experienced teacher, or the school principal.

Professional Organizations

Professional organizations are available in almost every subject field for professional development and assistance. These organizations may have local and state headquarters, and all have national offices and annual conferences. Most of these organizations publish professional journals with current research and teaching suggestions. The following is a partial list of some of these organizations.

- American Alliance for Health, Physical Education, Recreation, and Dance (www.aahperd.org)
- American Association of Physics Teachers (www.aapt.org)
- American Chemical Society (www.acs.org)
- American Federation of Teachers (www.aft.org)
- Council for Elementary Science (unr.edu/homepage/crowther/cesi.html)
- Council for Exceptional Children (www.cec.sped.org)
- International Reading Association (www.reading.org)
- National Art Education Association (www.naea=reston.org)
- National Association for Bilingual Education (www.nabe.org)

- National Association for Gifted Children (www.nagc.org)
- National Association for Music Education (www.menc.org)
- National Association for Research in Science Teaching (www.narst.org)
- National Association of Biology Teachers (www.nabt.org)
- National Council for Geographic Education (www.ncge.org)
- National Council for History Education (www.history.org/nche)
- National Council for the Social Studies (www.socialstudies.org)
- National Council of Teachers of English (www.ncte.org)
- National Council of Teachers of Mathematics (www.nctm.org)
- National Education Association (www.nea.org)
- National Science Teachers Association (www.nsta.org)

Participation in School and Professional Organizations

The sooner you get involved in school committees, the easier it will be to get acquainted with other teachers and help set policy for your school. Not only do you need to become acclimated to your new professional life, but members of the school community need to acquaint themselves with your talents. You will feel more comfortable as an active member of the school community.

The professional organizations in the preceding list offer many professional development opportunities through their committee structure, journals and newsletters, and national and state conferences. Many school districts will help finance attendance at national conferences. Class work at a national conference can sometimes be used for university credits, which also helps you in your school district's salary scale.

The two national groups that attract large numbers of teachers, the American Federation of Teachers (AFT) and the National Education Association (NEA), provide members with political information, leadership, and services. Both have national publications, as do most of the subject field organizations. Though membership in national professional organizations is not compulsory, it is a fine means to participate in your profession and obtain continuing and current professional education. Still another way to improve your professional skills and be recognized for your accomplishments is National Board Certification.

How Is National Board Certification Accomplished?

Four underlying assumptions are made by the National Board for Professional Teaching Standards (NBPTS):

1. There is a common core of professional knowledge and skills applicable for all teachers.
2. There is knowledge of human development and **pedagogy** that is distinctive to students at particular stages of development.

3. There is knowledge of pedagogy that is subject-matter specific.
4. There is a need for teachers to demonstrate depth of content knowledge as well as breadth (NBPTS, 1990, p. 40–41).

Assessment for certification includes demonstration of competence appropriate to the teacher's level of teaching and based on whether the teacher is a generalist or a subject field specialist. Levels of teaching include early childhood (ages 3–8), middle childhood (ages 7–12), early adolescence (ages 11–15), and adolescence and young adulthood (ages 14–18). Specializations refer to specific subject fields, such as mathematics, social studies/history, art, and humanities. Elementary teachers are considered generalists.

Did You Know That . . . ?

> The certification process strengthens teaching competencies and professional judgment, enhances professional confidence, improves the teacher's ability to examine and analyze instruction, and helps teachers focus on student outcomes. New teachers are particularly attracted to the opportunities national certification provides (Bohen, 2001).

There are two parts to the assessment; the first includes a portfolio of students' work, videotapes, and a variety of teaching artifacts. It is important that the candidate describe the purpose of the students' work and reflectively comment on and critique it in terms of the teacher's instructional goals. This is the **self-study** component. The second part of the assessment is performed at one of the 200 technology centers around the country. In this part of the assessment, the candidate must demonstrate both breadth and depth of content knowledge in the selected area of expertise, using both multiple-choice questions and simulated contexts that pose instructional dilemmas requiring instructional decision making.

Criteria for assessment are related to the standards defined by the NBPTS. These standards include five core propositions:

1. Teachers are committed to students and their learning.
2. Teachers know the subjects they teach and how to teach those subjects to students.
3. Teachers are responsible for managing and monitoring student learning.
4. Teachers think systematically about their practice and learn from experience.
5. Teachers are members of learning communities (NBPTS, 1990, pp. 14–15).

Many teacher preparation programs use these standards to evaluate their coursework and their students' performance.

What Should Teacher Portfolios Contain?

The most significant purpose for preparing a professional portfolio is that it encourages the individual to reflect on his or her own instructional practices. Portfolio development is not a novel approach to professional practice. Architects, public relations specialists, artists, photographers, and even dentists and plastic surgeons engage in portfolio preparation. Though many of these professionals use the portfolio to "show off" their achievements, the process of preparation is intended to initiate reflective self-study.

For teachers, portfolio preparation requires study of their own instructional decision-making process. Reflection should entail consideration of the learning environment for students, content of lessons, teaching methods, appropriateness of the lesson, reasons for success or failure, verification of students' learning, and what you learned from the process. Figure 13.3 identifies some of the reflective questions teachers must ask themselves to analyze their work.

One of the most important aspects of preparing your portfolio is to share your thinking process about teaching and the ways you believe students learn. You are sharing your internal dialogue not only for others to understand the world of teaching as you perceive it, but to clarify your beliefs and accomplishments for yourself and learn from them.

- Why did I choose this particular concept (lesson) to teach at this time?
- What do I know about my students that made me select this concept?
- What teaching strategy did I choose and was it appropriate? (How do I know?)
- In what ways did the environment of the classroom support the lesson? (Were resources appropriate and adequate?)
- What did the students learn from this experience?
- Did the students learn what I expected and planned?
- Did I provide for individual differences?
- How do I know what I accomplished? (What did I observe while I taught and while students worked and participated?)
- Did I teach according to my beliefs about the ways teachers ought to teach?
- What mistakes did I make? (What would I do if I were to repeat the lesson?)
- What surprised me?

FIGURE 13.3 Self-Study Questions

Your portfolio should be aligned to the National Board Professional Teaching Standards. The standards provide a meaningful system to help you organize your evidence. Most teachers begin with a personal statement about their beliefs about pedagogy and how they believe students learn. You may want to share the challenges that confront you in your school setting.

Photographs of your classroom and video tapes of the lessons you describe should be included. In addition, you may want to include case studies and annotated records about teaching situations. Letters to and from parents are appropriate. Unit lesson plans and the integration of technology help to enrich the portfolio presentation.

Teaching Hints

1. Team with a colleague to critique lessons and pedagogy.
2. Identify examples of your own lessons that fit National Board for Professional Teaching Standards.

Professional Ethics

People can hear you! This means that when you are at the market, standing in line at the movies, shopping at the drugstore, or eating in the teachers' cafeteria, when you talk about your students or their parents you are being disrespectful and forgetting commonsense rules of privacy. You would not appreciate it if your health care professional told other patients about your physical problems; the same holds true for teachers.

In loco parentis means that in the absence of the student's parents, schools are responsible for students from the time they leave home until they return home. In elementary schools teachers should act as the parent would act by reminding students to wear sweaters on cold days, tie their shoelaces, and eat their lunches. Teachers should demonstrate empathy when students have problems or are hurt, just as a parent would do. Teaching about substance abuse is another example of teachers acting in the best interest of students.

Teachers also have the obligation of understanding students' rights (Edmonds, 1992, p. 205). Teachers need to do the following:

- Learn what human rights are
- Help young people understand their rights
- Examine the problem of universality and global multiculturalism
- Create a classroom and school in which children's rights are achieved (see Lemlech, 2002)

Balancing Personal and Professional Responsibilities

Sometimes beginning teachers labor too long on their lesson plans and stay up too late to create the perfect lesson. As a consequence, the next day can be disappointing if the lesson does not go well or you are too tired to carry it out the way it was intended. Another consequence of this pattern is that it affects your relationships with family members.

It is extremely important that you plan your work schedule so that you are not intruding on family time and leisure activities. Though it is difficult to think about planning lessons at the end of the school day, there are decided advantages to doing so. First of all, the students' needs and the prior lesson are fresh in your mind. Second, you have access to the resources that will be needed for the lessons, and taking them home is too much of a nuisance. Third, when you go home you will be able to "turn off" your school work day and concentrate on home activities.

The well-rounded teacher has time for fun reading, enjoying the movies, engaging in recreation and sports, participating in political activities, and in general keeping in good shape. The balance between personal and professional activities is important for your well-being mentally, socially, and physically.

Chapter Summary

This chapter discusses professional relationships and some of the problems that confront new teachers. The focus of the chapter is on how colleague teachers can help each other improve the quality of teaching and learning, but there are occasions when new teachers need assistance from more experienced professionals. Assistance and support are discussed, with insight on who to ask for different needs. Typical new-teacher problems are identified with examples of ways these problems can be alleviated. The chapter concludes with criteria for National Board Certification, portfolio evaluation, and how to engage in self-study.

Teaching Problems

1. Marge did not relate well to her teacher-mentor. Her mentor taught at the same school, but was on a different calendar schedule. As a consequence he was rarely at school at the same time as Marge. During the first semester he visited the classroom only once and Marge's lesson did not go well. Marge really does need some help; what should she do? Whom should she ask for help and how can she explain her poor relationship with her mentor?
2. Bill is an aggressive young teacher who wants to be involved in school committee work. His principal is hesitant to assign him to a schoolwide committee because of his lack of experience and typical new-teacher problems. Is the principal correct in her judgment? Why is involvement in school activities important for beginning teachers?
3. Rhonda is a high school teacher in the social studies department. She has not been assigned to teach in her area of expertise because other teachers have seniority in selecting the subjects they want to teach. The department chairperson makes these deci-

sions. What are the issues involved here? Should the department chair cater to the more experienced teachers or attend to Rhonda's needs? Why?

4. Suppose that you are judging another teacher's portfolio and you need to assess the quality of students' work and the quality of teaching. What will you look for? What questions will you ask as you assess students' work and the teaching that influenced the students' work?

5. A colleague is gossiping about a student in her class. She is disrespectful and others are in hearing range. What should you do?

Appendix A

Answers to Selected Problems

Chapter 1—Chapter Review

Diversity	All things big and small
Democratic community	Student involvement, choice, decision making
Authoritarian teacher	Supreme deity
Punishment	Student compliance
Rewards and consequences	Means to assert teacher control
Stimulus/response	Skinner's theory
Discipline systems	Positive and negative reinforcement
Token economy	Credits and debits
Rules	Standards for classroom government
Pedagogy	Instructional approaches to teaching
Student control	Student choice, decision making
Teacher control	Teacher knowledge, democratic control
Milieu	Environment
English language learners	Second-language learners
Laissez-faire	No controls
Culturally responsive teaching	Sensitivity to students' experiences and backgrounds
Assertive discipline	Names and checks

Chapter 3—Teaching Problems

2. **a.** Linguistic, language arts
   b. Interpersonal, bodily-kinesthetic, social studies
   c. Logical-mathematical, mathematics
   d. Spatial, geography, social studies
   e. Linguistic, social studies
   f. Logical-mathematical, health, science

Chapter 11—Teaching Problems

4. a
5. c
6. b
7. b
8. d
9. a
10. a
11. b
12. c

Appendix B

John Washington's Health, Physiology, and Physical Education Unit

Using factors such as differentiation of learning, multiple intelligences, sequence of lessons, interdisciplinary content, integration, and assessment, discuss the following teaching unit.

Unit Goals

- Develop students' physical capabilities and their awareness of them.
- Develop students' research skills.
- Encourage family participation in physical fitness.
- Develop students' problem-solving capabilities.

Theme

John knew that the theme of a teaching unit should focus on the significant ideas that would be emphasized in his lessons and that the theme should introduce broad concepts that would give meaning to his unit. He decided on the theme of *physical fitness*. To give added meaning and dimension to his theme he wrote a generalization about it: *Every individual has distinctive patterns of behavior that affect well-being.*

Content Outline

1. Physical fitness is affected by our body structure and habitual patterns of behavior, including nutrition, exercise, and water intake.
2. Behavioral patterns can be changed through awareness and practice.
3. Physical strength and flexibility are important to people of all ages and improve health and happiness.

Unit suggestions were contributed by physical therapist Michele Zeolla.

Key Questions

To focus his lessons and learning experiences, John decided to list his key questions to help him plan activities for his unit.

1. How can fitness be described?
2. What does the body need to be fit?
3. How does nutrition affect our well-being?
4. What social factors and societal demands affect the individual's well-being?
5. What are some ways to control our health and improve overall fitness?

Learning Experiences/Activities

When the students entered the classroom they noticed a number of mats on the floor. Mr. Washington asked for their attention and then selected several students to sit on the mats. He asked them if they could demonstrate sit-ups, push-ups, and several other exercises. Two of the students did very well; three others had difficulty. Mr. Washington thanked them and assured other class members that they too would have an opportunity to try out the exercises. He then explained what they would be doing over the next several weeks. The following table identifies some of the experiences and activities that Mr. Washington anticipated in planning his unit.

Key Questions	Learning Experiences and Activities
How can fitness be described?	• Large-group discussion about the meaning of fitness. (Students' responses focused on feeling good, having energy, not getting sick often, and being muscularly strong.)
What does the body need to be fit?	• Students divided into groups with varied resources to research physical needs.
	• Class discussion of findings revealed consensus on the need for good nutrition, exercise, and water.
What do we mean by good nutrition? How does nutrition affect our well-being?	• Students responded that nutrition means the foods that we eat; they identified the categories of proteins, fats, carbohydrates, minerals, and vitamins, but could not describe the effects or amounts that should be eaten.

(continued)

Key Questions	Learning Experiences and Activities
	• Small-group research using national resource departments to study the food pyramid; the discussion focused on a healthy diet.
	• Groups drew examples of the food pyramid and historical changes in it.
Students are asked to record what they eat both at home and at school for a week.	• Students weighed and measured themselves in class and began to classify foods they eat into the food categories
Teacher helps students learn to study food labels.	• Students used a variety of food labels to record ingredients, calories, sodium, fats, carbohydrates, proteins, and fats.
	• Students calculated from their weight, height, and general build what their approximate intake of calories should be.
	• Students were asked to discuss a healthy diet plan with their families and bring a plan to class identifying appropriate lunches to be eaten at school.
Weil, *Eating Well for Optimum Health*, (2000) is discussed.	• Discussion focused on diet fads and associated problems. Discussion culminated with the meaning of a "balanced" diet.
Skeleton is displayed in classroom and students are invited to study bones and muscles. Students are asked how muscular fitness can be measured.	• Students were given outlines of the body and filled in the skeletal system and major muscles of the body.
	• Divided into groups, students tested each other's performance on various tests for muscular fitness (abdominal test, psoas test, upper back, lower back, hamstring test). Each student kept his or her own record.
	• Using tape measures students measured each other's arms, hips, thighs, knees, calves, ankles. Information was added to student's individual record sheet.

(continued)

Key Questions	Learning Experiences and Activities
How can flexibility be determined?	• Teacher demonstrated ways to find out where tightness exists. Working in groups, students helped each other check flexibility, and each student recorded his or her own information.
	• Both muscular and flexibility exercises were demonstrated in class, and students were given opportunity to practice.
	• Class discussion focused on the benefits of physical exercise and the need for drinking an adequate amount of water.
	• Students were asked to share information with family and spend time at home practicing specific exercises to improve performance.
What social factors and societal demands affect the individual's well-being?	• Students identified some of the environmental causes and motivations for poor eating habits (fast food, parents' work, television programs and commercials, homework assignments, home responsibilities).
	• Students were given a study to read about adolescents' needs for sleep and its effect on school success.
What are some ways to control our health and improve overall fitness?	• Students reviewed what they learned about the need for water to lubricate joints and muscles, good nutrition, and sleep.
	• Students discussed other aspects of fitness, including "what's fun," what they like to do, and experiences they have had.
	• Students were asked to develop individual plans for exercise needs and identify the times of day when they could practice the exercises.
	• Teacher talked about the "overuse" of muscles and how the body gets hurt when individuals exceed sport limitations.

(continued)

Key Questions	Learning Experiences and Activities
	• Students suggested that their families be invited to class to see their charts and to demonstrate what they have learned.
	• Students suggested that they remeasure themselves and retest themselves at the end of the next month.
Culmination/evaluation	• Student discussion, charts, parental visits.

Professional Lexicon

advance organizer A framework for organizing and structuring new knowledge to facilitate meaningful acquisition of information via graphics, presentations, concrete objects, and readings.

anecdotal record An informal record maintained by the teacher to study specific behavior exhibited by a student(s).

arranged environment The placement in the classroom of motivating materials and realia to initiate a unit of study.

assessment The process by which teachers use a variety of means to gather information and insight concerning students' work. Using the evidence that is gathered, the teacher can judge the student's performance.

authentic assessment A form of assessment in which students' everyday tasks and projects are included in the evidence used to judge students' performance. It is considered authentic or *natural* because the tasks are constructivist.

authentic teaching Teaching that is related to students' experiences, knowledge, and culture, and is relevant to real-life applications.

authoritarian A style of teaching in which the teacher has sole power and control of classroom and expects students to be obedient and compliant.

authoritative A style of teaching in which the teacher has knowledge and responsibility for the classroom and allows students to make choices and decisions.

backward problem solving An inquiry process that motivates students to think divergently about an ideal solution and the means to accomplish it.

balance Consideration of the entire curriculum or subject field so that equity among subject fields or aspects of study is achieved.

behavior modification system A discipline system based on the belief that desired behavior can be strengthened through rewards and undesirable behavior extinguished through punishment.

bullying Behavior that is overbearing and takes advantage of another individual.

case study narrative A type of observation in which, writing in narrative style, the observer describes every aspect of classroom life that relates to a specific question or problem.

checklist a structured observation instrument with predetermined categories to focus on either teacher or student behavior.

classroom management The orchestration of classroom life: planning curriculum, organizing procedures and resources, arranging the environment to maximize efficiency, monitoring student progress, and anticipating potential problems.

clinical supervision Supervision of a teacher's on-task performance in the classroom; involves a preconference to assess teacher planning, observation, analysis of the lesson, and a postconference to discuss the observation.

co-action A back-and-forth conversation between two individuals, such as the teacher and a student.

collegiality The establishment of a professional relationship for the purpose of service and accommodation through the mutual exchange of perceptions and expertise.

community A classroom environment in which students work together to achieve cooperative goals, mutual respect, and reflective caring attitudes.

concepts Categories (labels) that help to organize and structure information.

concept attainment An inquiry strategy designed to help students understand specific concepts by comparing and contrasting attributes; this strategy encourages students' use of metacognition.

conservation The concept that shaped containers can be equal in volume; according to Piaget's theory, children have difficulty recognizing this concept.

constructivist learning theory An approach to teaching and learning that recognizes that information can be transmitted, but understanding depends on the learner.

content standards Measures related to subject field disciplines that are used to judge what is to be taught to students at varied levels of education.

continuity Reiteration of significant content at different levels to achieve depth in conceptual understanding.

convergent questions Questions that involve students in recalling basic facts and actions.

culturally responsive A style of teaching that is sensitive to the backgrounds, experiences and contexts of students.

differentiation A means to individualize and personalize the teaching and learning process by modifying content, process, products, and environment.

direct instruction A teaching model designed to teach specific knowledge or skills efficiently using three major processes: presentation, practice, and feedback.

discipline (1) A content field; (2) behavior that can be good or bad.

discipline system A theory of classroom management to ensure teacher control and student obedience.

divergent questions Questions that involve students in abstract, reflective thinking; they usually require analysis, synthesis, evaluation, judgment, and characterization.

egocentrism The inability to see others' viewpoints, according to Piaget's theory, egocentrism is a characteristic of preoperational learners.

environment The surroundings of the classroom; its milieu, culture, and patterns of behavior.

ethnography A type of observation, similar to the case study, in which the observer describes through narrative accounts classroom/school life, interviews students and teachers, and tries to understand both the social environment and the cognitive learning experiences of students.

expository teaching Communicating knowledge by controlling the input process. The learner's task is to consume knowledge using visual and auditory means.

generalization Expression of the meaning of the theme to communicate goals and provide direction for the selection of learning experiences.

guided practice In order to acquire knowledge or skills, students use practice materials while the teacher monitors and provides feedback.

heterogeneous Grouped according to dissimilar skills, abilities, or characteristics.

homogeneous Grouped according to similar skills, abilities, or characteristics.

independent practice Classroom work in which students work independently, with a peer, or a group to apply knowledge or skills that has been taught, preferably in a relevant or new way.

initiation The motivating teaching strategy used to begin a unit of study.

in loco parentis In the place of a parent; instead of a parent; charged factitiously, with a parent's rights, duties, and responsibilities.

inquiry The search for data to examine, verify, and guide questions, ideas, beliefs, and knowledge in order to develop meanings and theories.

inquiry teaching models Teaching strategies that help students use alternative ways of thinking about any problem or situation.

integration The linking of subject fields and learning processes to facilitate learning by helping the learner to recognize relationships.

interaction Classroom activity in which several individuals express thoughts to communicate with each other. The discussion that transpires may be cooperative or combative.

interdisciplinary teaching A teaching style in which a teacher plans curriculum concepts from varied subject fields to demonstrate learning through different lenses.

learning style The individual's preferences and characteristics for ways to learn.

monitoring Purposeful observation of students' work and general behavior to detect problems in teaching and students' practice and application of work tasks.

multiple intelligences The individual's special abilities or capacities.

overlapping behavior A teaching behavior in which, while teaching a lesson, the teacher attends to more than one incident in the classroom simultaneously.

pedagogy Methods of teaching; instructional approaches.

performance standards Standards in which students' work is judged using what they have produced.

portfolio An exhibit of student or teacher work that includes reflective analysis of performance.

prejudice The act of making a judgment about others that is unwarranted and self-gratifying.

problem-based learning A teaching model in which curriculum is organized around a problem that is relevant to the students and helps create a learning environment in which the teacher can coach and guide student inquiry.

project-based learning A teaching model in which students engage in producing a product that has depth, takes time to complete, and is complex.

realia Real objects such as costumes, diaries, or transportation are used to create an environment that motivates students' interest and relates to real life.

refocusing A classroom activity in which the teacher or a group member reestablishes the purpose of a discussion, plan, or assignment by reiterating and clarifying meanings when students are on the wrong track or off task.

reversibility The concept that the number of objects in a collection is not affected by the ordering process; according to Piaget's theory, the preoperational learner may not grasp this concept.

ripple effect A phenomenon in which contagious misbehavior is often caused by the teacher engaging in public discipline that embarrasses other students.

rubrics Criteria statements used to guide learning activities and special projects. Rubrics may be written by the teacher or jointly by students and teacher.

scripting A type of observation in which the observer takes notes to record everything that is happening in the classroom; when possible the observer quotes participants.

self-study The process by which teachers assess their own professional development.

sequence The order of content in a teaching unit.

sheltered English A strategy using simplified language to help the student who is learning English understand content in the second language.

specially designed academic instruction in English (SDAIE) A teaching model in which the teacher uses simple language, provides many examples, and uses gestures to help English language learners comprehend the lesson.

standardized tests Norm-referenced tests that allow students' achievement to be compared with the performance of other students at the same grade level, regardless of place of residence, culture, or language and reading ability.

stereotyping Holding an opinion that is oversimplified or generalized about another group or people.

structured practice A classroom activity in which, after a presentation, the teacher controls practice by asking short-answer questions and elicits responses to verify student understanding of what is to be learned.

synomorphy Arranging the classroom so that the physical environment and the learning experiences are compatible.

theme A unit-organizing concept that represents the big ideas, overarching concepts, and unifying constructs or underlying assumptions for the unit of study.

valid decision making A classroom model in which students are involved in making significant decisions that affect their learning and life in the classroom.

webbing A graphic means to demonstrate the connection of ideas; used to brainstorm a teaching unit.

with-it-ness The quality of a teacher who demonstrates to students awareness and alertness to their task engagement and general behavior.

zone of proximal development The developmental level at which, according to Vygotsky's theory, children can learn to complete tasks with assistance from others prior to independent task completion.

Bibliography

Acheson, K. A., & Gall, M. D. (1997). *Techniques in the clinical supervision of teachers* (4th ed.). New York: Longman.

Allen, R. (2000). *Education Update*. Reston, VA: Association for Supervision and Curriculum Development.

Allport, G. W. (1954). *The nature of prejudice*. New York: Addison-Wesley.

Alton-Lee, A., Diggins, C., Klenner, L., Vine, E., & Dalton, N. (2001). Teacher management of the learning environment during a social studies discussion in a new-entrant classroom in New Zealand. *Elementary School Journal, 101*(5), 549–566.

Anderson, J. R., Reder, C. M., & Simon, H. A. (1997). Applications and misapplications of cognitive psychology to mathematics education. Unpublished manuscript, Carnegie Mellon University, Pittsburgh, PA.

Association for Supervision and Curriculum Development. (Summer 2002). Promises and perils—how genetic literacy will affect students' lives. *Curriculum Update*, pp. 4–5.

Ausubel, D. P. (1963). *The psychology of meaningful verbal learning*. New York: Grune & Stratton.

Barranti, J. (2001). *How has the requirement to implement content standards affected the instructional program in the schools and classroom?* Unpublished dissertation, University of Southern California, Los Angeles.

Bateson, M. C. (2001). Learning in layers. In R. Soder, J. L. Goodlad, & T. J. McNanson (Eds.), *Developing democratic character in the young*. San Francisco: Jossey-Bass.

Becker, H. (1992). Computer-based integrated learning systems in the elementary and middle grades: A critical review and synthesis of evaluation reports. *Journal of Educational Computing Research, 8*(1): 1–41.

Biddle, B. J., & Berliner, D. C. (2002). Small class size and its effects. *Educational Leadership, 59*(5): 12–23.

Bohen, D. B. (2001). Strengthening teaching through national certification. *Educational Leadership, 58*(8): 50–53.

Bowman, D. H. (2002a). Experts ponder September 11: Effect on school violence. *Education Week, 21*(41): 118.

Bowman, D. H. (2002b). School connectedness makes for healthier students, study says. *Education Week, 21*(32): 16.

Brooks, J., & Brooks, M. (1993). *The case for constructivist classrooms*. Reston, VA: Association for Supervision and Curriculum Development.

Bruner, J. S. (1966). *On knowing*. Cambridge, MA: Harvard University Press.

Canter, L., & Canter, M. (1992). *Assertive discipline: Positive behavior management for today's classrooms* (2nd ed.). Santa Monica, CA: Lee Canter & Associates.

Condon, M., & McGuffee, M. (2001). *Real ePublishing. Really publishing!* Portsmouth, NH: Heinemann.

Coulter, B., Feldman, A. & Konold, C. (2000). Rethinking online adventures. *Learning and Leading with Technology, 128*(1): 42–47.

Crocco, M. S. (1998). Crafting a culturally responsive pedagogy. *Theory and Research in Social Education, 26*(1): 123–130.

Darling-Hammond, L. (1997). *The right to learn*. San Francisco: Jossey-Bass.

Deci, E. L., Koestner, R., & Ryan, R. M. (2001). Extrinsic rewards and intrinsic motivation in education: Reconsidered once again. *Review of Educational Research, 71*(1): 1–15.

DeVries, D., & Slavin, R. E. (1978). Teams-games-tournament: Review of 10 classroom requirements. *Journal of Research and Development in Education,* 12: 28–38.

Dewey, J. (1916, 1944). *Democracy and education.* New York: Free Press.

Dewey, J. (1938). *Experience and education.* New York: Collier Books.

DiRocco, M. D. (1999). How an alternating day schedule empowers teachers. *Educational Leadership,* 56(4): 82–85.

Dodge, B., & March, T. (2003). Site overview. Available: http://webquest.sdsu.edu/overview.htm.

Eisner, E. (2002). The kind of schools we need. *Phi Delta Kappan,* 83(8): 576–594.

Emmer, E. T., & Gerwels, M. C. (2002). Cooperative learning in elementary classrooms: teaching practices and lesson characteristics. *Elementary School Journal,* 103(1): 75–91.

Encinas, M. (2001). *The elementary program quality program review: A case study.* Unpublished dissertation, University of Southern California, Los Angeles.

Freeman, J. G., McPhail, J. C., & Berndt, J. A. (2002). 6th graders' views of activities that do and do not help them learn. *Elementary School Journal,* 102(4): 335–347.

Gandal, M., & Vranek, J. (2001). Standards: Here today, here tomorrow. *Phi Delta Kappan,* 59(10): 7–13.

Gardner, H. (1993). *Multiple intelligences—the theory in practice.* New York: Basic Books.

Gardner, H. (1995). Reflections on multiple intelligences: Myths and messages. *Phi Delta Kappan,* Nov. 1995 (77): 200–209.

Glasser, W. (1986). *Control theory in the classroom.* New York: Harper & Row.

Glasser, W. (1996). *Quality schools: Managing students without coersion.* New York: Harper & Row.

Glassman, M. (2001). Dewey and Vygotsky: Society, experience, and inquiry in educational practice. *Educational Researcher,* 30(4): 3–14.

Gordon, T. (1974). *Teacher effectiveness training.* New York: McKay.

Griffith, J. (2000). School climate as group evaluation and group consensus: Student and parent perceptions of the elementary school environment. *Elementary School Journal,* 101(1): 35–62.

Hannaford, B., Fouraker, M., & Dickerson, V. (2000). One school tackles the change to block scheduling. *Phi Delta Kappan,* 82(3): 212–213.

Hertzog, H. S. (2002). When, how, and who do I ask for help? Novices' perceptions of problems and assistance. *Teacher Education Quarterly,* 29(3): 23–40.

Hertzog, H. S. (2004). Integration of technology for teaching and learning. In J. K. Lemlech (Ed.), Columbus, OH: Merrill/Prentice Hall.

Hodgkinson, H. (2002). Standards and the students of the future. *Education Update,* 44(1): 7.

Holloway, J. H. (2002). What do students know? *Educational Leadership,* 60(2): 85–86.

Hornbeck, D. (2000). Service learning and reform in the Philadelphia public schools. *Phi Delta Kappan,* 81(9): 665.

International Society for Technology in Education. (2002). *National educational technology standards for teachers: Preparing teachers to use technology.* Eugene, OR: Author.

Johnson, C. R., & Taylor, R. (2001). Excellence for all in Minnesota. *Educational Leadership,* 58(6): 55–59.

Johnson, D. W., & Johnson, R. T. (1996). Cooperative learning and traditional American values: An appreciation. *NASSP Bulletin,* 80(579): 63–65.

Johnson, D. W., & Johnson, R. T. (1999). *Learning together and alone: Cooperative, competitive, and individualistic learning.* Boston: Allyn & Bacon.

Johnson, D. W., Johnson, R. T., Holubec, E. J. & Roy, P. (1984). *Circles of learning.* Alexandria, VA: Association for Supervision and Curriculum Development.

Johnson, S. M., & Kardos, S. M. (2002). Keeping new teachers in mind. *Educational Leadership,* 59(6): 12–17.

Jonassen, D. H. (2000). *Computers as mindtools for schools.* Upper Saddle River, NJ: Merrill/Prentice Hall.

Jones, V., & Jones, L. (1986). *Comprehensive classroom management* (2nd ed.). Boston: Allyn & Bacon.

Joyce, B., & Weil, M. with Calhoun, E. (1999). *Models of teaching* (6th ed.). Needham Heights, MA: Allyn & Bacon.

Kawaka, B., & Burgess, B. (2001). *V-trip travel guide*. Eugene, OR: International Society for Technology in Education.

Klein, M. F., Tye, K., & Wright, J. E. (1979). A study of schooling: Curriculum. *Phi Delta Kappan*, 61: 244–248.

Klonsky, M. (2002). How smaller schools prevent school violence. *Education Week*, 59(8): 65–69.

Kohn, A. (1996). *Beyond discipline*. Alexandria, VA: Association for Supervision and Curriculum Development.

Kohn, A. (1999, September 15). Confusing harder with better. *Education Week*.

Kohn, A. (2001, September 26). Beware of the standards, not just the tests. *Education Week*, 21(4): 52, 38.

Kounin, J. (1970). *Discipline and group management in classrooms*. New York: Holt, Rinehart & Winston.

Langer, J. A. (2001). Beating the odds: Teaching middle and high school students to read and write well. *American Education Research Journal*, 38(4): 837–880.

Lemlech, J. K. (1999). *Classroom management: Methods and techniques for elementary and secondary teachers* (3rd ed.). Prospect Heights, IL: Waveland Press.

Lemlech, J. K. (2002). *Curriculum and instructional methods for the elementary and middle school* (5th ed.). Upper Saddle River, NJ: Merrill/Prentice Hall.

Lemlech, J. K., Hertzog, H. S. & Hackl, A. (1994). The Los Angeles professional practice school: A study of mutual impact. In L. Darling-Hammond (Ed.), *Professional Development Schools* (pp. 156–175).

Lemlech, J. K., Hertzog, H. S. & Pensavalle, M. (1998). Staff development and workshop experience in Los Angeles and Orange Counties.

Lemlech, J. K., & Kaplan, S. N. (1990). Learning to talk about teaching: Collegiality in clinical teacher education. *Action in Teacher Education*, 12, 13–19.

Leu, D. J., & Leu, D. D. (2000). *Teaching with the Internet: Issues for the classroom*. Norwood, MA: Christopher Gordon.

Lewin, K, Lippitt, R., & White, R. (1939). Patterns of aggressive behavior in experimentally created social climates. *Journal of Social Psychology*, (10): 271–299.

Linn, M. C., Lewis, C., Tsuchida, I. & Songer, N. B. (2000). Beyond 4th grade science: Why do U.S. and Japanese students diverge? *Educational Researcher*, 29: 4–14.

Lou, Y., Abrami, P. C. & d'Apollonia, S. (2001). Small group and individual learning with technology: A meta-analysis. *Review of Educational Research*, 71(3): 449–521.

Mackenzie, J. (2000). *Questions and questioning: The most powerful technologies of all*. Bellevue, WA: From Now On.

Madden, N. A., Slavin, R. E., & Stevens, R. J. (1986). *Cooperative integrated reading and comparison: Teachers' manual*. Baltimore: Johns Hopkins University Center for Research in Elementary and Middle Schools.

Manzo, K. K. (1999, May 17). Whole language model survives despite swing back to basics. *Education Week*.

Marzano, R. J. (2000). *Transforming classroom grading*. Alexandria VA: Association for Supervision and Curriculum Development.

Marzano, R. T., Pickering, D. J., & Pollock, J. E. (2001). *Classroom instruction that works*. Alexandria, VA: Association for Supervision and Curriculum Development.

Meier, D. (2002). Standardization versus standards. *Phi Delta Kappan*, 84(3): 190–198.

Moss, S., & Fuller, M. (2000). Implementing effective practices: teachers' perspective *Phi Delta Kappan*, 82(4): 273–276.

National Board for Professional Teaching Standards. (1990). *Toward high and rigorous standards for the teaching profession* (2nd ed.). Washington, DC: Author.

National Council of Teachers of Mathematics. (2000). *Principles and Standards for School Mathematics*. Reston, VA: Author.

Nieto, S. (2002). Language, culture, and teaching: Critical perspectives for teacher education. Annual Charles De Garmo Lecture. American Educational Research Association meeting, New Orleans, LA.

Noddings, N. (1999, February). Renewing democracy in schools. *Phi Delta Kappan*, 80: 579–583.

Nussbaum, E. M. (2002). How introverts versus extroverts approach small group argumentative discussions. *Elementary School Journal*, 102(3): 183–198.

Nuthall, G. (1999). The way students learn. Acquiring knowledge from an integrated science and social studies unit. *Elementary School Journal, 99*(4): 303–341.

Nuthall, G., & Alton-Lee, A. (1995). Assessing classroom learning. How students use their knowledge and experience to answer classroom achievement questions in science and social studies. *American Education Research Journal, 32*(1): 185–223

Ochoa-Becker, A. S., Morton, M. L., Autry, M. M., Johnstad, S. J., & Merrill, D. (2001). Decision making in three elementary classrooms: A pilot study. *Theory and Research in Social Education, 29*(2): 261–289.

Olweus, D. (2003). A profile of bullying at school. *Educational Leadership, 60*(6): 12–17.

Osterman, K. F. (2000). Students' need for belonging in the school community. *Review of Educational Research, 70*(3): 323–368.

Pastor, P. (2002). School discipline and the character of our schools. *Phi Delta Kappan, 83*(9): 658–661.

Pensavalle, M. (2002). *Observation of student teachers and master teachers.* Unpublished manuscript, University of Southern California, Los Angeles.

Pettig, K. L. (2000). On the road to differentiated practice. *Educational Leadership, 58*(1): 6–11.

Piaget, J. (1969). How children form mathematical concepts. In N.J. Vigalante (Ed.), *Mathematics in Elementary Education* (pp. 135–141). New York: Macmillan.

Popham, W. J. (2003). The seductive allure of data. *Educational Leadership, 60*(5): 48–51.

Raywid, M. A., & Oshiyama, L. (2000). Musings in the wake of Columbine: What can schools do? *Phi Delta Kappan, 81*(6): 444–449.

Resnick, L. B. (1999, June 16). Making Americans smarter. *Education Week*

Roblyer, M. D. (2003). *Integrating educational technology into teaching.* Columbus, OH: Merrill/Prentice Hall.

Rosenshine, B., & Furst, N. (1973). The use of direct observation to study teaching. In R. M. Travers (Ed.), *Second handbook of research on teaching* (pp. 122–183). Chicago: Rand McNally.

Routman, R. (2002). Teacher talk. *Educational Leadership, 59*(6): 32–35.

Rowe, M. B. (1969). Science, silence, and sanctions. *Science and Children*, (6): 11–13.

Rowe, M. B. (1974). Wait-time and rewards as instructional variables: Their influence on language, logic, and fate control: Part One. Wait-time. *Journal of Research in Science Teaching,* 81–94.

Ryan, A. M., & Patrick, H. (2001). The classroom environment and changes in adolescents' motivation and engagement during middle school. *American Education Research Journal, 38*(2): 437–460.

Sanders, M. G. (2001). The role of community in comprehensive school, family, and community partnership programs. *Elementary School Journal, 102*(1): 19–34.

Schon, D. A. (1983). *The reflective practitioner: How professionals think in action.* New York: Basic Books.

Schwab, R. L., & Foa, L. J. (2001). Integrating technologies throughout our schools. *Phi Delta Kappan, 82*(8): 620–624.

Shepard, L. A. (2000). The role of assessment in a learning culture. *Education Researcher, 29*(7): 4–14.

Simmons, R. (2002). *Odd girl out: The hidden culture of aggression in girls.* New York: Harcourt Brace Jovanovich.

Simone, G. (2001). Space to learn. *Educational Leadership, 59*(1): 66–69.

Sizer, T. R. (1992). *Horace's school: Redesigning the American high school.* Boston: Houghton Mifflin.

Slavin, R. E. (1983). *Cooperative learning.* New York: Longman.

Slavin, R. E. (1986). *Using student team learning* (3rd ed.). Baltimore: Center for Elementary and Middle Schools, Johns Hopkins University.

Slavin, R. E. (1989). Cooperative learning and student achievement. In R. E. Slavin (Ed.), *School and Classroom Organization.* Hillsdale, NJ: Lawrence Erlbaum.

Taba, H. (1967). *Teacher's handbook for elementary social studies.* Palo Alto, CA: Addison-Wesley.

Takenaga-Taga, D. (1999). Empowering science department teachers by sustaining their work. Unpublished manuscript, University of Southern California, Los Angeles.

Tomlinson, C. A. (2000). Reconcilable differences: Standards-based teaching and differentiation. *Educational Leadership, 58*(1): 6–11.

Torp, L., & Sage, S. (1998). *Problems as possibilities: Problem-based learning for K–12 education.* Alexandria, VA: Association for Supervision and Curriculum Development.

Trotter, A. (2002, April 3) Plagiarism controversy engulfs Kansas school. *Education Week, 21*(29): 5.

Vygotsky, L. S. (1994). The development of concept formation in adolescence. In R. van der Veer and J. Valsiner (Eds.), *The Vygotsky Reader.* Oxford, England: Blackwell.

Wassermann, S. (2001). Quantum theory, the uncertainty principle and the alchemy of standardized testing. *Phi Delta Kappan, 83*(1): 28–40.

Weil, A. (2000). *Eating well for optimum health.* New York: Knopf.

Wolfe, P. (2001). *Brain matters: Translating research into classroom practice.* Alexandria, VA: Association for Supervision and Curriculum Development.

Yeh, S. S. (2001). Tests worth teaching to: Constructing state-mandated tests that emphasize critical thinking. *Education Researcher, 30*(9): 12–17.

Zehr, M. (2002, September 4). Early bilingual programs found to boost test scores. *Education Week, 6*(22): 1.

Zorpette, G. (2001, November) The Asian paradox: Huge classes, high scores. *Scientific American,* 84.

Name Index

Abrami, P. C., 277
Acheson, K. A., 40, 44
Adazzio, Karen, 23, 244, 254–255
Allen, R., 82
Allport, G. W., 148
Alred, Gerry, 4, 5, 7, 9–11, 28, 33–37, 41, 56, 58, 64, 65, 76–78, 94, 118, 135–136, 149, 164, 166–167, 181, 186, 197–200, 204, 207, 243
Alton-Lee, A., 47, 48, 61
Anderson, J. R., 177
Ausubel, D. P., 172
Autry, M. M., 21

Bacon, Mavis, 277
Barranti, J., 255
Barrett, Helen, 282
Barry, Shirley, 232
Bateson, M. C., 150
Becker, H., 268
Bemis, Ben, 139, 140
Berliner, D. C., 133
Berndt, J. A., 141
Biddle, B. J., 133
Blum, Robert, 228
Bohen, D. B., 303
Bowman, D. H., 151, 228
Brooks, J., 56
Brooks, M., 56
Bruner, J. S., 199

Canter, L., 12
Canter, M., 12
Cantor, Jean, 28, 33, 36, 38, 43–44, 51, 86–88, 136, 182–184, 210–212, 214–215, 240, 246, 276
Cathcart, W. G., 37n
Conold, C., 272
Coulter, B., 272
Crocco, M. S., 19

Dalton, N., 47, 48
d'Apollonia, S., 277
Darling-Hammond, L., 9, 17, 21, 142
Davies, Mike, 154–155
Deci, E. L., 91
DeVries, D. L., 177
Dewey, J., 11, 21, 24, 33, 121
Dickerson, V., 92
Diggins, C., 47, 48
DiRocco, M. D., 92
Dodge, B., 271–272

Echols (Ms.), 155–157
Eisner, E., 211
Emmer, E. T., 231
Encinas, M., 289
Epstein, Joyce, 82

Feldman, A., 272
Foa, L. J., 269
Fouraker, M., 92
Franklin, J., 220n
Freeman, J. G., 141
Fuller, M., 94
Furst, N., 42

Gall, M. D., 40, 44
Gandal, M., 251, 252
Gardner, H., 57, 58
Gerwels, M. C., 231
Glasser, W., 13
Glassman, M., 25
Gordon, T., 12
Griffith, J., 41

Hackl, A., 288
Hannaford, B., 92
Hertzog, Hillary H., 267n
Hertzog, H. S., 134, 288, 292
Hodgkinson, H., 188

Holloway, J. H., 249
Holubec, E. J., 176
Hornbeck, D., 75

Ives, Roger, 28, 33, 35, 36, 38, 41, 45, 76, 77, 130–132, 173–174, 177, 189, 220–225

Jenkins (Ms.), 28, 29, 31
Jensen, Lee, 88–89
Johnson, C. R., 16
Johnson, D. W., 175, 176, 177
Johnson, R. T., 175, 176, 177
Johnson, S. M., 296
Johnstad, S. J., 21
Jonassen, D. H., 268, 269
Jones, L., 13
Jones, V., 13
Joyce, B., 158, 199

Kaplan, S. N., 290
Kardos, S. M., 296
Klein, M. F., 31
Klenner, L., 47, 48
Koestner, R., 91
Kohn, A., 13, 132, 251–252
Kounin, J., 117, 133, 134

Langer, J. A., 222, 227
Lemlech, J. K., 17, 112, 173, 215, 221, 232, 251, 288, 290, 292, 305
Leu, D. D., 282
Leu, D. J., 282
Lewin, K., 10
Lewis, C., 195
Linn, M. C., 195
Lippitt, R., 10
Lou, Y., 277

Madden, N. A., 178
Manzo, K. K., 17
March, T., 271
Martin, Lucia, 28–29, 31–33, 35–41, 44, 89–90, 127–130, 135, 167–169, 171, 180, 181, 194–195, 200, 207, 229, 253–254
Marzano, R. T., 76, 175
McKenzie, J., 270, 272
McPhail, J. C., 141
Meier, D., 300
Merrill, D., 21
Mitchell, Andrea, 79
Morton, M. L., 21
Moss, S., 94

Nelson, Dave, 228, 230, 239–240, 248–249, 255, 259, 276
Nieto, S., 75
Noddings, N., 5
Nussbaum, E. M., 197
Nuthall, G., 61

Ochoa-Becker, A. S., 21, 24
Olweus, D., 143
Oshiyama, L., 151
Osterman, K. F., 25, 169

Pastor, P., 140
Patrick, H., 132, 179
Pensavalle, M., 222, 292
Pettig, K. L., 102
Piaget, J., 24, 54, 56, 76, 121
Pickering, D. J., 76, 175
Pollack, William, 144
Pollock, J. E., 76, 175
Popham, W. J., 242

Raywid, M. A., 151
Reder, C. M., 177
Resnick, L. B., 18
Roblyer, M. D., 275, 278
Rosenshine, B., 42
Routman, R., 290
Rowe, M. B., 183
Roy, P., 176
Ryan, A. M., 132, 179
Ryan, R. M., 91

Sage, S., 275
Sanders, M. G., 82, 83
Schon, D. A., 298
Schrock, Kathy, 270
Schwab, R. L., 269
Shepard, L. A., 240
Sierra, Jim, 19, 70–72, 95, 96, 99–101, 103, 104, 113–117, 122, 123, 135, 172–173, 194, 201–209, 233–235, 239, 269–270, 273–274, 279
Simmons, R., 144
Simon, H. A., 177
Simone, G., 228–229
Sizer, T. R., 9
Skinner, B. F., 12, 140
Slavin, R. E., 177, 178
Songer, N. B., 195
Stevens, R. J., 178

Taba, H., 208–210
Takenaga-Taga, D., 288

Taylor, R., 16
Tomlinson, C. A., 100
Torp, L., 275
Trotter, A., 194n
Tsuchida, I., 195
Tye, K., 31

Vine, E., 47, 48
Vranek, J., 251, 252
Vygotsky, L. S., 24, 56, 76, 121

Washington, John, 311–312
Wassermann, S., 258

Weil, M., 158, 199
White, R., 10
Wolfe, P., 37, 73
Wooden, John, 165
Wright, J. E., 31

Yeh, S. S., 241

Zehr, M., 241
Zeolla, Michele, 311n
Zorpette, G., 118

Subject Index

Abstract learning, 73
Accountability, 145–146
Additive bilingualism, 75
Administrators, relationships with, 287, 293, 300
Advance organizer teaching model, 172–174
American Alliance for Health, Physical Education, Recreation, and Dance, 301
American Association of Physics Teachers, 301
American Chemical Society, 301
American Federation of Teachers, 301, 302
Anecdotal record in classroom observation, 46
Application phase of lesson, 168
Application questions, 181
Appropriateness in unit planning, 100
Arranged environment technique, 99
Assertive discipline, 12
Assessment. *See also* Standards
   authentic, 239–240
   in concept attainment model, 200–201
   definition of, 239
   in direct instruction teaching model, 168
   judging and grading, 259–261
   portfolio, 247–248, 280, 282
   rubrics, 248–251, 259, 280
   of student communication skills, 245–246
   of student content knowledge and understanding, 242–245
   of student ideas and ways of thinking, 240–241
   technology as tool for, 280, 282
   tests, 255–259
   types of, 240
   in unit planning, 101
   what teachers learn from, 246–247
Attention, maintaining, 133–134
Audiotaping, in classroom observation, 46
Authentic assessment, 239–240
Authentic teaching, 164–165

Authoritarian regulations, 9
Authoritative schools, 9
Authority/autonomy relationships, 169

Backward problem solving, 105, 107, 210–211
Balance, in unit planning, 103–104
Banked time, 93, 289
Base group, 177
Behavior, overlapping, 133
Behavioral monitoring, 231–232
Behavior modification systems, 12–13
Behavior problems. *See* Disruptions and misbehavior
Belonging
   developing sense of, 118–119
   factors affecting sense of, 169
Benchmarks for Science Literacy, 254
Bilingualism, additive, 75
Block scheduling, 92–93
Bloom's *Taxonomy of Educational Objectives: Cognitive Domain*, 181
Bodily-kinesthetic intelligence, 58
Book report, writing, 252–253
Buck Institute for Education, 276
Bullying, 143, 243
   gender differences in, 144
   helping victims of, 144
   signs of, 144

California's program quality review, 289–290
Case study approach, 214–215
Case study narrative observation, 47–48
Caucus group role play, 158
Center for Problem-Based Learning, 275
Certification, National Board, 10, 302–305
Challenge 2000 Multimedia Project, 276
Charts, data retrieval, 105, 106, 202
Checklists, in classroom observation, 47, 48
Citizenship, preparation for, 4–5
Classification skills, rubric for assessing, 250

Classroom
  democratic. *See* Democratic classroom
  teamwork in, 15–16
  trust, respect, and responsibility in, 4
Classroom community
  monitoring, 228–229
  student responsibilities for building, 7–9
  teacher responsibilities for building, 5–7
  teaching and learning in, 9–10
Classroom environment. *See* Environment
Classroom management, 23–24
  attention, maintaining, 133–134
  class size and, 133
  definition of, 112
  discipline versus, 11, 112–116
  elements of, 113
  example problem in, 139
  field trips and, 203
  for group investigation, 207
  in large-group instruction, 119–120
  motivation and, 132
  novice teacher problems with, 134–135
  problem solving, 135–136
  school socialization and, 132
  in secondary classroom, 130–131
  teaching hints on, 129
Classroom observation. *See* Observation, classroom
Class size, 133
Climate. *See* Environment
Clinical supervision, 293
Clubs, recreational, 149–151
Clustering of questions, 181–182
Coaching
  peer, 25, 291–292
  student, 227–228
Co-action, 185
Collaborative learning, 15. *See also* Cooperative learning; Group work
  in lesson plan, 77–78
Collegiality, 290
Collegial relationships, 290–293
Communication
  assessing student skills in, 245–246
  encouraging in classroom, 15–16, 24–25
  technology as tool for, 282
Communities of learners, 228–229
Community, classroom. *See* Classroom community
Community participation, planning, 82–83
Community schools, 152–153
Comprehension questions, 181
Comprehensive teaching model, 169–171
Computer-assisted instruction (CAI), 268

Computer-based learning (CBL), 273–275
Computer technology. *See* Technology
Concept attainment model, 197–201
  concrete representation in, 200
  motivation and assessment in, 200–201
  phases of, 200
Concept map, 105
Concepts, 198
  importance of, 207–208
  process for gaining, 208–210
Concrete experience, 73
Concrete operations stage of development, 55
Conferences
  parent-teacher, 232–236
  teacher-parent-student, 236–237
  unplanned, 236
Conflict resolution, 154
  controversial issue, 155–158
  personal, 154–155
Conservation, developmental concept of, 54
Constructivist learning theory, 56–57
  in assessment, 240
  in lesson planning, 72
Constructivist teaching model, 194–195
  inquiry teaching models and, 192–193
Content, 6, 8
  assessing student knowledge of, 242–245
  lesson planning and, 64–66
  observing, 31, 38–39
Content standards, 251–252. *See also* Standards
  English language arts, 252–253
  mathematics, 253–254
  performance versus, 188–189
  science, 254–255
Continuity
  curriculum concept of, 93
  in unit planning, 100
Contracting systems of discipline, 12
Controversial issues, conflict over, 155–158
Convergent questions, 180–181
Cooperative Integrated Reading and Composition (CIRC) model, 178
Cooperative learning
  advantages and disadvantages of, 176
  elements of, 175
  English language learners and, 180
  group investigation versus, 206–207
  inquiry-oriented, 174
  jigsaw strategy, 206
  models of, 177–178
  motivation in, 178
  research related to, 176–177
  roles played in, 179

sense of belonging and, 169
skill-oriented, 174
skills students need to learn in, 178–179
student behaviors in, 175
teacher behaviors in, 175
Copyright, 271
Council for Elementary Science, 301
Council for Exceptional Children, 301
Creative thinking, 210–213
Creative writing skills, rubric for assessing, 250
Critical thinking, 210–213, 225
Cuing students, 183
Cultural differences
   classroom behavior and, 63
   failure in teaching, 249
Culturally responsive teaching, 19, 63
Curriculum, standards and, 249, 251–255
Curriculum concepts, lesson planning and, 93–95
Curriculum planning, 22–23. *See also* Lesson planning; Unit planning
   classroom management and, 113–114
   process of, 101

Databases, 278
Data retrieval charts, 105, 106, 202
Decision making
   student, 21, 24–25
   valid, 141
Decision points, 114
Defiance, 144–145
Democratic classroom
   characteristics of, 20–21
   discipline in, 11–14, 112–116
   discussion strategies for, 184–188
   leadership in, 10–11
   valuing, 42–43
Desktop publishing, 277
Developmental considerations in learning
   constructivism, 56–57
   learning styles, 60–62
   multiple intelligences, 57–60
   stages of development, 54–56
Diagnostic assessment, 240
Diagramming interaction, in classroom observation, 44–45
Differentiation of instruction, 18, 65–66, 223
   factors affecting, 100
   in lesson planning, 72, 102
   monitoring and, 229
   technology and, 273–275
Direct instruction teaching model, 165–169
Discipline, classroom management versus, 112–116

Discipline systems, 11–14
Discussion
   democratic behavior during, 185–186
   problems in, 187–188
   strategies for, 184–188
   teacher's role in, 186
   variations in, 186–187
Disruptions and misbehavior, 141–143
   bullying, 143–144, 243
   interruption and speaking out, 146–147
   nonaccountability, 145–146
   novice teachers and, 295–296
   rudeness and defiance, 144–145
Divergent questioning model, 195–197
Divergent questions, 181
Diversity
   in classroom, 16–17
   in cooperative learning groups, 177
   novice teachers and, 295
Domain names, 273
Drill-and-practice software, 268, 274

Effort, student, 18–19
Egocentrism, 55, 56
English language arts, standards for, 252–253
English language learners (ELL), 17
   in class discussions, 188
   classroom management and, 136
   gestures and, 213
   in group work, 125
   judging and grading, 261
   monitoring, 223–224
   novice teachers and, 295
   partner work and, 227
   planning for, 75–76, 100
   problems of, 159
   research on teaching, 241
   specially designed academic instruction for, 180
   tests and, 256–257
Environment
   arranged, 99, 115
   classroom, 6, 7–8, 24, 37
   controlling classroom, 222
   organization of classroom, 31–35, 40–41
   school, and violence, 153–154
   social/emotional, 35, 179
Essay tests, 257
Ethics, professional, 305
Ethnography, in classroom observation, 48–49
Evaluation, in group work, 122–123, 126
Experience
   concrete, 73
   hands-on, 73

Experiment report, writing, 253
Expository instructional strategies, 161
   questioning strategies for, 180–184
Extrinsic motivation, 178

Family participation, planning, 82–83
Feedback, for homework, 230–231
Field-dependent learners, 61–62
Field-independent learners, 61–62
Fields, database, 278
Field trips
   classroom management and, 203
   planning, 81
   student learning from, 204–205
   in unit planning, 100
First-day planning, 127
   elementary classroom, 127–130
   secondary classroom, 130–131
Formal groups, 177
Formal operations stage of development, 55
Free discussion, 186
Freedom, self-control and, 140–141

Gangs, 149–151
Gender, bullying and, 144
Generalization, 95
Gestures, 213
Grading, 259–261
Graphics, multimedia and presentation software, using, 278–279
Graphs, as advance organizer, 173
Group investigation model, 201–207
   classroom management in, 207
   cooperative learning versus, 206–207
   phases of, 204–205
Group work. *See also* Collaborative learning; Cooperative learning
   duration of assignments, 77
   grouping students for, 76–77, 116
   large-group instruction, 117–118
      advantages and disadvantages of, 118
      classroom management in, 119–120
      sense of belonging in, 118–119
   monitoring, 224–225, 226, 231
   novice teachers and, 296
   partner work, 227–228, 229
   small-group instruction
      advantages and disadvantages of, 122
      beginning, 121–123
      evaluation in, 122–123, 126
      group procedures, 123–124
      group roles, 123
      group size, 123
      problems in, 124–125
      teacher responsibilities during, 126
   types of groups, 177
Guided practice, 167, 168, 225–226

Hands-on experiences, in lesson plan, 73
Heterogeneous grouping, 76
Homework, 230–231
Homogeneous grouping, 76

I messages discipline system, 12
Impulsive learners, 61–62
Inclusion, in group work, 125
Individuals with Disabilities Education Act (IDEA), 224
Individual work, monitoring, 222–223
Informal groups, 177
In loco parentis, 305
Inquiry-oriented cooperative learning, 174
Inquiry teaching models, 114, 161, 193–194
   constructivist teaching and, 192–193
   resources for, 214–215
Instruction, differentiation of. *See* Differentiation of instruction
Instructional games, 274
Instructionally beneficial data, 242–243
Instructional strategies, 23. *See also* Teaching models
   expository, 161, 180–184
   inquiry, 114, 161, 192–194, 214–215
   jigsaw, 206
   novice teachers and, 297
INTASC. *See* Interstate New Teacher Assessment and Support Consortium (INTASC)
Integration, curriculum concept of, 93, 94, 99
Intelligences, multiple, 57–60, 72, 99, 125, 172
Interaction, 7, 8–9. *See also* Social skills and interpersonal relations
   diagramming, in classroom observation, 44–45
   increasing, 184
   learning and, 121
   providing, 225–226
Interdisciplinary teaching, 94, 99
International Reading Association, 252, 301
International Society for Technology in Education, 269, 276
Internet
   class Web site, 282–283
   domain names, 273
   evaluating Web sites, 270–271
   plagiarism and, 271

portfolio assessment resources on, 280, 282
research using, 270–273
rubrics on, 280
WebQuest, 271–272
Interpersonal intelligence, 58
Interpersonal relations. *See* Social skills and interpersonal relations
Interruptions
  lesson planning and, 102
  student, 146–147
Interstate New Teacher Assessment and Support Consortium (INTASC)
  issues and standards, 4, 28, 54, 70, 86, 112, 139, 164, 192, 220, 239, 268, 287
  licensing by, 10
Interviewing, in classroom observation, 44
Intrapersonal intelligence, 58
Intrinsic motivation, 91, 178

Japan
  classroom management in, 118
  constructivist/inquiry teaching in, 195
Jigsaw cooperative learning strategy, 206
Judging, 259–261
Jurisprudential teaching model, 158

Keyboarding skills, 277
Key questions, 96
Knowledge questions, 181

Laboratory materials, planning, 80
Large-group instruction, 117–118
  advantages and disadvantages of, 118
  classroom management in, 119–120
  sense of belonging in, 118–119
Leadership, in democratic classrooms, 10–11
Learning
  abstract, 73
  collaborative, 15, 77–78
  concrete experience, 73
  cooperative. *See* Cooperative learning
  developmental considerations in, 54–62
  in-depth, 79–80
  representational, 73
  societal considerations in, 62–64
  subject matter considerations in, 64–66
  symbolic, 73
  teaching quality and, 9–10
Learning styles, 60–61
  in lesson planning, 72
Lesson planning. *See also* Curriculum planning; Unit planning
  concepts in, 83

considerations in, 102–103
curriculum concepts and, 93–95
for English language learners, 75–76
failure of, 101
for family and community participation, 82–83
for group work, 76–77
for hands-on experiences, 73
for in-depth learning, 79–80
multiple intelligences and, 58–60
of novice and experienced teachers, 71–72
novice teachers and, 294
parts of plan, 72–73
for problem solving experiences, 74
resources and, 80–81
scripting plan, 44
for service learning, 74
societal problems and, 64, 86–91
subject matter considerations in, 64–66
technology in, 80–81, 280–282
time management and, 91–93
Linguistic intelligence, 57
Literacy education, 4–5
Logical-mathematical intelligence, 57

Management, classroom. *See* Classroom management
Manipulative materials, planning, 81
Mathematics, standards for, 253–254
Mentors, for new teachers, 287, 292–293, 299
Methodologies, teaching, 6, 8
Milieu. *See* Environment
Misbehavior. *See* Disruptions and misbehavior
Models, teaching. *See* Teaching models
Monitoring
  behavioral, 231–232
  communities of learners, 228–229
  controlling classroom environment, 222
  definition of, 221
  English language learners (ELL), 223–224
  group work, 226, 231
  homework, 230–231
  partner and three-person teams, 229
  student contributions to group assignments, 224–225
  student performance, 115–116, 220
  students with special needs, 223–224
Motivation
  classroom management and, 132
  in concept attainment model, 200–201
  in cooperative learning, 178
  extrinsic, 178
  intrinsic, 91, 178

336 Subject Index

Multiple-choice tests, 256
Multiple intelligences, 57–60
   in group work, 125
   in lesson planning, 72
   in planning advance organizer, 172
   in unit planning, 99
Musical intelligence, 58

National Art Education Association, 301
National Assessment of Educational Progress, 249
National Association for Bilingual Education, 301
National Association for Gifted Children, 302
National Association for Music Education, 302
National Association for Research in Science Teaching, 302
National Association of Biology Teachers, 302
National Board Certification (NBC), 10
   how to accomplish, 302–303
   teacher portfolios for, 10, 304–305
National Board for Professional Teaching Standards (NBPTS), 10, 302–303
National Council for Accreditation of Teacher Education (NCATE), 10
National Council for Geographic Education, 302
National Council for History Education, 302
National Council for the Social Studies, 302
National Council of Teachers of English, 252, 302
National Council of Teachers of Mathematics (NCTM), 38, 188, 253, 302
National Council on Education Standards and Testing, 249
National Education Association (NEA), 269, 302
National Science Teachers Association, 302
Naturalistic intelligence, 58
Nonaccountability, 145–146

Objects
   as advance organizer, 173–174
   in concept attainment model, 200
Observation, classroom
   by administrators, 293
   analysis of, 39
   casual versus focused, 42
   of environment, 31–35
   identifying what isn't there, 49
   by mentors, 292–293
   of organization, 31–35, 40–41
   by peers, 290–291
   of rules, 50–51
   of students, 31, 36
   of subjects, 31, 38–39
   of teachers, 31, 37–38
   techniques for, 43–49
   what to look for, 28–31
Ongoing, formative assessment, 240
Organization
   classroom, 31–35, 40–41
   unit, 99
Organizations, professional, 301–302
Outcome standards, 251
Overlapping behavior, 133

Parents, sharing student work with, 232–237
Participation
   family and community, 82–83
   in planning, 102–103
   student, 18–19, 24–25, 184
   webbing and, 104–105
Partner work, 227–228
   monitoring, 229
Peer coaching, 25, 291–292
Peer relationships, 287–290
People resources, in lesson plan, 81
Performance, student. See also Assessment; Monitoring
   teacher responsibility for, 221
Performance standards. See Standards
Pictures, as advance organizer, 173
Plagiarism, 271
Planning
   first-day, 127–131
   lesson. See Lesson planning
   semester, 104
   technology, 283–284
   unit. See Unit planning
Portfolios
   student, 247–248, 280, 282
   teacher, 10, 304–305
Practice, 165
   drill and, 268, 274
   guided, 167, 168, 225–226
   structured, 167, 168
Precision questioning, 181
Prejudice, 148–149, 164, 166–167
Preoperational stage of development, 54
Presentation phase of lesson, 167, 168
Principals, 293, 300
Print materials, planning, 80
Probes, 183–184
Problem-based learning, 275–276
Problems, anticipating, 116
Problem solving
   backward, 105, 107, 210–211
   in lesson plan, 74

management-focused, 135–136
resources for, 214–215
software for, 274
technology and, 275–276
Professional development for novice teachers
administrator relationships, 287, 293, 300
balancing personal and professional responsibilities, 306
collegial relationships, 290–293
ethics, 304
funding for, 289
help with problems, 294–299
mentors, 287, 292–293, 299
National Board Certification, 10, 302–305
peer relationships, 287–292
program quality review in California, 289–290
time as inhibitor of, 288–289
who to ask for help, 299–302
Professional ethics, 305
Professional organizations, 301–302
Profiles of Student Behaviors, 258
Program quality review in California, 289–290
Project-based learning, 276
Project work, rubric for assessing, 251

Questioning strategies
for expository teaching lessons, 180–184
Taba, 208–210
Questions
application, 181
clustering of, 181–182
comprehension, 181
convergent, 180–181
divergent, 181, 195–197
general rules for, 182–183
knowledge, 181
as means for critical and creative thinking, 210–213
precision, 181

Race, classroom behavior and, 63
Realia, 81
Reality therapy, 13
Real-life problem solving, in lesson plan, 74
Recreational clubs, 149–151
Reflection in action, 298
Reflection on action, 298
Reflective learners, 61–62
Reinforcement, 184, 229
Relationships
administrator, 287, 293, 300
authority/autonomy, 169
collegial, 290–293

with more experienced teachers, 297–298, 299
peer, 287–292
teacher-mentor, 287, 292–293, 299
Relevance, planning for, 102
Representational learning, 73
Resources and tools, 7, 8
for inquiry and problem solving, 214–215
organizing, 114–115
planning, 80–81, 283–284
Responsibility, developing student, 14–15
Reversibility, developmental concept of, 54
Review, California's program quality, 289–290
Ripple effect, 117
Role play, caucus group, 158
Roles, group, 123, 179
Rubrics, 248–251, 259, 280
Rudeness, 144–145
Rules
analysis of, 50–51
authoritative versus authoritarian, 9

Satiation, 79
Scheduling, block, 92–93
School connectedness, factors influencing, 228
School environment. *See also* Environment
violence and, 153–154
School policies and procedures, novice teachers and, 298–299
School socialization, classroom management and, 132
Schools within schools, 152–153
School violence. *See* Violence
Science, standards for, 254–255
Science experiment report, writing, 253
SCORE project, 275
Scripting, in classroom observation, 44
SDAIE (specially designed academic instruction in English), 180
Self-control
developing student, 14–15
freedom and, 140–141
Self-study, teacher, 25, 303, 304
Semester planning, 104
Semistructured discussion, 187
Sensorimotor stage of development, 54
September 11, 2001
lesson planning and, 86–91
questioning examples for discussing, 182
Sequence, curriculum concept of, 93
Service learning, in lesson plan, 74
Sex roles, 63
Sheltered English, 136

Simulations
  computer, 274
  in unit planning, 100
Skill-oriented cooperative learning, 174
Small-group instruction
  advantages and disadvantages of, 122
  beginning, 121–123
  evaluation in, 126
  group procedures, 123–124
  group roles, 123
  group size, 123
  problems in, 124–125
  teacher responsibilities during, 126
Social interaction. *See* Interaction
Socialization, school, and classroom management, 132
Social skills and interpersonal relations, 147. *See also* Interaction
  bullying, 143, 144, 243
  in cooperative learning, 175, 176
  gangs and recreational clubs, 149–151
  prejudice, 148–149, 164, 166–167
  what teachers can do, 148
Societal considerations in learning, 62–64
Societal problems, lesson planning and, 86–91
Software
  databases, 278
  desktop publishing, 277
  evaluating, 274–275
  multimedia, 278–279
  presentation, 278–279
  problem solving, 275
  spreadsheets, 278
  Web site, 282
  word processing, 277
Spatial intelligence, 58
Speaking experiences, assessing, 245–246
Speaking out, 146–147
Specially designed academic instruction in English (SDAIE), 180
Special needs, students with, 159, 223–224, 300
Spreadsheets, 278
Standardized tests, 257–258
Standards, 5
  content, 251–252
  content versus performance, 188–189
  English language arts, 252–253
  INTASC, 4, 28, 54, 70, 86, 112, 139, 164, 192, 220, 239, 268, 287
  mathematics, 253–254
  NBC, 10
  NCATE, 10
  NCTM, 38, 188
  outcome, 251

  research on effects of, 255
  school curriculum and, 249, 251–255
  science, 254–255
  teaching with, 188–189
  technology, 269
Stereotyping
  prejudice and, 148
  sex role, 63
Storytelling, 245–246
Strands, 253
Strategies, instructional. *See* Instructional strategies; Teaching models
Structured discussion, 187
Structured practice, 167, 168
Student portfolios, 247–248
Students
  aggressive, extroverted talkers, 187
  control of, in classroom, 10–11
  in cooperative learning, 175, 178–179
  cuing, 183
  decisions by, 21, 24–25
  disinterest of, 102
  effort of, 18–19
  inhibited, 187–188
  interaction with, 7, 8–9, 44–45
  interviewing, 44
  monitoring. *See* Monitoring
  observing, 31, 36
  participation of. *See* Participation
  preferences of, 20
  responsibility of, 14–15
  self-control of, 14–15
  with special needs, 159, 223–224, 300
  understanding, 23
Student Teams Achievement Divisions (STAD) model, 177–178
Subject field content, 6, 8
  assessing student knowledge of, 242–245
  lesson planning and, 64–66
  observing, 31, 38–39
Subject field knowledge, 22–23, 242–245
Substitute time, 289
Summative assessment, 240
Supervision
  clinical, 293
  violence and, 153–154
Symbolic learning, 73
Synomorphy, 31

Taxonomy of Educational Objectives: Cognitive Domain (Bloom), 181
Teachable moment, 94, 164
Teachers
  characteristics of effective, 22–25

Subject Index   339

control of classroom by, 10–11
learning from assessment, 246–247
novice. *See* Professional development for novice teachers
observing, 31, 37–38
preknowledge of, 173
responsibility of, for student performance, 221
role of, in cooperative learning, 175
role of, in discussion, 186
student interaction with, 7, 8–9, 44–45
Teaching hints
  advance organizer teaching model, 174
  assessing student ideas and thinking processes, 241
  bullying, 144
  case study approach, 215
  caucus group role-play, 158
  classroom management, 120, 126, 129, 207
  coaching, 292
  comprehensive teaching model, 171
  concept attainment, 201
  conflict resolution, 155
  creating small community schools, 153
  democratic learning community, 39
  developmental considerations, 54
  direct instruction, 166
  discipline, 14
  English language learners, 76, 180, 261, 223–224
  gestures, 213
  instructional goals, 131
  monitoring individual skill practice, 223
  National Board Certification, 305
  portfolio assessment, 247–248
  prejudice in classroom, 149
  print material planning, 80
  specially designed academic instruction in English, 180
  student involvement, 9
  student questions and creative thinking, 211
  success, meaning of, 64
  Taba questioning strategy, 208–210
  unplanned conferences, 236
  violence, 154
  webbing, 104
  Web sites, choosing, 272
Teaching methodologies, 6, 8
Teaching models. *See also* Instructional strategies
  advance organizer, 172–174
  comprehensive, 169–171
  concept attainment, 197–201
  cooperative group learning, 177–178
  direct instruction, 165–169
  divergent questioning, 195–197
  expository, 161, 180–184
  group investigation, 201–207
  inquiry, 114, 161, 192–194, 214–215
  jurisprudential, 158
Teaching strategies. *See* Instructional strategies; Teaching models
Teaming, teacher, 289
Teams-Games-Tournament (TGT) model, 177–178
Teamwork, encouraging in classroom, 15–16
Technology
  as assessment tool, 280, 282
  as communication tool, 282
  computer-based learning, 273–275
  databases, 278
  desktop publishing, 277
  development of, 268–269
  Internet. *See* Internet
  multimedia software, 278–279
  planning for, 80–81, 283–284
  presentation software, 278–279
  problem-based and project-based learning, 275–276
  spreadsheets, 278
  standards for, 269
  for student learning, 269–273
  as student tool, 276–279
  as support tool, 280–282
  as teaching tool, 279
  word processing, 277
Tests
  essay, 257
  fear of, 259
  multiple-choice, 256
  standardized, 257–258
  teacher-made, 255–257
  true/false and yes/no, 256
Theme, 210
  clustering lessons around, 94–95
Thinking skills
  assessment of, 240–241
  creative, 210–213
  critical, 210–213, 225
  encouraging complex, 223
Time
  banked, 93, 289
  as inhibitor of professional development, 288–289
  substitute, 289
  in unit planning, 100
  wait, 183, 197

Time management
  novice teachers and, 295
  teacher planning and, 91–93
Token economies discipline systems, 12
Tolerance, 166–167
True/false tests, 256
Tutorials, 268, 274

Unit planning, 95–101. *See also* Curriculum planning; Lesson planning
  backward problem solving in, 105, 107
  balance in, 103–104
  data retrieval charts in, 105, 106
  example plan, 311–315
  novice teachers and, 294
  process of, 95
  semester or yearlong, 104
  webbing and, 104–105
Unstructured discussion, 186
URLs, 273
U.S. West Foundation, 269

Valid decision making, 141
Values, 149
Videotaping, in classroom observation, 44

Violence, 151
  conflict resolution, 154–158
  large schools versus small schools, 151–152
  school environment and supervision, 153–154
  schools-within-schools concept, 153
  what schools can do, 152–153

Wait time, 183, 197
Walk-throughs, 293
Webbing, 99, 104–105, 210–211
WebQuest, 271–272
With-it-ness, 134
Word processing, 277
Writing skills
  assessing, 246, 250
  book report, 252–253
  science experiment report, 253
  word processing and desktop publishing, 277

Yearlong planning, 104
Yes/no tests, 256

Zone of proximal development, 56